Debate held by a branch of the PT [Partido dos Trabalhadores] in Salvador, September 1982.

This book is more a kind of travel journal than a work of philosophy, psychoanalysis or politics. Suely wrote it after we went through Brazil on the lookout for individuals, groups, intensities and desires coming our way. These fragments, blocks of ideas, confidences, snippets of conversations, of letters, of conferences—Suely's montage of words, mine, hers, of so many others—aim to break loose from the individualization of enunciation. They are a declaration of love for the intelligence and the collective sensibility of that country.

— Félix Guattari

(Text written for the back cover of the first Brazilian edition)

SEMIOTEXT(E) FOREIGN AGENTS SERIES

Published by Semiotext(e)
2007 Wilshire Blvd., Suite 427, Los Angeles, CA 90057
www.semiotexte.com

Originally published as: *Micropolítica: Cartografias do desejo*. Petrópolis: Vozes, 1986; 6th ed. 2000; out of print. (Petrópolis: Vozes, 7th ed., 2005: expanded and revised edition with a new preface).

Special thanks to Jean-René de Fleurieu (who sponsored part of the translation), Robert Dewhurst, Amir Mogharabi and Andrew Berardini.

Revision by Rodrigo Nunes.

Cover Art by Clarissa Tossin
Design by Hedi El Kholti

ISBN-10: 1-58435-051-2
ISBN-13: 978-1-58435-051-4

Distributed by The MIT Press, Cambridge, Mass. and London, England
Printed in the United States of America

MOLECULAR REVOLUTION IN BRAZIL

Félix Guattari and Suely Rolnik

Translated by Karel Clapshow and Brian Holmes

\<e\>

Contents

Suely Rolnik

PREFACE TO THE 7TH BRAZILIAN EDITION

"YES, I BELIEVE THAT there is a multiple people, a people of mutants, a people of potentialities that appears and disappears, that is embodied in social events, literary events, and musical events. I'm often accused of being exaggeratedly, stupidly, stubbornly optimistic, and of not seeing people's wretchedness. I can see it, but… I don't know, perhaps I'm raving, but I think that we're in a period of productivity, proliferation, creation, utterly fabulous revolutions from the viewpoint of this emergence of a people. That's molecular revolution: it isn't a slogan or a program, it's something that I feel, that I live, in meetings, in institutions, in affects, and also through some reflections." This is how Guattari referred to what he had glimpsed in Brazil in 1982.

The atmosphere of that time was marked by the political campaign for the first direct elections after nearly two decades of military dictatorship.[1] What Guattari found so stirring about the reactivation of public life was not only the macropolitical dimension, predictable in this type of situation, but above all its micropolitical vitality, the force of what was happening in the politics of desire, of subjectivity, of relationship with the other. A silent molecular revolution was taking place within discourse and, even more, in people's gestures and attitudes: the first steps toward the disinvestment of a politics of subjectivation constructed over five hundred years of Brazilian history, since the country's foundation. A period in which regimes of exclusion and segmentation—colonial, slave-holding, dictatorial and capitalist—

were overlaid to form a perverse, powerfully established social hierarchy. Profoundly inscribed in subjectivities, this cartography is so cruel and so passively accepted that the country ranked (and continues to rank) near the top of the list of the world's most unequal societies.

The book documents this movement of collective elaboration, its dialogue with Guattari, and through him, its dialogue with a similar process that had taken place in Europe during the preceding decade, in which he had intensely participated. Despite conceptual and strategic differences, what these situations had in common was a possibility to articulate macro and micropolitics both theoretically and pragmatically, so that the dynamics behind the forces of resistance and creation then being activated could be indissolubly joined to construct new outlines of reality. This was one of the greatest challenges of those decades of post disenchantment with the experiences of really existing socialism.

In addition to the return of democracy, not only in Brazil but in various Latin American countries, the early 80s were also a time when the logic of the capitalist order changed on an international scale. In retrospect it is striking that Guattari would have already pointed not only to the installation of this new order—he called it *Integrated World Capitalism* (IWC)[2]—but also to the central role it would assign to subjectivity turning the forces of desire, creation, and action into a major source for the extraction of surplus value (replacing the mechanical force of physical labor). This situation would be confirmed throughout the following decades, becoming one of the central themes of contemporary theoretical and political debate.

Our month-long journey across various regions of Brazil took place in the heat of this process. We talked of politics but also of clinical practice; of class struggle but also of subjectivity and desire; of the state, the party, and the union, but also of autonomy. We talked about the importance of articulating the struggles on a larger scale but also, and above all, of the need to articulate movements that would not be subject to the state/party/union formula; we talked about identity and individuality, but as ways to move more effectively towards singularity; and finally, we talked about the bankruptcy of bourgeois conjugality, the flowering of feminism and the gay movement but also about a new smoothness that seemed to be surfacing in the politics of love relationships. It was important that these different dimensions be recorded in the book; more important still was recording the fact that they were all interwoven, threads of a single fabric. The organizing principle of the book answers this double need: hence its particular form.[3]

The discussions presented here were an active part of the broad and heterogeneous social movement that shook Brazil at the time. Published in 1986, the book itself became an important reference for some movements of the 1980s and 1990s, and went through six printings. The book was a landmark in the significant changes accomplished within the field of clinical practice, in the struggles against state mental health policies (which led to the ratification of psychiatric reform legislation).[4] It also affected their most invisible expression: a wholly other theoretical and practical stance that spread through consulting rooms and psychiatric institutions (particularly public ones), all the way to higher education. In fact, Brazil is the country where the ideas of Guattari, Deleuze, Foucault—and the entire philosophical tradition they carry with them, Spinoza and Nietzsche in particular—have received the most explicit incorporation in clinical practice (psychoanalysis included).

With Lula's presidential victory in Brazil[5] and, beyond the country's borders, the reactivation of critical forces spreading across the earth since the mid-1990s,[6] the book took on yet another dimension. It offers certain clues for a genealogy of the present. It provides an opportunity to observe the beginning of the collective process that led Lula and the PT[7] to the presidency of Brazil twenty years later. This is, however, just the tip of the iceberg for a much broader and deeper change that has been taking place in Brazilian society and which concerns, among other elements, the dominant politics of subjectivation. A micropolitical change that follows its probably irreversible course; one that is, up to a point, independent of the directions the state takes during or even after the current government.[7] It likewise provides an opportunity to verify the degree to which the theoretical and strategic issues then being formulated helped to prepare the soil where the current movements have germinated. The overcoming of the dissociation between micro and macropolitics, a problem confronted at that time, continues to be the order of the day—although for the current movements such a conquest has ceased to be the desired point of arrival as it was from 1960s to the 1980s, to become the starting point instead. Finally, the book also bears witness to Guattari's participation in this genealogy, in Brazil as in Europe.

The book's status as a historical document became evident at the same moment of its first publication outside Brazil. Hence the need to revise and augment it for its translations, and also for the seventh Brazilian edition, in order to provide more detailed information, especially on groups, movements and historical facts mentioned in the text.[8] Also included in this new edition is a conversation between Lula and Guattari that took place during the intense traveling schedule of 1982.[9] We had originally decided not to incorporate this conversation in the book, but to make it available immediately as a small, separate publication,[10] because we wanted it to be part of the debate surrounding Lula's campaign for governor of the State of São Paulo, which was underway at that time.[11] The booklet sold out in a few weeks and this conversation is now being republished here for the first time.

The dialogue between Lula and Guattari reflects their astonishing ability to foresee, twenty-two years ago, what is happening now—not only the ascension of Lula and the Workers' Party to the Presidency of Brazil, but also France's swerve to the right after

Mitterrand. One is equally struck by their insightful identification of the knots being loosened in Brazil and tightened in France, so as to finally bring about this arrival; but also by their perspicacious identification, even then, of other knots that threatened to appear in the future which has become ours today.

Guattari's writing in this book may appear different from his usual style. But that is only an appearance: what we can see here is certainly present in the invisible source of all his texts. Throughout his life, writing for him was always an uncontrollable impulse meant to register the sensations of his dense involvement with everything he did: his involvement with clinical practice (particularly in collective situations, whether institutional or not); but also—and with the same quality of total availability—his engagement with politics and social movements of resistance of every sort, wherever they arose (hence the seven visits he made to Brazil between 1979 and 1992, during the last fourteen years of his life). To accompany the dizzying pace at which he processed events, Guattari made a wild use of words, inventing concepts in a torrential flow with ferocious intelligence and breathtaking rapidity. On more than one occasion, Deleuze remarked upon his partner's speed and the fact that he "treats writing like a schizo flow that carries all kinds of things along with it."[12] Therein, precisely, lies the striking power of Guattari's thinking, its originality and beauty.

This book has a different rhythm. Not that it presents a tamer, more palatable or even pedagogical Guattari—which would neutralise the critical power of his thought. On the contrary, it is like a slow-motion picture of his thought at work, revealing its very movement—from encounters to sensations and, from there, to attempts at elaboration, back again to encounters and so forth. A living thought that participated in the collective tracing of cartographies for the imperatives of his time. And it is precisely because of this quality that Guattari's writings continue to be a part of such a tracing in our time.

— São Paulo, February, 2004

FÉLIX GUATTARI
« DOMAINE VAUGOIN »
DHUIZON
41220 LA FERTÉ-SAINT-CYR

dimanche

Chère Suely

Le livre est le plus beau cadeau qu'on m'ait jamais fait! Je le lis chaque jour, par petites doses, avec bonheur.

Merci mille fois

*Envoie des choses pour "L'Auto Journal".

"Dear Suely, This book is the most delightful present that I have ever been given! I read it every day, in small doses, with happiness. Thank you a thousand times." (Paris, May 10th 1986).

Suely Rolnik

FOREWORD

THIS BOOK WAS NOT JUST WRITTEN with four hands. Many more were involved.

It all began in 1982, with the idea of inviting Guattari for a tightly packed trip around Brazil. The country was experiencing a moment of incontestable revitalization: the first direct elections after almost two decades of military dictatorship. Not only the social and political consciousness of Brazilian society were revitalized in this process of redemocratization, but also the country's unconscious. It was the kind of situation that could make you think of Guattari, for as Deleuze once said, they both write for "unconsciouses that protest"; these are the allies they seek.[1]

What mysterious protest of the unconscious is this? One not related—at least, not directly—to the protests of conscious minds and their interests, or the protests expressed in marches and public gatherings, such as one finds in an electoral campaign. If we understand the unconscious as the place where the territories of existence, their cartographies and micropolitics, are produced by the operations of desire, then the enigma dissolves: there are all too many reasons to justify such a protest. There is no difficulty in identifying them: we all live in an almost constant state of crisis, in fact an economic crisis, not just of material economics but also of the economy of desire, with the result that no sooner do we succeed in articulating a certain way of living than it becomes obsolete. We are constantly out of synch with the actuality of our experiences. We are on intimate terms with this ceaseless scrapping of modes of existence: every day we develop our ability to make adjustments in order to maintain a minimum of balance amidst it all, and to gain more skill in the art of assembling territories.

However, this process is intensified by the capitalistic market which makes and unmakes worlds whose nature is not arbitrary: we find ourselves under constant pressure from all quarters to invest in the powerful factory of serialized subjectivity, the producer of the kind of humans we are, reduced to the condition of a support for value—even (especially) when we occupy the most honored places in the hierarchy of values. Everything leads to this type of economy. Very often there is no other possible outcome. For when, in the process of disassembly, we find ourselves perplexed and disoriented, and become fragile, we tend to adopt merely defensive positions—for fear of the marginalization in which we risk being confined whenever we dare to create some kind of singular territory. A fear that this marginalization will come to compromise our very possibility of survival. To avoid this risk, often we end up demanding a territory inside the edifice of recognized identities, even if it is in dissonance with our own consciousness and its ideals; thus we ourselves become the very producers of certain sequences on the assembly line of desire.

But things are not that simple: sometimes—and now, with increasing frequency—the unconsciouses protest. Strictly speaking, we cannot call it a "protest." It would be better to speak of an "invention": they divest from the assembly lines of subjectivity, to invest others, creating other worlds inside this world. Whenever this happens, the principle of the current system, the standardization of desire, suffers a blow. And when it happens (something of the kind was happening then in Brazil) we find an "ally" in Guattari. Not as a founder or master of a school with which we might align ourselves and thereby find reassurance, but as a certain quality of presence that mobilizes within us the will and courage to express the singularity of our experience, not only in speech but also in action.

It was with this in mind that I invited Guattari to visit us then. I organized a full schedule of activities in five different states, in August and September of 1982.[2] I included not only a series of talks, round-table discussions, and public debates (which always filled the places where they were held), but above all meetings, encounters, interviews, and formal or informal discussions with individuals, groups, movements and associations. All this was recorded, to later be transformed into a book. The selection of themes and places was made on the basis of the possibilities for meeting people who, whether institutionalized or not, had dissident subjectivities at that time.

Imagining where, how, and with whom constituted the beginning of the trip. A first assemblage was formed, which began to intersect other trajectories and form further assemblages. That's how the trip took shape, and with it, the texture of this book.

The initial idea was that the book would be a kind of travel diary, a simple process of editing from over a thousand pages of transcripts. But a different project emerged from them. It was an opportunity to record a certain aspect of Guattari that does not appear in his books. He himself defined this aspect as the feeling of being constantly riding "waves that carry us, surfing on the articulation of all kinds of vectors of collective intelligence."[3] This book would make it possible to keep alive in print the Guattari who was passionately involved in individual and collective adventures of invention—often the starting point for his process of creating concepts, the work in progress that he took up again tirelessly from day to day. The encounters that made up the trip and the theoretical elaborations they mobilized were what I wanted to make present in this book.

For three years I lived and dialogued with the transcriptions of the talks. The different materials gradually came together, while others were introduced: letters that Guattari and I exchanged during this time; texts he was writing at the time; texts I wrote to makes connections and construct crossings. A cartography was traced.

The book is organized by themes. Each one is made up of texts of different origins and treatments, which can be grouped in three kinds. The first and most frequent type consists of "blocks of ideas." The second type includes fragments of conversations, debates, discussions, interviews, round-table talks, and letters. The third type corresponds to longer fragments by Guattari, myself, and others, which were presented as small essays; also in this category were texts written independently by Guattari or myself during the preparation of the book.

Some texts are signed, and others not. The texts unsigned, which make up the greater part of the book—whether blocks of ideas, lectures, or essays—are generally the result from a montage involving fragments of Guattari's talks on a particular theme, recorded on different occasions, brought together and rewritten by myself; the interventions made by Guattari in the course of discussions received this kind of treatment as well. Just a few of these texts are direct quotes of Guattari's statements.

Guattari's name was only added in the case of interventions in debates during the trip and texts written by him afterwards. In the latter case, date and source are also provided. Contributions by other people, myself included, are preceded by the name of the speaker or writer, to differentiate then from Guattari's interventions. When they are part of a discussion or conversation, date and location are indicated. Materials I subsequently wrote have my name and a title. Some contributions are anonymous, either because the speaker's name was not recorded, or because the speaker wished to remain anonymous.

In a way, this book is dated: it belongs to a certain period and so are the assemblages that generated it. First, the Brazil of 1982.

The intensification of the process of macro- and micropolitical redemocratization: electoral campaigns for governors, representatives and councilors, the proliferation of organized minority groups, using of the term "alternative" to designate dissident social practices, echoes of the 1970s. Then events that took place during the three years of the book's preparation. Cartographies of these experiences and their confrontations constitute its raw material. On the one hand, the book is a testimony of these experiences, and on the other its cartographic character makes it go beyond its simple datation: as in any other cartography, whatever its time and place, it addresses strategies for the constitution of new territories, other spaces of life and affect, a search for ways outside of territories seemingly without exits. A search of those unconsciouses that impertinently "protest," the allies Deleuze mentioned in the interview quoted earlier:

"We address ourselves to unconsciouses that protest. We seek allies. We need allies. And we have the impression that those allies already exist, that they did not wait for us, that there are many people who have had enough, who are thinking, feeling, and working in similar directions: they have nothing to do with a trend, but with a more profound 'spirit of the age,' in which convergent investigations are taking place in very different domains."[4]

This book seeks to be one of those investigations. Its domain is the strategies of desire in the social field. Guattari call them "micropolitics." The book follows the movement of some of those strategies—the ones that arose in the encounters experienced during the trip and those that were added afterwards. Its real author is the collective intelligence set in motion in this process.

— São Paulo, January, 1986

1

CULTURE: A REACTIONARY CONCEPT?

THE CONCEPT OF CULTURE is deeply reactionary. It is a way of separating semiotic activities (orientation in the social and cosmic world) into spheres to which people are referred. These isolated activities are standardized and capitalized to suit the dominant mode of semiotization—they are cut off from their political realities.

Everything in Proust's work revolves around the idea that it is impossible to treat music, the visual arts, literature, architecture, or the microsocial life of salons as if they were autonomous spheres.

Culture as an autonomous sphere only exists in terms of markets of power, economic markets, and not in terms of production, creation, and real consumption.

What characterizes *capitalistic*[1] modes of production is that they do not operate solely in the register of exchange values, values that are of the order of capital, monetary semiotics, or modes of financing. They also operate through a mode of control of subjectivation, which I shall call a "culture of equivalence," or "systems of equivalence in the sphere of culture." From this viewpoint, capital operates in a way that is complementary to culture as a concept of equivalence: capital concerns itself with economic subjection, and culture with subjective subjection. When I speak of subjective subjection I am not referring only to advertising for the production and consumption of goods. *It is the very essence of capitalist profit to not be restricted to the field of economic surplus value: it also resides in the seizure of the power of subjectivity.*

Mass culture and singularity [2]

The title I suggested for this debate at the *Folha de São Paulo* was "Mass culture and singularity." It was repeatedly announced as "Mass culture and individuality"—and perhaps this is not simply a problem of translation. Perhaps it's difficult to hear the term *singularity*, and translating it as *individuality* seems to bring into play an essential dimension of mass culture. This is precisely the theme that I would like to consider today: mass culture as a basic element of the *"production of capitalistic subjectivity."*

Mass culture produces individuals: standardized individuals, linked to one another in accordance with hierarchical systems, value systems, systems of submission—not visible, explicit systems of submission, as in animal ethology, or as in archaic or precapitalist societies. These systems of submission are much more hidden. I wouldn't say that they are "internalized" or "interiorized," an expression, very fashionable at one time, implying that subjectivity is something to be filled. On the contrary, it is *produced*. Not just individuated subjectivity—subjectivity of individuals—but social subjectivity that can be found at every level of production and consumption. And, what's more, an *unconscious* production of subjectivity. In my view, this huge factory, this mighty capitalistic machine also produces what happens

singularization

to us when we dream, when we daydream, when we fantasize, when we fall in love, and so on. In everycase, it seeks to occupy a hegemonic function in all these fields.

I would set against this subjectivity-producing machine the idea that it is possible to develop singular modes of subjectivation—what we might call *"processes of singularization"*: a way of rejecting all these modes of preestablished encoding, all these modes of manipulation and remote control, rejecting them in order to construct modes of sensibility, modes of relation with the other, modes of production, modes of creativity that produce a singular subjectivity. An existential singularization that coincides with a desire, a taste for living, a will to construct the world in which we find ourselves, and the establishment of devices to change types of society and types of values that are not ours. So there are certain trick words (such as the word "culture"), barrier-notions that prevent us from understanding the reality of the processes in question.

The word "culture" has had various meanings in the course of history: its oldest meaning is the one that appears in the expression "cultivating the mind." This is "meaning A," which I shall call "value culture" because it corresponds to a value judgment that determines who has culture and who doesn't; or whether one belongs to a cultured milieu or an uncultured milieu. The second semantic nucleus embraces other significances concerned with culture: it is "meaning B," which I shall call "collective soul culture," synonymous with civilization. Here we no longer have the "having or not having" binary: everyone has culture. This is a very democratic culture: everyone can claim their own cultural identity. It's a kind of a priori of culture: people speak of black culture, underground culture, technical culture, and so on. It's a rather vague kind of "soul," one that's hard to grasp, and that in the course of history has lent itself to all kinds of ambiguity, because it's a semantic dimension found both in Hitler's party, as the notion of *Volk* (race), and in numerous freedom movements that seek to reappropriate their culture and their cultural background. The third semantic nucleus, "meaning C," corresponds to mass culture, and I shall call it "commodity culture." Here there is no value judgment, and no more or less secret collective territories of culture, as in meanings A and B. Culture is all assets: all the facilities (such as cultural centers), all the people (the specialists who work in those facilities), all the theoretical and ideological references concerning their working—in short, everything that contributes to the production of semiotic objects (such as books and films), distributed in a particular market of monetary circulation or in the state sector. This culture is disseminated in the same way as Coca-Cola, cigarettes, cars, or anything else.

Let's go back to the three categories. With the rise of the bourgeoisie, value culture seems to have replaced other segregative notions, ancient systems of the social segregation of the nobility. We no longer speak of "people of quality": what is considered is the quality of culture that results from certain work. This is what is referred to by Voltaire's formula of "cultivating one's garden," which becomes a kind of slogan at the end of *Candide*. The bourgeois elites derive the legitimacy of their power from the fact that they have carried out a certain kind of work in the field of knowledge, the field of the arts, and so on. This notion of value culture also has various meanings. It can be considered to be a general category of cultural value in the field of the bourgeois elites, but it can also be used to designate different cultural levels in sectoral value systems—so that people speak of classical culture, scientific culture, or artistic culture.

This brings us gradually to definition B, soul culture, a pseudoscientific notion elaborated at the end of the nineteenth century with the development of anthropology, especially cultural anthropology. At first, the notion of the collective soul was very close to a segregative and even racist notion: great anthropologists such as Lévy-Bruhl and Taylor reified this notion of culture. For example, it was said that so-called primitive societies had an animist conception of the world, a "primitive soul," a "primitive mentality"—notions used to describe modes of subjectivation that are really quite heterogeneous. Later, with the evolution of the anthropological sciences, with structuralism and culturalism, there was an attempt to do away with these ethnocentric systems of appreciation. Not all the authors of the culturalist movement made this attempt. Some maintained an ethnocentric vision. Others, however, such as Kardiner, Margaret Mead, and Ruth Benedict, with notions such as "basic personality," "basic personality of a culture," and "pattern of culture," sought to free themselves from ethnocentrism. Nevertheless, although it attempted to abandon ethnocentrism, abandon a general reference to white, western, male culture, what it really established was a kind of cultural polycentrism, a multiplication of ethnocentrism.

This "soul culture," meaning B, consists in isolating what I shall call a sphere of culture (domains such as those of myth, worship, or numeration), which contrasts with other levels considered to be heterogeneous, such as the field of politics, the field of structural kinship relationships—everything to do with the economy of goods and influence. This eventually leads to a situation in which what I would call "activities of semiotization"—every production of meaning and semiotic efficiency—is separated into a sphere that comes to be designated as that of "culture." To each collective soul (nations, and ethnic and social groups) a culture is attributed. Nevertheless, these nations and ethnic and social groups do not live these activities as a separate sphere. In the same way that Molière's bourgeois gentleman discovers that he "makes prose," the so-called primitive societies discover that they "make culture"; they are informed, for example, that they make music, dance, perform activities of worship, mythology, and so on. And they discover this especially when people come and take what has been produced to display it in museums, or sell it on the art market, or introduce it into the scientific anthropological theories that are circulating. But they do not make culture, or dance, or music. All these dimensions are entirely linked together in a process of expression, and also linked with their way of producing goods, with their way of producing social relations. In other words, in no way do they accept the various categorizations of anthropology. The situation is identical in the case of what is produced by an individual who has lost his references in the psychiatric system, or in the case of children when they become part of the school system. They play, articulate social relations, dream, produce, and sooner or later they will have to learn to categorize these dimensions of semiotization in the normalized social field. Now it's time to play, now it's time to produce for school, now it's time to dream, and so on.

The commodity-culture category—the third nucleus of meaning—claims to be much more objective: culture here is not the creation of theory, but the production and distribution of cultural goods, in principle without taking into account the distinctive value systems of level A (value culture), and also without worrying about what I shall call territorial levels of culture, which belong to level B (soul culture). This is not an a priori culture, but a culture that is constantly produced, reproduced, and modified. In which case, a kind of scientific nomenclature can be established to attempt to assess this production of culture in quantitative terms. There are very elaborate scales (I am thinking of the ones used by UNESCO) with which one can classify the cultural levels of cities, of social groups, and so on, according to data concerning the number of books produced, the number of films, or the number of cultural venues.

marginal subjectivities

My idea is that these three meanings of culture which appear successively in the course of history are still simultaneously in operation. There is a complementarity between these three types of semantic nuclei. The production of the means of mass communication, the production of capitalistic subjectivity, generates a culture with a universal vocation. This is an essential dimension in the creation of collective labor power, and in the creation of what I call the collective force of social control. However, apart from these two major objectives, it is quite prepared to tolerate subjective territories that, to some extent, escape this general culture. For this it is necessary to tolerate margins, sectors of minority culture—subjectivities in which we can recognize ourselves, recover ourselves in an orientation foreign to that of Integrated World Capitalism (IWC). This attitude, however, is not just one of tolerance. In recent decades, this capitalistic production has made an effort on its own to produce its margins, and in some way it has prepared new subjective territories: individuals, families, social groups, minorities, and so on. All this seems to be very well calculated. One could say that Ministries of Culture are now beginning to spring up everywhere, developing a modernist perspective whereby, in an apparently democratic manner, they propose to increase a production of culture that will enable them to join the rich industrial societies. And also encourage particularized forms of culture, so that people will have some sort of feeling that they are in a kind of territory and not lost in an abstract world.

In fact, things don't really work quite like that. This dual mode of production of subjectivity, this industrialization of the production of culture according to levels B and C, has not renounced the system of valorization of level A, not at all. Behind this false democracy of culture the same systems of segregation based on a general category of culture continue to be enforced in a deeply underlying way. In this modernist perspective, the Ministries of Culture and the specialists in the cultural facilities declare that they do not seek to categorize the consumers of cultural objects socially, but only to distribute culture in a certain social field, which supposedly operates according to a law of free exchange. However, what's left out here is the fact that the social field that receives the culture is not homogeneous. The distribution of products such as books or records does not have the same meaning at all when it's carried out in the milieus of social elites or in the milieus of the mass media, for educational purposes or for local cultural activities.

The work of sociologists such as Bourdieu shows that there are groups that already have a metabolism of receptivity for the productions of culture. A child that has never lived in an environment with reading, the production of knowledge, and appreciation of the visual arts obviously does not have the same kind of relation with culture as someone like Jean-Paul Sartre, who was literally born in a library. Even so, there is a wish to maintain the appearance of equality in relation to the production of culture. In fact, we preserve the ancient meaning of the word "culture," value culture, which forms part of the aristocratic traditions of scions of good families, people who know how to deal with words, attitudes, and systems of etiquette. Culture is not merely the transmission of cultural information, the transmission of systems of modelization; it's also a way for the capitalistic elites to exhibit what I would call a general market of power.

This is not only a power over cultural objects, or over the possibilities of handling them and creating something, but also a power to attribute cultural objects to oneself as a distinctive sign in one's social relations with others. For example, the meaning that a banal statement may acquire in the field of literature varies in accordance with the person to whom it is addressed. The fact that a student or a primary teacher in a small town in the provinces says commonplace things about Maupassant doesn't alter his system of self-promotion as a value in the social field. But if Giscard d'Estaing talks about Maupassant in one of the leading literary programs on French television, however banal what he says may be, it immediately becomes an indication—not of his real knowledge about the writer, but of the fact that he belongs to a field of power, the field of culture.

I shall take a more immediate example, situated in what I am considering to be the Brazilian context. It is customary to insinuate that Lula as a person and the PT as an organization are very likeable, but that they will certainly prove to be completely incapable of managing such a highly complex society as that of Brazil, because they don't have the technical capability, they don't have the appropriate levels of knowledge for the task. I was in Poland recently, and found that the same type of argument is used against Lech Walesa. Leaders of the Polish Communist Party use every means possible to try to discredit him. Especially an obnoxious character called Rakowski,[3] who tells Western journalists that he has a great liking for Walesa, with his seductive, charming personality, but he believes that, separated from his advisors, from his regular entourage, Walesa is nothing, he's simply incompetent.

What is being brought into play is not really those levels of competence. For a start, the level of incompetence and corruption of the elites in power is notorious. In fact, in capitalistic assemblages of power it's always the most stupid who are at the top. Just look at the results: the management of the world economy today brings hundreds and thousands of people to hunger and desperation, to a way of life that is intolerable, despite the technological advances and extraordinary productive capabilities that are developing in the current technological revolutions.

Therefore, we cannot accept that what is being pointed to or having a certain impact on public opinion is really competence. Moreover, this argument promotes a certain embodied function of knowledge—as if the intelligence required in the crisis that we are experiencing could embody some supposed talent or transcendental knowledge. This argument simply dodges the fact that all the procedures of knowledge and semiotic efficiency in the present world participate in complex assemblages that never fall within the competence of a single specialist. It's well known that any system for the modern management of vast industrial and social processes involves the articulation of different levels of competence. In this respect, I don't see why Lula should be incapable of undertaking such an articulation; and when I speak of Lula I'm really speaking of the PT, of all the democratic formations, all the minority movements that are agitating at this time of electoral campaign in Brazil. Therefore, there's no reason to think that these different potentialities of competence couldn't do what the elites now in power do—as well or even better.

I think that the key issue is not competence, but concerns Lula's relation with culture, as a quantity of information. Not soul culture—because it's obvious that, in this respect, he has the culture of São Bernardo,[4] working-class culture, and we're not going to take that away from him—but a certain kind of capitalistic culture, one of the fundamental mechanisms of power. The people of the PT, and Lula in particular, don't participate in a certain quality of the dominant culture. It's much more a question of style and etiquette. It could even be said that it's something that functions on a level that comes before the end of a sentence, or the formation of an utterance. These people are not part of the dominant capitalistic culture. From this starting point a whole vector of culpabilization develops, because this conception of culture impregnates all levels of society and production.

Consequently, these people cannot claim to have the legitimacy to manage capitalistic processes, an idea that they themselves also end up accepting.

What gives a character of strangeness to the political and social rise of people like Lula is the fact that we feel very sure that it is not only a case of a phenomenon of rupture in relation to the management of social and economic flows, but also a practical exercise of a kind of subjectivation process different from the capitalistic one, with its double register of the production of universal values on the one hand, and of reterritorialization in small subjective ghettos on the other. It puts into practice the production of a subjectivity that is capable both of managing the reality of "developed" societies and of managing processes of subjective singularization that don't confine the various social categories (sexual, racial, cultural, or other minorities) within the dominant control grid [*quadrillage*] of power.

The issue that arises now is therefore no longer one of "who produces culture," or "who will be the recipients of these productions of culture," but of how to assemble other modes of semiotic production in order to allow the construction of a society that is simply able to maintain itself. Semiotic modes of production that will make it possible to ensure a social division of production without thereby shutting individuals into systems of oppressive segregation, or categorizing their semiotic productions into different spheres of culture. Painting as a cultural sphere primarily has to do with painters, people with experience as painters, and people who disseminate painting commercially or in the mass media. How can one ensure that these so-called "categories of culture" are at the same time highly specialized, and singularized, as in the case of painting that I just mentioned, without there being some kind of hegemonic possession by capitalistic elites? How can music, dance, creation, and all forms of sensibility belong fully to the totality of the components of society? How can a right to singularity be proclaimed in the field of all these levels of so-called "cultural" production without this singularity being confined to a new kind of ethnicity? How can one ensure that these different modes of cultural production don't become just specialties, but are articulated with each other, articulated with the whole of the social field, articulated with all other kinds of production (what I call *machinic production*—the revolution of computers, telecommunications, robotics, and so on)? How can one open up, and even break apart, these ancient cultural spheres that are closed in upon themselves? How can one produce new assemblages of singularization that work through an aesthetic sensibility, by changing life on a more everyday level and, at the same time, by social transformations in terms of the great economic and social structures?

I would like to conclude by saying that the problems of culture must necessarily escape from the articulation between the three semantic nuclei that I mentioned earlier. When the mass media or the Ministries of Culture talk about culture, they always seek to convince us that they aren't dealing with political and social problems. They distribute culture for consumption, in the same way that minimum food rations are distributed in some societies. But assemblages of semiotic production on all these artistic levels, creations of all kinds, always involve, correlatively, micropolitical and macropolitical dimensions.

I could also talk about the impact of this conception in France now, with the Mitterrand government, how the Socialists are going round in circles with this category of culture. Because their attempt to democratize culture is not really connected with the processes of singular subjectivation, with active cultural minorities—so that, despite good intentions, a privileged relation is always reestablished between the state and the various systems of cultural production. Some people in France, among whom I include myself, consider it very important to invent a mode of cultural production that radically breaks up the current schemas of power in this area, which the state now has at its disposal through its collective facilities and its media.

How can we get culture to leave these spheres that are closed in upon themselves? How can we organize, make available, and finance processes of cultural singularization that dismantle current particularisms in the field of culture and, at the same time, enterprises of the pseudodemocratization of culture?

———

In my view, there is no such thing as popular culture and highbrow culture. There is capitalistic culture, which permeates all fields of semiotic expression. That is what I am trying to say when I speak of the three semantic nuclei in the term culture. There is nothing more horrifying than making a eulogy of popular culture, or proletarian culture, or whatever. There are processes of singularization in certain practices, and there are procedures of reappropriation, of cooptation, carried out by the various capitalist systems.

There is only one culture: capitalistic culture. It is a culture that is always ethnocentric and intellectocentric (or logocentric), because it separates semiotic universes from subjective production.

There are many ways for culture to be ethnocentric, and not only in the racist relation of a male, white, adult type of culture. It can be relatively polycentric or polyethnocentric, and preserve the postulation of a reference of value culture, a pattern of general translatability of semiotic productions, completely parallel to capital.

In the same way that capital is a mode of semiotization that makes it possible to have a general equivalent for economic and social productions, culture is the general equivalent for the productions of power. The dominant classes always seek this double surplus value: economic surplus value, through money, and power surplus value, through value culture.

2

SUBJECTIVITY AND HISTORY

SUPERSTRUCTURE-IDEOLOGY-REPRESENTATION OR PRODUCTION

Rather than speak of *ideology*, I always prefer to speak of *subjectivation*, or the *production of subjectivity*.

The subject, according to a tradition of philosophy and the humanities, is something that we find as an *être-là*, something in the domain of a supposed human nature. In contrast, I propose the idea of subjectivity of an industrial, machinic nature—in other words, one that is essentially manufactured, modeled, received, and consumed.

The machines for the production of subjectivity vary. In traditional systems, for example, subjectivity is manufactured by machines that are more territorialized, on the scale of an ethnic group, a professional association, or a caste. In the capitalistic system, however, production is industrial and takes place on an international scale.

Briefly, I would say that, in the same way that we manufacture milk in the form of condensed milk, with all the molecules that are inherent in it, representations are injected into mothers and children, as part of the process of subjective production. Many fathers, mothers, Oedipuses, and triangulations are required to recompose a restricted family structure. There is a kind of recycling or ongoing education in order to become a woman again, or a mother, to become a child again—or, rather, to *become* a child, because adults are infantile. Children manage not to be infantile for a while, as long as they do not succumb to this production of subjectivity.

All these issues of the collective economy of desire no longer appear utopian once we no longer consider the production of subjectivity to be simply a case of a superstructure dependent on the weighty structures of the production of social relations; once we consider the production of subjectivity as the raw material of the evolution of productive forces in their most "developed" forms (the leading sectors of industry). This is the raw material of the very movement that is animating the current world crisis, a kind of will for productive power that revolutionizes production itself through scientific and biological revolutions, through the massive incorporation of telecommunications, computers, and robotics, and through the increasing weight of collective facilities and the media.

Marxists and progressives of all kinds did not understand the issue of subjectivity because they became glutted with theoretical dogmatism, but this is not the case with the social forces that administer capitalism today. These forces understand that the production of subjectivity is possibly more important than any other kind of production, more essential than the production of petroleum and energy. This is the case in Japan, which has no petroleum, but which certainly does have production of subjectivity. It is this production that allows the Japanese economy to establish itself in the world market, to the point that it receives visits from hundreds of corporate delegations that want to "Japanize" the working classes in their own countries.

Such mutations of subjectivity operate not only in ideologies, but also in the very hearts of individuals, in their way of perceiving the world, of interacting with the urban fabric, with machinic work processes, and with the social order that supports those productive forces. If this is true, it is not utopian to consider that a revolution, a social change on a macropolitical and macrosocial level, also has to do with the production of subjectivity, which should be taken into account by liberation movements.

These issues seemed to be marginal, belonging to the domain of psychology, philosophy, or psychiatric hospitals, but with the birth of vast minorities that, taken as a whole, constitute the majority of the world's population, they become fundamental. I do not consider that there is a theory or a general cartography of the way in which these problems are semiotized. For me this point is fundamental, because theoretical and ideological representation is inseparable from social praxis, inseparable from the conditions of that praxis: it is something to be sought in movement itself, and even in the set-backs, reevaluations, and reorganizations of references that may have proved necessary to it. In my view, this is the condition for assessing how certain elements such as the *orixás* in *candomblé*[1] can be taken into account in the mode of cartography, of semiotization, of apprehension of the problematics here in Brazil.

Everything that is produced by capitalistic subjectivation—everything that comes to us through language, the family, and the facilities around us—is not just a question of ideas or of transmission of meanings by way of signifying statements. Nor can it be reduced to models of identity, or identifications with maternal and paternal poles. It has to do with systems of direct connection between the great machines of production, the great machines of social control, and the psychic agencies that define the way of perceiving the world. "Archaic" societies that have not yet incorporated the capitalistic process, children who have not yet become part of the system, or people who are in psychiatric hospitals and are unable (or unwilling) to enter the dominant system of signification, have a perception of the world utterly different from what is customary within the dominant schemes. This does not mean that the nature of their perception of values and social relations is chaotic. It corresponds to different modes of representation of the world, which are undoubtedly very important for the people who use them in order to live, but not just for them—their importance can extend to other sectors of social life, in another kind of society.

I am not opposing the relations of economic production to the relations of subjective production. In my view, at least in the more modern, advanced sectors of industry, production involves a kind of work that is both material and semiotic. But this production of competence in the semiotic domain depends on its creation by the social field as a whole: it is clear that, in order to produce a specialized worker, more is involved than the intervention of professional training organizations. There is everything that comes before that, at elementary school and at home: a kind of apprenticeship that consists in going about the city from childhood, watching television—in short, existing within a completely machinic environment.

The production of manufactured goods cannot really be reduced to one sphere, the sphere of the factory. The social division of labor involves an enormous quantity of paid work outside the productive organization (in collective facilities, for example), and unpaid work, especially work done by women. What I call production of subjectivity in IWC does not consist solely of the production of power to control social and productive relations. *The production of subjectivity is the raw material for any and all production.*

The notion of ideology does not allow us to understand this *productive* function of subjectivity. Ideology remains in the sphere of representation, whereas the essential production of IWC does not simply concern representation, but also a modelization of behavior, sensibility, perception, memory, social relations, sexual relations, imaginary phantoms, etc.

The production of subjectivity can be found increasingly in what Marx called the infrastructure of production. This is very easy to verify. When a power such as the United States wants to create possibilities for economic expansion in a country of the so-called Third World, the first thing it does is work on processes of subjectivation. Without this preliminary work on the way forces of production and consumption are being shaped, without this work on all the milieus involving economic, commercial, and industrial semiotization, local social realities cannot be controlled.

The problematics of micropolitics don't involve the level of representation but the level of the production of subjectivity. They have to do with modes of expression that involve not only language but also heterogeneous semiotic levels. Thus, it is not a question of creating some kind of interstructural general reference, a general structure of signifiers of the unconscious to which all specific structural levels would be reduced. Despite of the systems of structural equivalence and translatability, it is the opposite operation that will impact on points of singularity, on processes of singularization, because they are the very productive roots of subjectivity in its plurality.

All the important phenomena at present involve elements of desire and subjectivity. If we take the cases of Iran or Poland, it is not possible to explain what is taking place in those countries without understanding the extent to which there is a collective production of subjectivity which is expressed, with great difficulty, as a rejection of a certain type of social order. Traditional academic and political references, classical Marxism, or a Freudian-Marxist patchwork do not explain these problems of desire on a collective scale.

Various religious phenomena that are currently appearing—such as the one that binds the people of Afghanistan together in their struggle against the Soviet oppressor, or the one that can be seen in Iran—cannot be explained solely in terms of ideology. In my view, they concern certain processes of the constitution of collective subjectivity, which are not the result of the sum of individual subjectivities, but of a confrontation with the ways in which subjectivity is now manufactured on a world scale.

Those who are conventionally known as "social professionals"—journalists, psychologists of all kinds, social workers, instructors, cultural organizers, people who carry out any kind of pedagogical or cultural work in poor communities, public housing, etc.—work in the production of subjectivity. But, in fact, who does not work in the social production of subjectivity? I do not see this as a problem, because at this point it is inevitable. I do not think it would be possible, or even desirable, to go back to a production of subjectivity that involved, for example, regulating the transition from one age group to another by means of initiation systems—which are certainly systems of celebration and of marvelous representations, but are also extremely cruel.

We embarked on this process of the general social division of the production of subjectivity, and now there is no turning back. But for that very reason, we have to question all those who occupy a teaching position in the social and psychological sciences or in the field of social work, all those whose profession consists in taking an interest in the discourse of the other. They are at a fundamental political and micropolitical crossroads. Either they are going to play the game and reproduce models which do not allow us to create outlets to process singularization, or they are going to encourage these processes as much as they can, and within the assemblages that they are able to mobilize. This means that there is absolutely no scientific objectivity in this field, nor any neutrality, as it is supposed to exist in psychoanalysis.

These theories simply serve to justify and legitimate the existence of specialized professions and segregative facilities, and the actual marginalization of some sectors of the population. People in therapeutic systems, or in the universities, who consider themselves to be mere depositories or channels for the transmission of scientific knowledge, have already made a reactionary choice. Despite their innocence or goodwill, they really occupy a position that reinforces the systems of production of the dominant subjectivity. It does not have to be that way. In France, this issue was debated in 1968, and the "psy" professionals (psychologists, psychiatrists, psychoanalysts) and social workers in general were systematically considered as "gendarmes."

There is no profession that is essentially of a police nature other than the police profession itself, and even that is debatable. From the point of view of micropolitics, any praxis may or may not be of a repressive nature; no scientific body, and no body of technical reference can guarantee a correct orientation. Nothing guarantees that a processual micropolitics, one that constructs new modes of subjectivation that singularize, can be found in that kind of education. The guarantee of a processual micropolitics can only—and should only—be found at each step, on the basis of the assemblages that constitute it, and through the invention of modes of reference and modes of praxis. This invention makes it possible to elucidate a field of subjectivation, and at the same time, to intervene effectively in that field, both within it and also in its relations with the outside. For the social professional, everything depends on the ability to work with assemblages of enunciation that assume their responsibility on the micropolitical plane.

Debate held by a branch of the PT in Rio de Janeiro, September 11, 1982:

Mauricio Lissovski: One of the most important political issues at present is how to invest in the process of the production of capitalistic subjectivity "desiringly." This issue has traditionally been linked with the notion of ideology. If we think of Brecht, his project involved a criticism that started in the consciousness of the politician-actor and was meant to reach the consciousness of the masses. But if we seek to subvert subjectivity, we have to act critically and abandon proposals such as those of Brecht. We have to abandon the notion of ideology, and, with it, the problematics of consciousness.

A person that pursues the subversion of subjectivity in order to allow an assemblage of "desiring" singularities must invest in the very heart of dominant subjectivity, making a move that reveals it instead of denouncing it. This means that, instead of seeking freedom (a notion indissolubly bound up with that of consciousness), we have to reclaim farce, produce and invent delirious subjectivities capable of clashing with capitalist subjectivity and make it crumble.

Any revolution on a macropolitical level also concerns the production of subjectivity.

SUBJECTIVITY AND INDIVIDUAL

Instead of speaking of a *subject*, a subject of enunciation, or of Freud's psychic agencies, I prefer to speak of a "collective assemblage of enunciation." A collective assemblage does not correspond either to an individuated entity or to a predetermined social entity.

Subjectivity is produced by assemblages of enunciation. The processes of subjectivation or semiotization are not centered on individual agents (on the operation of intrapsychic, egoic, microsocial agencies) or on group agents. These processes are doubly decentered. They involve machines of expression that can be of an extrapersonal, extra-individual nature (machinic, economic, social, technological, iconic, ecological, ethological, or media systems, in other words, systems that are no longer immediately anthropological), or of an infrahuman, infrapsychic, infrapersonal nature (systems of perception, sensibility, affect, desire, representation, image, and value, modes of memorization and production of ideas, systems of inhibition and automation, corporal, organic, biological, or physiological systems, and so on).

The question is how the real assemblages of enunciation can connect these different agencies. I am not making all this up: this problem perhaps is not yet theorized, really, but certainly it is fully in action throughout the whole development of society.

It would be advisable to separate radically the concepts of individual and subjectivity. For me, individuals are the result of mass production. The individual is serialized, registered, and modeled. Freud was the first to show how precarious the notion of the totality of an ego is. Subjectivity is not susceptible to be totalized or centralized in the individual. The individuation of the body is one thing, the multiplicity of subjective assemblages is another. Subjectivity is mostly manufactured and modeled in the register of the social. Descartes wanted to attach the idea of conscious subjectivity to the idea of the individual, and that equation has infected the entire history of modern philosophy. But this does not change the fact that the processes of subjectivation are fundamentally decentered in relation to individuation.

I could give other examples. In the mode of subjectivation of dreaming, it is easy to note an explosion of the individuation of subjectivity. In a car, it is not the person as an individual, as an egoic totality, who is driving; the individuation disappears in the process of servomechanical articulation with the car. When driving flows smoothly it is practically automatic, and the consciousness of the ego, the consciousness of the Cartesian *cogito*, does not intervene. Then, suddenly, there are signs that require the intervention of the entire person (such as danger signs). Clearly, the individual's body is always recovered among these different components of subjectivation; the individual's own name is always recovered; there is always the ego's desire to reassert itself in continuity and in power. But the production of speech, images, or sensibility, the production of desire has nothing to do with this representation of the individual. That production is adjacent to a multiplicity of social assemblages, a multiplicity of processes of machinic production, and mutations in universes of value and universes of history.

Therefore, a micropolitics of molecular transformations should rely on other foundations that involve radically questioning these notions of the individual as a general reference for processes of subjectivation. It may be better to start out from a broad definition of subjectivity, such as the one I am proposing, and then go on to examine the individuations of subjectivity as special cases: moments when subjectivity says me or super-me (ego or superego), moments when subjectivity recognizes itself in a body or part of a body, or in a system of collective corporal belonging. But here, too, we find a plurality of approaches to the ego, so that the notion of the individual continues to explode.

Capitalist profit is basically the production of subjective power. This does not imply an idealistic vision of social reality: subjectivity is not situated in the individual field, but in every process of social and material production. What one might say, using the language of computers, is that an individual always exists, but only as a terminal; this *individual terminal occupies the position of a consumer of subjectivity*. It consumes systems of representation, sensibility, and so on—which have nothing to do with natural, universal categories.

Here is an obvious example. Young people walking in the street with Walkmans establish a relation with music that is not "natural." In producing this kind of instrument (both as a means and as a content of communication), this highly sophisticated industry does not simply transmit specific music or organize natural sounds. What it is doing is *inventing* a musical universe, a different relation with musical objects: music that comes from within and not from somewhere outside. In other words, what it is doing is inventing a new perception.

Children are another example. They do perceive the world through the people around them in their own home, but this is only partly true. Most of their time is spent in front of the television, absorbing relations through images, words, and meaning. These children will have their entire subjectivity modeled by this kind of device.

Yet another example can be found in experiments conducted by anthropologists in so-called primitive societies. They presented videos to some tribes, and discovered that the video was perceived as an object that could even be amusing—but it was just another object. This reaction shows us that the kind of behavior that consists in remaining wholly focused on the apparatus, on a relation of direct communication, only exists in our society. It is our society that produces it.

I set out from the idea of a collective economy, collective assemblages of subjectivation, which are individuated in some circumstances and social contexts. Let's take language. Ferdinand de Saussure was one of the first linguists to establish the social character of language, a social fact embodied in individuated utterances and agents. Obviously, we don't have here two individuals, a transmitter and a receiver, who invent language as they speak. Language exists as a social fact, and the speaking individual exists. The same is true of all the facts of subjectivity. *Subjectivity* is in circulation in social complexes of various sizes: *it is essentially social, and is assumed and experienced by individuals in their particular existences.* The way in which individuals experience this subjectivity oscillates between two extremes: a relation of alienation and oppression, or a relation of expression and creation. In the first one, the individual submits to subjectivity just as he receives it; in the second, the individual reappropriates the components of subjectivity, eliciting a process that I would call *singularization*. This hypothesis, if we accept it, doesn't simply circumscribe social antagonisms to the fields of economics and politics, or the aim of the struggle to the reappropriation of the means of production or of political expression: it must enter the field of subjective economy and not remain restricted to political economy.

In light of this system of intrinsic mediation of the processes of desire by language, it becomes necessary to develop a different conception of how subjectivity is produced, how statements are produced in relation to this subjectivity. A conception that has nothing to do with postulating intrapsychic agencies or agencies of individuation (as in theories of the ego), or agencies modeling iconic semiotics (such as we find in all theories about the way an image functions in the psyche). An example of the latter is Freudian theory: Freud set out to build a social economy of subjectivity based on systems of identification and the problems of ego ideals.

What the structuralists say is not true: it is not language or communication that produce subjectivity. Subjectivity is manufactured just as energy, electricity, and aluminum are. An individual is the result of a biological metabolism in which his or her father and mother participate. Things can be viewed in this way, but in reality it also depends on the biological industry, and even on genetic engineering. It is clear that had this industry not launched the ongoing race to respond to the viruses that regularly sweep across the planet, human life would have been wiped out. The spread of AIDS started a treasure hunt of enormous scope, a permanent race to find a response. *The perfection and production of immunological responses currently forms a part of the creation of life on this planet.*

There is no "recipient" subjectivity in which external things are placed and then "internalized." These "things" intervene in the actual syntagmatics of unconscious subjectivation. Examples include: a certain way of using language, of connecting with the mode of collective semiotization (especially in the media); a relation with the world of electric sockets, in which it is possible to get electrocuted; a relation with the world of circulation in the city. All of these elements make up subjectivity.

In my view, the individual stands at a crossroads of many components of subjectivity. Some of these are unconscious. Others belong more to the body, a territory in which we feel good. Others yet belong more to what American sociologists call "primary groups" (the clan, band, or group). Yet others belong to the production of power: they stand in a relation to the law, the police, and similar authorities. My hypothesis is that there also exists a subjectivity that is even more extensive. It is what I call capitalistic subjectivity.

It would be useful to define subjectivity in another way, totally giving up on the idea that society and the phenomena of social expression are the result of a mere agglomeration, a mere sum of individual subjectivities. On the contrary, it is individual subjectivity that results from an intersection of collective determinations of various kinds, not only social but also economic, technologic, the media, and so on.

Debate at the Psychoanalysis School of the Sedes Sapientiae Institute, São Paulo, August 31, 1982:

Mário Fuks: From what I understand, you say that the changes, the variations, in the methodology of modelization correspond, in the final analysis, to general changes in the production of subjectivity. My question is: is there a direct link (and, if so, to what degree) between the transformations that have been occurring in the production of subjectivity and the changes in psychoanalytic models that have been taking place during the course of almost a century of the history of psychoanalysis?

Guattari: A subjective fact is always engendered by an assemblage of heterogeneous semiotic levels. The historic modelizations of the unconscious corresponds to a tremendous drift of the modes of subjective territorialization. Some modes of subjective reference, or modes of production of subjectivity, were literally swept away from the planet with the rise of capitalist systems. One could say that there is a general movement of deterritorialization of subjective references. Until the French Revolution and Romanticism, subjectivity remained bound up with territorialized modes of production—in the extended family, guild systems, castes, and social segmentarity—which didn't make subjectivity operational at the individual level.

With the emergence of a new kind of collective labor power, and with the delimitation of a new kind of individuation of subjectivity, the question of inventing new coordinates for the production of subjectivity arose. Historians such as Philippe Ariès, Donzelot, and others have shown that a confinement of the family and a delimitation of childhood were taking place. In the systems prior to capitalist formations, the production of subjectivity in the child was not entirely centered on the conjugal family. A complex economy of integration between age groups and of articulation with the surrounding social field kept subjectivity in relations of permanent dependence. The disparities were always in some way complementary. We have various literary witnesses for this complementarity. One could be the relation between Don Quixote, the master, and Sancho Panza, his servant. But perhaps it is not the best example, because this work in fact provides an outline of the deterritorialization that the master-servant relations were already experiencing at that time.

Individualized responsibility is a late notion, as also are the notions of error and internalized guilt. At some point, a generalized confinement of subjectivities took place, a separation of social areas, and a breach of all of the old forms of dependence. With the French Revolution, not only did every individual become legally—

although not really—free, equal, and brothers (losing their subjective adherences to clan and primary group systems), but they also had to account to transcendental laws, laws of capitalistic subjectivity. Under those conditions, it was necessary to provide other foundations to the subject and his relations: the relation of the subject with thought (the Cartesian *cogito*), with moral law (the Kantian numen), with nature (a different way of feeling it and conceiving it), with others (the conception of the other as object). In this general drift of territorialized modes of subjectivation there developed not only psychological theories concerned with the faculties of the soul, but also a permanent rewriting of the procedures of subjectivation in the general field of social transformations.

The evolution of the novel as a whole can be traced back to those different attempts to create systems of reference for the new modes of production of subjectivity. It is interesting to note how systems of modelization in the novel are always related to the systems of modelization of the psyche. Freud always looked for references in ancient mythology, yet he translated them to a kind of family novel much closer to the work of Goethe. However, I think it is clear that the greatest psychoanalysts are not Freud, Lacan, Jung, or anyone of that kind, but Proust, Kafka, or Lautréamont. They were able to take subjective mutations into account much better than the supposedly scientific attempts at modelization.

The systems of modelization present in the organization of social struggles are related to the systems of modelization of the psyche. One has only to think of the types of subjective production engendered in the workers' movement by the Second International, or Leninism, or Maoism. It may be something much less thrilling than novelistic expressions of sentiment, but it undoubtedly points us to a mode of expression that has nothing to do with the evolution of bourgeois subjectivity.

If we look at what really takes place with artistic and scientific creation, we never find systems of centralization, institutions that totally control creative processes. They proceed from assemblages of enunciation that sometimes cross not only institutions and specialties, but also countries, and even eras. There is always a kind of multicentering of points of singularization in the field of creation. That does not prevent the appearance of a creative individual or a school at one time or another—but one always returns to a phylum of production that intersects another phylum. Only generals and despots of culture harbor the idea that it is possible to program a revolution, even a cultural one. *By its very essence, creation is always dissident, transindividual, transcultural.*

SINGULARITY OR INDIVIDUALITY

Meeting at the Freudian Institute of Psychoanalysis, Rio de Janeiro, September 10, 1982:

Question: You say that the entire process of transformation takes place through singularization. Does that mean that every change is individual?

Guattari: No, I'm trying to say exactly the opposite. Collective subjectivity is not the result of a sum of individual subjectivities. The process of singularization of subjectivity is accomplished by adopting, associating, and agglomerating dimensions of different kinds. Processes of singularization that convey vectors of desire may meet processes of individuation. In such a case, there are always processes of assignation of social responsibility, culpabilization, and entry into the dominant legal system. I think that the relation between singularity and individuality is best presented in this way, and not as an absolute disjunction, which would imply a mythic return to pure singularity, a pure conversion to the primary process. There is a permanent intersection at which the issue specifically arises: how can the process of singularization that takes place at the fantasmatic level of the object of desire, or at any other pragmatic level, be articulated with the processes of individuation that take hold of us from all sides?

But what processes of individuation are these? A first, more obvious level of individuation is the fact that we are biological individuals, committed to processes of nutrition and survival. A question that arises then is how one can prevent it from becoming a passion for death, of the kind that we find in anorexia or melancholy. Another level of individuation is sexual division: we are men or women or homosexuals, but at any rate something perfectly classifiable. Yet another level is individuation in social-economic relations, the social class that we are compelled to assume. All these examples show us that individuation itself confronts various processes of integration and normalization. The question that arises is how the micropolitics of singular processes can be articulated with these processes of individuation. The entire development of philosophy since Descartes, or psychology since theorists such as Taine and Wundt, tends to relate subjectivity to an individual identity. They consider family and social groups like superstructures in relation to individuated subjectivity. I think that this lies at the root of all the reductionist views in the field of phenomenology and of psychology. However, forms of behavior and engagements in value systems never come from this individuation.

———

The relation established between the ego and the social and legal person always tends to put responsibility on subjectivity. A social reification of subjectivity takes place, with all its countereffects of repression, culpabilization, and so on. We are totally imprisoned by a kind of individuation of subjectivity. In this respect, the question is not really one of recovering the level of our individuality, because we can go on spinning around it as if we had a terrible toothache, without being able to release processes of singularization on an infrapersonal, or on an extrapersonal level. Because in order to do so, it is necessary to connect with the outside.

When I speak of a "process of subjectivation" or of "singularization," it has nothing to do with the individual. In my view, there is no clear unity of the person: the individual, the ego, or the politics of the ego, the politics of the individuation of subjectivity, are correlated with systems of identification that are modelizing.

THE ASSEMBLY LINE OF SUBJECTIVITY

IWC asserts itself through a double oppression in modalities that vary according to the country or social stratum. First, by direct repression, both economic and social—controlling the production of goods and social relations through external material coercion and the suggestion of meaning. The second oppression, perhaps greater than the first in intensity, consists in the installation of IWC in the very production of subjectivity: *an immense machine producing a subjectivity standardized on a world scale has become a basic element in the formation of collective labor power and the force for collective social control.*

Machines are acquiring increasing importance in production processes. Relations of intelligence, control, and social organization are increasingly closer to machinic processes; through this production of capitalistic subjectivity the classes and castes that possess power in industrial societies seek to ensure increasingly despotic control over production systems and social life.

The production of subjectivity by IWC is serialized, standardized, and centralized around an image, a subjective consensus relating to and overcoded by a transcendental law. It is this gridded control of subjectivity that makes it possible for it to be propagated at the level of the production and consumption of social relations, in all milieus (intellectual, agricultural, industrial, etc.) and at every single point of the planet.

Vast state machines control everything, from their own agents to the people who earn minimum wage, or people lost in regions such as the arid zone of northeast Brazil. Individuals are reduced to mere mechanisms concentrating on the value of their actions, a value that responds to the capitalistic market and its general equivalents. They are like solitary, anguished robots, increasingly absorbing the drugs that power offers them, and allowing themselves to be increasingly fascinated by promotion. Each rung of promotion offers them a certain kind of home and a certain kind of social relation and prestige.

The current tendency is to equalize everything by means of broad unifying, reductive categories—such as capital, labor, a certain kind of wage system, culture, or information—which prevent people from noticing the processes of singularization. All creativity in the social and technological field tends to be crushed, every microvector of singular subjectivation is coopted. A general drift of the territorialized modes of subjectivity is taking place everywhere. Millenary traditions of a certain kind of social relation and cultural life are rapidly being swept from the planet. All supposed residual cultural identities are contaminated. All the modes of valorization of existence and production are threatened in the current development of societies. Even the most traditional and most strongly anchored values such as work are being undermined from within by industrial revolutions. If we closely analyze what happens with people who invent rich, personalized semiotics such as *candomblé*, we see that they are not completely impermeable and autonomous in relation to the dominant models.

The production machine of capitalistic subjectivity is in place right from childhood, with the child's entry into the world of dominant languages, with all the imaginary and technical models which the child must enter.

Culpabilization is a function of capitalistic subjectivity. The root of capitalistic technologies for culpabilization consists in always proposing an image of reference that serves as a basis for questions such as: "Who are you?"—"You who dare having an opinion, on behalf of what do you speak?"—"What are you worth on the scale of values recognized by society?"—"What does your discourse correspond to?"—"In what category do you put yourself?" And we are obliged to accept the singularity of our own position with the greatest possible consistency. But it is often impossible to do this alone, because a position always implies a collective assemblage. However, the slightest hesitation in response to this demand for a reference pushes you into a kind of hole, forcing you to wonder: "After all, who am I? Am I just a piece of shit?" It is as if your right to exist were to collapse. And so you think that the best thing to do is to shut up and internalize those values. But who says so? It is not necessarily the teacher or the explicit external master, it may be something that is part of us, inside us, something that we ourselves reproduce. Agencies of the superego and agencies of inhibition.

In my view, it is very important not to confuse these procedures of culpabilization, systematically produced by all the systems of modelization or formation of subjectivity, with a kind of sado-masochistic mechanism that in Freudian terms would be of an intrapsychic nature (a kind of Eros/Thanatos conflict). In other words, *dealing with these problematics does not involve an extended psychoanalysis, but micropolitical procedures setting up particular devices that dissolve these elements of culpabilization in capitalistic values.*

Segregation is a function of the capitalistic subjective economy that is directly linked and culpabilization. Both presuppose the identification of any process with imaginary frames of reference, encouraging all kinds of manipulation. It is as if, in order to maintain itself, the social order had to establish systems of unconscious hierarchy, systems of scales of value, and systems of discipline, albeit in the most artificial manner possible. These systems provide a subjective consistency to the elites (or the supposed elites), and open up a whole field of social valorization in which the various individuals and strata of society have to find their place. This capitalistic valorization essentially takes a position not only against the systems of use value, as described by Marx, but also against all modes of valorization of desire, of singularities.

Another function of the capitalistic subjective economy, and perhaps the most important of all, *is infantilization.* They do our thinking for us, they organize production and social life for us. Moreover, they consider that everything that has to do with extraordinary things—

speaking and living, growing old and dying—should not disturb the harmony at the workplace and within the positions of social control that we occupy, starting with the control that we exercise on ourselves.

Infantilization—of women, of the insane, of certain social sectors, or of any dissident behavior—consists in making sure that everything that is done or thought, or that might be done or thought, is mediated by the state. Any kind of economic exchange, any kind of cultural or social production, tends to pass through the mediation of the state. This relation of dependency on the state is one of the essential elements of capitalistic subjectivity.

Collective facilities—not only services for physical or mental health (such as health clinics and health centers) or cultural life (such as schools and universities), but also the media—tend to acquire undue importance. They reinforce the state in its extended function. The function of these facilities, like workers on a machine for the formation of capitalistic subjectivity, is to integrate human, infrahuman, and extrahuman factors, creating a real articulation between agencies as different as those at work in libidinal economy (such as family systems) and in semiotic productions (such as the media).

The capitalistic order is projected on the reality of the world and on psychic reality. It has an impact on patterns of behavior, action, gestures, thought, meaning, feeling, affection, etc. It has an impact on the assemblies of perception and memorization, and the modelization of intrasubjective agencies—agencies that psychoanalysis reifies in the categories of ego, superego, ego ideal, and all that paraphernalia.

The capitalistic order produces modes of human relations even in their unconscious representations: the ways in which people work, are educated, love, have sex, and talk. And that's not all. It manufactures people's relations with production, nature, events, movement, the body, eating, the present, the past, and the future—in short, it manufactures people's relations with the world and with themselves. And we accept all this because we assume that this is "the" world order, an order that cannot be touched without endangering the very idea of organized social life.

The appropriation of the production of subjectivity by IWC is draining all knowledge of singularity. It is a subjectivity that does not know the essential dimensions of existence such as death, pain, loneliness, silence, or the relation with the cosmos and time. Feelings such as anger are surprising and scandalous. Similarly, an uncontrollable disease such as cancer is something that leaves us bewildered. The same is true of the relation with aging. This process is so inconceivable that a chain of "micro-gulags" is created for old people, simply in order to isolate them. And people accept this isolation. It is scandalous that the elderly are passively handed over to a fate that takes them to those fields of desperation, which in some cases are nothing but "killing fields" in their modern version.

Everything that pertains to the domain of rupture, surprise, and anguish, but also desire, the will to love and to create, somehow has to fit into the registers of dominant references. There is always an arrangement ready to prevent anything that might be of a dissident nature in thought and desire. There is an attempt to eliminate what I call the processes of singularization. Everything that surprises, however mildly, has to be classifiable in some area of framing or reference. Not only teachers but also the mass media (particularly journalists) are very skilful at this kind of practice. I am convinced that if extraterrestrials landed in São Paulo tomorrow, there would be experts, journalists, and all sorts of specialists to explain that there is nothing so extraordinary about it, that there were already plans for it, that a special committee has been dealing for a long time with the subject, and, above all, that there is nothing to get upset about, because the government is there to take care of these things.

With the help of computers, the programming of childhood in France is now able to calculate what the rate of delinquency will be for entire sectors of the population ten, fifteen, or twenty years from now. So, before the deviation is experienced in a genetic program, it is overcoded by this programming of subjectivity. In which case, all that remains for people is to live a prestructured "possible" where they happen to be. For example, if you are a woman of a certain age and class, you have to conform to certain boundaries. If you don't do it, either you are a delinquent or you are mad.

The capitalistic order has an impact on modes of temporalization. It destroys ancient life systems and imposes a time of equivalences, beginning with wage labor, through which it gives value to different activities of production. Those that enter commercial circuits, productions of a social order or highly valued productions, are all overcoded by a general time of equivalence.

Phenomenologically, we realize that this time of equivalence is something that depends on a certain social order: time does not follow the same rhythms or the same "ritornellos" in an oneiric assemblage, in a melancholy or manic assemblage, in an assemblage of dance or collective social production. These are, in fact, specific modes of territorialization. All of these internalized ways of measuring the equivalence of time are not just a subjective fact, but also basic elements for the formation of collective labor power, and for the formation of the collective force for social control. What has been said about the mode of temporalization could also be said about the mode of spatialization. Nowadays, all relations between space, time, and the cosmos tend to be mediated by imposed schemes and rhythms, framed by systems of transportation, by the modelization of urban space and domestic space, by the car-television-collective facilities triad, and so on.

What gives strength to capitalistic subjectivity is that it is produced both by the oppressors and by the oppressed. In this respect it can be distinguished from the systems of social classes or ancient aristocratic and religious castes. Japan is a good example, because it is a country where subjectivity tends to be totally enslaved by the machinic process, where there is a passion for production, even among the most exploited workers. A kind of relation of complementarity and dependence is established between the various social categories, which ultimately dismantles class alliances and social alliances.

If I insist on the mode of production of capitalistic subjectivity, my purpose is not intended to describe a state of reality toward which we are inexorably heading, or because I wish to celebrate the anniversary of Orwell's *1984*, but because I believe that this development brings as well immense possibilities for diversion and reappropriation. This can be understood once one recognizes that the struggle is no longer restricted to political economy, but also includes subjective economy. No longer are social confrontations merely of an economic order, they also take place among the different ways in which groups and individuals choose to live.

Suely Rolnik: There are many authors who devote themselves to an analysis of the processes of subjectivation characteristic of capitalism, and of their political implications. And many of them consider these processes to be like a subjective assembly line disseminated throughout the whole social body, conveying a violence of a different type than the more directly perceptible violence of the relations of domination and exploitation.

What seems to me original in the work that Deleuze and Guattari have developed is, firstly, the recognition of this production as the basic industry of the capitalist system itself (or of the bureaucratic socialist system). Then these authors' sensitivity to the points of rupture within this complex device for the production of subjectivity, points at which, according to them, many present-day social movements are inscribed. Finally, they recognize these points of rupture as focuses of major political resistance: they attack the logic of the system, not as an abstraction or representation, but as a lived experience. There is an opening up of new possibilities in this position that is quite rare nowadays.

MOLECULAR REVOLUTIONS: DARING TO SINGULARIZE

The attempt at social control on a world scale through the production of subjectivity clashes with considerable factors of resistance from processes of permanent differentiation that I would call "molecular revolution." But the name is not important.

What characterizes the new social movements is not only a resistance against this general process serializing subjectivity, but also an attempt to produce original, singular modes of subjectivation, processes of subjective singularization.

Vast areas of the planet are pervaded by the function of singularization, by processes of reappropriation of subjectivity: both in the so-called Third World at an international level, and also in the other Third World that is developing within the so-called "developed" countries. In this respect, it can be said, briefly, that there is a kind of vectorization of the general problematic of components of molecular transformation.

The function of autonomization in a group corresponds to the capability of carrying out its own work of semiotization, of cartography, inserting itself into local power relations, making and unmaking alliances, and so on.

What characterizes a process of singularization (which, at one time, I called the "experience of a subject-group") is that it is self-modeling. In other words, it captures the elements of the situation, it constructs its own types of practical and theoretical references, without remaining dependent in relation to global power, whether in terms of economy, knowledge, technology, or segregations and prestige that are disseminated. Once groups acquire this freedom to live their processes, they acquire an ability to read their own situation and what is taking place around them. It is this ability that will give them at least some possibility of creation and make it possible to preserve this very important character of autonomy.

The idea of molecular revolution concerns every level synchronically: infrapersonal (at work in dreaming, creation, etc.), personal (in relations of self-domination, what psychoanalysts call the superego), and interpersonal (in the invention of new forms of sociability in domestic, romantic, and professional life, and in relations with neighbors and school).

Free radio stations, challenging the system of political representation, questioning daily life, and reactions that refuse work in its current form, are viruses contaminating the social body in its relation with consumption, production, leisure, communications media, culture, and so on. They are molecular relations creating mutations in the conscious and unconscious subjectivity of individuals and social groups.

A molecular revolution consists in producing conditions not only for collective life but also for the embodiment of life for oneself, both materially and subjectively.

What I am describing as processes of singularization is something that frustrates mechanisms internalizing capitalistic values, something that can lead to affirm values in a specific register, irrespective of the scales of value that surround us from all sides and keep watch on us.

The possibility of reappropriating the media, for example through free radio stations, can subvert the modelization of subjectivity.

The trait that the various processes of singularization have in common is that their differential becoming rejects capitalistic subjectivation. It can be felt in a warmth of relations, in a certain way of desiring, in a positive affirmation of creativity, in a willingness to love, in a willingness simply to live or survive, in the multiplicity of these willingnesses. It is necessary to open up space for this to happen. Desire can only be lived in vectors of singularity.

Revolutionary microprocesses may not be of the same nature as social relations. For example, an individual's relation with music or painting can stimulate a totally new process of perception and sensibility.

There is a kind of social resistance that should be opposed to the dominant modes of temporalization. It could go from rejecting a certain pace in the processes of wage labor, to the fact of certain groups realizing that they should produce their own sense of time— as in music or dancing. Some theorists in the Autonomia[2] movement in Italy insisted precisely on differentiating between modes of temporalization. The same can be said of modes of spatialization.

Some attempts at singularization are difficult and problematic, and they may eventually be aborted. But despite their precariousness and failures—we may all be dispersed and lost, overcome by anguish, madness, and wretchedness—they break away from the industrial production of subjectivity by IWC. They trigger off processes capable of reappropriating subjective territories, and there is more to them than a mere defensive attitude. These attempts may also appropriate mutant aspects of what I call "machinic processes" (theoretical and literary machines, machines of sensibility, etc., and not just technical tools found in production). It is true that there is no possibility of a common front in all this; and it is true too that we have been taking a beating for quite some time. However, there still is a huge potential for resistance, and even offensive, and these will tend to acquire increasing importance in the historical events that are yet to come. First we must nevertheless recognize that the enemy is to be found not only in the dominant imperialisms, but also in our own allies, in ourselves, in this insistent reembodiment of the dominant models not only in the most dearly loved political parties or in the leaders who defend us in the best possible way, but also in our own attitudes, on the most diverse occasions.

Questioning the capitalistic system is no longer the exclusive domain of large-scale political and social struggles, or of the affirmation of the working class. It also concerns what I have attempted to group together under the heading of "molecular revolution," whose enemies or antagonists cannot be clearly classified. A relation of complementarity and segmentarity makes us simultaneously allies and enemies of other people.

Is it possible that between these new types of struggle involving social movements and industrial society there could only be a Manichean relation through opposition? Could it be that molecular revolutions, by definition, will always remain on the defensive, or be demanding recognition? Will they always remain prisoners of the absurd antagonism between accepting neoliberalism and the wonders of capitalism or ending up in the "gulag"? Are the people who control IWC—in which I include not only the Americans, but also the Russians, the oil-producing nations, and others—really carrying out a transformation of productive forces, aimed at resolving a series of basic problems for the entire planet? The current crisis or war shows us precisely the opposite. None of the basic problems on the planet are about to be resolved. On the contrary, there is an ever greater gap between the revolution in manufacturing, computers, telecommunications, and robots on the one hand, and the social forms that IWC maintains by force on the other hand. There was a time in the history of capitalism when a series of bourgeois revolutions profoundly transformed social relations and at the same time transformed economic relations. It seems that this parallelism is totally lacking in the current crisis. In that respect the world movement of molecular revolutions is far better attuned to the transformations of production and computer technology that are currently being carried out, and to the evolution of scientific and aesthetic relations; better adapted to the transformations that are underway in those fields than the sclerotic structures of the universities and official organizations, both in the East and in the West.

They want to convince us that we are heading to some kind of disaster. It is all the more important to show that, in symmetry with the apparent omnipotence of IWC, an entire range of possible paths are open to us leading to transformations at every level.

The question arises whether one could conceive of an organized society, not a utopia, capable of producing modes of subjectivation on different bases than those on which world industrialization is established. I don't think we should return to the archaicism of a cultural *déjà-là* of subjectivity in order to recover it; on the contrary, we should create conditions for the production of a new kind of subjectivity that becomes singularized and finds the paths of its own specification.

As long as movements that seek to change society fight the omnipotent production of capitalistic subjectivity with archaic practices based on a Manichean vision, they will be leaving the field wide open to it. In order to trigger processes capable of reappropriating subjectivity—

among psychiatrized people;[3] among groups trying to organize their life differently; among social minorities resisting the systems of coercion that seek to modelize them; among women who want to free themselves, even on a small scale, from a system that has subjected them for thousands of years; or among creative workers eager to free themselves from standardizing systems in their field; or even children who refuse the educational system and the way of life that are proposed to them—all these groups must create their own modes of reference, their own cartographies, invent their praxis in order to make breaches in the dominant system of subjectivity.

Everybody should assert the singular position that they occupy, making it live, articulating it with other processes of singularization, and resisting any attempt to level out subjectivity. Because it is through those attempts that imperialism is now asserted by the manipulation of collective subjectivity at least as much as by economic domination. Irrespective of their scale, the way they are expressed or assembled, these attempts to question the system producing subjectivity have a definite political impact.

Every becoming-singular, every attempt to achieve an authentic existence, come up against the wall of capitalistic subjectivity. Sometimes these becomings are absorbed by the wall, sometimes they undergo a veritable implosion. It is necessary to build a different logic in order for this wall to be simultaneously perceived as a target that one could penetrate. It is possible to know how formidable the wall is, and how arduous it would be to bring it down without falling into fascism, and still keep on developing new assemblages and territories where people feel good. In my view, if we fail to preserve these two dimensions, we will run a double risk of impotence: either by letting the huge machines of the State control everything, or else let the systems of power and leadership manipulated by the media reappropriate our everyday life.

Assemblages capable of building up their own modes of subjectivation involve two kinds of attitude:

> —the normalizing attitude, which follows two different but complementary ways: either it systematically ignores those assemblages, dismissing them as ancillary problems or archaisms, or else it recovers and integrates them.
> —the attitude of recognition, which preserves their specific character and their common traits in order to make their articulation possible and produce a real change in the situation.

Any emerging singularity brings about two kinds of micropolitical response: a normalizing response or an attempt to use that singularity to initiate a process that may change the situation, and perhaps not just locally. I will cite as an example something that happened here a short while ago. We were absorbed in a collective discourse that seemed to be flowing on its own, like a computer spewing out files. Although no one had made any objection, we could feel the presence of something that was hard to capture, an affect, a kind of malaise, as if the question "What are we talking about anyway?" were hovering in the air. We felt that there was no common thread. That is what I would call "an indicator of singularity." There was something happening there and we didn't know what to do or say about it. Two different attitudes were possible. We could say: "Let's be patient, we just began, so let's go on and anyone who isn't pleased can leave." Very often, that is what happens. On the other hand, one could deal with the phenomena of singularity present in the situation.

Here's another example. A child sitting at the back of the class gets bored and starts throwing gum or pellets at other kids' heads. We usually put the disruptive child outside the classroom, or try to give him as little chance as possible to act up. Or else, in more sophisticated systems, we may send him to a psychologist. It is very rare for us to ask whether this act of singularity concerns the class as a whole. To do so would be to question our own position in the situation, and recognize that perhaps other children also are bored, but don't show it in the same way.

In other words, a point of singularity can be steered towards a stratification that cancels it out completely, or it can also enter a micropolitics that turns it into a process of singularization. In my view, this is where the importance of analyzing the problematics of the unconscious lies.

Capitalistic cultural systems seek to coopt the value of singularity. This is done through a process of integration. For example, certain traits of singularity in black music are integrated into jazz, which is distributed throughout the social field and becomes a kind of universal music. Another example is the use of certain traits of singularity revealed by feminist movements or gay movements as local axioms, and contribute to improve the production of subjectivity in the system.

Meeting at the Freudian School of São Paulo, August 26, 1982:

Question: I would like to know how this process that causes singularity to emerge can take place in a system that is permanently bureaucratized, a system that establishes its social control in terms of production.

Guattari: I think that this problem is raised by business managers themselves, especially in basic industries, and by research organizations and advertising agencies. They all know very well that, in addition to improving the workers' mental health, breaking up routine repetition and finding ways of articulating various existing modes of subjectivation can also have considerable economic, technological, and scientific consequences. During the time of Stalinism, the condemnation of cybernetic research had huge consequences for the Soviet Union. The rejection of creativity in a technological or social field (it comes to the same thing) can trigger considerable crises.

Nowadays we can see in many places, especially in Japan, that corporate leaders are trying to create conditions for at least some singularization to be possible in the vectors of production. This means that in these stratified structures an attempt is being made to create sufficient margins to allow for these processes, as long as the system capable of coopting them remains absolute. In a way, progress in the technology of basic industry depends on the modulation of degrees of singularization and freedom.

In the current social system, the complex of stratified social forms is clearly incapable of responding to machinic changes, which are constantly reterritorialized and restratified. In a course given by Merleau-Ponty that I attended, he said that during a visit to a school inspired by the Freinet method, a child asked his teacher: "Next year, will we still have to use these free texts?" It's always the same thing: universes of "possibles" keep encountering subjective stratifications until they reach a point at which a dialectical transformation of the other levels of social life can be established. Otherwise, the rigidity of the stratified structures becomes even greater. This is what has brought the generations born after the 1960s (specifically, after May 1968) to invest in a much greater conformism than previous generations had done—Freudians would call that "counterinvestment." In the case of 1968, it happened because the transformations did not affect the structures as a whole.

It is precisely the points of singularity, the processes of singularization, that are the productive roots of subjectivity in its plurality.

There is always something precarious or fragile in processes of singularization. They always run the risk of being coopted, either by institutionalization or by becoming-sectarian. A process of singularization may appear active at the level of the assemblage, and at the same time may close off into a ghetto.

Minority groups could have a discourse and a way of operating that are completely ossified and undistinguishable from traditional sectarian groups, and yet find themselves in the position of carrying out sequences of molecular revolution—due to the totality of the dynamics of the processes of social and economic transformation. What may be at work in this kind of circumstance is a set of processual problems capable of bringing about mutations in the unconscious social field, independently of the discourses held by these. To account for such phenomena, however, it would be necessary to redefine the concept of the unconscious. Looking at it in this way, what is at work in these minority groups goes totally against the idea that they are missionaries, the bearers of some redeeming truth. At any rate, what I am saying has nothing to do with that kind of focus.

Interview by Pepe Escobar for the "Folhetim" section of the* Folha de
São Paulo, *September 5, 1982:*

Pepe Escobar: Can life be invented if all the images are produced
beforehand?

Guattari: Yes, take the example of chemists. They work with the
same material every day: carbon and hydrogen. It's like the situation
of a painter who buys his paints at the same store. What matters is
what he does with them. The main thing is to free oneself from this
kind of redundancy, seriality, mass production of subjectivity, the
constant prompting to return to the same point.

———

What I think is interesting about punk groups is that they seem to
be completely imprisoned by the dominant means of expression.
They use material manufactured by the mighty media industry
(instruments distributed in hundreds of thousands throughout the
planet). They are also totally dependent on commercial systems to
record or give concerts. This dependency even extends to the places
where they can rehearse. In Paris it takes them some time to find a
place, and when they find one the neighbors complain, and sooner or later the police evict them. I don't know if the same thing
happens here. Apart from that, punks are, unconsciously, tribu-
taries of the dominant systems of expression: their themes are the
themes of commercial music, their melody lines are reproductions
of those found everywhere. It's easy to see the extent to which they
are polluted by images from film and television, the extent to
which they incorporate a certain representation of the star system,
a whole ego ideal. Not to mention the phallocratic relations that
make even second-rate rock and punk music an impossible field of
action for women.

If we consider all these elements together, we could say that it is an undertaking that has been completely coopted, that it is imploding, running the risk of declining into microfascism. Nevertheless, despite all the heterogeneous, mass-produced character of its components (in which everything seems to have been borrowed from the dominant oppressive systems), these components can constitute elements in a process of singularization. Hundreds of groups live out and embody their desire in collective undertakings such as rock and punk, which for them can be of absolutely vital importance. Although they convey elements of meaning of the dominant ideology, and although they are prisoners of numerous systems of modelization, they express—on a certain unconscious level, although we would have to agree on the meaning that we assign to this term—what I call a "vector of molecular revolution," which can subvert the modelization of subjectivity.

Even when a two-year-old child tries to organize its world, construct its own way of perceiving social relations, and appropriate relations with other children and with adults—that child, in its way, participates in molecular resistance. And what does it find? A function of the subjective facilities of television, family, and school systems. Consequently, the micropolitics of the child involve the people who are in a position of modelization in relation to it.

It is possible to subvert this position. People who have seriously experimented with other educational methods are well aware that this infernal mechanism can be dismantled. With a different kind of approach, the whole wealth of sensibility and expression natural to the child can be relatively preserved.

Autonomy is a function. The "function of autonomy" can be embodied effectively in feminist, black, ecological, homosexual, or other groups. But it can also be embodied in machines for struggle on a large scale—as in the case of the PT at this time of electoral campaign.

I really believe that organizations such as parties or unions can be fields in which to exercise the function of autonomy. There are also other fields, microscopic ones: the relations of daily life in a neighborhood, a community, a school, a theater group, or a group that sets up a free radio station. Or even the relations between activists of any kind, between men and women, between races or between generations.

So what is this "function of autonomy" that can bring together so many different levels of social life? I would not define it as something that sets out from a program or a general axiomatic, but as something that is expressed at a micropolitical level—precisely that of the production of subjectivity.

A process of singularization of subjectivity can acquire tremendous importance, in precisely the same way that a great poet, a great musician, or a great painter, each with their unique visions of writing, music, or painting, can trigger off a mutation in the collective systems of hearing and seeing. In saying this, I don't mean that any maladjusted child or any person classified as schizophrenic is automatically a great artist or a great revolutionary.

The way in which the current forms of struggle are being experimented with involves great precariousness, with highs and lows, mediocre things and brilliant things. It is like a laboratory where a new kind of struggle is being created by means of a complex dialectic of trial and error. Examples of this are what the Italians experienced in their various experiments with autonomy, the totally original organization that the Poles are trying out in the Soli-darność (Solidarity) movement, or even what Brazilians are probably going through now with the activities of the PT, minorities, and so on.

Interview by Sonia Goldfeder, August 31, 1982:

Sonia Goldfeder: Can you give examples of where what you call molecular revolution is happening now?

Guattari: Poland is a country that is now going through a complete subjective change. There is a rejection, a discrediting, of everything about the way things work in the country. This forms part of sensibil-ity, the unconscious, fantasies. It can even be seen in the jokes that are told there. One that I remember is the story of three dogs—one Bel-gian, one Russian, and one Polish. The Belgian dog says: "My country is great, just bark and they bring a steak." The Polish dog asks: "But what's a steak?" And the Russian dog asks: "What's barking?"

At the same time as they were even changing their sense of humor, the Poles organized a protest movement that they call a "union." It's obvious that it isn't a union; Jaruzelski is right. Why? Because, while it is a movement that wants to change society, a kind of party that represents society, it is also a way of organizing daily life, even the forms of Solidarity's struggle against repression. They publish books, they argue, there's a whole metabolism of what is happening among students, workers, and intellectuals. All this is completely new. It's something that clearly accepts the three levels of molecular revolution: the infrapersonal level, the way in which one lives the relation with society, and the presence of the relations between political forces. This is what gives them their fantastic power—because in Solidarity you have not just ten million people but a whole population. They have even reinvented Catholicism. The old Church, the episcopate, still exists, but alongside it they have invented a kind of Catholicism that is not a real religion. The molecular revolution is the awakening of this notion of desire, both on a microscopic level and on a social scale. Once the fuse had been lit, they said: "That's it! Stop! We won't take it anymore!"

For a long time we believed that history was made by parties, by leaders, by large social and economic movements. Now we see that it is also made by this kind of molecular wave. If we don't take this into consideration, we remain outside events. In Iran, I agree that there is an atrocious struggle against those fascistic types led by Khomeini. But that doesn't prevent there being a fantastic element of subjective mutation there. The appearance of a series of religious phenomena unites a whole nation against an oppressor. People went to their death in their thousands because there was an explosion, because there was a subjective revolution. It all became institutionalized under Khomeini, and even so it hasn't ended. The whole Muslim Arab world rejects capitalistic subjectivity. This doesn't mean that they are progressives: it means that the supremacy of capitalistic production in history is not so clear. The real social revolution involves being able to articulate oneself and to allow the process of singularization to assert itself.

———

In West Germany—in Berlin, Frankfurt, Hamburg, and all the main cities—there are alternative sectors that are very highly developed and well structured. There is a very elaborate reappropriation of daily life.

The goal of the production of capitalistic subjectivity is to reduce everything to a tabula rasa. But it is not always possible, even in "developed" capitalist countries. What characterizes political life in

France, for example, is the development of collective forms of subjectivity that capitalism considered to have been completely overcome. I am referring to struggles like those of the Bretons, the Basques, the Corsicans, but also the struggle of a vast mass of young people who utterly refuse to join the dominant process of culture and production, and the dominant organizations, including the communists and socialists.

In Brazil, although the country is committed to the capitalistic process and is on the way to becoming a great power, there are huge areas of the population who are "not guaranteed," who escape this kind of control grid and this kind of production of subjectivity, and that is very important.

Round-table discussion at the Folha de São Paulo, *September 3, 1982:*

Laymert Garcia dos Santos: We cannot consider the role of the communications media in Brazil using precisely the same categories that theorists in the industrialized countries use when they consider the problem. For one very simple reason: they do not apply here in the same way. In the United States or in Europe, the starting point is a twofold question: on the one hand, what the media produce for the mass of depersonalized, anonymous, interchangeable, decoded individuals, the category of the "free worker"; and, on the other hand, what the free worker *produces* from that production, in other words, what he *manufactures* with the statements and images that constantly bombard him. The terrain on which this reflection moves always places the free worker as a basic requisite, constituting one of the two basic elements of capitalism—the other, clearly, being capital.

In naming the "free worker" one has named the basic element for the operation of the media. For, as the German theoretician Hans Magnus Enzensberger states, the industrialization of the mind implies four conditions:

1) a philosophical prerequisite: rationalism;
2) a political prerequisite: the proclamation of human rights, especially equality and liberty;
3) an economic prerequisite: the accumulation of capital;
4) technological prerequisite: industrialization.

Thus, what is necessary for the media to be able to act is the existence of the free worker, the depersonalized individual, the individual who, from the viewpoint of the capitalist system, only counts as labor power, although he spends all his time saying "me, me, me." It is as though capitalism depersonalized on the one hand, while simultaneously proposing models created on the basis of an abstract equality to fill the gap, the nonexistence of people, so that the subject, semiotized by models, can speak of "myself."

The communications media work in this process. The media constitute a kind of wall of language that ceaselessly proposes models of images to which the receiver can conform—images of unity, images of rationality, images of legitimacy, images of justice, images of beauty, images of scientificity. The mass media speak through and for individuals.

This process of individuation—depersonalization and repersonalization—is quite sophisticated in the advanced capitalist countries, and Guattari speaks about it infinitely better than I do. But it seems to me that in Brazil things do not take place in precisely the same way. Here, a tremendously modern capitalism is conjugated with precapitalist and even anticapitalist forms, which the movement of the mode of production is itself responsible for conserving, updating, and creating. Nothing exemplifies Brazil better than the automatic photo booth. In Europe and the United States, these machines are automatic. The individual comes along with the local currency, adjusts the seat, sits down, puts in the money, takes the picture, the machine does everything, and the person goes away. In Brazil, there is someone who positions our face, adjusts the seat, sells the token, and after the machine has done everything the attendant takes the strip of photos, dries them, cuts them up, and puts them in a little package. I think that Brazil is this association, this conjunction. We could find a thousand examples, but this one expresses well the way things are.

This conjunction of ultramodern forms with incredibly archaic ones can be found everywhere in big Brazilian cities. But it is not just outside, above all it is in the mind. Behavior and language reveal this very well. I am thinking, for example, of an expression that is used a great deal in Brazilian life, which is the famous "Do you know who you are talking to?" (*Você sabe com quem está falando?*). The analysis that Roberto Da Matta[5] makes of this sentence shows how pejorative the notion of the individual is in Brazil, because "Do you know who you are talking to?" reveals the opposite of the American question "Who do you think you are?", or the French equivalent "Who do you take yourself to be?" (*Pour qui tu te prends?*). In the last two cases, the question indicates that the fundamental rule is equality, that everyone has the same rights, and therefore that someone who thinks he or she is superior should give up that pretension. In the case of "Do you know who you are talking to?" the attitude is the opposite. The question places the person who uses it in a superior position, immediately establishing hierarchy and social inequality. In Brazil, the person appears to be more important than the individual, for being an individual is a stigma, it means being anonymous, being a "nobody."

The question "Do you know who you are talking to?" permits precisely this transition from the individual to the person. That is, from the domain of the impersonality of capitalist relations to the hierarchic, authoritarian system of personal relations, the territory of favors, consideration, respect, and prestige, with its hotshots, its big names, its godfathers, and its personal contacts. In this respect, what makes someone a *person*, what gives him social identity, is not simply the economic criterion but also, and above all, personal relations. A person is someone who *counts*. As the saying goes, "you can know a man by the shoes he wears." And when *persons* know each other, they don't ask "Do you know who you are talking to?" because everybody already knows their place.

So, in Brazil, two worlds live side by side and combine in the same drama: the world of *persons*, where everyone is somebody, everyone is in one way or another above the law, the world of personalized social relations with its highly elaborate code. Those who don't know the code risk being made inferior, put in their "proper place" by receiving up front a "Do you know who you are talking to?" On the other hand, there is the impersonal world of *individuals*, ruled by an egalitarian, universalizing law. As Roberto Da Matta maintains: "The laws apply only to individuals and never to persons."

The working hypothesis that I would like to discuss here is the following: it seems that the mass media in Brazil do not work with precisely the same assumptions as their counterparts in advanced capitalist countries. In other words, they do not work with the hypothesis of a society in which the predominant notions are of equality and universality and the individual who is simultaneously depersonalized and ready to be repersonalized, to be modeled. Here, from the viewpoint of the mass media the issue is not one of modeling, because there is not even a recognition that capitalism works in terms of depersonalization-repersonalization. The media do not create models so that individuals can speak of "myself," because the individual does not count.

The mass media speak of the world of persons, whom they even transform into superpersons. In newspapers and magazines, on the radio and on television, the individual only appears in police reports, personalized through violence. Or during Carnival, when the individual becomes a character in a national historic event. Or even in mysticism or in soccer, when the individual stands out as having special gifts or superior powers. Here, the media only set out to exhibit and reinforce the world of persons, turning it into a spectacle, making it even more glossy and glamorous, increasing the gap. Or else, in so-called "popular" programs such as *Povo na TV* (People on TV)[6] or *Gil Gomes*,[7] they seek to denounce and repress in advance anyone who wishes to infringe the social code or who attempts to force their way from individual to person.

This does not mean that modelization ceases to take place. On the contrary, it seems that the impact of the media, and particularly of TV, is even greater. The empathy seems to be much stronger. Because persons recognize one other in the images presented, while individuals have a chance, at least in their imagination, of becoming persons. Perhaps that is the meaning of the photo published in the *Folha de São Paulo* a couple of days ago, where we saw two homeless women in their "living room" in a public square in the poor São Paulo neighborhood of Bom Retiro. Under a tree, on a table, was a television that didn't work...

To conclude, a movement that seeks to confront the problem of domination in Brazil may have to act on two fronts: on the one hand, it will have to make a critique of the individual, the abstraction of the free worker, the basic assumption of capitalist society; but it will also have to undo and divest from the code of personal relations, the authoritarian, hierarchizing code expressed in "Do you know who you are talking to?" In the field of culture, for example, this is what happens in the songs of Luís Melodia[8] or the films of Julinho Bressane.[9]

Another example of what I am saying is Lula's way of speaking in a televised debate with the other presidential candidates. I notice that Lula's way of speaking does not come from the same register as the discourse of the other candidates, which is a discourse of persons. His way of speaking is action, while that of the others is representation. When Lula responds, all of a sudden the tone changes, the diction is different, and also the behavior—everything is different. His way of speaking is movement, a segment of a much broader movement. And so it can't be imitated. Reading the transcript of the debate one finds, for example, that Montoro[10] took up a number of Lula's statements. But only on the level of expression, to embed them within his own discourse—a process that diluted them completely. Perhaps that is why we feel that there is a huge gap: on one side there is Lula, with the singularized speech of a movement, and on the other there is the representative discourse of the candidates-persons.

Question: You say that Lula is action, performance, and also a new way of *being*. This leads one to think that there may be a dynamic now in which people are being more performative, in other words, they are more disposed to go out on the street and establish their individuality. But does this correspond to something new that is emerging, of which Lula is a spokesman, or is it a mere formalism?

Laymert G. dos Santos: You raise the question in terms of an alternative: either it's a formalism or it's a new way of being. It doesn't seem to me that it's a formalism, but it isn't my place to form a judgment. On the other hand, it also doesn't seem to me that Lula is a new way of being, that he is action and movement. What I was highlighting was not that, but the fact that Lula is a segment of movement. And the strength and impact of his discourse lies precisely in the fact that it is not the discourse of Lula himself (the discourse of a "person") but speech in action, speech that comes from a movement of which Lula is an important segment and not its spokesman. He is only an element that amplifies this other speech, the speech of the movement.

In this sense, I would say that the movement by which Lula is empowered and in which he intervenes is indeed a new way of being. But I don't agree with you that this new way of being involves imposing individuality. It seems to me that Lula has perceived very well what I am referring to: it is necessary to fight on two fronts. If there is someone who knows what an abstract individual is, it is someone who works in a factory, and Lula is one of them. At the same time, Lula has this other component, very often absent in other kinds of leadership, which is a sort of detachment from this code of personal relations and social hierarchy. Let's say that Lula doesn't have the proper respect that persons demand, and it's precisely because he doesn't have that proper respect that he doesn't try to modulate his discourse according to the person that he's talking to. The singularity comes precisely from that fact: he's someone who criticizes the process that makes us abstract individuals, and at the same time criticizes the code of being a "person" in Brazil.

But Lula is only an example. We could take the examples that I gave: Luís Melodia's music or Julinho Bressane's films, which show precisely how people existing on the fringe of society—small-time crooks and scroungers in Rio de Janeiro, people living in Estácio[11]— divest from the two codes at the same time, and in so doing produce a speech that is new and different.

Round-table discussion at the ICBA (Brazil-Germany Cultural Institute),[12] *Salvador, September 13, 1982:*

Marcus do Rio: In youth movements, one of the things that seems fundamental to me is *the discovery of the political use of humor.* I think that political youth movements, from the 1960s to the present day, have discovered the extremely subversive potential contained in humor. But I don't see anything of this either in Lula or in the leadership of the PT. I have never seen a single photo of Lula laughing, and when the PT candidates speak I really get depressed; humor is totally banished from their discourse.

Break-out and break-in:[13] a sign of a process of singularization?
Suely Rolnik

The break-out of rioting and the break-in of looting that formed part of our life in Brazil for some months in 1983 is the kind of phenomenon that lends itself to a reading in terms of the processes of singularization with their disruptive potential, but also with their seductive promises and perils.

We all remember those times when hordes of people suddenly irrupted into the streets in the big city centers, invading, looting, and overturning everything that lay before them. It was particularly noticeable that at first they only stole food, but very soon they moved on to another stage in which they stole anything, sometimes not even for consumption but just for the savor of divesting from the dominant code that free access to things provided.

In this circumstance, as was to be expected, the cities panicked and promptly responded by closing their doors. In the newspapers and on the radio and television there was a procession of deeply worried technical experts and scientists, lay people and specialists, atheists and religious people, civilians and military personnel, intellectuals and business leaders, politicians of the left, center, and right. They all repeated the same refrain: "We can understand that the unemployed demonstrate and demand jobs. Nothing could be more fair and honest. We can even understand that the unemployed and underemployed dare to steal food and clothes—after all, the community owes them at least food and clothing; we can't let our workers die of want. But stealing jewels, candies, or stereos is rioting. It's certainly being led by criminals or professional agitators (fascists, according to the left; communists, according to the right). In which case, there is no way that we can let this behavior go unpunished."

In fact, there were some people who only dared to take clothes and food (in order to work). And it is also true that they were not the real agitators, they were not the bearers of the "breakdown," despite the importance and legitimacy of their struggle. The disruptive effect lay in the gesture, made up of humor and violence, which shattered a certain conception of the relation between work and leisure; which shattered the criterion of productivity as the principle of the organization of time and space; which shattered the principle of private ownership of the means of production and consumption—a gesture that did not show respect for a life reduced to hierarchical values organized in accordance with general equivalents, and that manifestly divested from man, reduced to the condition of a neutral support for values dissociated from sensible experience.

And, beyond all that breaking and smashing, what was also broken down was a certain conception of political struggle that reduced it to a polarized confrontation between interlocutors authorized and recognized by a state machine. The disruptive effect lay, above all, in breaking away from that dependent, infantilized, demanding posture, a "weaning" from the state as a universal provider, a privileged interlocutor, a certified translator of all desires. In the tumult of the rioting, what seemed to be shattered was basically the mode of production of subjectivity that characterizes contemporary societies.

However, although in this phenomenon there was a courageous affirmation of life, a creation of new social assemblages, signs of a process of singularization being prepared, on the other hand it also brought with it a danger: of taking dissolution as the goal instead of the path necessary for creation. It would not be the first time that people have succumbed to the fascination of destruction taken to its final consequences, as a response to the violence committed against life in the world we live in. It would not be the first time that people have said "If we have to live as precariously as this, it would be better to be the authors of our own death." This danger is what Guattari calls "microfascism."

But this was not the danger that so shocked a large part of the population. This was not the fear that was voiced in the media. What was unbearable was the destruction in itself, and not the danger that it might become a goal. What was unbearable in all this was the danger of the breakdown of the principal mechanisms of the society in which we live. For those who viewed the events in that way, changes are only conceivable on the molar plane, the plane of forms and their representations, whereas each and every change of molecular texture is invariably experienced as conveying a danger of violence and chaos. The preservation of the texture of a particular social order is confused with the preservation of *the social order* as such, whatever its nature may be; and, implicitly, the preservation of the texture of a particular psychic world is confused with the preservation of *the psychic world* as such. In other words, what was confused in this case was the preservation of a particular figure of oneself with the preservation of one's supposed essence. From this viewpoint, the rioting conveyed something much more violent and distressing than having one's property looted. *The fear of losing houses and objects is nothing in comparison with the terror of losing oneself.*

It was probably a fear of this nature that caused the government of the state of São Paulo to occupy the streets of the city with the forces of the law and define a restricted area for the movement. The movement, which had been rebelliously agitating the city, affirmatively and autonomously, once again lined up to express its pleas to the state and to capital in a civilized way. Overcoded, the movement was now under control. The break-up of the pleading position was broken. The cruelty of life, its ineluctable violence that destroys worlds and demands the construction of others, was temporarily silenced: the violence against life that characterizes capitalistic sub-jectivity had reconquered its space and power.

Two fears, and two measures. Some, indeed many, deprived of resources to deal with the almost daily exercise of life's cruelty, do not equip themselves to experience changes and fear any kind of break. They fear the cruelty with which life revolts against every-thing that confines it. This fear is cowardice. They were the ones who, united (and in the majority, as they almost always are), decid-ed to put an end to the rioting at whatever cost, in the same way that they would resist any sign of singularization. Others, the few, recognized the creative potential in the disruption, and if they feared something it was precisely that this potential might be lost: that it might simply be denied, for example by reducing the move-ment to its macropolitical dimension; or else, worse still, that it might be lost in pure destructiveness as a result of not being able to find ways to articulate forms of life that embodied the consistency of the process being experienced. One way or another, what was feared in this case was not the cruelty of life but the violence against it. Yet this kind of fear is a sign of life. Those who felt it, although apprehensive, accepted the rioting with silent joy, in complicity with the possible process of singularization that it announced.

At the time of the rioting I wrote to Guattari to comment on the event. This is what he replied: "With regard to the 'savage hordes' that you describe in your last letter, I have an intuition that in the long term this kind of phenomenon heralds the reconstitu-tion of a new kind of 'autonomous-communist-anarchist' movement—not having any one specific focus, but all that at once. Toni Negri and I are writing a kind of 'manifesto'[14] about it" (letter of May 27, 1983).

Round-table discussion at the Folha de São Paulo, *September 3, 1982:*

José Miguel Wisnik: I would like to mention two things that, in my view, represent singularities in the Brazilian situation with respect to the European situation. The first is the fact that in Brazil today there is, I believe, a process of wild molecular proliferation—in the sense of a process that is outside police control, in a way, and outside the control of explanation. I am referring to the appearance, everywhere and all the time, of forms of violence that are expressed in very different ways, basically by assault. Armed assault, which is proliferating everywhere, seems to me to correspond to a specific molecular form of gestural response that indicates a movement of forces in Brazil. We witness or live with the proximity of assault everywhere, and at the same time we also live with forms of violence whose goal is not simply the appropriation of an object that belongs to someone else, but which also express themselves as symbolic acts. For example, last year it was reported that here in São Paulo, near the huge ABC[15] industrial complex, groups of people who live in *favelas* (shanty towns) were going to pedestrian bridges (walkways over Via Anchieta and Imigrantes)[16] and throwing paving stones at the passing cars. They were blocks of granite, deadly in some cases, and in a way they seemed to be a sign: they were not there as part of a classic assault, but as a form of recreation, a weekend pastime, in other words, as "culture." There is a kind of awful contiguity between that industrial complex, which makes automobiles, and that kind of behavior, that way of acting above that automobile machinery in action—which seems to be a kind of response.

This proliferation of destructive molecular forms—not easily subject either to police control or to a theoretical control that might explain the meaning of the gestures and seek to channel them—is different, in a way, from the minority movements that seek to express desire in a common form of political language.

How can we understand this difference? What political consequences can we draw from it?

On the other hand, in Brazil, the issue that involves the relevance of desire as collective production seems to me to have been worked on and elaborated in various manifestations of art and popular music before being actually discussed in the field of thinkers, the university, and the politicians; hence the advanced state of that discussion in Brazil now. In a way, popular music raises the question of desire in many forms, not only of verbal expression but also of gestural and corporal expression. It does so with a penetrative capacity that creates a new situation, a singular situation: the possibility (which is also ambivalent) of discussing, raising, and elaborating this molecular issue within the so-called culture industry. There is a song by Caetano Veloso that is called *Ele me deu um beijo na boca* (He Kissed Me on the Mouth), which in a way is a condensation or variation of the philosophical discussion in *Anti-Oedipus*. I think that in Brazil this theory can have more dialogue with this kind of song than with the essays that have been written. This issue is often expressed poetically, in an irreducible form, in music and in dance. Moreover, Brazilian popular music raises this issue in connection with other sources (for example, the forces and flows of black music), other matrixes, far from the European matrix that produces this theory. In these other matrixes, the issue is raised not only from the standpoint of thinking that is in some way rationalist and inherited from the Enlightenment, which is European thinking, but also from that of other matrixes—affective, corporal, and religious—which in some way launch this problem toward other planes. In this connection, I would like to conclude by asking Guattari the following questions, inviting him to receive them as a "kiss on the mouth": Who are your gods? What are they like? Are your gods the "iridescent surface of the hollow bubble," or are they more "like babies' heads without a bonnet?"[17]

Guattari: At present, in Brazil, the invention of modes of semiotic expression of different natures, which has been mentioned by everyone in this debate, constitutes some kind of possible reserve of expressiveness, of totally unforeseen, unexpected means with which to struggle against all the hardened, bureaucratized languages. In response to José Miguel Wisnik's remarks, I would say that the way to avoid deadly expressions of desire (such as throwing paving stones as a weekend pastime), the way to avoid the risk of the accumulation of microfascism, the risk of the development of fascist cancers, clearly does not consist in creating systems of control and overcoding. It consists in establishing devices that articulate dissident modes of expression to the dominant modes of expression, giving them a certain strength in real power relations. Instead of a kind of fascist steamroller, we would then have the creation of rhizomatic forms of connection and articulation. We would also have a deepening of processes in their singularization, without this causing them to become impotent in real power relations.

As for the question of who my gods are, I might say that they are miraculous gods, somewhat reminiscent of President Schreber's divinities,[18] but also—and perhaps in a more historical, more real way—my gods are contexts of social struggle and transformation, such as what is taking place in Brazil at present.

IN SEARCH OF IDENTITY

Is it possible that what organizes a form of behavior, a social relation, or a system of production is the fact that it is limited to an identity? Or that it has a tag glued to it? Or even that it is exercised in accordance with preestablished laws of regulation? Could it be that the founding relation of the ego, what gives us the feeling that we are ourselves, lies in our obedience to the code of a microsociety or the laws of a society? Or else in a reference to an ideology of a religious, political, or some other nature? Is that what enables us to live, not only in the sense of being able to respect one another but also, and above all, in the sense of being able to have creative relations? Is that what enables us to organize a division of labor? Is that what enables us to produce, both in the material field and in the subjective field, the conditions of collective life and, at the same time, the conditions of embodying life for ourselves (what I call the process of singularization)?

It is precisely this kind of problem that I think is very poorly put when considered in these terms—in terms of an identity, in terms of the power that the ego has of controlling unconscious drives, under the control of the superego, the law, and all the systems of social control. I think that, on the contrary, the way in which the ego, individuals, and social groups are modeled by contemporary capitalistic systems is much more a vehicle of disorder and entropy than the systems of sensibility (what I call modes of pre-personal semiotization), systems that can develop without submitting to domination by the structures of identity.

What is produced by capitalistic subjectivity, what comes to us through the media, the family, and all the resources that surround us, is not just ideas; it is not just the transmission of meanings through signifying statements; nor is it models of identity, or identifications with maternal and paternal poles, and so on. More essentially, it is systems of direct connection between, on the one hand, the great machines of production and social control and, on the other, psychic agencies, the way of perceiving the world.

The problematics of identities—as psychoanalysts perceived in the course of the history of psychoanalysis—do not just involve a tracing of identities, or processes of identification. What is rich and fruitful in the evolution of the theory of the object in the history of psycho-analysis is that, despite all the interpretive reductions with which the question of the relation of the object was treated, there has been a reconsideration—particularly in Kleinian theories—of the idea that there might be points of subjective singularity beneath the structures of the ego and identifying structures. Also in Lacanian theory, one of the formulations that has continued to be most operational for me is the idea of the object "a" as a function of singularity in psychic processes. The point on which I do not agree with Lacan's references is the use he makes of the matheme of the object "a"; especially the way in which he articulates it in his theory of the fantasy, which final-ly reincorporates it in the problematic of representation.

The current level of the debate is not very important: if there is something valid in the teachings of psychoanalysis, it is, at least, the fact that it has tended to cause the legitimacy of the notion of identity to explode. At the beginning of psychoanalysis, these problematics exploded spectacularly. In Freud's first analyses—especially in his studies on hysteria—he discovered that, beneath the discourse of identity and the discourse of the ego, modes of subjectivation can be incarnated in the body, in discourses of images, in discourses of symptomatic relations, social relations, and so on. Hence, what we need to ask ourselves is whether we are going to be content with making the notion of identity explode *inward*—making it implode toward the theory of "partial objects"—or whether we are also going to try to make it explode *outward*, toward things such as Winnicott's "transitional objects," or institutional objects, toward any economic object, any machinic object that inhabits the social field.

To settle this issue, I think it is opportune to set out from a radical twofold decentralization of the notion of subjectivity in relation to the notion of identity. Subjectivity seems to be characterized in a twofold manner: on the one hand, by the fact that it inhabits infra-personal processes (the molecular dimension), and, on the other, by the fact that it is essentially assembled in terms of concatenations of social, economic, and machinic relations, that it is open to all socio-anthropological determinations and economic determinations.

Debate on "The Unconscious and History," Olinda, September 14, 1982:

Djanira Cavalcanti: An issue that was raised at the beginning of the debate is worrying me considerably. It's the question of the recognition of minorities, of the credibility that can be given to them. I don't know whether, in practice, a request for recognition is actually presented by these minorities. But if it is, I think it shouldn't be. In these minority movements, what takes place on the plane of desire goes beyond the reproduction of spaces, and of the dominant existing affects—which are recognized only too well. In our women's movement here in Olinda, and not only here, what we're seeking is not recognition. We're no longer concerned about that. We're relaxed about it. Really, what we're seeking is to appropriate a social space, an existential space of our own. A space where we can recognize and get to know one another, where we can create a good affective atmosphere among us. I think it's important to talk about this.

Guattari: We are revolving around a question of identity and recognition, which is really not surprising: identity is often linked to recognition. When the police ask for someone's identity card, it's precisely in order to identify them, to recognize them socially. The point at which the problematics of the unconscious link up with political problematics lies precisely in the idea that it is not just a question of identifiable or identified subjectivities, but of subjective processes that are not grasped by identities.

IDENTITY OR SINGULARITY

Identity and singularity are completely different. Singularity is an existential concept, whereas identity is a concept of referentiality, of the limiting of reality to frames of reference, frames that may be imaginary. This referentiality will lead both to what Freudians call the process of identification, and to police procedures relating to the identification of the individual—in terms of his identity card and fingerprints. In other words, *identity is what causes singularity to pass from different ways of existing to a single identifiable frame of reference.* When we experience our own existence, we experience it with the words of a language that belongs to a hundred million people; we experience it with a system of economic exchange that belongs to a whole social field; we experience it with representations of modes of production that are completely mass-produced. However, we live and die in a completely singular relation with this intersection. What is true for any creative process is true for life itself. A musician or painter is immersed in everything that makes up the history of painting, everything that painting is around him, and yet he reconsiders it in a singular way. That's one thing. Another thing is the way in which that existence, that creative process, will later be identified in socio-historic coordinates; that does not coincide with the meaning of the process of singularization. What interests capitalistic subjectivity, however, is not the process of singularization, but precisely this result of the process: its circumscription to the modes of identification of the dominant subjectivity.

What I call processes of singularization—simply being able to live or to survive in a particular place, at a particular time, and to be ourselves—has nothing to do with identity (things such as: my name is Félix Guattari, and I am here). It has to do with the way in which, in principle, all the elements that constitute the ego function and are articulated; in other words, with how we feel, how we breathe, how we want to speak or don't want to, being here or going away.

CULTURAL IDENTITY: A TRAP?

Interview by João Luiz S. Ferreira for the Bahian Cultural Foundation, Salvador, September 13, 1982:

João Luiz S. Ferreira: The interest in this interview arose when you used the concept of cultural identity as a concept to be disdained. I thought your criticism of the cultural agency was improper because here in Bahia it's an essential issue. I feel—and perhaps this may not really be true, but at any rate it's the impression I have—that some European countries don't have the kind of cultural identity that Bahia has, which is specific, even in relation to the reality of São Paulo, the most dynamic center of capitalism in Brazil. I believe that—at least here, in our case, for a number of reasons—this idea would not result in the development of a liberation movement, or anything like that.

In the Northeast, specifically in the case of Bahia, capitalist dynamics and what you call the production of capitalist subjectivity come from Brazil's Central-Southern region, with television and the whole mechanism that's familiar to us. In some cities in the interior of Bahia, it's thought that actors on Globo TV are foreigners; the word "foreigner" is used—and it seems to me that this is a politically important issue.

I think that the racial relation in Bahia is not just a relation at a social level; the racial relation in Bahia also raises the question of culture. It's even a problem that has emerged within the black movement: an antagonism between those who proposed a cultural movement and those who proposed a line that was directly political. Now, after some years of experience, what we see is that the Movimento Negro Unificado (Unified Black Movement)[19] doesn't have the slightest influence here in Bahia. Recently it's been going through a process of break-up, or fragmentation. Although I think that the black movement in Bahia, and even the cultural movement, is going through a period of a kind of decline, what has happened in recent years is a radical transformation of the whole black community, mainly based on "racial pride" and cultural pride. A series of items emerged in the cultural question, some that are debatable—as in the case of the cult of Africa—and others that are very important, such as the recognition of *candomblé* as a central element in the structure of black resistance. I believe that this is a basic fact, in terms of the process of the recovery of identity, especially in the black sector of the population in Bahia, which, after all, is the majority. This doesn't mean that the process isn't also taking place in the emerging white middle class. But I think that the whole critical sector of the middle class—whether Marxist or anarchist, the political line doesn't matter—lacks this consciousness, and its ideologies (even those of the PT), clearly elaborated in the more developed industrial centers, function for me as an impediment to this process of interaction, integration, and a more radical awareness of reality. The importation of this discourse functions as a substitute for an awareness of reality. This is why I think it would be interesting to try to reach a better understanding of the criticism that you made of this concept.

Guattari: I'm not going to go into an analysis of the phenomena that you're describing, phenomena that are taking place in the Bahian context, because I'm not familiar with them. The only observation that I'm in a position to make is that it seems to me that *the concepts of culture and cultural identity are profoundly reactionary*: every time we use them, without realizing it, we transmit modes of representation of subjectivity that reify it. The result is that they don't allow us to recognize that subjectivity has a composed, elaborated, manufactured character, like any other merchandise in the field of capitalistic markets.

In their real functioning, semiotic universes do not exist as separate universes. People in archaic societies (or in a society such as the one that you're describing, in Bahia), people whose activity of expression takes place in different ways, don't separate their modes of semiotization into spheres of creation: the sphere of music, or dance, artistic representation, theater, religious activities, economic activities, the sphere of an ethnological field, and so on. All of this constitutes their production of subjectivity, indissociably.

So I think that things would change if we treated the different elements that you describe in the situation in Bahia in terms of production of subjectivity instead of making them isolated spheres, reified entities. In fact, it's this same reifying attitude that leads to describing people from São Paulo or Rio de Janeiro as "foreigners": the conception of a reified entity is correlative with the notion of cultural identity, which implies the identity/otherness binary.

Instead of reifying a notion such as that of the culture of a social group, perhaps we could more profitably speak of an *assemblage of processes of expression*. On the molar level these processes are actually antagonistic in relation to the productions of capitalist subjectivity, but what their reification does not allow us to perceive is the fact that on the molecular level they are perfectly indistinguishable in relation to other semiotic productions. Not only those that take place in Africa but also those of punks or rock groups on the outskirts of Paris, or of a poet or musician from Japan, or from anywhere in the world.

It's very important to consider that, on the one hand, these processes of singularization can be captured by circumscriptions, by power relations that give them the figure of identity—never forgetting that this involves a deeply reactionary concept, even when handled by progressive movements. On the other hand, these same processes can function concomitantly in the molecular register, totally escaping the identitarian logic. This kind of ambiguity of concepts exists in all fields.

The idea of singular collective subjectivation does not necessarily refer to an immanent or transcendent soul that is considered to be the soul of a social group: all of these conceptions that refer subjective phenomena to cultural identities always have an undercurrent of ethnocentrism. A subjectivity can be involved in processes of singularization—such as the subjectivity of homosexual groups, or the subjectivity of blacks who reinvent a particular religious system such as *candomblé*—without thereby having to project the reference of a cultural identity on that production of subjectivity. Such a reference is mythical, although mythical isn't precisely the word I would like to use, because this is an extremely functional myth: it involves a kind of subjective production that fits in very well with the business activities of capitalistic societies.

The reappropriation of cultural elements of a very heterogeneous origin which is found in phenomena such as *candomblé* is normally treated as belonging to a separate cultural identity that is being recovered. However, everything indicates that, on the contrary, this practice has a creative character: the invention of a kind of religion in a context that is really very modernist. Indeed, it seems to be a characteristic of the situation in the Latin American continent in general. It has not been completely devastated by capitalistic semiotics, and it possesses extraordinary reserves of non-logocentric means of expression, capable of articulating themselves in completely original forms of expression.

Sometimes during this trip, especially in Bahia, I have heard people speak of the Brazilian "soul," or the soul of a region of Brazil. And I asked myself whether they were referring to something deeply inscribed in the ways that people here feel, think, and express themselves, or to some kind of recomposition of a certain cultural subjectivity in reaction to the dominant subjectivity. I asked myself this question because this dominant subjectivity exists, whether we like it or not, in any region of Brazil (even in Bahia), because Brazil has become a great capitalist power.

If we compare this with the situation in France, we see that there, regions have been reconstituted within a perspective of autonomy (I am thinking of Corsica, Brittany, and the Basque Countries), recreating a "cultural identity." Really it is a cultural pseudoidentity, which adopts a position of reaction to the capitalistic movement, a movement that, in one way or another, has already contaminated all modes of subjectivation. It is very important to realize this, so as not to go on thinking that really, basically, "we Brazilians are not going to let ourselves be caught by the kind of control grid that exists in the 'developed' industrial countries." Other countries that had millenary traditions of a certain kind of social relation, and a certain kind of cultural life, were swept away within a decade, precisely by the production of capitalistic subjectivity. One has only to think of what the Japanese experienced in the space of forty years. In certain parts of Japanese society, even in urban systems, there is still a cultural quality specific to Japan, particularly an etiquette of social relations, a way of articulating the relation of written language, body language, or the language of the face, but all perfectly integrated into the process of production of capitalistic subjectivity. I have no doubt that one day you will have a Ministry of Cultural Personalities here, the responsibility of which will not be to crush all the specific modes of expression of the various regions of Brazil but, on the contrary, to develop them, to provide incentives for them—provided, of course, that they do not interfere with serious things, with matters concerned with production and politics.

Cultural identity constitutes a level of subjectivity: the level of subjective territorialization. It is a means of self-identification in a specific group that conjugates its modes of subjectivation in relations of social segmentarity. But at the same time, one could consider other levels of subjectivity, where it functions in multiple transverse relations: not only in transcultural relations, but also in what one might call transmachinic relations. That is why, for example in the anthropology of African societies, one can have the embodiment of a social group in a "basic personality"—to go back to the terminology of cultural anthropology—and at the same time one can have an extraordinary "diffusionism," which has been traversing the whole of Africa for thousands of years. A diffusion both of machine techniques as such, and also of ritual techniques (such as geomancy), linguistic and mythic issues, and so on.

The notion of "cultural identity" has disastrous political and micropolitical implications, because what it fails to grasp is precisely the whole wealth of the semiotic production of an ethnic or social group, or a society.

MINORITIES: THE BECOMINGS OF SOCIETY
Identity or becoming-woman, becoming-homosexual, becoming-black

What minority groups demand is not just recognition of their identity. The difference between homosexual groups today and those of *la belle époque*, for example, is that their issue is not sectoral. They are working so that their process, their becoming-homosexual, will be introduced into society as a whole, because in fact all relations are worked on by becoming-homosexual.

There is the same thing in feminism. Apart from placing the problem of the recognition of women's rights in some particular professional or domestic context, it is also the vehicle of a becoming-feminine that concerns not only all men and children but, deep down, all the mechanisms of society. It is not a question of symbolic problematics—along the lines of Freudian theory, which interpreted some symbols as phallic and others as maternal—but of something that lies at the very heart of the production of society and of material production. I describe it as becoming-feminine because it has to do with an economy of desire that tends to question a certain kind of goal in the production of social relations, a certain kind of demarcation that makes it possible to speak of a world dominated by masculine subjectivity, in which relations are marked precisely by the prohibition of that becoming. In other words, there is no symmetry between a masculine or masculinized society and a becoming-feminine.

In his *Illuminations*, Arthur Rimbaud spoke of a "becoming-black." In a way, this becoming-black also concerns other ethnographic categories. There is a becoming-black in painting, a becoming-black in music, just as one might say that there is a becoming-minoritarian in literature—literature's refusal to be inscribed in the dominant forms.

In other words, the idea of "becoming" is bound up with whether or not it is possible for a process to singularize itself. Feminine, poetic, homosexual, or black singularities can break with the dominant stratifications. That is the mainspring in the problematics of minorities: they are problematics of multiplicity and plurality, rather than a question of cultural identity, of return to the identical, of return to the archaic. If there is a revival of archaic traits, such as traits of African religions that existed hundreds of years ago, it is not as archaisms that they acquire a subjective impact, but in their articulation with a process of creation. This is the case with what is most lively in jazz. It incorporates certain traits of singularity from black spirituals to make an authentic form of music that corresponds to our sensibility, our instruments, and our modes of distribution, until this music, too, runs into the wall of the state.

To sum up, against the idea of recognition of identity I would set an idea of transverse processes, subjective becomings that establish themselves through individuals and social groups. And they are able to do so because they themselves are processes of subjectivation, they shape the very existence of those subjective realities. But they cannot exist by themselves. They can exist within a processual movement; and that is what gives them their potential for traversing all stratifications—stratifications of matter, meaning, machinic systems, and so on.

So we could say that *every time that problems of identity or recognition appear in a particular place, at the very least we are faced with a threat of blocking and paralysis of the process.* It is within this logic—which may seem somewhat paradoxical—that it is possible to conceive of the existence not of a common program, a front, a unification, but of corridors of passage, corridors of unconscious communication between the black question and the feminine question, between becoming-child and poetic becoming. Becomings that literally permeate these different modes of subjectivation.

If problematics such as those of the subjectivation of blacks in Brazil or homosexuals in France are raised now, this does not mean that there is a black nature or a homosexual nature in the human species, or universes of blackness and universes of homosexuality that must be recovered. It means, firstly, that social assemblages in Brazil seek to construct their subjectivity on the basis of the articulation of various elements. The homosexuality that homosexuals construct is not something that specifies them in their essence, but something that directly concerns the relation with the body, the relation with desire of all the people who are in touch with homosexuals. It does not mean that homosexuals are seeking to proselytize, or establish a dictatorship of homosexuality. It simply means that the problematic that they singularize in their field does not belong to the domain of the particular, and still less to that of the pathological, but to the domain of the construction of a subjectivity that is connected and interlaced with problems in other fields, such as literature and childhood. It is precisely these elements that would lead to speaking of a north-south that traverses all countries, a blackness that traverses all races, minor languages that traverse all dominant languages, a becoming-homosexual, a becoming-child, a becoming-plant that traverse demarcated sexes. These are the elements that Deleuze and I group together under the heading of a "molecular dimension" of the unconscious.

Countless processes of minoritization traverse society: processes of minoritization and infantilization, which affect women in certain sectors of society, which affect certain elements in their behavior, which affect sexually dissident forms of behavior, which affect certain conceptions of the relation with production, of the relation with nature, conceptions that are not recognized by society as a whole (such as those of the ecology movement); one could extend the list by adding the psychiatrized, drug addicts, and so on. In a way, to want to be a poet or make poetry already implies participating in a minority, an oppressed minority, unless, for example, that poetry fits into certain academic and publishing standards.

The processes of marginalization traverse the whole of society. From their terminal forms (such as prisons, asylums, and concentration camps) to more modern forms (the social control grid), these processes lead to the same vision of poverty, despair, and abandonment to fatality. But this is only one aspect of what we are experiencing. Another aspect is what creates the quality, the message, and the promise of minorities: they represent not only poles of resistance, but also potentials of processes of transformation that contain the possibility of being taken up again, at some time or other, by entire sectors of the masses.

The feminist movement in France has been able to achieve some possibility of intervention now, in some of the state's mechanisms of power, which is good. But the feminist movement is not simply that, just as it is not simply feminist groups. The movement only has meaning insofar as it is articulated with the whole complex of feminist microrevolutions that are at work throughout the fabric of society.

Round-table discussion at the ICBA, Salvador, September 13, 1982:

Luís Mott: At the beginning of this discussion, a colleague questioned our desire to be here at this table. What I really wanted was to overturn the table, not to be at the table, because in Brazil even the slightest desire simply to carry our aspirations outside the tiny ghetto in which we live is always barred. By a coincidence, about three months ago, despite all my university qualifications, I was prevented from giving a talk at this very location. The subject was "The struggle against sexual discrimination in Germany from the nineteenth to the twentieth century" (and it wasn't even homosexual discrimination that was being discussed). And so I, as a homosexual, am taking advantage of Guattari's respectability as an "international personality" in order to be here at this table, to legitimize the right to expression of the homosexual movement.

This isn't the first time that the question of "being at the table" has been raised in relation to homosexuals. At the 32nd conference of the Sociedade Brasileira para o Progresso da Ciência (Brazilian Society for the Promotion of Science), held here in Salvador last year, people said that the acronym SBPC stood for "Sociedade de Bichas Procurando Cartaz" (Society of Gays Seeking Fame), because the homosexual movement was very visible, appearing on television and being very active. For two thousand years, thousands of homosexuals were unable to appear if they wished to avoid being burnt at the stake, or forcibly psychiatrized (I was forcibly psychiatrized when I was young, because I had a homosexual tendency and my family didn't accept it). We who were oppressed by slavery, by "heterosexism" (an important word to introduce in Brazil), want and have the right to appear and be respected. Obviously it's not me, this short, fat person, that wants to appear and be respected, but the cause of all the thousands of homosexuals (one has only to consult the "Kinsey Report" to find out that there are 10 or 15 million gays in Brazil).

I agree with Guattari: what we want is for people not to see themselves as blacks, not to see themselves as homosexuals, not to see themselves as women; we want people to see themselves as human beings who have the right to sleep with whoever they want. The fact of being black doesn't imply discrimination, the fact of being a woman doesn't imply inferiority: so, those who are white and macho, or who participate in the world of white machos, please don't hassle the oppressed, don't prevent us from sitting at the table and appearing. What we want, deep down, is an egalitarian society, a society in which there are neither oppressors nor oppressed, a society in which, as Guattari says, "let desire manage as best it can"—it's a phrase of his from an article called "I Have Even Met Happy Travelos."[20] What we homosexuals are struggling for is precisely the right to freedom of desire. As Guattari said, our struggle doesn't just concern homosexuals, fags, and lesbians. Our struggle extends to the whole of society, inasmuch as what we want is freedom of sex, sexuality without labels.

I'll conclude with a quote from one of Guattari's French colleagues, Guy Hocquengheim, who declared: "My asshole is revolutionary."

Guattari: I am going to talk about something that happened to me four years ago, when I came to Brazil for the first time. I was with a group of friends from the left (or one could even say the far left), in a very warm, friendly environment, and at about midnight a black woman who had been in the audience from the start raised an issue. She said: "The black movement is beginning to organize seriously in Brazil, and I would like to give you some documents." Later I realized (actually it was a friend who drew my attention to it) that during the 10 or 15 minutes when we were talking the audience dispersed.

It is through these tiny things that one realizes what is happening. Everything indicated that there was a total divestment from the black issue here, at least at that time; I don't know if things have changed since then. I realized that, on the unconscious level, the issue of racism was very far from being resolved in Brazil—even in the minds of those who have perfectly correct political positions in relation to it.

The point I would like to raise is that a parallel can be drawn between the way that blacks suffer racism (even from people who say that they've overcome it), the way that women suffer phallocratism, and even the way that homosexuals experience the real, profound gap that exists between, on the one hand, declarations and conscious adoptions of a position and, on the other, the unconscious economy in questions of homosexuality. We could extend the list by talking about people who have been psychiatrized, or who have a mental functioning different than what is considered normal. Why does it seem important to me to establish a relation between these different situations? Because they are not simply of the nature of localized cultural problematics, racial problematics, or social problematics; my hypothesis is that there are unconscious passageways between these different forms of racism, these different forms of segregation.

One of the conditions for the maintenance of capitalistic societies is that they should be modeled on a certain axiomatic of subjective segregation. If blacks did not exist, it would be necessary to invent them somehow. In Japan there are no blacks, but they invented the blacks of Japan: there are totally marginalized ethnic minorities, such as the Koreans, who are like the North Africans in France. What seems to me to be important in these issues is to get away from a purely defensive character in the struggle of minorities—"we are victims, nobody recognizes our rights"—and, on the contrary, to develop an offensive position that, as in the work of Rimbaud, evokes a "becoming-black," a becoming that concerns all races. We can all enter a becoming-black, a becoming-Indian (which actually was precisely the funny, brilliant point of the Metropolitan Indians[21] in Rome), a becoming-woman, a becoming-homosexual, or a becoming-child.

It is these becomings that seem to me to be the real response to the problems of racism: they consist in striking at the root of the problem. In other words, addressing the problem not at the level of the great cultural and ideological organizations, but at the level where the construction and production of subjectivities is really articulated. It is the level of all the racism between man and woman (imposed practically since birth), all the dichotomies in relations of semiotization (such as play activity versus school activity), all the systems of punishment that ensure that only profitable activities are selected by a certain system of social hierarchy. It is the level of projection of all the collective fantasies of the danger of so-called marginal people ("people who are insane are dangerous," "blacks have an extraordinary sexuality," "homosexuals are polymorphous perverts," and so on). It is this way of capturing the processes of singularization and immediately framing them in references—affective references, theoretical references introduced by specialists, references of segregatory collective facilities. It is in these becomings that there is an articulation between the molecular level of subjective integration and all the political and social problems that are now appearing all over the planet.

Meeting at the premises of the Grupo de Ação Lésbico-Feminista (Lesbian-Feminist Action Group),[22] São Paulo, September 2, 1982:

Question: In one of the articles in *Pulsações Políticas do Desejo*[23] you identify three levels of homosexuality: the first is clandestine, the second is that of the more avant-garde militantism, and the third, more molecular, seeks points of passage between the various sexual minorities. I wanted to understand what those "points of passage" might be.

Guattari: Perhaps I said that in the article, but I think that this passage doesn't take place only between sexual minorities. It's also a passage (a becoming) that can traverse different fields, not only microsocial but also in literature, or music. So it's a molecular becoming in the sense that it configures a certain kind of universe that is going to affect not only the relation between the sexes but also the relation between all the systems of otherness, the systems of perception, the syntax of writing, or music. It's no accident that the greatest creators in art, literature, or drama—I'm not going to make a list—were homosexuals. It has nothing to do with a problem of sublimation, or "openly assuming" marginality. The way in which someone like Shakespeare articulated what we might now call his "scripts," the way in which he organized his characters, the way he modulated his writing from poetry to narrative text, for example— that way is a becoming of literature that participates in the same becoming-homosexual. And the passage from that becoming of literature in Shakespeare to becoming-homosexual takes place just as much as the passage from becoming-homosexual to becoming-woman, becoming-child, or becoming-cosmic.

One always has to start with something, in other words, one always has to have a minimal cartography. In this respect, for people who are socially categorized as homosexuals the best cartography is one that is configured along the lines of a becoming-homosexual, and not cartographies like the psychoanalytic one, which revolves around a salad consisting of sublimation and all that drivel.

Question: I belong to a homosexual group. In some of your talks you have said that singularities should be affirmed. So I ask: how can I affirm my singularity as a lesbian, without reaffirming an impermeable homo/hetero opposition?

Guattari: I'm going to repeat—and it's a bit silly to keep repeating, because it makes me rather professorial, which bothers me—that it seems to me much more appropriate to speak of a "process of singularization" than to speak of singularity, in the sense that what we have are differential processes. For example, a feminist group may be following a differential process in relation to other existing groups. But you as a woman, in your becoming-homosexual (and we would have to see whether that's really what it is), in your becoming-singular, are introducing another differential process of singularization, an infraindividual process. The whole question has to do with knowing how these different processes of singularization that you are experiencing are articulated. And perhaps there's even a third level in the process of singularization: that of Brazilian society in relation to everything that's happening.

Micropolitics is precisely the attempt to assemble things in order to avoid something about which I've spoken many times: a process of singularization in a group of homosexuals that in certain circumstances leads to the reification of an individual becoming-homosexual. The attempt to assemble things in such a way that the processes of singularization are not mutually neutralized, not coopted in the reconstitution of molar pseudoentities. On the contrary, micropolitics consists in creating an assemblage that allows these processes to support each other, so that they become stronger.

Comment: This reification (the "gay" personological model) reminds me of a passage in *Anti-Oedipus* where you speak of perverse reterritorializations in artificial paradises. I also remember that when we discussed the question of becoming-woman in a study group, some people understood that it was about a becoming-woman-as-object.

Comment: I'm one of the people who understood it like that, because you also say in the same text that women are the only authorized depositories of becoming-sexual-body.

Guattari: On the macrosocial, molar level, I believe that's true.

Comment: It doesn't seem true to me, because in our society it's men who can express sexuality openly.

Guattari: If we keep to this idea of processes of differential singularization, it's possible to conceive that in a completely phallocratic society perhaps the first rupture—before a becoming-poet or a becoming-homosexual—might be the rupture of this first level of molar classification. Breaking away from this machine of the production of individualized people, and the binary division of the sexes.

I'm convinced that becoming-homosexual is heterogeneous in relation to becoming-woman. On the other hand, it's conceivable that at a certain stage the universes of homosexuality can only be described in terms of this semiotization of a becoming-woman. Which the classical Freudians revealed unwittingly: if you're not in the dominant becoming-man, then it's because you're a woman. But that's where we get stuck. You may be familiar with an admirable article by Pierre Clastres called "The Bow and the Basket."[24] The differentiation in the society to which he refers is absolutely clear: either you carry the bow or you carry the basket. We find this again in all the theories related to the phallus.

Question: But isn't that also a Manichean opposition: either you're on one side or you're on the other?

Guattari: That's right, that's precisely what I'm trying to say. It's an impermeable opposition, but at the same time it's a differential opposition in relation to the dominant oppositions. If I can't join the initiation to a certain dominant sexual position, if I can't semiotize my singularity—which may not be man, woman, plant, animal, or anything like that—then, all right, I'll be a woman. However, that won't enable me to singularize. I can certainly prance about, carry a bag gracefully, wear makeup: in the most forced way possible I can imitate the pseudotraces of woman's singularity. Even so, there's a process of differentiation—in this field there are never absolute singularities, except death. We are always involved in differential processes of singularization: the whole point is not to allow ourselves to be captured, not to succumb to those modes of categorization and structuration that block the process.

Comment: Perhaps I haven't understood the answer properly, because I find it strange that for you, as far as the body is concerned, a woman has more freedom. I think the opposite is true.

Suely Rolnik: I think that the point is not to assess who has more freedom, man or woman, but to circumscribe and problematize the model that to this day permeates the figures of both man and woman, the phallocratism in whose logic they are both imprisoned. And if what I'm saying makes any sense, combating that dominant sexual politics means targeting a figure of man (the macho in any of its versions) and a figure of woman (bride or whore, wife or lover). The resistance here consists in embarking on processes of differentiation of all of these figures, because in that way what we are divesting from is phallocratism itself. It's precisely those processes that we could call, to quote Guattari, "becoming-woman": the becoming-woman of man, the becoming-woman of woman—in short, the becoming-woman of society.

What I mean is that the basis of this society is a "phallocratic" mode of production of subjectivity—a politics of desire in which the accumulation of capital, prestige and power are the sole guiding principles, and the other is an instrumentalised object. This mode of production involves an increasingly accelerated process of breaking down the prevailing forms and mass-producing new forms, but dissociated from the demands of life. If we agree on this, it doesn't take much effort to realize that what is repressed in this mode of pro-duction is the possibility of creating forms of existence based on sensitivity to the processes that are experienced, forms as multiple and varied as the processes. In other words, what is repressed is a kind of "pregnancy function"—the power of being fertilized by otherness, of functioning as a channel for the incubation of forms of existence that impose themselves on each new configuration of experience. So isn't it precisely that "becoming-woman" that is being repressed? In which case, any break with society's present mode of functioning must involve a becoming-woman.

And feminism? Is it one of these experiments with a becoming-woman? That depends on where we place ourselves. In feminism there was, first of all, a whole dimension of demands for rights, a reaction against inequality, a revolt against exploitation and domi-nation, and the achievements in this domain are undeniable. But it's only one side of the story, the molar side. On the molecular plane, although it's true that feminism created a ground for a more protected proliferation of this becoming-woman of women, at the same time it has had the opposite effect: the tendency to confuse becoming-woman with the position of exploited/dominated figure of woman in the current cartography. This meant a disqualification of that becoming, which contributed to restraining it through the effect of culpabilization. In this way, instead of embarking on a becoming-woman—an implosion of the figures of both man and woman in the dominant mode of subjectivation—many women invested in the position of man, and in so doing succumbed com-pletely to phallocratism. I have the impression that today this type of feminism has been surpassed by the new generation of feminists, who tend to incorporate and develop a micropolitical vision; in this case we would in fact be experiencing a becoming-woman of women, or rather of both men and women, while the struggle for equal rights still goes on.

Question: I would like to understand more about this question of becoming, thinking mainly of the "becoming-poet" of which Guattari spoke.

Guattari: Let's start with a clean slate, setting out from a general reduction of all the dominant significances that lead to the affirmation that there are men and women, adults and children, an animal order and a plant order. Let's throw all that out and consider that there isn't any body or identity, because that's all categorized in a specific mode of representation.

However, let's consider that there are singular objects, involved in a general process of deterritorialization, objects that are poetic inasmuch as they are breaks with perception, compositions of processes of sensibilities and heterogeneous representations, which at a given point organize themselves according to a particular profile that can't be linked to the ordinary references of the dominant significances.

What I like about my becoming-woman may be a way of striking the heel of my shoe on the floor, a way of capturing the intensity of a relation of organs (in the most indefinable sense of the word "organ"), a way of territorializing something, of turning towards someone who is looking at me. They are different systems of intensity that are not necessarily articulated in a significance of woman, and which cannot necessarily be categorized in a mode of representation of woman. But at the same time, I may also be involved in a "sadomasochistic trip," in which case I may ask my lover to articulate these different systems of intensity and incorporate them in the scene. After all, especially in this case, it's very likely that I wouldn't be able to perform this articulation, given the intrinsic nature of the sadomasochistic contract: it's a process whose aim is precisely to abolish itself as such. These systems of intensity, these kinds of objects, taken in these different relative processes, may belong to totally heterogeneous singularities. They may belong to the domain of an ethological semiotic: it's a question of capturing something (such as a completely deterritorialized object) and having the intensity of that capture, which in ethology would be called a grasping[25] function. They may also belong to the domain of artistic representation, or musical representation, the domain of a corporal semiotic, a caress, or they may even be incorporated in a fantasmatic scene, causing the same scenes to be constantly repeated (also in the sense of "making a scene," and always the same scene).

In other words, such elements of molecular singularity may coexist and be involved in totally heterogeneous levels, according to the nature of the processes in which they are incorporated. It's the same as piloting and processing a singularity that will play a part in a becoming-poetic, or a becoming-homosexual, but that will also play a part in a becoming-man-of-letters, in a becoming-power within a given social group.

Question: I would like to know whether you have more information about the process that the feminist movements in Europe have been experiencing. How do you see that process?

Guattari: I don't have much information. But in any case I think that the movements in question certainly were and still are a support for problematic processes and analytic processes that have to do with women's issues. At the same time, from the little I know, these groups very often function like sectarian groups. However, one thing doesn't rule out the other. It's the same as what I've been saying about the PT: it may be completely engulfed in a political game, a media game, and at the same time it may be partially the vector of molecular problematics.

Question: Do you have any information about the relation between the French homosexual movement and the feminist movement? To what extent do they support each other, show solidarity toward each other, or work together? Another thing I'm interested in knowing about is the relation between these movements and political parties. Do you think it's useful for them to have contact with political parties, or should they ignore them completely? And a third question, for which I imagine it's not possible to receive a reply: What do you think of this wave of "macho homosexual," "macho gay," "macho man"? Won't this damage the homosexual movement in relation to feminists, given that it distances them from each other? I've been told that in the United States there's a very macho homosexual movement.

Guattari: There is, and there's also a very macho feminism. I think that currently there isn't very much politics or micropolitics in common between the feminist and homosexual movements in France. France still hasn't emerged from a process of oppression, repression, and depression that coincided with the whole period of Giscard d'Estaing's rise to power. And, after more than a year since the left's accession to power, I can still say that on the whole there's a kind of passivity that lingers on—everyone doing their thing in their own corner. At any rate, there's no equivalent to the processes that seem to be developing here.

Question: I'd like to know whether the homosexual groups in France—the men who are militant—are feminists, whether they're interested in feminism.

Guattari: They may make declarations of that nature, but I don't think that it occurs in practice.

Comment: Until a few years ago, it was common for a homosexual man to have feminine traits, and be very feminine. Now I have the impression that they no longer want to have so-called "feminine" characteristics. They're the macho men who were mentioned just now.

Guattari: Do these macho homosexuals segregate transvestites?

Comment: Not only transvestites but also queens, the more overt homosexuals.

Question: I read in a French book about sexuality (I don't remember the author's name) that the "macho gay" in the United States emerged as a reaction to the image that heterosexuals had of homosexuals: the homosexual was considered a crazy fag, a queer, that whole story. So they began to cultivate a masculine image to show that it had nothing to do with what hetero society imagined. I'd like to know what you think of this.

Suely Rolnik: I don't know if I agree with this story that the macho man is a reaction by the homosexual to the effeminate image that's attributed to him. I think it's more akin to a kind of proliferation of sadomasochism that reproduces, or simply perpetuates, what very frequently happens in the heterosexual conjugality of family life. Except that, when shifted to a homosexual territory and intensified there, the sadomasochism appears more clearly. But why is this politics of desire reproduced or perpetuated? I think it's because the panic generated by the giddy process of deterritorialization of the family that we are all experiencing (and which obviously implies the deterritorialization of a certain image of man, and woman, and the relations between them: the romantic image of "love") brings about the defensive appearance of countless forms of denying the situation and perpetuating this kind of territory. It's in this process that I would situate the reproduction of what are almost caricatures of the dominant figures of man and woman and their conjugality in the field of homosexual relations: the "becoming-macho" (macho man) of men, the "becoming-bride" or "becoming-wife" (the fag, the queer), and "becoming-whore" (the transvestite).

What I mean is that these clones of little devoted wives proliferate among heterossexuals as well as gays. I mean melancholy, masochistic women that are forever crying, waiting to be favored by their husband's desire, or whorish lovers compulsively "made up" to conquer and reconquer the male, prisoners of their own role as transgressors. Similarly, the clones of husbands or pimps, those men who are eternally escaping, treating women sadistically with their threatened or real absence, proliferate among heterosexuals and gays alike. They are the macho men who discriminate against the queer homosexuals and transvestites that you mentioned.

What happens is that an existence that is initially configured by the triangle of "the husband, the wife, and the other" is gradually reduced to a mere form, inflated and drained out by capitalistic deterritorialization, reconstituted in silicone or in planned *mises-en-scène*, pretending that nothing has changed. However, in Brazil, familialist love of the Fordist, Holywoodian type is still "current coin," and this kind of conjugal territory predominates, even though its duration has decreased perceptibly and the partners are periodically replaced.

Guattari: I think it's you who should be explaining this macho man business to me. What I ask myself in connection with this issue is whether, irrespective of this character of modelization and countermodelization, there isn't also a conjugation with sado-masochism, as Suely suggested. Something that alarms me (and it was almost by accident that I realized it) is the considerable increase, in the prostitution districts in Paris, in the number of women equipped with sadomasochistic material—whips and so on. I think it's quite a new phenomenon. I have the impression of not having seen it before, at least not so openly in the streets. I believe that in the United States the sadomasochist groups have been strong for some years, and that's something that hasn't changed, nor has it affected the new homosexuals.

Leaving that on one side, I'm going to say something about what you asked, about articulation with political parties. I'm going to repeat my opinion, at my own risk. I think that, at this time of political campaign, all the minority movements should get deeply involved with this business of the PT. Not in order to get ahead in the party, of course, but to find their modalities of insertion, to try to develop a nebula of expression, an agitation, a lifestyle that goes beyond all the sectarian group structures that stick to this process like clams and limpets.

Comment: You support the idea that the movements should join up with the PT. But from what I've seen, those processes of integration in political structures tend to wind up with some kind of spontaneous, disorderly madness.

Guattari: If that's the way it is, the craziness can't be very solid.

Comment: That's just it. I think that the important thing in what you're introducing is this category of desire. If these groups were capable of doing a reading of politics in terms of desire, it might be different.

Guattari: I agree with you, I fully agree.

Comment: To give you an idea of how this is being manipulated here, there are candidates who include in their platforms things like "let blacks live their blackness, women their femininity, homosexuals their desire."

Guattari: I think you're absolutely right to criticize the "sloganeering" side of this. This work only makes sense if it corresponds to a collective consciousness-raising about a project of this kind. But in my view, that's one more reason for raising the problem, at least talking about it, even if nothing gets done.

Comment: The debate is about whether we should do it from within or from outside.

Guattari: As far as I'm concerned, there's no law and no slogan. Either you feel really committed, with an urge to intervene here or there, or else you don't—and that's it. It's not a question of going out and distributing pamphlets in São Paulo, calling for homosexuals to join the PT!

Comment: That's right, long live homosexuality!

Guattari: There are two levels in this business, and both are very important. First, there's the question of the recognition of rights. That's a battle for lawyers, politicians, and so on. In France there's a group of homosexuals that engaged in a struggle of this kind with incredible tenacity, having to do very unpleasant things, and yet managing to achieve results. They studied the texts, and went to see representatives, senators, and other politicians. In other words, they lobbied. But I think the problems shouldn't be reduced to that level. There's a second aspect, which is that, with or without recognition, there's a living presence of homosexuals, feminists, and so on. There's a whole affirmation, a performance of a different way of talking, seeing, and behaving. This dimension can be very important.

Comment: It's good that you mentioned those homosexuals who worked within the system as lawyers and succeeded in shaking it up. Here, everyone looks down on the institutional part.

Guattari: That's silly.

Comment: They think that dealing with the institutional side is reformism, that it doesn't change anything. As far as they're concerned, the institutions should be ignored because only one kind of thing is worthwhile, anarchism—which I question deeply. I think it's very naïve, as you yourself say, to ignore the state on the basis that "it's useless," or "it oppresses us," and therefore to leave it aside and try to do something totally from outside, as though it might be possible for us to destroy it like that.

Suely Rolnik: This malaise in relation to institutions is nothing new; on the contrary, the feeling is particularly strong in our generation which, since the 1960s, has taken institutions as one of its main targets. But it's true that the malaise has been especially pronounced in Brazil over the last few years, and in my view this must have to do with an absolutely objective (and obvious) fact, which is the hardness of the dictatorship to which we were subjected for so long. The rigidity of that regime is embodied in all the country's institutions, in one way or another; in fact, that constituted an important factor for the permanence of the dictatorship in power over so many years.

But I think that this antiinstitutional malaise, whatever its cause, doesn't end there: the feeling that the institutions are contaminated territories, and the conclusion that nothing should be invested in them, is often the expression of a defensive role. This kind of sensation is, in my view, the flip side of the fascination with the institution that characterizes the "bureaucratic libido." These two attitudes really satisfy the same need, which is to use the prevailing forms, the instituted, as the sole, exclusive parameter in the organization of oneself and of relations with the other, and thus avoid succumbing to the danger of collapse that might be brought about by any kind of change. Those are two styles of symbiosis with the institution: either "gluey" adhesion and identification (those who adopt this style base their identity on the "instituted"), or else repulsion and counteridentification (those who adopt this style base their identity on negation of the "instituted," as if there were something "outside" the institutions, a supposed "alternative" space to this world).

Seen in this light, both "alternativism" and "bureaucratism" restrict themselves to approaching the world from the viewpoint of its forms and representations, from a molar viewpoint; they protect themselves against accessing the molecular plane, where new sensations are being produced and composed and ultimately force the creation of new forms of reality. They both reflect a blockage of instituting power, an impossibility of surrender to the processes of singularization, a need for conservation of the prevailing forms, a difficulty in gaining access to the molecular plane, where the new is engendered. It's more difficult to perceive this in the case of "alternativism," because it involves the hallucination of a supposedly parallel world that emanates the illusion of unfettered autonomy and freedom of creation; and just when we think we've got away from "squareness" we risk succumbing to it again, in a more disguised form. In this respect, I agree with you: the institutions aren't going to be changed by pretending that they don't exist. Nonetheless, it's necessary to add two reserves. In the first place, it's obvious that not every social experimentation qualified by the name of "alternative" is marked by this defensive hallucination of a parallel world. And secondly, if we think about the context of the dictatorship, it's self-evident that in order to bear the harshness of an authoritarian regime there is a tendency to make believe that it doesn't exist, so as not to have to enter into contact with sensations of frustration and powerlessness that go beyond the limit of tolerability (indeed, this is a general reaction before any traumatic experience). And in order to survive, people try in so far as possible to create other territories of life, which are often clandestine.

Comment: I'd like to go back to the formula "long live homosexuality," because there was an argument in our group between really "being homosexual" and temporarily "going homosexual." Whenever we affirmed ourselves as homosexual, or raised the issue of repression, some people thought it was reactionary, because in that way we were reconstructing a new pattern, or a new identity, and negating a process of coming to be. But not doing it, not presenting oneself as a homosexual, means leaving out a set of problems that exists. It doesn't matter whether you really "are" lesbian or gay or just temporarily "go" lesbian or gay, because even if you consider that I'm just "going" lesbian and not "being" lesbian, "going" lesbian has palpable consequences just as complicated as those of "being" lesbian.

Comment: At the level of the struggle we're obliged to identify ourselves, to present ourselves as lesbians, because we have to speak out against police discrimination, discrimination at work, and so on. Creating a new pattern is something different, because we have to identify ourselves—and that's what bothers us. So there was an argument about this question of "being" or "behaving" lesbian—an argument that is sometimes rather sterile, because it separates us from other movements.

Comment: This was mentioned quite a bit by everyone. From what I understand of what Guattari thinks, the most transformative way would be the existence of various molecular revolutions, in other words, a multiplicity of feminist groups, lesbian-feminist groups, black groups, and other groups, questioning patriarchal or phallic structures. But the party reproduces the patriarchal structure. So I don't think that the most productive thing would be to spend my energy on that kind of structure, but rather to try to construct new forms of performance, assemblages that seek to question those power structures.

Guattari: Perhaps you're right. If the movement works like that, OK. But there might also be situations in which it falls apart. I'll give a historical example: all the different components of the Autonomia movement in Italy broke down, and often because of this kind of discourse. We can imagine how unfortunate it was. One of the elements that exploded was Lotta Continua,[26] which had nothing special about it, but it was important in the Italian movement. The crucial point in its explosion consisted in the fact that one day all the feminist militants of Lotta Continua left the movement with precisely this same discourse. They organized themselves in structures—very interesting ones, actually, such as publishing houses and cooperatives—which within a few months became completely depoliticized. The Lotta Continua movement experienced this as a kind of hangover of guilt: it lost its main driving force, it fragmented, and only the newspaper remained. No doubt this process would have appeared at some point in history, one way or another. Nevertheless, a different script could have been written: the autonomization of the feminist members operating as a factor to reinforce the effectiveness of movements like Lotta Continua, instead of contributing to its collapse into a black hole. Just imagine if all the women in the PT (whether or not they were feminists, or lesbians) suddenly decided to say: "That's it, we've had enough of Lula and all that, we're off."

Comment: And then they'd organize themselves into women's groups. I think that would be great!

Guattari: Maybe. But to think it great that a movement like the PT should disappear is debatable, to say the least.

Minority Experiments in Psychiatry

Meeting with the International Network of Alternatives to Psychiatry, São Paulo, August 28, 1982:

Guattari: The creation of the International Network of Alternatives to Psychiatry constituted a break with what had been taking place until then in this field in Europe. A break that was certainly not embodied in a real social practice, but which at any rate caused psychiatric issues such as psychological and psychoanalytic techniques for assistance to the community or for children to become a subject of public debate. The subject in question was not only of interest to certain minority experiments in the field of psychiatry, such as therapeutic communities. It also mobilized various other sectors, and not just in the field of the "psy" professions. In England, for example, groups of psychiatrized people organized themselves, mainly to fight against arbitrary committals. The subject was widely discussed among leftist groups. In the media, the movement had a considerable repercussion. But at that point, in the time of antipsychiatry, there was a considerable discrepancy between the discourse presented by the media and the everyday psychiatric reality. This discrepancy caused a malaise among those who were working in the field. At the time of the creation of the Network this malaise was becoming more pronounced, and it became the focus of considerable controversy.

From the outset, the Democratic Psychiatry movement,[27] for example, tried to raise the issue in other terms. For a start, Basaglia[28] always rejected the term "antipsychiatry." He considered that activity in this field could not be carried out only through small minority groups: that it was necessary to find a mode of articulation with what was taking place within psychiatric establishments. That provided the theme for a book that was very successful at the time: *L'Istituzione Negata*.[29] By definition, specific questioning of the institutions along these lines can only be carried out through articulation with political and social movements, in terms of their becoming aware of these problems.

At the time of the creation of the Network some people found themselves at the intersection of these tendencies and believed that the theoretical debate shouldn't be bracketed, but should create conditions for exchanges and confrontations in the practical field, so that the debate would go beyond minority groups. Programs of action were proposed at the level of psychiatric practice and at the level of state structures and laws related to psychiatry. The idea was to create conditions to develop tactics, a strategy, that would involve the effective participation of all kinds of components: the promoters of antipsychiatry, of course, but also mental health workers, groups of psychiatrized people, alternative movements that were addressing these issues, and, where possible, various leftist political and union groups interested in these issues.

In 1975, we decided to meet in Brussels to discuss these issues. The whole team coordinated by Basaglia and Giovanni Jervis in Italy was there, the whole group that was working with Mony Elkaïm in Brussels, and groups from England and from France, Laing, Cooper, Robert Castel, and other theorists of these issues were also present. The meeting, which was supposed to be restricted, immediately turned into a very extensive and important encounter. The fact was that, despite us, a process had been triggered off.

There were various subsequent meetings. The Paris meeting was incredible, a spectacular shambles. Part of the district of Les Halles was literally occupied by the Network. It was so surprising, going so far beyond what had been planned, that it was impossible to have a proper discussion. But that wasn't the most important aspect. At the meeting in Trieste, which must have had some five or six thousand people, we were able to have some discussion despite the difficulties; but the event took place during a very heated time of social struggle in Italy, with all the effervescence of the Autonomia movement.

The fact is that at first the Network was essentially European, with components that were extremely different from each other. It was very difficult to keep them together without a nucleus of catalyzing friendship that would prevent the traditional reflections of collective paranoia that are inevitable in this kind of undertaking—things like "we'll end up being coopted by the people from Italy, more or less tied to the Italian Communist Party," or "we'll be manipulated by the British antipsychiatrists," or "we're going to waste time with these alternative movements, which are all very well but don't tie in with social reality"; a whole host of narcissistic, personal problems.

Despite all this, however, and, it must be said, to our great surprise, the European network continued to grow. There were no extraordinary results or achievements, because it developed precisely at a time when there was a general decline in the importance of social struggles in Europe. But in a way, it had the merit of creating a kind of line of resistance that sometimes made it possible to organize a specific defense against repression. There was a great deal of interchange; a real network was organized in terms of alternative European structures.

I'm thinking, for example, of the case of Spain at the end of the Franco regime, when a strong repression clamped down on alternatives to psychiatry: people with a broad range of action in this respect were particularly targeted by the repression. The fact that this was rapidly publicized by the activity of the Network served as a way to pressure the local power relations. There were other struggles against repression in countries such as Germany and Belgium, with situations different from the one in Spain. There were also struggles of the Italian type. At any rate, there was very considerable popularization of these struggles through the Network—for example with Bellocchio's films[30] (I don't know if they were distributed in Brazil).

Basically, what now seems to me to have been most important is the fact that these problems were raised for the first time on a European scale, in new terms, and with interlocutors who were totally different than the ones to whom we were accustomed. That's the situation now, with the difference that in France there's the possibility of a legal struggle, especially after the abolition of laws such as those that govern committals. The young psychiatrists who are at the head of the National Union of Psychiatry (which is very well established in France) have been engaged in legal activity together with members of the Magistrates' Union (a leftist organization). They're in touch with the Network. There are also new components of the Network in Europe—especially in Holland and Sweden—which are concerned about these problems. There are structures for study, structures for transforming laws at a European level, structures articulated to confront what's developing in this field.

As for the links with Latin America, since the beginning of the Network there have been various Mexicans and Brazilians interested in these issues; they took the initiative to create a network, with ways of operating that were not identical, but similar. Perhaps this invention of other resources may enable the Network in Latin America to overcome the kind of difficulties that I mentioned, in other words, the risk of turning into sectarian groups of some kind, or formal academic groups.

Suely Rolnik: It was in this spirit of a network that in São Paulo, around 1980, we created a group called the Social Psychology and Psychiatry Nucleus, which met at the Sedes Sapientiae Institute. The initiative mobilized many people, far more than we had expected. It was a bit like what happened in Europe: we discovered, with some surprise, how great a demand there was in this regard, especially in São Paulo, the city where we were meeting. Many people and groups from other states also contacted us. The number of experiments not identified with the dominant systems of reference in the field of psychiatry was very considerable. And most of them were operating in total isolation. I remember that group in particular because it had the specific aim of creating a network among the alternative practices in psychiatry. But the same aim obviously existed implicitly in other, earlier initiatives, and of course not only in São Paulo. The Nucleus dissolved after two years of existence. Later, a group was created that was officially linked to the International Network, which was joined by various initiatives of this kind scattered throughout Brazil. This is the group that Guattari was referring to when he said he hoped that forms of organization would be found to overcome certain difficulties in the European Network. I'm not so sure....

Guattari: I didn't talk about the way the European network was organized, and that aspect is very important. The Network quickly began operating on an international plane, not only in terms of the debates, but also in terms of the structures and the actual meetings themselves. For example, in France there has never been a unified secretariat: it's at the European level that there is a grouping of the subsets of the Network. The approximately sixty communities of alternatives to psychiatry that exist in southwest France are much more closely linked to the community movements in Holland than to the supposedly alternative psychologists, psychoanalysts, and psychiatrists in Paris, with whom these communities don't have much in common. Similarly, the jurists who are interested in matters of legal changes organize things between themselves, without going through national secretariats. The same is true for the movement of people who have been psychiatrized. I think this point is very important, and I imagine that, at least in this respect, the problems must be the same in Latin America.

The Network doesn't exist so that everyone will come to an agreement, or create a front, a common program for jurists, the psychiatrized, or the "psy" professionals of whatever category. The Network exists to create conditions for a real dialectic, on the assumption that in this way ideas can advance with different rhizomes, different levels of construction. That's what happened at the meeting of the Network in Cuernavaca, in Mexico, three and a half years ago. It's what happened the following year, at the meeting held in San Francisco, the initiative for which came from movements of the psychiatrized in the United States. Those two meetings were more a way for the various components to get their bearings in relation to each other. But the real foundation of the Latin American network took place last year, in Cuernavaca, because over twenty delegations were present there. With that meeting they went beyond the initial character of making contact. There were very lively work groups.

Question: How does this asymmetry of multiple participations work? How did it work in the French experience?

Guattari: I hope the debate will focus not so much on French and European problems as on Brazilian and Latin American problems. Of course, I'm not going to evade the question, but I shall be very brief. What happened really is that in the French context of 1977— also bearing in mind the terrible Parisian centralism—for a long time the Network was fragmented by sectarian group phenomena. This prevented it from functioning on a French level, on a national level, and it was the best thing that could have happened, because the Network actually became multicentered, with contacts on a

European scale. It was only recently, at the last meeting in Geneva, that a French secretariat was reconstituted, because of the imminent coming to power of the Socialists, which created an urgent need to develop proposals for mental health on a national level. At times like these it becomes hard to maintain the spirit of encounter and elaboration of ideas, because there are deadlines at stake. The best way of dealing with the situation is for the various sensibilities to delegate the mandate for dialogue with the political and trade union formations to a restricted or relatively restricted group. But it has to be made quite clear that it isn't a question of a political secretariat, or an organization that will formulate a theory or program to unify all the components. It's a transitory organization with a perfectly defined goal. Outside this kind of situation, basically, one of the criteria for the Network's vitality is the fact that it can cut off its national head without changing anything: in one way or another, it goes on living.

To prevent the paralysis of initiatives, it's important for there to be not just one secretariat but a proliferation of secretariats, as many secretariats as there are different lines of initiative. In this way, a whole series of apparent contradictions ceases to exist. But a multi-centered structure isn't necessarily always the most suitable. Situations such as those in France or Brazil at present involve at least a small level of agreement and coordination, and even representation of the Network on a national scale.

For Brazil now it's clearly very important that a light and highly efficient structure should affirm the problematics of the psychiatric alternative. First by affirming itself in relation to itself, as a movement; affirming itself as a force with proposals for dialogue with formations of the left such as the PT; and also, of course, affirming itself as a force of opposition to traditional psychiatry, opposition to the powers of the state, and all the traditionalist conservative forces in this field— and when I say "conservative," I include a part of the working class that's directly involved in these issues, workers in the field of psychiatry. I imagine that in this respect there isn't much difference between the Latin American situation and the European situation: part of the working class is really conservative.

Question: From what I understand, you're defining psychiatry as social control. I would like to know whether the Network has arrived at the conception of an alternative to psychiatry. I know that, for example, the anti-asylum model currently being proposed in the countries that are most backward in terms of mental health seems to be reverting to even greater social control in countries such as France. Does the Network propose an alternative model?

Guattari: Going back to what I tried to explain before, it's never a question of proposing an alternative model. But on the contrary, of trying to articulate alternative processes when they exist. Especially on a European scale: the situation of psychiatry in some countries there is completely archaic and practically penitentiary, while elsewhere, especially in Scandinavian countries, the sophistication of psychiatric control has been raised to an unimaginable level. In Denmark and Sweden, the state pays mothers, and allows special times for workers to participate in psychotherapy groups: there are whole villages in which life revolves around therapy. There's nothing absurd in this; on the contrary, it's very astute.

In the Network, the coexistence of these systems in their diversity generates a reciprocal enrichment: the "underdeveloped" structures can read the future that awaits them; the "highly developed" structures can see how certain forms of struggle and intervention in the more archaic structures are viable and can be effective.

Comment: The emergence of an antipsychiatry struggle in Brazil doesn't strike me as being very viable. Here, although there's some spontaneity among the working masses to deal with the issue of mental health, it is limited to "spontaneously" calling in at the police station when there are problems of this kind. Moreover, we're fully engaged in fighting for the *physical* health of the population, because even that isn't respected. The discrepancy in relation to the European situation is huge; there, the problems of physical health have largely been resolved. That makes it possible for you to be concerned about mental health, and even propose a form of spontaneous organization of the struggle in that respect.

Guattari: I don't think that anyone before you spoke of "spontaneity"; at any rate, I didn't use that word. On the contrary, the Network's problem is the search for an organization with maximum efficiency. The fact is—just check it out—that all the political, union, university, and traditional structures haven't changed anything in the field of psychiatry in the last forty years, at least in Europe, but also, on top of that, they've merely consolidated the situations of oppression, developing pseudoreforms, actually working with the very mechanisms of disappropriation of these problematics in the real social field.

Perhaps the situation is different in Latin America and in Brazil. If they were to tell me that there are organizations of the left in the medical field now (such as political or union organizations) which at least consider this issue, and not in terms of a vague program to improve facilities, increase the number of psychiatrists, raise salaries, and so on; if they were to tell me that those organizations really link up with the viewpoint of those concerned (such as the psychiatrized, or children), then there would really be no point in seeking structures that would make it possible to articulate the singularities, the various positions that are in conflict. What would be the point, if it already exists?

I want to emphasize that in what I've just said there's no hostility in relation to parties and unions. On the contrary, I insist on the need for them to create conditions for dialogue in the field in which these issues arise. To create structures that are actually sensitive to these problems, connected with real practice, even if they are minimal, so that a true dialectic is established between these components of struggle which, by definition, are on different levels.

I'm reminded of the problems that arose in Spain in 1976 and 1977. The fact that the rise of the leftist formations didn't coincide with a genuine dialogue about these problematics caused the health issues that the left proposed to be far removed from reality. It's necessary to take advantage of times when there are conditions for the development of a general dialogue. Which all goes to show, as I say, that there is absolutely no cult of spontaneism in this kind of proposal.

Letter from Guattari to Suely Rolnik, Paris, May 24, 1983:

I sense that the Network of Alternatives to Psychiatry, in both Europe and Latin America, is in the process of being coopted by the same kind of people close to the Communist Party. Great! There's no reason to hang on to the Network! What's important is to go on with our own networks and reinvent an international way of working that enables us to have access, in the least bad conditions possible, to the tremendous period that lies ahead—for better and for worse!

Psychiatric facilities in France have been modernized: there is a broad policy for opening up the situation, for developing outpatient facilities and sectorization.[31] This policy of sectorization is reformist, it has not resolved any of the basic problems. Firstly, because it reinforces the grid system that exists in all the other registers of social control. And also because the reform that it introduced in France failed. What happened was a multiplication of facilities of a different nature, but the great bastions of psychiatry remained untouched. The result is that in France there is a psychiatric machinery that costs a colossal sum of money, together with a crisis perceived by everyone, including those responsible in terms of state power. For the Ministry of Health, the Socialist government chose a minister who made promissory declarations of principle about the suppression of the 1838 law (the law that affects committals), which would imply radical changes in psychiatric facilities. But at present it's impossible to foresee how it will turn out.

Some communities that offer alternatives to psychiatry—about thirty groups in the South of France, in the Cévennes, a very pretty, mountainous region—agreed to take in people leaving psychiatric hospitals, or children with difficulties. This movement grew out of the events of 1968. Now the state finances these groups, without asking for anything in return, such as control. One might say "Great, this is a nice, useful form of recognition." But in fact these groups gradually become absorbed into structures that are much more subtle than those of a psychiatric hospital. The group carries out its own self-regulation, its own training, and its own discipline. In my view, this would be completely positive if it could lead to a modification of the reality of psychiatric oppression in France. In reality, the power of the state uses this sector as a kind of escape valve. The people who engage in these activities are not at all threatening for the powers that be, because, even if they have dissident conceptions and different practices, so far, at least, this has not produced a dialectic that might lead to a transformation of the situation in the psychiatric field.

These issues are frequently discussed in the Network: we came to the conclusion that it was positive to go on with this kind of experimentation, but that it would only be meaningful if it was articulated with the movements of protest against psychiatry in the large asylums, in sectorization, and so on.

Thirty years ago, when La Borde[32] began (in the context of a traditional structure in its relations with the state, with social security), microprocesses of transformation were experienced, often with passion and enthusiasm. In this context, La Borde made a series of small changes that had a certain degree of effectiveness in transforming the relations between specialists and patients, and also between the specialists themselves.

I am not going to give a talk about what La Borde was like then, but let's say that our experience reflected the problems of mental health at that time. However, this process did not succeed in sweeping away the wall of the state; it ricocheted.

The microprocesses experienced at La Borde did not lead to a more general process of transformation: they went on revolving in a vacuum, as it were, working upon themselves. It's like a breakthrough in the domain of painting that just continues to revolve around itself, shut up in a museum that school groups visit on Saturday afternoon; there is a paradox between small miracles such as the work of Modigliani, on the one hand, and the scandal of compelling children to bore themselves by visiting it, on the other. Of course, I'm not seeking to compare Modigliani to La Borde. Nevertheless, sometimes there are people who come to visit La Borde as if they were going to a museum. I can't say to them "What a shame, you should have come thirty years ago, this isn't the best time to visit La Borde." Even though, thirty years ago, it was in fact a "wealth of possibles" that might have led to something else, different than what

La Borde is today. History decided: La Borde became one of the institutions that have not been directly coopted by the power of the state, but with which the power of the state gets on very well. The only exception to this took place during certain very difficult points in the Giscard period in France, when the power of the state really wanted to close down La Borde, and arrest many of the people who were working there. But the arrests did not have anything to do with the psychiatric problems: there were other problems at stake.

In Belgium, a group of Latin Americans connected with the Network carried out an experiment that is worth mentioning. The group contacted the unions (for example, the union federation of employees of commercial establishments), not only to make demands for things such as social security but also, and above all, to ask them to support the incorporation of people leaving psychiatric institutions into certain sectors of production. Actually, the matter was not put in terms of reincorporation in production. It was like the experiment in Parma, in Italy, where there was an attempt to get people with Down's syndrome and other severe neurological disturbances accepted by groups of workers, not in order to become part of the production process but simply to be with them in the factory. This kind of specific intervention in problematics can affect ideas much more than any discourse.

The groups did retain some traits of sectarian dogmatism (not just political but also psychoanalytical), but these traits do not prevent the experiments from having a mutational nature, a micromutational character, which has to be detected through recognition of the processes, even if they are very small. Only in this way can one evaluate what went right and what went wrong.

Minority Experiments in School

It is surprising that Freud, who discovered the period of latency (the period of depression, and of draining of meaning from the world, which follows the Oedipus complex and the castration complex) did not realize that this period coincides with the age of schooling, the child's entry into the modelizing productive facilities, the entry into the dominant languages. And the child, who has an extraordinary ability to dance, sing, draw, and so on, loses all that wealth in just a few months. The child's creativity drops to a kind of degree zero: he begins to make stereotyped drawings, and to model himself in accordance with the dominant attitudes.

The people who have tried to experiment seriously with other educational methods know very well that it is possible to dismantle this infernal mechanism; they know very well that with another kind of approach this wealth of sensibility, this wealth of expression, can be relatively preserved.

Meeting with "alternative"[33] *preschools in São Paulo, August 27, 1982:*

Guattari: In Europe, and particularly in France, people who work in day-care centers, in schools, or even in parallel structures (alternative structures) always have a direct or indirect relation with the state. The relation may be direct insofar as the people are paid by the municipality or the state, or indirect, when they receive subsidies, or simply what in France we call systems of "deferred salary" (social security, retirement, unemployment benefits, family pension, etc.). To this extent, salaries and investments are always, in a way, derived directly or indirectly from the financial control of the state. To this we can add the fact that the training of the specialists is also extensively controlled by the state. Thus, in Europe, the state is massively present in schools.

What I see as interesting in these experiments of self-managed preschools that you are experiencing here in São Paulo is, at the same time, their difficulty. You've succeeded in acquiring autonomy in relation to the dominant regulations. However, this involves a counterpart, which is the fact that, for example, you can't accept people who are unable to pay; so you end up being fenced in by the prevailing systems of social and racial segregation.

It seems to me to be really necessary for all pedagogic or microsocial experimentation to take up a position in relation to this kind of problematic. To be unaware of it means running the risk of it intervening in the modelization, the transmission of models to the children—first of all, through those factors of social difference, difference of economic status, or of racial status. One of the questions that should be raised, for example, is whether there are black children in these schools, and one should inquire into all the implications that this might have in the libidinal economy of these children. These are limitations in initiatives of the kind that you are developing. However, this clearly doesn't mean that there is not a margin of perfectly valid, original experimentation. What is important is to try to capture the specificities, the true, original characteristics of each experiment.

It seems that there are various figures involved in these undertakings. One can make out at least four important figures. First of all, the children, who are the principal figures. There's also the alternative figure, who adopts a position in relation to his own expressions, who wants to create a small space of freedom, and who—for that very reason—runs the risk of creating a ghetto, that is, of not being able to articulate this space of freedom with what's happening in the social field, with what's happening on the level of the state. The third figure is the state, which, at least in the contexts that I know, is always ready to colonize everything, serialize everything, coopt everything (including alternative experiments) whenever possible. The fourth figure is the neighborhood, the population, the environment.

I personally don't have much experience in relation to the problems of day-care centers, but the alternative structures in psychiatry, which is a field that I know better, run up against precisely this kind of problem. The psychiatrized are always squeezed between the state figure and the alternative figure, which frequently has an indirect dependence on the power of the state. And when these undertakings reject that dependence—which was the case, for example, in Ronald Laing's first communities in England—they risk becoming some kind of elite community, even if they live in poverty; the one does not prevent the other. To get away from this, it's necessary to articulate a vast sector of experiences of this kind, which creates power for negotiation with the state. It's somewhat like the situation in Germany, for example, where there is a whole sector of the population that runs schools, and also cooperatives, and so on, and that collectively negotiates their needs for financial resources with the public authorities. In my view, that's the only way of reaching a consolidation of these alternatives.

If we accept this idea of four figures, we see that it's very difficult to evaluate initiatives like yours unilaterally. For example, what would lead the population of a neighborhood to consider it really necessary to venture into an undertaking like yours? It's the fact that these undertakings correspond to their desires, their needs. And so they have to be sufficiently elaborated to be able really to propose some small alternative.

It's in this sense that I believe that—even though your initiatives may, in a way, be in a situation that's closed in and sometimes even like a ghetto—they could come to have tremendous importance in a different social context, they could become nomads, emigrate, change their character, be taken up and reinterpreted by other milieus.

Question: I think that the universities could be a channel for this kind of pedagogical experiment, outside the limits of the middle class. But the universities here only use the poorest neighborhoods to conduct research. I'd like to know if the universities in France are as disassociated, as detached from the community, as they are here.

Guattari: In any part of the world the university is disconnected from social reality—and that is actually its function. So there's no reason to be shocked. On the other hand, however, there are gigantic social substitutes, multiple collective facilities, which perform an increasingly perceptible function of social control. There's a program to build a database, not only about confirmed delinquency but also about any kind of disturbance, any deviation, however small it may be. So, in some housing projects on the outskirts of Paris, it's common for a family, or a mother, to have to receive a series of visits from 10, 15, or 20 different types of social workers.

Suely Rolnik: … educators in the street, school and day care center, social workers and psychologists in the workplace but also at school, in the day care center, etc. In short, a horde of social workers who come crashing down on a family that sometimes consists of only three people.

Guattari: The application of a psychological and medical control grid during early childhood and at school is constant. If a child shows any kind of "disturbance," however insignificant it may be, it's a reason for the child to be placed in a special class. Suely can say something about this.

Suely Rolnik: I worked in one of those institutions when I lived in Paris. The "special class," within the school itself, is just the first step on a long road that excludes 50% of French children from "normal" schooling. Each neighborhood has about six types of collective facilities for children: from school to psychiatry, ranging through different types of combinations of pedagogy, psychoanalysis, psychiatry, and medical care. The state comes down heavy.

Guattari: The role of the university in all this is precisely to define distinct and highly segregating formations. The power of the state or of equivalents to state power, through collective facilities, is acquiring increasingly excessive importance. That's why I keep saying that experiments like yours are also important for "developed" countries. They raise the question of the reappropriation of all the relations of children with each other, and of children with adults; reappropriation of educational, health care, psychological, and cultural problems; reappropriation carried out by the fabric of society without passing through the mediation of the state, which is assuming ever greater proportions and is developing a mode of subjective production that is increasingly alienating and serialized.

If we go back to the four figures, what you are proposing (to create a process of meetings to consider all these issues) could be embodied in a three-fold or four-fold affirmation. *An affirmation related to yourselves and the children with whom you work*: a collective awareness that you are not in small, privileged sectors, and that this experiment represents a movement of transformation and creativity. *A second affirmation, related to the power of the state*, which involves an articulation with the workers in the public education sector. On this level there is a tremendous amount of work of interchange to be carried out, with all the paranoias that can develop in a relation of this kind. This problem arose for the alternatives to psychiatry. They set out to establish a relation with the nurses and psychologists working in the hospitals, the very people who generally say things like "this is minority work, completely out of touch with reality, it serves no purpose." *A third affirmation, related to the formations of the left*, related to the parties, for them to become aware of these problematics. *There is one last affirmation*, even more important, *related to the totality of social groups directly interested in these initiatives*, so that the project may have credibility and acquire consistency.

This proposal of yours reminds me of a story that it would be interesting to relate. It concerns an experiment that took place in France a few years ago, which was very significant, although short-lived. Some instructors collected some children (perhaps older than the ones you work with), and, in addition to proposing common activities (and you can imagine what they were), they had the children prepare a joint letter containing their own demands (of course the adults helped). A book was published about the experiment. It was a very interesting project, because the children were able to affirm, almost like a "children's bill of rights," a kind of mini-French Revolution—mini, but very significant. One can imagine that the organization that you are proposing could also be developed in parallel in terms of children: establishing systems of interchange and dialogue among them.

Comment: In this discussion, there's something that has been bothering me from the start: it's the limiting of "alternative" pedagogy to these middle-class experiments in São Paulo. There are many experiments like these. Outside this cordon of the Latin Quarter, the route that runs from the Catholic university to the state university, a new life is being built. For an experiment to be pedagogical, it doesn't have to be formalized as a school.

Question: My experience tells me that it's not quite like that. Within a formal institution it's also possible to create an alternative space for action. On the other hand, you can work in a *favela*, for example, and be terribly authoritarian, and even reproduce many of the state structures. It would be interesting to understand why there is this hostility between those who work within the institution and those who work outside it. Why is there this special valorization of work done outside the institution?

Guattari: I don't think that there can be an all-encompassing formula for what we are calling alternative. It's precisely because of this that the analysis of the limits of each experiment seems to me fundamental. It isn't a question of modesty. But it's a question of apprehending the true formations of the unconscious that we are taking as a starting point to work from. Obviously, when I speak of "formations of the unconscious," I include racial and social segregation, and similar problems. An alternative on a limited scale is perfectly conceivable. I can think of some initiatives in France, for example in the Freinet school, which developed some very original techniques. The Freinet experiments originated mainly in the countryside, in small villages totally cut off from the more general French social reality. That didn't prevent them from being valid experiments. An experiment totally restricted to the *favelas* can learn things from the social field that are certainly fundamental. But it's also possible for certain kinds of techniques and a certain kind of representation to develop there, completely separate from certain realities of industrial societies, and therefore presenting a character of limitation of a different kind.

What defines an alternative experiment is its processual character. And in order for the small coefficient of freedom that we have available to function to the maximum, it's necessary to analyze the conscious and unconscious impacts of those four figures at each point. The impact in terms of the most immediate contact with the children, in terms of institutional micropolitics with the group, with the neighborhood, and so on. This is because *the more those four figures are repressed in the field considered, the more active they will be in the modelization of behavior.*

In my opinion, therefore, it's only by dealing with those four figures that we will be able to break the boundaries and develop this work of collective elaboration, alliance and change in power relations that we want so much.

Minority Experiments in the Media

Interview with Félix Guattari for the Journalism course at the Pontificial Catholic University (PUC), São Paulo, August 26, 1982:

PUC: Could you tell us something about the situation of French radio before the phenomenon of the free radio stations emerged?

Guattari: In France, radio and TV were both under state supervision during the whole postwar period. In fact, you can't separate one from the other: the administration of radio became subservient to the enormous machine of the TV sector—a machine for industrial media production. This machine incorporates the parties, which have a certain conception of the state; it also incorporates a large number of salaried workers.

I can't say exactly how many people work in radio in France, but in the production sector alone there must be thousands. It was these professionals who most strongly defended the monopoly when the Giscard government wanted to decide whether to maintain state supervision or not. At that time the monopoly had three official stations: France Antenne, with a large audience, Fipa, which offered popular music, and a "highbrow" station, France Musique (I'm not questioning the level as such, but the conception of "highbrow"). In addition to these monopoly stations there were also three stations outside the state monopoly: RTL, Europe I, and Sud Radio. In fact, even these stations are not wholly private.

Europe I, for example, is a mixed company in which the state has a majority share.

Recently, with the rise of Giscard, the weight of radio and TV became increasingly greater on the political level. Giscard d'Estaing, who has an exceptionally narcissistic personality, made systematic use of TV. This produced strong resistance, a widespread feeling of being "fed up" that made a reversal of the situation possible, as occurred during the last elections. Which shows that the problem of the escalation of power with the aid of the media is not a linear phenomenon.

Another longstanding factor in the questioning and transformation of the monopoly is the commercial advertising function of these state radio stations. Until Giscard there was no advertising on the monopoly radios. Advertising was introduced slowly on state TV, with considerable problems, limitations, control, and a whole restrictive legislation. The financial and commercial milieus had been working on the question of advertising for a long time. For thirty years the financial sector had been leading an offensive to impose advertising on radio. This offensive became an important aspect in the issue of these free radio stations: the advertisers wanted to run commercials on the large radio networks, aimed mainly at local and sectoral populations, which would give them the desired return. When the free radio movement began in 1977, we, in our naïveté, did not realize that many of the people who supported us with great energy basically had a perspective very different than ours: they wanted this leverage in order to develop their own commercial radio stations.

A final factor to consider in the period prior to the phenomenon of free radio is that, in the realms of both TV and radio (much more in TV), there was an incredible bureaucratic "padding" of the broadcasting organizations. I could tell a thousand anecdotes about the way in which the production sectors and the technicians operated, and about the weight of the unions and the technocrats in this machine, which is a veritable bureaucratic monster. A monster that will really only be liquidated when there's a mutation.

PUC: Did Mitterrand use the free radio stations before he was elected?

Guattari: First I want to make an observation about the question itself: no one could "use" the free radios to campaign before the elections, because they were intercepted, embargoed, closed down—they were objects of persecution. They were vehicles that did not convey anything in terms of content. However, it's also true that the free radio stations became one of the most important topics in Mitterrand's electoral campaign.

At first it was just a minority. The people working in the free radios were a bunch of crazies, a bit like Don Quixote attacking the great monopoly. It was scary. It was as if the people here were to decide to attack a military post. The phenomenon quickly acquired incredible power, producing an impact on the mighty media, as if this act of illegality had created a split in the monopoly's structure. It seemed that, *suddenly, doubts had been raised about the legitimacy of the monopoly*. It was as if a cracked window pane had been totally shattered by the impact of a mere pebble.

Briefly, the stages were as follows: this small group of comrades, directly inspired by the Italians (more than inspired, because it was mostly Italian equipment that they used), saw their initiative spread rapidly throughout France. Often, two or three people put the equipment in a kitchen and started broadcasting. Of the groups that were formed, some were folkloric and insignificant. Others, however, were very important from the very start. For example, the Fessen-heim group in Alsace had mobile equipment and started broadcasting in three languages: French, German, and the local language. The repression never managed to capture them. They probably kept moving from one mountain to another. Then the nonprofessional militant groups appeared. First came the ecologists, and the radio fanatics. Then came the neighborhood militants, for example from Saint-Denis (a Paris suburb), who invented a model of radio that immediately became very important. They were in touch with everything that was happening in the neighborhood—where, incidentally, there were many immigrant workers. The people came personally to the radio station to talk about what was going on, to criticize people by name. They used to broadcast during the day and at night—mostly at night, because at that time there's no competition, and the small media became bigger. This triggered off repression and, at the same time, a reaction against the repression, an intense mobilization on the part of the legal community and intellectuals.

There was a snowball effect: the more the free radio stations were repressed, the more they grew. While the workers' unions were totally loyal to the principle of the monopoly, union section groups began to use the free radio stations, which created an imbalance and generated a series of conflicts within the unions. The opposition parties became supporters of the free radio stations, saying: "We're in favor of the monopoly, but we don't want repression of the free radio stations." So we asked them to come and say so on our free radio stations. They came, the police followed, and they were prosecuted. Even Mitterrand had some brushes with the police—and everybody knows that Mitterrand is a law-abiding man! The contradictions within the Giscard majority grew, because there were substantial financial interests as well as local political interests that also began to question the monopoly.

So this phenomenon, which at first was insignificant, gradually sparked off a whole series of contradictions between the ossified state radio and the other radio stations; and also, on the other hand, on what I would describe as a molecular level, it brought

out a whole series of contradictions between a model of predictable listening and this thing that people began hearing and
that kept mutating.

Free radio is a completely different use of the radio media. It
isn't done in the same way as the dominant radio system—it doesn't
set out to do anything better or in the same way as the dominant
radio system. It's about finding a different use, a different listening
relation, a kind of feedback, and a way of getting minor languages
spoken. It's also about promoting a certain kind of creation that
can't take place anywhere else. For example, at the radio station
where I worked, Radio Tomate (Radio Tomato), we brought a
theater group to talk to us. But we brought the whole group, not
just the leader. And if we wanted to we would talk to them for two
hours or more. One can't imagine a commercial-style radio being
able to do that (a two-hour interview), because it depends on audience ratings, and on a certain assumption about how listeners will
receive the message. On the official radio stations, people speak the
way they think they should speak in order to be heard. That doesn't
happen on free radio. It isn't uncommon, in fact, to hear some state
announcers comment in shock: "On Radio Tomate I spoke in a way
that I'd never spoken before!"

PUC: But didn't the state radio stations themselves copy the free
radio stations?

Guattari: Once, on Europe I, they began to do broadcasts like the ones
on free radio, and it caused a big fight with the television people.

Radio Tomate was the first to put African immigrants on the air:
they promoted the music that they liked, which was totally unknown
at the time. They also had a very special presentation style. On the
official radio stations we're now beginning to hear the same kind of
music, and the same presentation style. The difference is that the

African comrades on free radio were undisciplined, they arrived late, and so on, and on the official radio stations they just can't do that.

PUC: How did the Radio Tomate group originate?

Guattari: Immediately after the Socialists came to power, a core group of intellectuals and jurists from the CINEL[34] brought together elements from various free radio stations that had existed since 1977, incorporated elements of the autonomous movement, and illegally occupied some premises in the center of Paris. Then there was an extraordinary growth, because the people in the neighborhoods, the local kids, began to come to this place, and there was an incredible mixture of neighborhood people with intellectuals, militants, and so on. Sometimes, even beggars turned up. Once, I tried to bring the Minister of Culture, Jack Lang. He accepted, but didn't want to go to where the radio station was located.

It was an extraordinary experience, and sometimes surprisingly violent. There were scenes of conflict, personal problems, sometimes mixed up with drug problems, there was a lack of money, and so on.

PUC: What was the repression like before? Were people jailed?

Guattari: Jail, no, but so many charges were brought against us that the judges became fed up. Once, I published a letter in the newspaper *Libération*, informing the judge that I would no longer respond to his summonses. Through a lawyer, the judge said that I could refuse to respond, as long as I didn't make my disobedience public.

PUC: How did they intercept broadcasts in the Giscard period?

Guattari: There was an electronic system that located the broadcast and wiped it out with static. But we were never completely jammed.

We only needed to change the wavelength and *voilà*! Or else, if we were near the location of an official radio station, the jamming wiped them out, too. One way or another, it's a very complicated problem. Not to mention that the fact that jamming could also operate as information. You would turn the knob on the radio and constantly hear "censored, censored, censored."

PUC: Did the radios of the far right play any part in this movement?

Guattari: At the time, not at all. Now, with the free radio law, there are no more radios of the far right, but there are right-wing radios: Radio Chirac, for example, and some Zionist stations, one of which is particularly reactionary. But as far as I know, the fascist groups never occupied the free radio stations. Once, a station created a space for everyone. Anyone who wanted to could speak. You just had to call, and you could talk for ten minutes. Then the fascists used that opening. At the time, it was understood as the birth of fascist radio. People intervened immediately to prevent it from happening again.

PUC: Currently, in France, various groups are requesting a radio station. But the time comes when the dial no longer has room for the number of requests. How is that problem being solved?

Guattari: It's a complicated issue. The situation is very different in Paris compared with the rest of the country. With the exception of the big cities, such as Marseilles and Lyons, in the rest of the country it's still possible to satisfy all the requests. In Paris, there must be about 200 requests, and the possibilities are limited. The problem is knowing the limit. The Socialists worked out a maneuver and eventually imposed a kind of compromise, which consisted in allowing the installation of very powerful stations in the Paris region, instead of accepting radios with a range of 5 to 8 kilometers (which is quite a lot in a very densely populated area like Paris). They started with the idea that 7 or 8 stations could have a considerable range (about 30 km), and 10 stations could have a range of 15 km, which was sufficient for complete saturation of the space of the Paris region. A different technical approach, more compatible with the spirit of free radio, proposed using private frequencies, such as those of the army and others, which would allow the functioning of at least 50 stations with a shorter range. The important thing was to set up a barrier against the commercial stations and the stations of the big organizations and newspapers that monopolize the media. With 50 transmitters, a process of fusion and association could be devised that would cover the demand. Now, with only 15 stations able to operate, there's a real war in that sector.

PUC: Are alliances being formed? Are different tendencies able to operate from the same radio station?

Guattari: There's a committee of technocrats and representatives of the movement, which is behaving like a matchmaker, trying to make forced marriages. This has given rise to interminable conflicts. Radio Tomate, at any rate, didn't want to get married, or didn't get married in time, and now it's on a waiting list, waiting for decisions.

PUC: Why did the free radios only occupy FM and not the short and medium bands?

Guattari: Mainly for economic reasons. You can set up a 300-watt system, which has a range of 10 kilometers, for only 10,000 francs. But if you want to switch to AM you need enormous aerials and much more expensive equipment.

PUC: Who sells the equipment?

Guattari: Previously, it was imported illegally from Italy. Now, much of it is made in cottage operations by electronic whizzes. For years, we were the object of a campaign of denigration on the technical front. It's important to have a good command of the technical aspect because if one day a free radio movement develops in Brazil, this problem will certainly arise. The experts say to us: "What you're doing is dangerous. You're irresponsible. You might enter the frequency of aviation routes, ambulances, and the police. You could trigger off an urban disaster." In fact, nothing like that happened. They were scared that there might be a mess on the social level, and that this kind of radio might have the same function as in Italy: acting as a sounding board for very strong political movements.

PUC: Can it be said that this phenomenon has now been coopted or boxed in by capitalism in France?

Guattari: Not by capitalism, but by the power of the state, by local power, by traditional parties, and by the unions. The Socialist government resisted the incursion of the financial sector, and at the time there was a very lively debate in which the leftist forces also participated. Once the government had rejected the idea of introducing advertising on free radio stations, they became insignificant for private interests. Which doesn't prevent them from looking for other ways.

PUC: On the level of language, what changed? What did the movement represent from an aesthetic viewpoint?

Guattari: I have considerable reservations about the aesthetic impact. Everything depends on the criteria adopted. If you like the music of John Cage, just turn the knob and sweep all the stations. It produces a very special kind of music.

PUC: But isn't that precisely the noise that the free radio stations are ultimately seeking?

Guattari: In a way it is, because *it's about sweeping away the dominant redundancies*, a certain way of speaking: "Good evening, dear listeners of Radio XYZ! Once again it's time for program ABC." On the level of language, from the outset there was an important fact: dozens of languages began to be spoken on French radio. On Radio Tomate alone there was Spanish, Italian, German, Polish, Basque, Breton, and so on. Some programs are exclusively in those languages, others are bilingual. Another thing is the way the languages are spoken: the forms of syntax, rhetoric, and argumentation. None of it fits into the dominant molds (which doesn't mean that free radio doesn't create its own molds). In fact, that's one of the most interesting questions: what's the specific way of talking on free radio?

PUC: Are there statistics about the number of listeners?

Guattari: There have been some surveys, but they aren't very reliable. One of the best stations, Gay, devoted to the homosexual audience, must have from 100 to 150 thousand listeners, an audience not overtly homosexual. According to some surveys, Radio Tomate must have about 50,000 listeners. But what's more significant is the fact that the audience of the state radio stations dropped by about 50%. There's a terrible crisis in those stations. It's mainly because people aren't able to get the state stations because they have to go through the free radio transmissions. You think you're listening to one station and suddenly another one comes in on the same frequency, and it happens without you touching the dial. A lot of people are complaining now because they want to listen to classical music on France Musique and they can't tune in.

PUC: What have been the most important experiments with free radio in France?

Guattari: That's difficult to answer, because there's a great deal of diversity. There's the experiment of Radio 93 in the suburb of Saint-Denis, on which people presented their real-life problems. In general, they were people who were under siege, people holding out against the police in large housing projects. For example, people talked about being arrested for not making an installment payment. It's one thing to read about that kind of thing in a newspaper, but it's different to hear it directly from the person concerned. There were also experiments with regional radio, which were very important. The experiment of Radio Coeur d'Acier (Radio Heart of Steel), in Longwy, was fundamental. The most important thing that happened with that station, in a way, was what also happened at the Lip factories, where they went beyond the traditional directives and there was an experiment in self-management: this made it clear that the movements were capable of breaking up the union structure and its stereotypes, to the extent that at one point this station—which was connected with the CGT (General Workers' Confederation) and the PCF (French Communist Party)—became freer than all the other free radio stations in France. It was very difficult for the CGT to put an end to this experiment, because it wasn't just a small, leftist group that was involved, but a very extensive social movement.

I would like to reverse our relationship for a while, to let you talk about free radio in Brazil now. I spoke about this issue in Campinas with people close to the PT, and they told me that here not only would a free radio station be jammed, but also those involved could go to jail. My question is, if Lula were to create a Workers' Radio, would that lead to repression?

PUC: Certainly. At the very least, the station would be closed down. The problem here is that jamming isn't a matter for technical experts, as in France, but for the police. The people involved would be identified. On the other hand, one must bear in mind that a radio station run by an organized party such as the PT could have the support of fairly extensive popular movements, which would immediately give a political dimension of national proportions to any potential arrests. At any rate, a station of that kind could only arise as part and parcel of a political struggle in which the power relations were favorable to us.

Guattari: I'm going to make an observation that may be misinterpreted, coming from a French person who's just passing through here. It seems to me that in a large country and a great industrial power such as Brazil this issue has to emerge at some point. I don't see how it's possible that the question of the new media isn't raised here, even if only for the training of collective labor power. In a country such as Poland, which has been undergoing quite harsh repression, there are free radio stations, and they play an important part in resistance to the regime. I was in Poland recently, and I was informed that a large part of the police effort was concentrated on stopping clandestine broadcasts. Moreover, one also has to start to reflect on the role of free radio in democratic organizations.

PUC: The problems connected with the emergence of free radio in Brazil are not just of a police nature. There's also immense internal resistance within the leftist groups themselves. Their platforms simply ignore the question of the media, and don't indicate alternative ways of resisting their power. On the other hand, the people concerned about these problems aren't directly linked to political movements, and so they don't have their own political perspectives.

Guattari: This problem also arose in France. The militant Trotskyite, Maoist, and leftist groups of whatever nature were the last to face up to the possibilities offered by free radio. But this situation can be changed, and very quickly. If we were to wait for the traditional militant groups to become aware of the problem, we would risk waiting a long time. The transgressors are often isolated individuals, genuine "crazies." One of the ways of confronting this problem in France was to consider that the broadcasting facilities had to be prepared carefully right at the outset, and only brought into operation on very special occasions. For example: in the case of a strike with a factory occupation, if a free radio station broadcasts what's happening, this requires the police to confront a much broader social area than the factory in question, aggravating the problem. Or else, in the case of some specific event, the timely intervention of free radio can introduce different information, which can immediately be repeated by the major media. It's precisely in order to be able to intervene at the right moment that it's necessary to carry out the technical preparation of the equipment in advance. Otherwise, when a favorable situation arises, we generally don't have time to set up the technical conditions.

PUC: Brazilians should certainly face this issue more boldly. At any rate, the discussion has begun. Can you conclude by saying something about free radio in Poland?

Guattari: There are broadcasts made by the clandestine leadership of Solidarity. They're very short, recorded on cassette, and broadcast without the presence of the militants, running the risk that the material may be seized. There have been some arrests, which began with the arrest of a Belgian who took material there. A network that was working for Solidarity was seized, but eight days later the transmissions began again. Their content consists mainly of indications given by the Solidarity movement. Among other things, they include accusations that certain magazines and pamphlets have been published by the government using Solidarity's name. The radio operates as a guarantee of the authenticity of the movement's declarations. Fortunately, the government has not yet had the idea of making false broadcasts of Radio Solidarity. A further point is that it's very important for the population to hear the voice of the leaders.

Interview by Pepe Escobar for the "Folhetim" section of the Folha de São Paulo, *September 5, 1982:*

Pepe Escobar: Certain writers receive special attention in your books—Fitzgerald, Faulkner, Kafka, Kleist, Michaux, the beat generation—genuine visionaries, cosmic craftsmen capable of designing mutations of perception in relation to space, the body, and time. In Latin America, there are writers who plunge into the task of affirming subjectivity with equal passion. In most cases they are unknown even in their own countries. There are also musicians seeking to get away from conventional harmonic structures. Is it only in the domain of art that one can find elements to break through the seamless block—the "white wall," as you and Deleuze call it—or is it also possible through the small adventures of daily life?

Guattari: European or North American cultural ethnocentrism is an operation of systematic modelization of all cultural production— whether through art or not—that might threaten that order. But I question whether it's necessary for so-called marginal cultures to get involved in the "big scene." The problem doesn't have to do with transforming the system of mass mediatization. That's what was raised at the conference on culture that UNESCO recently organized in Mexico,[35] in which I participated as an observer. An idea that came up was to group Latin culture together—Latin-American, Latin-European—and prepare joint cultural programs. That has its importance of course, but at the same time it scares me: it goes back to the old problem of dividing the pie. The same problem exists in France with the question of free radio. Should we present requests to speak on the official radio stations or make our own stations? To a certain extent, the battle was won. There are hundreds of radio stations scattered throughout France. But a great paradox arose: the government came and proposed stations with a range of 30 or 40 kilometers—in other words, thousands and thousands of people— and insisted that the transmitters should be of "good quality." Thus state power strikes at the core of these stations, introducing a tendency to reproduce the old system. But people insisted that what they wanted were small, non-professional radios, because that's precisely what they like. There's a tremendous problem of…

Pepe Escobar: Cooptation.

Guattari: That's right. Look, I don't tend to get nostalgic about past times, about going back to nature, about the coexistence that can be found up to a certain point in history. I say this as a reminder that history has had periods of enormous distribution of mythical and cultural production without any mass communication industry, even in pre-Colombian America. We had cultures, texts, and so on that involved a system of multicentered production and distribution. Therefore, affirming the need for various social groups to reappropriate the means of expression doesn't necessarily mean particularizing culture and preventing the formation of a weave of cultural productions. When an idea is valid, when a work of art corresponds to a genuine mutation, articles explaining it in the press or on TV aren't necessary. It's transmitted directly, as fast as the Japanese flu virus. This idea of a great global projection screen as a general reference of mass mediation for cultural things strikes me as profoundly perverse.

It's important to try to broaden the customary notion of the media. The notion of the media as a display for products, as a kind of supermarket, is something that not only determines the forms of consumption of literature, art, and so on, but also modelizes the forms of production of art and literature.

For example, let's consider Kafka. It's very clear that Kafka never finished a work—or perhaps, at most, one or two stories. He had a certain ideal of literary form, rather classical really, but when he planned a novel, he thought of Dickens and Kleist. Even his most elaborately worked novels remained unfinished. It's remarkable that when one considers Kafka's work as a whole, one sees the extent to which the same elements of creation permeate not only his outlines of novels and stories but also his diary and his letters. And all of it is always marked by a kind of latent will for destruction, which is complemented by the fact that he never really finished anything. A few weeks before his death he was still recommending people close to him, those who knew his manuscripts, to destroy everything, even though he knew that probably they wouldn't take any notice. One can speculate that, with this desire for noncompletion of expression, what he was seeking was the identifiable forms of creation. There's a phrase in his diary, as far as I remember, that expresses a kind of illumination found in all Kafka's creation, something like "we can write everything." I think that this is what really interested Kafka: the fact that we can always write down everything that occurs in our existence. And when he succeeded in demonstrating to himself that he could capture in a statement something that initially seemed to him to be impossible to semiotize, at that point the work literally fell from his hands. He had achieved his objective, and the idea of going beyond it, of finishing a novel or a story, was of absolutely no interest to him. This is a paradox from the viewpoint of the media market in a broad sense.

It's this kind of fragmented work (and when one thinks of fragments, one immediately thinks of Nietzsche) that Deleuze and I call "minor." It's precisely this kind of work, breaking away from great literary identities, that has expanded tremendously in the media, perhaps much more than all the great works that have been put together and sealed and tied up in and about themselves.

I have the impression that in all the great authors we could find vanishing points of literary identity. Joyce produces the impression that there's a kind of vanishing point at the end of his work. *Finnegans Wake*, for example, seems to be on a kind of line of flight moving toward a production that is almost asignifying—or, at least, in this work Joyce tries to recompose a language that isn't spoken by anybody but that potentially could be heard throughout the planet.

In other words, this "minor" attribute that is used to describe a certain kind of expression of a local character, this notion of "minor expression" in the field of literary production, is not necessarily synonymous with a step in a supposed hierarchy of types of expression, a kind of division of literary labor. A hierarchy that would allow one to say things like: "If you want to write just for yourself or for your neighbor, that's fine, but others, by climbing more steps, are going to reach great literature and be able to conquer the great media markets." What really happens is the opposite: it's precisely the production of a person who doesn't write for anyone, not even for himself, and who even, in some cases, experiences his writing process as something foreign to his ego, a kind of productive intrusion, a process that may be threatening for his system of representation of the world—it's precisely this singular, minor production, this singular point of creativity, that will have a maximum impact on the production of mutation of sensibility, in all the different fields that I call molecular revolution.

The systems of distribution of the production of literature, art, and so on are always conceived as belonging to the domain of a pyramid of control and selection, which is embodied in the fact that there is always a teacher to correct the copies, a critic to select texts, an editor, and so on. This mode of distribution is very segregationist from the viewpoint of the productions selected. We can very easily imagine systems of media and distribution that don't belong to this pyramidal system. I don't think that this is at all utopian because, after all, for thousands of years the distribution of myths and stories and so on did not depend on the TV Globo network or on the two or three critics who lay down the law in the market. And those productions did not fail to find their maximum field of distribution.

The same problems arise in connection with the alternative press and free radio. The free radio movement in France suffered from the effects of the intervention of state power, once it stopped repressing the movement. The Socialist government in France said: "Very well, now you're going to produce free radio with no hassle, but all free radio stations are going to be subject to law. We'll subsidize them, but in order to qualify they have to have a minimum audience, quality, and social value." As a result, ninety per cent of the French free radio stations succumbed to the temptation, and plunged into the funnel, with the exception of a few small stations (twenty or thirty in the whole of France, including Radio Tomate). These stations said: "What we want is not to make big free radio stations, but to make *our own free radio stations*. What we want is not to broadcast with sophisticated devices, or to extend our range, but simply to stop being interfered with on our frequency. We're also not concerned about recognition or possible value judgments; we're not going after audience ratings, because whoever wants to can listen, and whoever doesn't can simply turn the dial. We want to be the only ones to guarantee what we like, what our production is, without referring to the new types of media evaluation that were established about a year ago." It's important to understand the following: when we refuse to submit to those parameters, and say that we don't want to produce professional radio, that doesn't mean that we want to be amateurs, or produce mediocre things, but simply that we don't want to become professionals in our practice—which doesn't prevent us from feeling like devoting ourselves to it completely.

Going back to Kafka: he never became a professional of Kafkaism. Later, many professionals of Kafkaism appeared, in the universities and all over the place.

Round-table discussion at the Folha de São Paulo, *September 3, 1982:*

Arlindo Machado: The discussion of the problematics of the media in Brazil is vitiated and archaic, it's a discussion that never manages to keep up with the evolution, the growth, the very rapid changes that take place in this sector. I'm not referring only to academic discussion, but also to discussion among the parties, the press (commercial and alternative), social movements, and even among the culture industry workers themselves.

Our backwardness in relation to the discussion in France, Italy, or the United States is all the more disconcerting if we consider that the role of the media in Brazil is much more centralizing and effective than in those other countries. Television is an instrument for modeling subjectivity, with an efficiency that goes far beyond old institutions such as political parties, schools, government machinery, and sometimes, even, certain religious institutions. What I'm saying is nothing new. It's been the subject of many university theses. But we haven't considered all the consequences: if the media in Brazil have this hegemonic role in the formation of subjectivity, how is it possible that the more progressive forces in society have not succeeded in creating a project to "perforate" this hegemony? The question of the media is not even addressed in the platforms of the political parties that are presenting themselves now as an alternative for our society. Perhaps this neglect of the media problem is the result of the unconscious sedimentation of the means of communication even within the most advanced forces in our society.

To illustrate this issue, we could say that the most advanced political struggle that sectors of the vanguard of intellectuality and political militancy are raising now (1982) in the field of the media is the fight against censorship. Censorship is clearly a state apparatus that uses the ideology of the current regime to intervene in the production of cultural merchandise, especially merchandise that has a far-reaching impact: it prohibits some, and lets others through. In very general terms, we could say that the question of censorship is only a particular phenomenon in the process of state intervention in the private sector. In this respect, when the struggle against censorship is set as an end in itself, it doesn't differ very much from the struggle that the liberal elements of the private sector are carrying out now against the general role performed by nationalization in Brazil. This kind of struggle is being led by groups that are directly linked to economic interests in the area of the production of cultural commodities. Although it's true that an occasional relaxation in censorship can create a greater space for debate, and allow some issues that are more controversial to be placed in circulation, it's also true that the struggle against censorship, when set as a goal in itself, hides and sometimes even eliminates the most important and fundamental point: the issue of ownership, and of the use of the means of cultural production.

About three years ago there was some relaxation of censorship in Brazil, and when we managed to have contact with various films, see a number of plays, and hear a range of music that had been banned for a long time, the general feeling was one of frustration. When censorship was removed, or at least was relaxed, it became obvious that things didn't change very much. We were seeing *A Clockwork Orange, Rasga Coração*,[36] or *Empire of the Senses*, but something was still missing. The communications media remained entirely in the hands of the trustees of the culture industry, in the hands of the financial conglomerates. Society remained separated from the communications media. At no point were we able to cross over to the category of active producers.

On the other hand—and here we enter more directly into the issue in question, that of the relations between mass culture and singularity—whenever symbolic production took place in a way that was marginal to the media system, and through the initiative of the social movements themselves, the issue was no longer raised in terms of censorship, as shown by the following example. During the first student demonstrations in 1977, and the first workers' strikes in 1978, the production of films described as "militant" proliferated in São Paulo. They were films financed by the very organizations that were involved in the struggle. They were films created as collective work operations, and their function was to serve as a tool, as an aggressive form of publicity to broaden the struggle. The films were hunted down and seized by the police, but at no time was censorship the pretext. When the police invaded a public screening and seized the film, even arresting the people who were organizing the projection, they never asked if the organizers had a certificate from the censor. It would have been ridiculous to raise the issue. At the time, some newspapers published lists of films banned by the censor, and sometimes they included in the lists some of the films produced in these circumstances. But it was a mistake, because those films had never been banned, they had never even come to the attention of the censor. It would have been an act of suicide if someone had taken one of those films to the Federal Censorship Department. The matter was simply not raised in those terms, because the issue of censorship was not very important either for the groups who were producing the films or for the police who were harassing them.

When symbolic production in the area of the media reaches a certain degree of radicality; when the role of this production is a destructive role, a role of rupture, a noise within the general system of the dominant media; and, especially, when the media are used in another sense, in a perforating sense; when the media begin to serve as a sounding board for broader emerging social movements—then the issue of censorship becomes totally obsolete. The question of the intervention of the state apparatus in the production of culture no longer has any point, and the whole problem of freedom of creation is placed on a completely different level.

If free radio stations or pirate radio stations began to proliferate in Brazil now, as happened in Italy and France, the traditional forms of control of cultural production would break down, because pirate broadcasting does not raise the problem of culture in the way that the system traditionally deals with it. Long before a pirate broadcast infringes the law of censorship, it infringes national security laws, it infringes the state monopoly of the use of radio waves, which only permit the operation of transmitters with a large coverage. Not to mention the fact that pirate broadcasting is completely outside the whole structure of business and com-merce—outside all the legal structures that give expression to cultural production in the area of economics.

It seems to me, therefore, that the issue of censorship only appears as a problem within the limits of traditional cultural pro-duction, that is, within the limits of cultural production produced directly for the media structure. *The issue of censorship only presents a problem for a kind of cultural production that, in the final analysis, does not question the very structure of the media.*

Question: I would like you to develop this comparison between the process of cultural piracy characteristic of Europe and the "Tupiniquim"[37] style of piracy characteristic of Brazil.

Arlindo Machado: Well, I wouldn't presume to answer the first part of your question, because as far as the process of cultural piracy in Europe is concerned, particularly in France, Guattari is better placed to answer than I am, especially as he is one of the leading organizers of the free radio movement in France. Now, with regard to the second part of the question, your expression "the Tupiniquim style" of performing cultural piracy seems to me very appropriate. I think it definitely is Tupiniquim, because it seems to me that the very people who are making the most creative use of the mass media in Brazil now are the Indians. You probably remember the comic episodes that involved Chief Juruna[38] some time ago, when he visited ministerial circles carrying a portable tape recorder and recording all the official speeches and promises. That was the way he found to call the men in government liars. His presence at official ceremonies carrying a portable tape recorder—a presence that came to be disconcerting—was a declaration, a way of making explicit the demagoguery of the men who were making the speeches. Chief Juruna's attitude was very similar, in my opinion, to the attitude of a child whose father gives him a toy piano so that he'll develop an early love for music; instead of striking the keys, as the design of the instrument requires, the child puts his hand underneath it and starts plucking the strings directly, or hitting the toy so that the strings vibrate and produce a pleasant sound. In other words, the child invents an entirely new way of relating with the instrument.

For me, that's what piracy is: it's inverting the use that's foreseen in the construction of the device; it's transforming a receiving device into a broadcasting device, for example. That's precisely what the indigenous peoples do, incredible as it may seem. Funai[39] distributed amateur radio transmitters (citizens' band radios) to some tribes in the north of the country (mainly those that were in difficult geographic locations), so that they could communicate and ask for help in the case of a tragedy (for example, an epidemic). But instead of asking for help, the Indians began making a different use of the radios. They began communicating with one another, eventually establishing a small communication network. That, in my view, is what piracy is. Another example is the use of videocassettes at a congress of indigenous people which was held in Peru in 1979 or 1980. The congress was a veritable Tower of Babel, because each tribe spoke a different language. One solution that was found in order to transmit their experiences, their struggles, their tradition, their culture was the use of the videocassette. The Brazilian tribes that took part in the event also took with them their experiences on videotape, with the aid of the Indian Defense Commission. That's piracy. That's the Tupiniquim way of using the mass media.

Meeting with minority groups, Olinda, September 15, 1982:

Question: What was the reaction of French companies to the Presidential decree that legalized free radio?

Guattari: There were various reactions. The peripheral stations, the ones that don't belong to the state but in which the state has great weight—such as Europe I—began to do a series of programs called Radio Libre (Free Radio); they began to imitate the kind of expression that had been experimented with in free radio, in order to recapitalize it immediately in their companies. On the other hand, other people in the corporate "movement" invested a lot of money in free radio, but so far the Socialist government has maintained a purist position, maintaining that there are to be no commercials on free radio. But nobody believed them. Then large commercial interests said: "OK, we won't do advertising, but we're going to get ready to do our own free radio broadcasts," completely convinced that the government would eventually give in and authorize advertising on free radio. And one also has to bear in mind all the regional broadcasting of video and cable TV, which would also probably operate with advertising budgets. And the third element is Radio France, the national radio organization, which didn't try to do free radio, and so lost fifty per cent of its audience.

Debate held by a branch of the PT in São Paulo, August 29, 1982:

Question: Doesn't the fact that the Mitterrand government legalized and institutionalized the free radio stations imply a drain on their creative capacity?

Guattari: I don't see a contradiction between institutionalization and creative capacity. It's true that, at present, the rights of the free radio stations are completely manipulated by France's new Socialist government; but it would be absurd to use that pretext to deny that there has been at least some small advance, in the form of no longer being arrested and taken to court, no longer suffering jamming in broadcasts, as occurred during the Giscard period. Let's take our conquest as a starting point. The free radio station where I work hasn't been recognized by the government, but that's not important. At heart, I even prefer it like that. That isn't going to interrupt our process of expression through free radio. In the final analysis, what will be decisive between succumbing to cooptation or nourishing the process of transformation will not be the laws approved by the Assembly, nor the programs adopted by the large traditional organizations. What will be decisive is a processual creativity that will make the laws clash in some way with the vitality of the movement in all its components.

Considerable care must be taken to avoid thinking of the activity of the media in the same way that information and communication theorists often do. In media activity, there is never a direct passage from the systems of production of statements to the individuals who receive those statements; there is never a direct passage between the producer and the receiver of the image. The media always act through the mediation of processes of subjectivation. Sociologists have demonstrated that the impact of the media on public opinion, for example, always operates through intermediary systems, which they call primary groups or "two step groups."[40] It is precisely these levels of intermediary subjectivation, these primary groups, that are targeted by the processes of production of capitalistic subjectivity. And the modelization of these groups is effected through the control of their leaders: that is the objective of the media.

In which case, it's not only the fact of creating free radio stations or making independent videos or Super-8s that will make it possible for groups to dismantle the production of dominant subjectivity. Considered by themselves, the phenomenon of free radio in Italy or France, and the phenomenon of video and Super-8 lend themselves to all possible forms of cooptation. What will make it possible to dismantle the production of capitalistic subjectivity is the fact that the reappropriation of the mass media is integrated in assemblages of enunciation that have a whole micropolitics and politics in the social field. A free radio station is only interesting if it is linked to a group of people who want to change their relation with daily life, who want to change the kind of relations that exist among them in the very team that is producing the free radio broadcasts, a group of people who develop a sensibility; people who have an active outlook on the level of those assemblages and, at the same time, do not shut themselves up into ghettoes on that level.

It is obvious that we can only change the relation with the media—with this mode of production of subjectivity—through some reappropriation of the means of communication. It is not a question of waiting for some leader or some party to authorize or create free radio stations, but of starting right away to create our own free radio stations ourselves, because it is now that the situation presents this possibility.

Free radio is like a kind of match that you strike and then everything catches fire. All it needs is for three or four free radio stations to appear in some corner of Brazil, and immediately thousands of free radio stations will begin to operate. That's where the problems arise on a large scale: problems of legislation, of the positions taken by the political parties, of the reactions of professionals (in radio, journalism, and so on), of coordination on the technical level and on the material level. It's the kind of problem that raises the issue of the complete autonomy of radio—autonomy in relation to parties, unions, municipalities, and so on—and does so on a large scale from the outset.

Minority, marginality, autonomy, alternative

Correspondence, February and September of 1983:

Suely Rolnik: When you refer to the processes of rupture with the mode of production of capitalistic subjectivity, you use a series of terms: process of singularization or autonomization of subjectivity, function of autonomization or minoritization, and even autonomy, minority, marginality, and molecular revolution. Are all these terms equivalent to each other, or do they designate different kinds of process, or different aspects of a single process?

Guattari: I agree that there's an equivalence in these formulas. But I would say this:

1) "molecular revolution" corresponds more to an ethico-analytico-political attitude (the same is true for "function of autonomy").
2) "process of singularization" would be the more objective event of a singularity detaching itself from layers of resonance and causing the process to proliferate and broaden, which may or may not find an intrinsic structure or system of reference.
3) "Autonomy" refers more to new territories, new social refrains.
4) "Alternatives" can be either macropolitical or micropolitical.
5) As for "minority" and "marginality," I see "minority" more in the sense of a becoming, a becoming-minority (examples: a becoming-minority for literature, which would be an escape from the dominant redundancies, a becoming-child, a becoming-crowd, etc.), while "marginality" would be more sociological, more passive.

Interview by Sonia Goldfeder, São Paulo, August 31, 1982:

Sonia Goldfeder: How would you define the question of marginality and minorities in current societies?

Guattari: First of all, it's necessary to distinguish between marginalities and minorities. It's a distinction of method. In ordinary language we can say that "marginal people" are the victims of segregation, and are increasingly controlled, watched over, and assisted in societies (at least in "developed" societies). That's what Foucault is referring to in the expression *surveiller et punir* (watch over and punish). Basically, everything that doesn't fit into the dominant norms is framed, arranged on small shelves, in individual spaces, which may even have a specific ideological theory. So there are processes of social marginalization as society becomes more totalitarian, and that is in order to define a certain kind of dominant subjectivity to which everyone must conform. This happens on all levels: from the clothes you use to your ambitions and your practical subjective possibilities.

Minorities are something different; you can be in a minority because you *want* to be. For example, there are sexual minorities that champion their nonparticipation in the values and modes of expression of the majority.

We can imagine a minority being treated as marginal, or a marginal group wanting to have the subjective consistency and recognition of a minority. And there we would have a dialectical combination of minority and marginality.

A very common representation in the dominant culture is that the problem of marginality/minority is important but particular; and therefore it's necessary to take particular measures for young delinquents, prostitutes, drug users, people who can't affirm themselves in the culture, and so on. I think that this is a way of not recognizing the nature of the process that led to marginalization— a process with which we are increasingly confronted—or to the politics of autonomization of minorities.

There aren't many women who are conscious of the problems of women's alienation, and fewer women still organized in feminist movements, and yet the problem tends to affect all women. There aren't many workers who revolt against the form of organization of labor, the hierarchy, the conception of the relation between work and leisure, and so on, and yet there's an increasing maladaptation of forms of work. In other words, those who express themselves in the "waveband" of marginality and minority undoubtedly raise problems that concern that waveband, but that also concern the whole of society.

The fact that the aim—undoubtedly pertinent—of people who want to change society is to increase salaries, democratize society, and achieve a majority in Parliament is all very well. But to what extent does their *way* of engaging in politics, engaging in unionism, or engaging in militant journalism intervene in the general problematics raised by minorities and marginalities? Unfortunately (and this often happens), people who want to change society transmit the same prejudices, the same phallocratic attitudes, the same total lack of knowledge of desires, which can only be constructed and experienced in certain vectors of singularity, or of autonomy—what we call it isn't very important.

Minorities and rhizome

The old marginalities have now been replaced by a process of marginalization that permeates all strata and components of society. I believe that nowadays it is the various minorities that are raising the most crucial problems with regard to the future of societies—particularly the problem of the world crisis. Not that minorities have a theory about it, or have means of intervention to change the various social orders, but they are the ones that take into consideration the problematics of unconscious subjectivity in the social field, without which one loses the principal motive of the crisis and the impasse into which our societies are plunged.

That is why I consider that a dialogue between minorities might have a much greater impact than a mere agreement between oppressed groups. Such a dialogue could lead to a very positive attitude, a much more aggressive attitude, which would consist in questioning the principal motive and the aim of current societies.

Molecular problematics are totally connected—both at the level of their repressive modelization and at the level of their liberating potentials— to the new kind of international market that has been established. In relation not only to the economic markets, but also to all the information markets, and all the image markets—with the result that the transmission of models ultimately tends to concern the whole surface of the planet. This may be interesting with a view to trying to conceive *a new dimension of internationalism.* There are mutations that were brought by minority movements, which do not need a central staff to be discussed and disseminated, because they are transmitted through other modes of communication. What operate there are not only programmatic transmissions of programs and ideas, but also *transmissions of sensibilities and experimentation* that, as I have said before, are not brought about by the establishment of an "international."

Debate at the Federal University of Santa Catarina, Florianópolis, September 17, 1982:

Question: It would be interesting if you would say more about the forms of organization that you spoke of, the forms of articulation of minority movements, for example. Forms that are not parties, that do not have centralized coordination, but that are also not spontaneous; forms in which power is diluted—in fact, everything that you call "rhizome."

Guattari: I'll take an example that isn't very ambitious, which is the free radio movement in Italy and France. In France, the movement didn't set out from a structured organization, set up as a sectarian group. It began to develop, very quickly, in 1978, in rather heterogeneous milieus: milieus of marginal people, national minorities (such as groups of people in Alsace), or movements of local workers' unions. It eventually brought about a total transformation in the way that the issue of the media was considered in France. However, there was no general program of intervention on the part of the free radio stations. There was a kind of molecular focus, if one can call it that, which raised the issue on all kinds of levels, to such an extent that it became quite important during the electoral campaign. The articulation of free radio stations was raised on the level of legal battles to change the laws about the monopoly, on the level of struggles of solidarity against repression, on the level of technical assistance to exchange or manufacture equipment. It was an articulation that was quite effective at responding to that kind of problem, without ever leading to unification—which would actually have been impossible and absurd as a project, going against the very spirit of the movement.

That's more or less the kind of articulation that I was talking about. I think we could transpose the same thing to the feminist movement in France and in Europe, which, irrespective of the divisions between its components, raised problems that changed the way in which a series of questions were raised, in terms of society as a whole. This doesn't mean that the movement achieved immediate, palpable results, but that the molecular focus that it brought into play—the questioning of a certain kind of man-woman relation, for example— is something that even the most reactionary parties couldn't escape.

The problem of the International Network of Alternatives to Psychiatry is also of the same nature. It's not a question of coming to an agreement, or even of creating an alliance between psychiatrists working in the public sector and people who experienced psychiatric hospitals in their lives and in their bodies for decades. Or people who are completely uninterested in the public structures of psychiatry, but who are in marginal community initiatives, shelter structures, outside the usual funding parameters. And yet the problem of the Network consists in finding a form of association that revolves around certain objectives, even though the means and the technologies may be different.

These are examples of devices that allow a new kind of articulation; devices that allow the creation both of defensive structures and also of more aggressive structures, devices that allow the creation of openings and contacts that are impossible to realize in isolation (when isolated, one is deprived of resources, and the tendency is to curl up for protection). They are *living* devices, because they are embodied in the social field itself, in relations of complementarity, of support—in other words, rhizomatic relations.

When we want to characterize the "alternative" in terms of its processual character, it is merely a sign that we cannot sum it up in a theory, an ideology, or a practice. This does not mean that we make a vague combination, a vague syncretism. On the contrary, we work out an understanding of the singular positions in which each individual is situated, an understanding without paranoia, without projection, and without culpabilization. We do this precisely in order to make it possible, through this articulation, to develop a process of reflection and analysis, a complete *activity of metabolism of the change in the perception of situations*, which may possibly lead to alliances. The alliances, in this case, would be characterized by constituting systems of "transversality"[41] whose criterion is the position of desire.

It is necessary to set up structures and devices that establish a totally different kind of contact. A kind of self-management or self-organization of a set of problems which does not start from a central point that arranges elements, inserts them into a control grid, or establishes an agenda, but that, on the contrary, allows the various singular processes to attempt a rhizomatic unfolding. This is very important, even if it doesn't work.

I was perplexed—and note that I was experienced with regard to sectarian groups—at the way in which things happened in the March 22 Movement, in France in May 1968. People talked, made all sorts of plans, and had lots of discussions, and in the end nothing was decided. The next day, sometimes the discussion was resumed by a group that had set itself up (without anyone having appointed it) and that had managed to get as far as preparing a plan. I am not saying that this is a strategy to be applied and imitated; it's simply an example of a totally different logic than that of a secretariat, or a politburo. The logic of a politburo or something like that consists in the fact that its members say: "On the basis of our analysis, we have decided to do such and such," and from that point the group, with its voluntarism, carries out the line of action that has been defined, with the whole militant dimension of attribution of blame that is always implied in that kind of undertaking. I am talking here about a different logic, completely different than that: we propose doing something, and if it works, OK; if it doesn't work, that's also OK, because maybe we can do it another way, another time. However, I think it is very important that there should be a structure of parameters, where one can keep an eye on the problematics as they appear, where one can express these kinds of collective investment of desire, where one can evaluate the consistency of these different projects together.

It is far from my intention to create a theory of minority movements in Brazil. In any case, I would be quite incapable of doing so.

3

POLITICS

MICROPOLITICS: MOLAR AND MOLECULAR

When I was young, I completed half the course to become a pharmacist. That is certainly what left me with this mania for using expressions such as "molar" and "molecular."

The micropolitical question—that is, the analysis of formations of desire in the social field—has to do with the way in which the level of broader social differences (which I call "molar") intersect with the level that I call "molecular." Between these two levels there is no distinctive opposition that depends on a logical principle of contradiction. It may seem difficult, but it is merely necessary to change the logic. In quantum physics, for example, it was necessary for physicists to admit that matter is corpuscular and undulatory at the same time. In the same way—*social struggles are molar and molecular at the same time.*

Meeting at the premises of the Grupo de Ação Lésbico-Feminista, São Paulo, September 2, 1982:

Néstor Perlongher: You speak of a blackness that traverses all races, a homosexuality that traverses all sexes, you speak in affirmation of singularity. Here in São Paulo there is a group called the Grupo Somos de Afirmação Homossexual (We Are Homosexual Affirmation Group). I would like to know how you see the difference between what you call "affirmation of singularity" and what takes place in this group. It seems to me that what is taking place there is an affirmation of individuality, a construction of identity that has a sense of normalization, and consequently a molar sense of reterritorialization, to use another of your and Deleuze's concepts that seems to me to be particularly interesting. In any case, what I am saying of this group is true of all minorities—they tend to constitute types of "mini-Zionism." Another question is whether this concept of "reterritorialization" could not also be applied to the process by which all these minority, fragmentary, molecular forces can be coopted or confiscated by political parties.

Guattari: Your mini-Zionism makes me think of missionaryism, and things like that. But first of all I would like to say that it is always necessary to mistrust our categories. This opposition between molar and molecular may be a trap. Gilles Deleuze and I always try to cross this opposition with another, the opposition between micro and macro. The two are different. The molecular, as process, can originate in the macro. The molar can be instituted in the micro. The problem that you're raising can't be reduced to just two levels, molecular and molar (the level of the politics of the constitution of major identities). This reduction doesn't enable us to understand problems such as individuality, identity, and singularity. For example, the fact that a woman has to behave in a certain way, model herself from childhood in her way of assuming standards of femininity, just as they're programmed in the social field as a whole, by what I call the "general function of collective facilities." And when I speak of collective facilities I'm not referring only to things like clinics or health centers, but also to magazines, and radio and TV programs aimed at women. It's this function of collective facilities that codifies conduct, behavior, attitudes, and value systems practically by remote control. But it can't be said that we are dealing with a process of individuation at this level. As an illustration, let's take the image of automobile salesmen. They have a range of models available for different budgets, which correspond to different social categories. This range of models intersects with the fact that you can personalize or "customize," as they say: you can choose seat coverings in leather, suede, or cloth, and you can also choose your favorite color. At this level, therefore, we could think more about the process of personalization.

The example of the car is important because perhaps that's what distinguishes the mode of consumption in industrial capitalist societies from the incredible mass production of consumer goods that exists in the countries of Eastern Europe. There are the same pants, the same cigarettes, the same stereos—in short, the same things with the same materials: except that in the capitalist world we personalize ourselves. In any case, these two types of society exude the same kind of tedium, the same kind of impossibility of escaping from this pseudo-personological siege. And in this case I think we can certainly speak of modelization, of a totally alienated production of subjectivity.

It's not my place to come here and give a course on the life of women who are completely confined to their domestic space with all its preestablished circuits—the corner supermarket, the soap opera at such and such a time, a weekend spent somewhere or other. Nor am I the appropriate person to talk about how this confinement frequently causes there to be a great superiority of men over women at work, because, however oppressive the field of work may be, there is always a certain degree of freedom there, however tiny. That's why, when the weekend comes, or a holiday or a vacation, people who work very often feel a kind of subjective boredom and unconsciously begin to hope that the break will soon be over, so that they can go back to their situation of insertion in work. This leads to an extraordinary paradox: the fact that sometimes it's in labor relations where there is the greatest degree of exploitation and submission that these frequently insignificant microdimensions with their coefficient of liberty and desire are preserved.

I know Japan a little, and this kind of thing is very sensitive in a society such as the Japanese one. There's a development of a whole kind of group Eros running alongside the large production organizations. At work itself, or after work, the employees, especially the men, meet up with other colleagues—including the boss—to drink sake and talk, creating a kind of sociodramatic situation. This kind of model shows us how the molar production of subjectivity is necessarily accompanied by some negotiation of molecular processes.

That's why it's necessary to mistrust this kind of molar/molecular categorization, which separates the fields too much. Capitalistic production machines function poorly, or even not at all, if this capturing of miniprocesses of desire, or freedom of singularization, or whatever you like to call it, doesn't take place. If there's one set of problems with which totalitarian systems—of the Soviet kind and others—have very great difficulty in dealing, this is it. On the other hand, knowing how to deal with these problems is one of the great superiorities of the production of subjectivity in capitalist countries: being able to use the media and a series of very complex systems to carry out this kind of ongoing cooptation of the microvectors of singular subjectivation.

If we go back to the example that you propose—a militant homosexual group—we see that this case, too, can't be mechanically classified into these two categories (molar and molecular). There will always necessarily be a certain functionality that is molar—for example, the fact that at some time or other one may fall into the trap of some kind of representativity, or the fact that feminist militants let themselves be carried away by the star system.

Basically, the processes of singularization cannot be specifically assigned to a macrosocial level or a microsocial level, or even to an individual level. That's why I prefer to speak of a "process of singularization" rather than singularity—and, once again, without presenting an apologia for the processes of singularization, because they can enter any kind of modality of systems of cooptation, systems of modelization. *Any micropolitical approach consists precisely in the attempt to assemble the processes of singularization on the very level from which they emerge.* This is in order to avoid their cooptation by the production of capitalistic subjectivity—either by the great network of collective facilities, or by structures of the kind that you indicated, of reappropriation through militant action. Militant action is also exposed to risks of modelization: the "alternative," for example, may be an equally oppressive modelization, but in another form. Consequently, an analytic micropolitics of singularities would have to traverse these different stratifications, these different levels.

Let's take the example of feminism. At a molar level, it can constitute an organization with a transitory program to protect itself against segregation, to demand rights, and so on. But at the same time, at a molecular level, the function of autonomy in feminism does not concern only those women who consider themselves feminists, but all women, and also the way in which the organization addresses women who are not members. And equally, of course, it concerns all men, if we consider that men are also, I repeat, immersed in a becoming-feminine. However, if the feminism in question becomes reduced to molar references—of capitalistic binary oppositions of the sexes, and not just that but also things like the vote, political proposals, tendencies—it loses its processual character (its function of singularization). Unfortunately, this has happened in Europe with many feminist movements that only conducted politics as a group and on a large scale. This often led them to function like completely classical sectarian groups, and in some cases even led to the adoption of a psychoanalytic posture within the group, which was catastrophic.

That is why I believe that there is a level in autonomous groups (the molar level) where they are enveloped by circumscriptions, and enter into power relations, which give them a figure of identity. But the only way of guaranteeing that they will not transform their processes of singularization into a banner (which would go against the very reality of those processes) is to attempt to preserve the function of autonomy. That is precisely where all the work can be done: at the points of coexistence of these n levels, the relations of which do not obey a binary logic of false/true and that kind of stuff.

3rd Congress of Black Culture of the Americas—PUC, São Paulo, August 25, 1982:

João Silverio Trevisan: I'm going to raise some issues that were already fairly confusing for me and that you have done me the favor of making even more confusing. I would like to apply what you call molecular movements to something that I know quite well. I'm referring to the homosexual movement, with which I was connected, and from which I more or less separated when I perceived that the only way to survive was precisely through the absorption of this singularity by the system. And so I ask: what am I to do with my confusion? For me it's not funny, because it also involves my personal life. It's not a problem that a political party can resolve. Moreover, I have the impression that it isn't exclusively a problem of homosexuals, at least in Brazil. I think that in all the movements that you call molecular there was a moment when they got out of step with Brazilian society, and I don't know when or why that lack of synchronization occurred. I know that the answer is very complex. I don't know if what I'm doing, really, is asking a question or just vomiting. But in any case, I think it's quite a serious problem, because I have the impression that all these movements in Brazil are currently in a cul-de-sac, and that's because of the cooptation of their singularity, a takeover that has already taken place.

Guattari: Would you like me to make some kind of response?

João Silverio Trevisan: I'd like you to say that I'm not totally lost.

Guattari: The issue that you raise is, by definition, the kind of issue to which I can't respond in depth: it's of the nature of what I call a micropolitical analysis, an analysis that can only be made by the individuals and groups concerned. I don't believe that there are any general models that can be applied. Either a model is useful for something (as a precise description), or else it must be set aside. If we apply the model of the relations of molar forces to the problem of a family, institution, or group, we discover that there is not a term-by-term opposition of the two vectors, molar and molecular—they intersect completely. On the contrary, there is always a coextensivity of these two dimensions: there may be a dimension of social resistance by a group against exploitation, against alienation, and against any kind of oppression, while at the same time, within the problems of the group, there may be microfascist processes on a molecular level.

In my view, the *problem of a micropolitical system of analysis lies precisely in the fact that one never uses just one mode of reference.* For example, I may be on this platform making great speeches about emancipation and liberation and at the same time have an investment of paranoid power impelling me to take over the auditorium and establish a relation of phallocratic seduction, racist seduction, or whatever. Let's suppose that I even become the leader of this group struggling for a just cause, and everyone applauds me and says "Félix will represent us for this cause," and at the same time there's no device for any attempt to analyze what other types of investment are necessarily at work in the situation on the molecular level. In this case, what will inevitably happen is that, sooner or later, the best intentions, the most favorable power relations, will have an appointment with an experience of bureaucratization, an experience of power. Inversely, if the processes of molecular revolution are not taken up on the level of the real power relations (social, economic, and material power relations), they may begin to revolve around themselves as imploding processes of subjectivation, bringing about a despair that may even lead to suicide, or madness, or something of the sort.

The micropolitical analysis takes place precisely at the intersection between these different modes of apprehension of problematics. It's clear that there are not just two modes: there will always be a multiplicity, because there isn't subjectivity on one side and material social reality on the other. There will always be a certain number of processes of subjectivation, which constantly fluctuate according to the circumstances, according to the composition of assemblages, according to the moments that come and go. And it is in these assemblages that the articulations between the various levels of subjectivation and the various levels of relation of molar forces must be assessed. On a theoretical level, what can be said about the gay group that you mentioned is that if there had been a device to try to grasp the nature of the various processes of subjectivation at work—for example, phenomena of leadership, or of internalization of the dominant models—perhaps it would have been possible to avoid the implosion that you indicated. At any rate, it's something to be able to raise this problem, instead of systematically denying it for the sake of some ideology or other—Marxist, psychoanalytic, microsociological, or whatever.

João Silverio Trevisan: Fine, but you haven't offered any new leads for my problem.

There is no logic of contradiction between the molar and molecular levels. The same kinds of elements and the same kinds of individual and collective components that operate in a certain social space may function in an emancipatory way at a molar level, and coextensively may be extremely reactionary at a molecular level. *The micropolitical problem is how we reproduce (or don't reproduce) the dominant modes of subjectivation.*

Thus, for example, a community work group may have a clearly emancipatory action at a molar level, but at a molecular level have a whole series of phallocratic, reactionary leadership mechanisms. This could happen in the Church, for example. Inversely, the action might reveal itself to be reactionary and conservative at the level of the visible structures of social representation, at the level of the discourse as articulated on the political or religious level or whatever, that is, at a molar level. And at the same time components of expression of desire, of expression of singularity, may appear at a molecular level, elements that do not in any way lead to a reactionary, conformist politics.

To oppose a molar politics of the large organizations that exist at any level of society (micro or macro) to a molecular function that considers the problematics of the economy of desire, equally present at any level of society, does not imply a valuation in which the molecular is good and the molar bad. The problems always arise on both levels simultaneously.

On the molecular level it is much more difficult to identify the enemy, because, unlike the situation on the molar level, it is not a class enemy embodied in some leader or other. The enemy in this case is something that is embodied in our friends, in ourselves, in our own ranks, whenever the problem leads to an assemblage of enunciation of a different kind.

For example, a militant feminist may have a disalienating attitude or practice in the man-woman relation, but suddenly discover that she has an incompatible and even microfascist behavior in relation to her child or in relation to herself. So we see that on this level of analysis of the formations of desire in the social field, on the micropolitical level, there is no Manichean logic operating, on the basis of which the "good" can carry out a programmatic grouping among themselves to attack the "bad." On this level, one can never definitively trust a leader, an organization, or a program. On the contrary, it is necessary to create devices so that the issue is constantly raised anew. I have no formula for this kind of device, but I have an observation to make about it: whenever, in an organization or a political struggle, we find ourselves saying things like, "Now we have to decide our line; only then will we be able to deal with the problems of the organization," whenever that occurs we can be certain that we are hiding problems on a micropolitical level. *The problems of organization are never mere problems of infrastructure.*

Let's take the example of the newspaper *Libération*. This newspaper tried to invent a new kind of journalism, a new kind of relation between the people who work there and, of course, between the newspaper and its readers. Later, this was gradually restricted until only a microscopic trace was left as an indication of the proposal. It was what was called the "copy-editor's notes." The copy-editor inserted a little message in the middle of any important declaration. This stirred up a lot of interest and was a great success. But it interfered considerably with the leadership that was being established at the newspaper; so they began to monitor the "copy-editor's notes": there were "good" notes and "bad" notes. Until, finally, they completely suppressed them. This kind of sign, this kind of symptom of a tendency, a problem that may seem to be secondary, is precisely what becomes an element of appreciation for an analysis of the processes of subjectivation and singularization.

One has only to turn one's eyes away for an instant from the representations of politics that the media provide and *examine what is taking place in the theater of affects*—follow the gestures, lip movements, facial expressions, the ungainliness of bodies—to discover that, most of the time, the *champions of freedom are as contemptible as the others, the defenders of conservatism*. And when this observation begins to operate at the lowest level, at the grassroots level, then we enter a possible process of validation of molecular social practices. Like a painter who discards his first vision in order to recover the reference elements that constitute the real weave of his painting. It's shadowy, close, warm, grainy and so on. It's the same with politics. Politics is a stage of analytic representation—in the sense of Artaud's theater of cruelty—in which we have to apprehend the deplorable elements that are before us, but also around us and within us. *It is through the cartography of subjective formations that we can hope to distinguish ourselves from the dominant investments of libido.*

Democracy may be expressed in terms of large political and social organizations; but it is only consolidated, and only takes on consistency, if it exists on the subjective level of individuals and groups, on all these molecular levels, new attitudes, new sensibilities, new praxises, which prevent the return of old structures.

To counter this kind of assertion it is common to use the famous argument that "if politics is everywhere, it is nowhere." To this I would respond that, in fact, politics and micropolitics are not everywhere, and that *it is precisely a question of placing micropolitics everywhere*—in our stereotyped relations of personal life, conjugal life, romantic life, and professional life, in which everything is guided by codes. It is a question of making a new kind of pragmatics enter all these fields: a new kind of analysis that actually corresponds to a new kind of politics. Nowadays, any important problem, even on an international level, is basically linked to mutations of subjectivity on the various micropolitical levels.

If it were a question of setting down the *first (and only) rule of micropolitics*, a kind of parameter for analysis of the formations of the unconscious in the social field, I would say the following: be alert to all the factors of culpabilization; be alert to everything that blocks the processes of transformation in the subjective field. These processes of transformation, which occur in various fields of social experimentation, may sometimes be very small and yet constitute the beginning of a much greater mutation. Or not.

These processes always have a problematic beginning, and therefore we often try to find parameters that lie outside our own experience, or to compare it with other experiences. This kind of attitude is precisely the result of the systems of culpabilization that operate as a factor inhibiting everything that escapes the dominant redundancies. However, these attempts always begin in difficult conditions, with relative objectives limited to the short term. The important thing is to perceive the field of possibles of which they are vehicles (especially in the context of the social and political changes that are taking place in Brazil), because it is through this kind of metabolism that the real vectors of social change are formed. That is why I think that *the practice of a social analysis of the attribution of guilt* is fundamental.

Interview by Pepe Escobar for the "Folhetim" section of the Folha de São Paulo, *September 5, 1982:*

Pepe Escobar: In what way is Kafka important for you?

Guattari: Kafka is my favorite author. It's interesting to see the extent to which there was an exploration of geopolitics and the science fiction story in Kafka. When he turns to America, it represents one kind of intensity. When he turns to Russia, it's another kind. When he turns to Africa, yet another. This cartography can be found, and I find it in my own way of fantasizing the world. When I was in the United States a few years ago, I had dreams of being a representation strolling in Manhattan. Kafka creates a global, geopolitical cartography of affective investments, reactivated by a series of pieces of information. And then there is also Kafka as a kind of futurologist about what was going to happen in Prague: a bureaucratic perversion, the possibility of the development on the social level of a way of exercising semiotic control over populations. This is true for every great writer as an analyst of politics, of subjective formations, of unconscious drives. We should always reflect on this point, *the invention of life.*

Nelson Rodrigues or the subtle art of a schizoanalyst
Suely Rolnik

The analysis of the highways and byways of desire in Brazilian society finds a fertile ground in the work of Nelson Rodrigues.[1] Nobody excels him, or has matched his sense of humor, in the observation of the nuances of the middle-class family of the 1950s, its profile and its poverty—which persist up to this day, even beyond the intense transformations that have marked the last three decades, so that his work remains highly topical. His writing distills a privileged sensibility for capturing the rigidity with which the prevailing social forms are preserved on the molar plane, even when they are utterly out of date; and on the molecular plane, the imperceptible movement of particles undermining everything, diluting all contours; and between the two planes, a total absence of transit, the tension of a polarity that inexorably leads to an irreversible destruction. The particles ceaselessly agitated by the intense movement of the molecular plane are never articulated in new social forms. They never constitute new territories of desire. The family implodes. But a form of organization beyond the family is unthinkable. "Family or death" is the motto of the kind of subjectivity that we can extract from the work of Nelson Rodrigues.

Nobody excels him, or has matched his sense of humor, in the observation of the nuances of the middle-class family of the 1950s, its profile and its poverty—which persist up to this day, even beyond the intense transformations that have marked the last three decades, so that his work remains highly topical. His writing distills a privileged sensibility for capturing the rigidity with which the prevailing social forms are preserved on the molar plane, even when they are utterly out of date; and on the molecular plane, the imperceptible movement of particles undermining everything, diluting all contours; and between the two planes, a total absence of transit, the tension of a polarity that inexorably leads to an irreversible destruction. The particles ceaselessly agitated by the intense movement of the molecular plane are never articulated in new social forms. They never constitute new territories of desire. The family implodes. But a form of organization beyond the family is unthinkable. "Family or death" is the motto of the kind of subjectivity that we can extract from the work of Nelson Rodrigues.

This is all recorded in the play *Álbum de Família* (Family Album). As we read through it we get to know the story of a family, step by step, in seven sequences. Each member of the family is presented through stereotyped visual and verbal images assembled by a photographer and a master of ceremonies. They are extemporaneous portraits of the supposed stability of an equally supposed domestic happiness, flashes immobilized in a photo album. But this is only the outset. Lines of flight soon begin to agitate the scene, dissolving forms and characters at an increasingly giddy pace, so that the photographer and the MC become more and more pathetic in their pretense to adjust appearances. This movement is only stopped by mutilation, death (crime and suicide), or madness. A hellish destiny, which makes the works of Nelson Rodrigues, as he himself declared, "pestilent and fetid, capable on their own of producing typhoid and malaria in the audience."[2] In the defeat of a way of life, it is life itself that always ends up defeated. But how?

On the molar plane, reality is imprisoned in a family album. Outside the family photo, only its negative is imaginable: the transgression of incest. But the prohibition of incest and its transgression are two faces of the same coin—the coin of the Oedipal triangle. As Nelson Rodrigues himself says in the play *Toda Nudez Será Castigada* (All Nudity Shall Be Punished), "all chastity is obscene." The plot of the sequences is always triangular: the game consists of a violent dispute in which one character has to be eliminated or subjugated in order to allow the fusion of the other two in an incestuous dénouement that is often enunciated as promise of shared death. Oedipus rules the stage, passing through obvious and crude images like that of

Guilherme, one of the sons, who reveals to Gloria, his sister, that he has castrated himself so as not to succumb to the temptation of his desire for her. Or the image of Gloria, who, on entering a chapel, sees in the "huge, completely disproportionate, floor-to-ceiling image of Our Lord"[3] the face of Jonas, her only passion, her father. The Oedipal images are so amplified—as in the case of this photo of the father in the daughter's desire—that their contours gradually dissolve, leaving only the grain. But although this transgression is part of Oedipus' destiny, as we said, by now we have already reached a point beyond that destiny. Oedipus dissolves. The fulfillment of the order at this point—the reiterated presence of Oedipus, so often and so grossly, so "screamingly obvious"[4]—functions as a veritable particle accelerator, which brings about an implosion of the molar representation and leads us to the molecular plane.

On this other plane, reality is imprisoned from outside the church or the family's home. Nonô lives there, the son who has gone mad, who, from time to time, as the author comments, lets out "a horrible, unhuman scream, the cry of a wounded animal,"[5] a scream that, in the words of his Aunt Rute, "isn't a scream, it's like I don't know what. It's like a howl or something...,"[6] "going round the house like a crazed horse..."[7] All we know of Nonô is his voice. The only picture of him is a photo taken the day before he went mad, when, as Nelson Rodrigues informs us, he even scared the unflappable photographer, demonstrating "hostility toward the respected professional."[8] In Nonô's voice a line of flight is traced, in which the family and its characters, its form and its meanings, disappear. But Nonô's noisy, insistent howls, which do not cease haunting the stage and the audience, are never intertwined with the other to make up a desiring mesh. Raw deterritorialization. Savagery.

The planes never work upon each other: on the molar plane we remain inflexible in the inhumanity of submission; on the molecular plane, in the unhumanity of a becoming-animal. The logic of the relation between the planes is that of the binary opposition between order and chaos, which are irreconcilable. In this kind of economy, life, oscillating between the two poles, can only wind up defeated. Once it becomes impossible to create territories of desire life gets irremediably lost. On the molar plane, transgression, the only imaginable movement, generates guilt and consequently mutilation, crime or suicide; on the molecular plane, demolition, leading nowhere, generates madness.

The ineluctable choice between these two irreversible paths haunts us throughout the whole play, embodied in the counterpoint of the two types of audio material that punctuate the entire plot like a Greek chorus, from the moment they enter the scene, in one of the first sequences, until the very last. From one corner, at the rear of the family house, come the agonizing moans of the ill-fated labor of a teenager whom Jonas has impregnated. It is a voice of resentment, blaming the family for its pain, and at the same time it also demands from it its salvation. The sound material reterritorialized in the family is the only possible dwelling the language of this drama can have. From the outside of the family house comes Nonô's laughs, cries and howls. Pure deterritorialized sound, going beyond language. Here the weight of the neurotic Oedipal moan of the lover, whose destiny is death. There, the lightness of Nonô's smile, whose destiny is madness. Two extremes, the poles between which oscillate the movement permeating the plot.

The voice of the speaker, the third voice of this chorus, stretched between the hoarse voice of transgression and the wild voice of madness, is an empty voice: at each increase of speed the presence of Oedipus, repeating and accentuating itself in an increasingly vertiginous acceleration, causes a character to die and the family to destroy itself a little more, until the play ends with a thread, a tenuous thread of schizo sound that escapes all meaning. The howl of Nonô, the wild son of Dona Senhorinha, whom the mother will meet in a promise of incest. And that is what we are left with.

Nelson Rodrigues is truly upsetting. The dry humor and incisiveness with which he conducts the micropolitical analysis destabilizes the comfort of confining oneself to an apprehension of reality reduced to its representation. A representation of a regime (sociopolitical, romantic, subjective, or whatever) which gives us the illusion that life can be "resolved" or "governed" under the auspices of consciousness. An illusion that everything works out in the end. Is it not this facile dream that is embodied in the droning voice of the master of ceremonies (the voice of public opinion, according to Nelson Rodrigues) or in the stupid gaze of the photographer, which becomes our gaze as we, the spectators, turn the pages of this family album? This is the happy dream that the biting Nelson Rodrigues attacks, with the subtle art of the schizoanalyst.

Class struggle and autonomy

The questioning of the capitalist system no longer belongs only to the domain of large-scale social and political struggles, but also to everything that I have grouped under the name of "molecular revolution." It is clear that the molecular revolution is not restricted only to minorities, but also includes all movements of individuals, groups, and so on that question the system in the dimension of its production of subjectivity.

If we accept the hypothesis that Integrated World Capitalism is also sustained by the control of the production of subjectivity, we are obliged to recognize that social antagonisms, which were previously confined to the fields of economics and politics, have now shifted. *It is no longer a question merely of reappropriating the means of production or the means of political expression, but also of leaving the field of political economy and entering the field of subjective economy.*

In this respect, the problematics of subjectivity are put in terms that are totally different than those of Marxism. For Marxism, questions such as those of desire, art, religion, and the production of ideas belong to the domain of a superstructure that depends dialectically on the infrastructures of production. But once the production of subjectivity is found precisely within these infrastructures of production, and with ever greater importance, it is impossible to maintain the opposition between infrastructure and superstructure. It is impossible to confine ourselves to a reading of political economy in order to understand and question Integrated World Capitalism.

It seems to me that the principal current historical events of the planet cannot be explained simply in terms of strategic relations, socioeconomic determinations, and so on. This kind of determination undoubtedly still exists. It is obvious that the social antagonisms based on strategic power relations—relations of class, caste, and so on—have not disappeared, and they depend on specific levels of analysis and reference. The approaches based on economic and social contradictions remain valid. But many phenomena, sometimes enthralling and sometimes catastrophic, are not explained by this kind of theory. I am thinking, for example, of the emergence of a series of religious phenomena with an extraordinary potential for struggle, in Iran, in Afghanistan, or in Poland. To understand such phenomena it is necessary to consider the problematics of the economy of desire, for otherwise we run the risk of letting that economy be manipulated by the more conservative tendencies—for example, tendencies that exist within the episcopate, whether it be progressive, Marxist, or bureaucratic.

Interview by Sonia Goldfeder, São Paulo, August 31, 1982:

Sonia Goldfeder: What is your position with respect to Marxism now?

Guattari: I have never belonged to any religion, I was never baptized, I'm not Catholic, or Marxist, or anarchist, or Freudian, or anything. That said, I go on using ideas and ways of making ideas work, drawn from any kind of theory, particularly from Marx. Marx was an extraordinary genius who interpreted history, economics, and the production of subjectivity in a way that was entirely new. What is paradoxical is that he has been used to concoct an appalling academic hotchpotch. It's part of the power of coopting or reterritorializing each and every movement of mutation in the world. Which, of course, is nothing new. If you try to decipher the theme of Christ in the Gospels and you look at what it produced, you get the same thing. In my view, what is fundamental is a radical questioning of the relation between theory (as expressed in books and taught in schools) and the way in which you specifically use, discuss, or articulate it, that is, the way in which you situate it in a specific reality.

The way in which Marxism is used now serves for undertakings of reduction, Manicheanisms that specifically crush molecular revolutions. However, I can see how it is possible to use Marx's thinking for some problems. I would say the same thing about Freud's thinking. The way in which psychoanalysts use Freud's thinking also revolts me. Nevertheless, in Freud's thinking there are surprising things, of a vigorous, youthful, dialectical nature, that provide us with great whiffs of oxygen. When you see the way in which the thinking of Marx and Freud is made to work in the universities, it makes you want to flee.

Round-table discussion at the ICBA, Salvador, September 13, 1982:

Question: The people at this meeting really have very different desires and concerns. They're mostly middle-class (they could be called "white Bahians"). They're able to discuss matters such as these issues of singularity and the right to individuality because they're not directly oppressed by a social group, or by a racial group, as we blacks are. They lead a life in which they don't have to face an unequal struggle in order to satisfy their elementary needs, such as food, housing—survival itself—and even leisure. But for blacks this discussion is meaningless. And not just for us. In Brazil we still have collective problems that only a deeper discussion of the whole structure that's determining them could help us to resolve. Only then, when we've acquired the tranquility to have a home, food, and greater access to technology itself, the very form of social organization that whites created and imposed on the world, will we be able to discuss in greater detail the matters that are being raised here.

Guattari: First of all, I'm going to insist once again on the idea that the processes of singularization—in the sense in which I use the term—has nothing to do with individuality. It's rather the reverse: *individuality is an effect of the alienation* of those processes. The problem that you raise has to do with *establishing a relation between the problematics related to hunger and those related to desire, not in terms of "both...and," but of "either...or."* It's precisely this alternative—movement "or" traditional militancy—that we have to try to dismantle. I believe it's necessary to get away from this logic that opposes the possibilities of singularization in the field of desire to the possibilities of a politics capable of confronting the power of the state, the great established social bodies.

The whole question has to do with the fact that if we refer only to the phenomena of molecular revolution, we can undoubtedly exert ourselves to transform our personal life (for example, the relation with the body, time, music, cosmos, sex, the environment), and even organize ourselves in groups of coexistence to get away from the dominant models. All this seems to me essential in order to escape from the modelizing systems of capitalistic subjectivity. And this can undoubtedly go quite a long way. In Germany, for example, in some urban centers this taking control of daily life is sometimes highly elaborate. But that's only one side of the story. It's also clear that this isn't going to make it possible to change the fact that a considerable part of the gross national product in Germany is wasted on arms production. And it's not going to make it possible to change the fact that entire regions of the Third World are devastated by the capitalist raw materials market. It's obvious that things like poverty exist and that, in order to struggle against this situation, the affirmation of molecular movements is not enough. The reverse is also true: a molecular movement can't survive for long without establishing a politics in relation to existing forces, economic problems, the media, and so on.

So we see that there's a considerable distance to be traveled between the problems of the social economy of desire and what casts thousands of people into terrible poverty and utter desperation. But we have to be careful not to lapse into the classic reasoning that consists in saying "All right, let's first resolve the problem of the power of capitalistic elites, and only afterwards will we deal with the problems of desire, because there are priorities." The machines controlled by capitalism (through the revolutions in robotics, computers, and telecommunications) tend to transform power relations radically, and increasingly marginalize considerable segments of the population—sectors of production, regions, and even whole countries. The forms of resistance to capitalistic subjectivity are increasingly threatened by the development of this machinism, and this lies at the very heart of the world crisis. For this reason the issues of the molecular revolution tend no longer to be marginal issues. The problematics of the old marginalities are somehow connected with all these processes of marginalization.

All of this goes back to the idea that the traditional forms of militancy will tend to be increasingly incapable of responding not only to the problematics of marginal groups, but also to the basic problems of most of society.

Meeting with minority groups, Olinda, September 15, 1982:

Comment: The organized homosexual movement in Brazil is an intellectualized elite movement of people with university education. People such as transvestites and poor fags remain marginalized.

The Grupo Gay da Bahia (Gay Group of Bahia)—the largest homosexual activist group in Brazil—is the only one in the country that has a very extensively promoted activity not only among transvestites but also among street homosexuals. The Recife-based group GATO[9] is quite different in terms of its activity, but it also has ideas on the question of people's social origins. Most of us were from the middle class, with the exception of a few transvestites, and so thinking about our class boundaries led us to operate in other social sectors. For example, each of us individually went to discuss homosexualism with people in the slums, with groups of mothers, and so on.

Comment: I'd like to raise something about the black movement. The movement here in Pernambuco is very much one of beautiful blacks from the universities, segregating poor, ugly blacks, in the same way that we're segregated by whites, because of our poverty and our color. The movement was created here by the kind of blacks that I call "dark-skinned," who are really white. They're the black minority that gets to buy books to read, or go to university. The initial proposal was not just to bring together chic blacks. The proposal was to support blacks who were rejected at work because of their color—which occurs frequently. If it happened, the person would inform the group, which in turn could inform the press. But the concern has become not so much that as to show that black hair is pretty, parading in the streets with beautiful "Afro" clothes (that is, for those who can afford them). And the movement began to shrink. Now it's trying to get back to that initial proposal, but there's still considerable difficulty in really reaching marginalized blacks.

Comment: The kind of middle-class discourse that dwells on cultivating a bad conscience, self-accusation, and guilt, attaching value exclusively to the problem of poverty, is boring, even though poverty here in the Northeast reaches tremendous proportions. It's true that in the Northeast, given the social structure, the middle class is much smaller, but that doesn't mean that minorities from that class don't have the right to organize in terms of their own situation, to have their own demands and express their interests. This rejection is not at all healthy: we connect with just one side, poverty, and lose something else that is also real. The condition of women, for example, the lack of space for their professional, individual, and existential expression is a reality, irrespective of social class. What's more, this reality is even more shocking in the Northeast, where the existing culture makes the space for women smaller than in other more metropolitan realities, at least in Brazil.

Comment: With a group of women from Recife and Olinda (the SOS),[10] not all from the feminist movement, we carried out an experiment of gynecological self-examination, together with groups of women from poor neighborhoods on the urban periphery. We discussed questions concerned with knowledge of the body, sexual relations, man-woman relations, pleasure, frigidity—in short, questions that affect the lives of all of us. An area of intimacy between women was created, one that hadn't existed before, and that's very important. This work with the body eventually proved to be a more real breakthrough for our acceptance by those strata of the population. Strangely, it was this work that made it possible (at least for me, who have been a militant in the feminist movement for four years) to escape from my middle-class confines. We didn't have access to the mass media, and it was difficult to break down prejudices about feminists along the lines of "feminists are dykes," or "feminists are man-haters," and so on. And it was this work with the body that made it possible to make contact with women from other socioeconomic spheres. The local left used to say that these issues of the body and sexuality aren't important for poor women. But it was precisely this work that made it possible to achieve affective contact with those women, and it also showed us clearly that the problematics of reality can't be reduced to a question of class.

Round-table discussion with PT candidates for the São Paulo City Council and State Assembly, September 2, 1982:

Question: I would like you to speak about the "Disobedience" campaign proposed by Caty Koltai, a city council candidate for the PT. What we propose is to combine an attitude on issues that concern daily life with the more general demands of the working class. The result is that we're often labeled as petty bourgeois by other party comrades.

Guattari: I would like to defend two opposite theses. The first is that in the evolution of the proletariat, the evolution of the collective labor power that forms an integral part of modern production, there's a whole modelization of the worker. There's a whole ideology of the valorization of work which doesn't take into account the fact that those conditions of the evolution of the proletariat lead precisely to an enormous rejection of work. Not of social labor as such, not of the work of social self-valorization—work that really does have some use in society—but of totally absurd work such as social control, arms manufacture, environmental and ecological destruction, and so on. This rejection forms the focus for the establishment of another kind of working class (or nonworking class)—the class of the unemployed, or the class of the *marginati* as they say in Italy (all the people who don't work because they don't have work, or because they simply don't want to work, or even those who work without working because the work doesn't interest them). However, the ideology of valorization of work that exists in the proletariat means that they don't take into account anything that seems to be that other kind of working class. In the workers' movement, this translates into the presence of a kind of axiom that runs through the whole history of the movement, an axiom according to which revolutionary militants have to be the best at work. We find exactly this kind of axiom in the texts of the PT: there is an extremely traditional clause (in the statutes, if I'm not mistaken) that proclaims that PT militants (it isn't put like that, but it comes to the same thing) have to be "good workers." So it seems to me that perhaps what you're doing in this "Disobedience" campaign is not at all marginal or minoritarian, but relatively at the forefront from the viewpoint of a raising of consciousness of a general process of marginalization that is increasingly tending to pervade the social strata of the country. I would even link this approach of yours to the consciousness raising that took place especially in the Autonomia movement in Italy, which embodied a new worker figure.

Now I'm going to defend the opposite thesis. If this "Disobedience" movement consists in including in the platform only slogans of rejection that in no way correspond (at least, in their form of expression) to what can be understood, felt, and heard by the great masses of the working class, the peasants, service workers, and so on, we may be running the risk of ending up with a radical break.

Incidentally, in this respect you would also be close to Autonomia Operaia. That movement's form of expression, and also its practice, were isolated in relation to the global understanding of the popular classes, the working classes, in Italy. Admittedly, this didn't happen with all the tendencies within Autonomia. There was a whole tendency that was called "desiring autonomy," such as the movements in Bologna connected with Radio Alice,[11] and the Metropolitan Indians in Rome, who always rejected this kind of "ghettoization" and confinement. Perhaps those tendencies were basically correct, but they ended up focusing on themselves, presenting themselves like tribes that were total foreigners to the whole social field. What eventually happened was a terrible repression by the government, and the repression was, in fact, broadly supported by the parties of the left, beginning with the Communist Party, inasmuch as they consistently maintained an aggressive policy against these movements.

Now, having presented these two theses, I shall perform a small dialectical pirouette: the avoidance of the kind of fate that I indicated, remembering the Italian example, will depend on the ability of this movement, or movements of this type, to find their medium of expression in the current struggles, and to act as a catalyst for a much broader raising of consciousness. *Abandoning the position of the scapegoat,* which constantly makes us run the risk of sinking into this kind of infernal logic, leading some movements to totally isolated actions, actions of armed struggle, actions of affirmation solely in the mass media, and so on—actions that ultimately play along with the strategy of the great forces of repression. I'm thinking particularly of what happened in movements such as the Red Brigades,[12] or Prima Linea.[13]

It would be illusory to think that there is any kind of similarity between the various social movements that we describe as autonomous in Europe, in the United States, and in Latin America.

Formally, it may be possible to find some points in common, because they often use the same language, and the same style. But having spent a month in Brazil circulating in various milieus, I think that there are profound differences in these things. Everything that developed in Europe and the United States in extending what was called the "new culture"[14] of the 1960s was generally characterized by a division between lower middle-class, marginal, or dissident elements and the great social struggles. In the United States, admittedly, this was covered up while there were major social movements against the war in Vietnam, which served, perhaps somewhat artificially, as a bridge between the various movements (in France, something similar happened after the war in Algeria). But immediately after the war in Vietnam all those movements dispersed, and only the "deep" social movements, such as the black movement, reorganized themselves. All the others remained confined to sectors. The feminists, for example, developed their own field of action, and sometimes their ideologies were very disconnected from the social field. The ecologists continued to create broad movements in some cases, but their political impact was always extremely diffuse, and was very often coopted by the power of the state, and by the traditional leftist parties.

I mention all this in order to say that, in my opinion, what is happening in Brazil now is of a different nature. There are struggles for the establishment of democratic politics, struggles of the working class for the affirmation of utterly basic rights—rights that in industrialized countries have been recognized for quite some time—struggles of the peasants (if one can speak of peasants), sectors that live in conditions of utterly extraordinary poverty and that make up a broad movement in Brazilian society. They're joined by particular, singular sensibilities, ranging from the sensibilities of minority group movements to those of people concerned about changing their relation with food, with the body, or with space.

In other words, it seems to me that there's a totally different situation than what there was in Europe, especially in France in 1968. I remember that enormous student demonstration going to the Renault factories and reaching the closed factory gates, gates that hadn't been closed by the bosses but by the unions, by the Communist Party, and also, we must realize, by a large part of the working class itself.

Going back to the initial question, I think that instead of looking for similarities it's necessary to try to differentiate the specific set-up of the struggles that are organized in each context. This makes me think that not only are there radical differences between what's happening in Europe and what's happening in Brazil, but also great care has to be taken to avoid generalizing about Brazil. The simple trip that we have made during these few days suggests to me that there isn't just one Brazil but several, and that the perception of these problems in the Northeast, for example, is very different from the perception that may exist in São Paulo or Rio.

Suely Rolnik: I agree with Guattari that it is necessary to be cautious when examining the relation between counterculture movements and large-scale social struggles, as this relation varies according to the contexts even in the same country, as in the case of Brazil. But I disagree with his reading concerning the counterculture movement in Brazil. Although it is true that, at the moment, movements of this kind, like the minority groups of the present, largely attach themselves to the PT, which functions as a binding and articulating axis, the same cannot be said about the countercultural movement in the 1960s and early 1970s in Brazil under the dictatorship. During that period there was a significant counterculture movement in Brazil alongside the guerrilla movement (unlike the rest of Latin America, where the guerrilla movement was generally predominant), but between the two there was a clear separation, and even more, an explicit and violent conflict. The only thing that they had in common was the courage of a generation to run serious risks for the sake of opposing a situation that had become absolutely intolerable—the risk of prison, torture, and death or exile that many of those who took part in the guerrilla movement or in the counterculture did in fact suffer. Not to mention the risk of a fragilization that could lead to madness. In the case of the counterculture, this risk derived not only from the traumatic experience of repression, but also from the radicality of an existential experimentation that broke away from the bourgeois lifestyle with brutality. Psychiatric internment was common, and many never recovered. I also disagree with Guattari when he says that changing the relation with food, the body, the affects, sexuality and space was specific to the Brazilian counterculture movement, as it was attitudes such as these that made up the existential experimentation, hallucinogenics included, and break from bourgeois life which fundamentally defined the counterculture everywhere, starting with California.

State and autonomy

The state fulfills a basic role in the production of capitalistic subjectivity. It is a "mediator state," a "providence state," through which everything has to pass, in a relation of dependence that produces an infantilized subjectivity. This expanded function of the state— much more wide-ranging than its administrative, financial, military, or police powers—is carried out by, for example, a support system that in the United States is called the welfare state. It is a system of "deferred salaries"; a system of subsidies that causes a group to be self-regulating, self-forming, self-disciplining; and a system of information, examination, control, hierarchy, promotion, and so on. The state is this set of ramifications, this kind of rhizome of institutions that we call "collective facilities." That is why the state is not afraid to speak of decentralization. It is also why the parties are not afraid to include self-management proposals in their programs. In France, for example, the political parties and the unions are all subsidized by the state, through officially established relations.

The whole attitude of the capitalists and also of the (classic and/or Marxist) socialist parties is to accelerate this process of entry into capitalistic flows, promoting "progress" in accordance with a particular conception. For them, it is very important that this function of the state should be developed, in other words, that there should be an increase in the classic collective facilities such as those that exist in Europe. As for the problems of making changes in daily life, in the economy of desire, they can come later. But history shows us that this division is not at all appropriate: the conception of a social struggle in various stages leads to the fact that the problematics of restoring the fabric of society, the problematics of self-management and social valorization are always delayed, always put off. What happens is that this function of capitalistic subjectivation and the state facilities that are established in the whole social field operate to the advantage of the new bureaucratic castes, the new elites, which do not have the slightest intention of being stripped of their power.

I must emphasize the fact that this does not take place only in relation to the functions of production. We also look to the welfare state to decide whether we should have sex or not, with whom, and how, and whether we should breast-feed or not, and how. This infantilizing function of state power takes place on an extremely miniaturized level, which is not limited to the control grids of behavior and social activity. This modelization also affects unconscious representations. Perhaps this is where the difference lies between this conception and Althusser's conception of the "ideological state apparatus." It is not a question only of these visible facilities, embodied in society. The state also functions on an invisible level of integration.

The assistentialist state begins by organizing a segregation that drives a considerable part of the population out of the economic circuits. In a second stage the state comes to the rescue, giving assistance to those people, but on condition that they go through the system of control. There can only be real autonomy and a genuine reappropriation of life to the extent that individuals, families, basic social groups, and primary social groups are able to choose for themselves the facilities they want in their neighborhood. So it is a question of taking over the management of these problematics, without constantly asking for subsidies, asking for the establishment of a post for some kind of psychologist or psychiatrist, asking for standardized facilities that the state comes and constructs somewhere or other.

Let's imagine a science-fiction script in which the formations of the left succeeded in taking power in Brazil. In such a case, it would be necessary to ask them the following question immediately: "Is it your intention to follow a modernist course along European lines?" That would mean that all the people here would have excellent salaries and status, and very well-built facilities. But it would also mean that they would all become workers in a machine to produce utterly crushing modes of subjectivation.

If the coexistence of these two types of objective—the affirmation of the processes of autonomy and the existence of great machines for struggle—continues to be prevented, I have the impression that, unfortunately, it will always be the same kinds of political formation—whether they are of the right or of the left—that will be responsible for the administration of the major problems, and that will take care of all the minorities. Depending on the situation, these formations may even say: "Relax, we'll sort out this question of minorities," and various ministries will spring up overnight: ministries for blacks, women, the insane, and so on. I say this because that is more or less the way things are happening in Europe now. We have personalities in the ministries whom we could call "Mr. Narcotics," "Ms. Women's Situation," "Mr.

Ecology," and so on. The marginalities even have a status. But it is precisely this recognition that makes them go into collective facilities and their equivalents, and in certain contexts makes them agents of the production of capitalistic subjectivity. And this often takes place in conditions of surprising ambiguity. Admittedly, we didn't succeed in inventing a political structure that was capable of developing these two types of struggle at the same time; and I think that's why the movements essentially became exhausted.

That's why I insist that, if the minorities of whatever kind—marginal people, workers in insecure jobs, all the people who reject the prevailing lifestyles and modes of discipline—were to keep politely waiting for state power (whether capitalist or socialist) to bring them solutions, we would risk having to wait a long time; we would risk coming once again to phenomena of the demoralization of that whole vital portion of society; and perhaps we would be running an even worse risk: that the situation might take such a turn that a right wing more extreme than the one we know might take power. And it would know very well how to keep that power.

How can one ensure that the processes of singularization—which are nearly on the tangent of the incommunicable—are maintained during a period of electoral campaign? By placing our singularity in the ballot box? In the vote? It would slip through our fingers. And yet it is obvious that if we want to overthrow this kind of stupid, reactionary regime—which thinks it can manage a society, a social order, in accordance with a knowledge of the laws that govern economics and politics—if we want to confront this kind of obstacle, we won't do it by making poetry in our own little milieu, or setting up little homosexual spaces where we can feel great, or inventing alternative formulas for children's education, and so on. We can put all those things together, but even then we wouldn't be able to overthrow the powers that be in Chile, or in other places. In that case, we would be exposed to the risk of a definitive, radical isolation of the people who are interested in the mere fact of being on the earth. It is very singular simply being on the earth, having to live, having to die, having to reproduce, having to get one's bearings in the world without accounting to the state, without depending on the state to know how to think, how to speak, and how to make love. We would be exposed to the risk of having a total separation between the processes of existential singularization and all those enormous, heavy, militarized, armed structures that organize the social field. And then, no doubt, we would be obliged to invent a new logic, a new pragmatics that allows the real energies of change and processual transformation to create devices that can undermine the kind of barbarity and stupidity that runs our societies. In my view, those are our biggest problems now.

Meeting with "alternative" preschools, São Paulo, August 27, 1982:

Comment: What we are doing in our pedagogical experiments in these "alternative" preschools is simply modernizing them, and that's because we really don't have a mobilized population that is able to impose its interests. It seems to me that being "alternative" here has much more to do with working politically to mobilize these interests than with directly carrying out work already linked to an institution.

Guattari: But the situation can alter and develop, and if that happens it's very important that groups like yours should have a viewpoint and represent a force in your proposals.

Comment: But we don't know whether the problems that we have raised here are the problems of the majority of our population. We lack connections.

Guattari: In my view, this can't be put in terms of a majority, or of consensus. The issue is something different. There are two kinds of model, one that always bears within itself an appeal for dependence on state powers, and another that sets out to bring about a fundamental transformation in the relation of society with the state, with all the difficulties and uncertainties that this represents. In the second case, it's necessary for the model to be sufficiently consistent and sufficiently palpable so that it can at least be heard by responsible politicians on the left, so that it can motivate people in their desire for change, and become a formula as important as those concerning things such as salary and housing. It's in this sense that I think the types of procedure in question here have great political importance in themselves, even if they are based on very limited experiments.

For these experiments of autonomization to be able to survive, it is necessary to discuss them with the staff in the supervisory organizations. The state does not have a structure armed from head to toe like the "statue of the Commander," the state is made up of bodies that have their own structure, and that have antagonistic relations between themselves, with the result that sometimes it is possible to find certain kinds of support, certain alliances, and even a certain complicity with some parts of it. It is also necessary to have discussions with the parties, the unions, and so on, but in this case the discussion is not on the basis of accusations such as "you're rotten, bourgeois, capitalist pigs, etc.," or on the basis of schematic programs, but on the basis of what we would call *diagrams concretely embodied by people and by experiences.* This can produce a much greater impact than any amount of talking.

Question: How does the alliance between the alternative community and the state work in Germany?

Guattari: The alliance functions on various levels. The communities are surrounded by systems of cooperatives in all kinds of areas, which gives them a much greater capability of collective resistance, and the possibility of permanent dialogue between different people, families, groups, and so on. It goes even further than that: they even have their own banking system, in addition to having succeeded in introducing a minority in the municipal councils, and that puts them in the position of arbiters in negotiations between the Social Democrats and the right wing in Germany, with all the risks that entails, of course. It's a question of knowing each time to what extent one can accept one risk or another without again lapsing into the traditional group operation, without losing the singular, processual character of these various initiatives.

Over a period of ten years it became the custom in France to disdain any kind of struggle to defend the rights related to traditional liberties. The mentality, the militant ideology, tended to say "that has to do with bourgeois law and it's not our problem." But with the Giscard regime, when we began to be persecuted daily, when our comrades were jailed by the dozen, when police checks were carried out in the subways and everywhere, then those problems of liberty began to be considered from another angle. So a discussion began with leftist jurists, lawyers, etc., in order to be able to fight on that ground too. This doesn't mean that we became lawyers, or that we adopted the mentality of magistrates. It simply means that we are in a much better position to assess the specific levels of the struggle, with their limits; to assess whether the processes of real autonomization, the processes of creating a different kind of subjectivity, a living subjectivity embodied in society, ensure that our viewpoint is not going to be coopted, that we are not going to succumb to the economy of images manipulated by the media, that we are not going to succumb to the formalism of laws or of great programmatic declarations.

In France, the people who do not usually engage in the activities of traditional politics were precisely the ones who constituted a large part of the electorate that enabled the Socialists to come to power. There was a surprising swing in the voting because suddenly that whole stratum of the population (substantial in France), which never participated in elections, actually joined up with the Socialists. However, now that the Socialists are in power, things take place such as the homosexual movement having to take to the streets in the middle of August (when everything in France comes to a halt), just to win the right to a small community radio station.

Very subtle, very subterranean "negotiations" are now going on between the old tendencies of the autonomy movement (which made very violent interventions a few years ago), to determine the extent to which the hostilities are going to be resumed or not. It's possible that none of this will take place and that it will lead to a cooptation process and things like that. I'm not a prophet, but I'm convinced that, if the Socialist government goes on like this, it will lose all the popular support that it acquired in the last election. We'll end up with a right-wing regime much more reactionary than anything we have ever known before.

What is very characteristic of the current situation, particularly in the "developed" European countries, is that professions such as those in the social or artistic fields are totally gridded and modelized into hierarchies by systems of exams, CVs, and so on. This means that the slightest pedagogical innovation, the slightest change in the field of art, is immediately placed in a frame. But that's not all. The hydras of the state are preparing a highly sophisticated technology in order to coopt and utilize anything that might constitute "Tupiniquim" vectors. There are real, active networks there, networks of community life and alternative life, and a multiplication of these primary groups and these microassemblages of singularization, just as is happening here. But there are also incredibly elaborate polices to create laws outside the law: for example, the French government is now trying to create a certain kind of relation that is not highly institutionalized, in order to fund initiatives such as the communities that are alternatives to psychiatry, or free radio stations. It is always a dilemma when one has to choose between continuing in a situation with scanty or even wretched resources, or letting oneself be seduced by the temptation of accepting subsidies, which are proposals without any obvious counterpart from the regulatory viewpoint.

For all these reasons I insist on the importance of the fact that here in Brazil people should now begin to think of a kind of strategy in relation to these issues. In France, a group of intellectual friends and I proposed discussing with the Socialist government the creation of a method of funding for all these marginal, minority sectors, a method that would no longer be directly government controlled. This was in order to try to escape from the accursed triad of "state/private capitalism (including foundations)/utter poverty." Perhaps it won't lead to anything, but what we are aiming for is the creation of a new kind of democratic, decentralized, sectoral foundation that will make it possible to resolve these funding problems. These foundations would not refuse contact and dialogue with the state, but the negotiations would take place at the level of the sectors or regions of the activities to be funded. These sectors could thus mix funding from the state, funding from private sources, and self-financing. In other words, it would be a question of setting the issue of self-management on a higher level than the one on which it is generally placed. In any case, the issue of foundations arises in the rich capitalist countries, and so the question of the reappropriation of these methods of funding arises in various sectors, with all the risks of cooptation, of course. But that risk can never be completely avoided. What is at issue here is the establishment of devices that can articulate living processes.

Letter from Guattari to Suely Rolnik, Paris, February 8, 1983:

Democracy is foolish, and this foolishness is important, even essential. The right to folly! Even stronger than the right to hysteria or madness. But singularity can only exist outside democracy. And so what? Dialectics all over again? No, just living with it—living with all of this, with all these people! The world is foolish, like the Cosmos. God is utterly stupid! (The state is a different kind of problem, it has nothing to do with democracy: it is the *Urstaat* that, like death, haunts machinic processes.)

Church and autonomy

Debate held by a branch of the PT in Rio de Janeiro, September 11, 1982:

Question: We have always seen the Church as reactionary. Now, in Latin America, it has become progressive. How can there be a relation with grassroots movements and with God at the same time?

Guattari: I always go back to insisting on the need for a different kind of logic. Using classical logic, we would say that to be developing the two policies to which you refer is an act of duplicity on the part of the Church, and also on the part of anyone who plays along with the Church to some extent in this respect. Perhaps this is more true in the context of Poland than Brazil. *But it is precisely this notion of duplicity that should be changed: we should speak of triplicity, quadruplicity, multiplicity.* On the one hand, there is the policy of the episcopate—which, incidentally, is also not homogeneous; there is the policy of all the levels of the Catholic hierarchy: there is the position of the practicing Catholics in the field, in different places, in urban or agrarian sectors. These positions are undoubtedly not decided in a Manichean manner. The positions adopted now can undoubtedly change abruptly. The Church is now going along with the progressive movement, but this partnership may be interrupted abruptly on the day when the clergy understand the gravity of its consequences.

My view is that it's difficult now to get one's bearings in this context. What is possible and necessary is to identify what's happening here and now. But it's not possible to predict what's going to happen six months or two years from now. So the question presents itself in the following terms: does the attitude of the Catholic Church, or the multiplicity of attitudes of the Catholic Church, offer possibilities for constructing a new kind of instrument of social struggle or not? Within what limits are such possibilities being offered? What is there, here and now, that implies a threat of cooptation? What does this involve in terms of an establishment of devices that oppose the micropolitics of cooptation? It's not a question of giving a general, programmatic response, as the members of sectarian groups may do; what is sought is something that presents itself in specific assemblages, in particular situations in connection with well-defined objectives, for example in a social struggle in a factory, in an electoral campaign, and so on. The mentality of sectarian groups is limited to analyzing power relations in terms of class. Of course, that discourse has a certain consistency. But it is true that there are also processes of subjectivation through religious phenomena. This is particularly true if we think of how those phenomena are reappropriated by the very fabric of society (and even how there is a reinvention of religiosity by that fabric), which represents a strong contribution of energy for the struggle in the social field.

It is a question, therefore, of knowing how the social movements here are going to articulate with that tremendous potential.

Debate held by a branch of the PT in São Paulo, August 29, 1982:

Question: I would like to know your opinion about the use of the banner of autonomy in hands that are, to say the least, dangerous, such as those of the Polish bishops, or the whole world Church.

Guattari: Poland is currently one of the most innovative places on the level of the collective production of subjectivity. A kind of extraordinary will to live and a kind of collective desire are leading those people to confront one of the most diabolical systems of repression with their bare hands, with courage and creativity. It is interesting to note that the issue of desire on a collective scale invests in traditional formations there, such as the Catholic Church. A great many members of the population recognize themselves in Catholicism, in one way or another, and this forms part of the process of molecular resistance in the present Polish situation.

One thing is the fact that the episcopate is trying to manipulate the situation as much as possible in all its dimensions, on both the national and the international level. Another thing is the fact that considerable masses, thousands of people, are making particular use of the Catholic Church to group together.

Two months ago I made a discreet and very nerve-racking trip to Poland. Together with many other comrades in Poland, I was led to rethink the reality of the intervention of the Church in the processes of the Polish people's struggle. The Poles told me that they had invented a new category of relation with religion. It is what they call "practicing nonbelievers," that is, people who take part in all the initiatives of the Church but are not believers. A kind of Catholicism that is not a true religion. I imagine that there are also nonpracticing believers. Which all goes to show that it is not a traditional religious phenomenon. Whatever the strategic and tactical attitudes of the leadership of the episcopate may be, it seems to me that there is an incontrovertible phenomenon: a certain mode of Polish subjectivation that utterly rejects the existing system and that cannot possibly be coopted, for example from the viewpoint of the Soviet Union. Hence the borrowing of symbols of religious semiotization (religious practices and social activities), which constitute a formidable force. Something along those lines might be said about what has happened and is happening in Iran. As for Latin America, that is for you to say.

Interview by Néstor Perlongher for the journal O Inimigo do Rei,[15] *São Paulo, September 1, 1982:*

Néstor Perlongher: There is a Third-Worldist theory which says that the Church gives Marxism the spiritual dimension that Marxism doesn't possess.

Guattari: That explanation seems to me to be particularly absurd, for the simple reason that, from many viewpoints, religious structures can be as authoritarian as bureaucratic Marxists.

Perhaps we could find an affiliation between democratic centralist apparatuses (or those calling themselves democratic) and the organization of the Jesuits. It would certainly be easy to include Jacobinism with them too. There's a certain model of formation of minds that makes it difficult for us to think that the Catholic Church contributes a bit of soul to Marxist organizations.

When I was young, I knew working-class priests who gave up the Church to engage completely in social activism, and within a few months had become the most bureaucratic characters one could image in that system. It's obvious that there are people in the Church who are not like that, and who, for example, live in a real relation with the peasants. But the structures of the Church that those people adopt remain completely conservative and reactionary, even when the Church develops a policy of defense of human rights. Which means that this democracy is only superficial, and is subject to cooptation.

Néstor Perlongher: You've said that the essential outstanding historic events of the present period correspond to collective expressions of desire, which do not enter the traditional frames of modelization. On the basis of that statement, how would you place this renaissance of the post-Council religious institution that has been taking place recently?

Guattari: To approach real problems, the historical problems of the present day, is much more difficult than to confine oneself to repeating the customary mechanical frames. In my view, it's necessary to broaden your question, because the phenomenon to which you refer concerns all religions, particularly the Muslim religion, which is experiencing an extraordinary revitalization, and also Jewish subjectivity—rather than Jewish religion—which is experiencing a period of revitalization (many intellectuals are reassuming their Jewish identity).

I think we must be careful not to interpret these phenomena unilaterally: although, on the one hand, this religious renaissance corresponds to a kind of archaism, on the other, as we see in Poland now, it is a kind of collective expression that borrows schemas from the Church, religious schemas, but attributes to them a content, a practical meaning, entirely different than the traditional one. We could say the same about the renaissance of nationalist languages such as Basque or Breton. In these phenomena, at the same time as there is a complete return to the past, often with conservative attitudes, there is also—and this is very important—an artificial construction of modes of subjectivation.

Party and autonomy

Debate held by a branch of the PT in Rio de Janeiro, September 11, 1982:

Question: I wonder whether autonomy may not be a stage in the struggle, a stage in which a lively questioning is maintained until a mass movement appears, until the organization confronts the issue of taking political power in a practical way. In saying this, of course, I don't want to downplay the importance of this stage.

Guattari: This logic of preservation and conservation, this business of saying that in times of difficulty it's necessary to conserve and preserve the avant-garde, smells to me of sectarian groups. It doesn't seem appropriate to me to transport this idea of conservation to the components of autonomy, because, by definition, one can't make a career for oneself in the autonomy movement. In fact, one also can't make a career in militancy, but that's another story. It's a fact that the preservation of nuclei of autonomy in various fields (ecology, feminism, homosexualism, free radio, etc.)—a preservation that is really artificial, like sectarian groups—is something that can lead to the neutralization of living processes, which is precisely what characterizes those nuclei. It's not a question of a mechanical renovation. The best comparison in this case would be with what happens in schools of painting. There may be a group of painters who discover an extraordinary process of creation in a certain situation, at a certain time, and this discovery is later captured by a process of conservation (what we call "a conservatory" in music), which clearly fulfills the function of a dam, a blockage, incomprehension or inhibition in relation to processes that we can see in a nascent state in other kinds of assemblages.

3rd Congress of Black Culture of the Americas, São Paulo,
August 25, 1982:

Question: The question that I would like you to discuss is whether it isn't necessary to go beyond movements (with their particular singularity) toward a larger social dimension, as a condition for the universalization of this singularity.

Guattari: I definitely don't see this in terms of going beyond anything. Subjectivity is always a process of singularization, but one that can be lost at the very moment when it passes into the order of the general. In this respect, I remember the example given by Trevisan: the experience of a homosexual group in São Paulo, which at a certain point linked up with general dimensions and thereby destroyed itself from the viewpoint of its subjective dynamic. I definitely do not believe in a dialectic that moves beyond the singular toward the general. At any rate, I do not believe that there is a need for this change in dimension, this qualitative rupture.

Flow concept
Suely Rolnik

My attention was always drawn by the fact that Guattari often used the term "dialectic"—for example, to designate the nature of the articulation between the different movements in their autonomy, or between them and broader social struggles, such as struggles for wage raises. I found it rather strange, because one of the fruitful results of his partnership with Deleuze was that he overcame "a kind of dialectic in which he was still trapped," as he put it,[16] although already before the encounter with Deleuze he had formulated his conception of desire as a machine, thus distancing himself from the dialectical conception of desire.

It seemed to me that he used the term simply as a synonym for a dynamic relation, as commonly employed in militant discourse of the left or in certain academic discourse. I realized later that this use of the term "dialectic" by Guattari was not at all unusual in relation to the use that he and Deleuze make of these concepts: in fact, it constitutes an important aspect of their work, one that is also intimately associated with the critique of dialectics that is not only conceptualized but also realized at the level of their writing itself. Let me explain: the text is never a coherent, conceptual construction closed in upon itself, constituting a representation or abstraction within which meaning resides, and in which each concept finds its place. The text is never that kind of burrow in which we could snuggle and have the impression that, whether dialectically or not, everything has always been under control, and is now, and will be evermore.

It is precisely from this tradition that the Deleuze & Guattari partnership seeks to break away. They counter the metaphysical mold of this confinement with a procedure in which the concept always has a meaning defined as a function of the field of experimentation with which it is articulated. It is unstuffy writing, exposed to the free air of the world—there is no reason to protect oneself from the world: on the contrary, one must experience it. It is in this experience that one concept or the other is convoked, invented, or reinvented. The term "dialectic," like any other, only acquires meaning in its variations.

I commented on this in a letter to Guattari. This is what he wrote:

"I don't know why I use the term dialectics. I don't want to go on trampling on words. During a certain period Gilles condemned certain words, and everyone around him followed suit. Words come to me as they will, and it no longer bothers me. When I spoke of dialectics I must have been thinking not so much of Plato or Hegel as of machinic phyla, in the dimension of the irreversibility of rhizomes..." (letter of August 25, 1982).

On yet another occasion, when I was translating "1933: Micropolitics and Segmentarity," one of the plateaus in *A Thousand Plateaus: Capitalism and Schizophrenia*,[17] I asked Guattari for information about a reference to "Joyce's 'letter'" that appears in the text, where "letter" might be either a missive or a letter of the alphabet. I needed the information to translate the word correctly in the text and to include a reference in a footnote. He answered as follows:

"I talked to Gilles about Joyce's letter, and we no longer remember it… But it's not important, Gilles said that you should delete the passage and be done with it" (letter of September 19, 1983).

That's how the "Deleuze & Guattari" partnership treats words, notions, and concepts. Writing is a field of vibration in which words appear, combine with others, and then separate, combine with yet others, or disappear, according to the flows with which the text is connected. *Text is flow. Its movement is physical.* As Deleuze once said in an interview: "Félix treats writing like a schizo flow that carries all kinds of things along with it. As for me, I'm interested that a page should escape at every edge and yet be closed in upon itself like an egg. And also that in a book there should be retentions, resonances, precipitations, and many larvae."[18]

Interview by Sonia Goldfeder, São Paulo, August 31, 1982:

Sonia Goldfeder: In your view, how does the participation of minority groups in a process of social mutation take place? Should they be coopted by society as a whole, or should they remain apart in order to maintain their difference?

Guattari: It's necessary to distinguish two levels of reality. Firstly, the level of present reality, in which minority groups are marginalized—their ideas and their way of life are repressed and rejected. Secondly, the level of another reality, where there is a linking up of the left, and where these groups are taken into account, listened to, and have some weight in society. Homosexual groups, for example, obtain new legislation, or groups of psychiatrized people question current methods. All this forms part of a normal, traditional logic of power relations, pressure groups, and so on. Does this mean a cooptation of everything that's dissident in the movement? That's the kind of thing I can't answer.

Will Lula's PT coopt the whole dissident movement that can be seen in part of its grassroots support? I hope not. I only know that among the final points of the PT program there's one that speaks specifically about "respect for autonomy." This kind of affirmation in a political program is extraordinary. I've never seen it anywhere. To reject this attempt because of a fear of cooptation isn't justified in the name of an incapacity to completely express our desire in the situation, in the name of a mythical ethics of autonomy, in the name of the cult of spontaneity. This is an attempt of great importance, and, if there is some justification for a fear of cooptation, it is simply because, if a movement plunges into this kind of relation, it loses its efficiency, it loses its capacity for openness, it ceases to be a channel in which singular traits of a mutation of subjectivity can be affirmed. It becomes a "mass organization" along the lines of a "PT's women's organization," or a "PT youth organization." In such circumstances the movement ages very quickly, it becomes deaf and insensitive. It no longer grasps anything. It's like a movie screen that becomes transparent and nothing else is imprinted on it.

If, in order to overthrow a dictatorship in practical terms, we create a tool that has the effect of crushing singularities, what is being crushed really is the very desire to struggle, the involvement: it will run into an impasse and implode. If we do not succeed in articulating these two dimensions, we will inevitably succumb either to a capitalism that devastates each and every subjectivity—with the exception of minoritarian elite subjectivities on the level of "value culture"—or to another variant, which is the "gulag."

Informal conversation, Florianópolis, September 17, 1982:

Question: Don't you think it's a bit over-optimistic to consider that this kind of good faith by the parties in relation to autonomy is possible?

Guattari: There's always the risk that the parties will crush the minorities. It's not a matter of optimism or pessimism, but of a fundamental, definitive questioning about all the systems of party, union, group, and sectarian group involved in the course of a liberation struggle. There's nothing that provides an a priori guarantee that they won't again transmit the dominant models in this field. Not their program, nor the good faith of their leaders, nor even their practical, concrete commitment to minorities.

So what might intervene to prevent this kind of "entropy" (a term that I don't much like, but I'll use it) in this field? Precisely the establishment of devices (which we can call whatever we like—analytic devices, devices of molecular revolution, of singularization, and so on), devices on the scale of the individual or the group, or even broader combinations, which would make us raise the issue of the collective formations of desire. And which would make us raise it before, during, afterwards, and definitively.

Situations like the electoral campaign do not mean that movements such as the International Network of Alternatives to Psychiatry should attach themselves to parties. What I say is that situations of this kind raise the issue of a dialogue, a contact, an insertion in the social dynamic that they signify. Should we take a purist attitude, along the lines of "I'm autonomous," "I don't eat this food," "All this will be immediately coopted," "I don't want to know about it"? Or else are we going to run the risk of a dialogue, but one of a calculated nature, a measured nature? That means running the risk of getting involved in this kind of social conflict, but at the same time it gives us the means not only to preserve autonomy but also to permit its expansion. That is, to act in such a way that the aims of the political movement as a whole are not reduced to the objectives of taking political power or presenting demands to counter the right wing, presenting social and legal demands. Acting in such a way that, through all the dialectics of these processes of autonomy in the social field, the political movement will lead to one of the basic aims of the struggle, which is precisely this issue of singularity and autonomy.

Considered thus, autonomy not only has to do with those people who propose to organize themselves in a new way, but also contaminates the dogmatic groups and traditional groups that are in the organizations. And it also goes beyond the framework of the party, finding bridges in the very fabric of society to link up this whole multiplicity of focal points of the collective will for singularity.

Meeting with groups working with communities on the outskirts of the city, Olinda, September 16, 1982:

Question: I'd like you to explain more about what you understand as dialogue between minorities and parties.

Guattari: I see no interest in raising the issue of minorities in terms of a "dialogue" with party formations. Because, if the dialogue is established, it will be false from the very start. The issue that I call molecular revolutions doesn't take place first and foremost through dialogue. These revolutions take place through the experience of the establishment of concrete processes that embody these problematics, irrespective of whether people think one thing or another.

Let's take as an example the supposition that we have to make a free radio station, with a proposal for multicommunity management. The issue that arises is not about a dialogue in order to reach an agreement about the content of what's going to be said at the microphone; everyone can say whatever he thinks best. The question is how it's going to function, how we're going to deal with problems such as money, space, and the leaderships of the various movements. The problematics will be embodied in this kind of thing.

What is of immediate importance is not to be unaware of this kind of issue, and perhaps to think about the processual steps that will make it possible to raise it in other terms. For me, much more important than discussing with God knows who, with the PT or the PMDB[19] (and discuss what, incidentally?), is setting up a system of dialogue, because if these steps are consolidated the question of dialogue will arise later on its own, obviously. Once the various minority components are embodied in a living activity (not only in their immediate field of life, but also with a capacity for intervention in other milieus), it's obvious that the weight of their words, their weight in social relations, will change in nature, irrespective of the ideological discussions. That's the only way in which I can conceive this whole issue.

I think that at this historical moment the liberation movements cannot do without the phenomena of images in the domain of the masses, such as Walesa or Lula. This issue must be addressed without any moral preconception (democratic or otherwise).

If I come to Latin America, I take a plane. That doesn't mean that I agree with this means of transportation, or with its technology. But if I travel merely in order to take a plane, then there's a problem: the trip is no longer the aim, which becomes the plane, the medium. I think that the phenomena of crystallization in the mass media—as happens with Solidarity in Poland, for example, or with Lula in Brazil—have to do with the reification of an image, and it's true that this can lend itself to a series of manipulations by the dominant media. But it can also lend itself to a series of manipulations by the very systems of molecular investment that are always crazy to invent idols, to dream with them, and to promote processes of expansion among the masses. The problem has to do with knowing whether, at the same time, we are capable of establishing devices for molecular revolution that maintain these phenomena of centralization around an image of subjectivity, in a well-defined space, and make the most rigorous possible functional use of them, with a view to defined objectives—for example, the construction of instruments that get away from this system of alienation by the media.

I think that this business of the PT has contradictory, antagonistic dimensions, but it would be a great mistake to leave the phenomenon of Lula to the Trotskyites and the priests. The various marginal minority assemblages must not take the attitude of yielding over their own territories, but must try—despite all the risks that this represents—to take advantage of this kind of huge machine that is being established precisely in order to publicize and launch, in the social field, processes of singularization capable of entering into extremely complex, rhizomatic dialectics. But it's obvious that this business is not at all simple, because the best intentions—mine, for example—are not exempt, a priori, from secondary interests and traps.

Debate held by a branch of the PT in São Paulo, August 29, 1982:

Luiz Swartz: I would like to make an observation. It seems to me that the great paradox in your whole explanation lies in the question of the coexistence of parties with autonomous movements. In your first statement you said that certain kinds of struggle should be routed through that kind of organization, the parties. And that another kind of struggle takes place autonomously. And now you've put the question in terms of the party being an instrument that has to be used at a certain point, and not used again afterwards. It seems to me that there's something very important here: perhaps there's an incorrect evaluation of the strength of the party. The party, in my opinion, doesn't lend itself to being used as an instrument, because it eventually acquires a bureaucratized, disciplinary dynamic of its own that practically prevents the continuity of these molecular struggles.

Guattari: I think the treatment of these issues calls for great prudence, because history shows us that this kind of view can have disastrous consequences. First of all, I would like you to understand that I'm not saying that the PT is the eighth wonder of the world, a miraculous solution, or that Lula is a reincarnation of Jesus or Buddha. I know that there are many problems precisely in relation to the articulation of these minorities with a certain relatively traditional conception of organization. I also know that a trace of what I would call "leaderism" is being established, leaderism that is embodied in the media, and that triggers off a whole series of mechanisms, precisely in the field of collective subjectivity. This, of course, always introduces a certain risk of reification of subjective processes. However, when all is said and done, I believe that even so, there is great novelty, great experimentation, in what is being done here in the PT. It's not my place to give lessons on revolution, for the good reason that, in my view, there are no possible lessons in this field. Nevertheless, there is at least one thing that I think Europe can try to transmit: the experience of our failures.

In France, after 1968, there was an intense movement of waves of molecular revolution on all levels—on the social level, on the level of artistic creation, on the level of new forms of sensibility. For example, in the field of prisons there was a very interesting attempt with the Prison Information Group (which included Foucault, Deleuze, and various intellectuals from the fields of psychiatry, education, urbanism, and so on). There were groups for reflection that set out to function at the same time as groups for research and intervention. The results of the experiments were not negligible. It all happened in parallel with the maintenance of the neighborhood committees, and the development of struggles in the immigrant worker sectors, and in feminist, homosexual, and other movements. But the problem was that none of those modes of action was able to pass to another level of struggle. The only link with that other level of struggle, the struggle of other sectors of the population, continued to be the old systems of sectarian groups, the old party and union systems. What happened was that the nonintellectuals who took part in those movements became intellectuals of a kind during the experiments. So there was a gradual agglutination of those non-intellectuals—some militant immigrants, for example, who, by the very nature of the movement, eventually became isolated from the rest of the immigrant population. More examples could be given in the field of prisoners, the psychiatrized, and so on. The problem with this kind of experiment does not have to do with the establishment of an intensive contact between intellectuals and a particular group. But if those groups are actually isolated from all the other social movements, if there is an absence of essential links, they eventually lead to processes of specialization and degeneration. It's like a kind of wave ceaselessly breaking on itself.

We could say the same about what happened in Italy, although with different characteristics, of course. For many years the question of articulation with other levels of struggle was raised in Italy, within various Italian components of Autonomia. Certain factions in the movement wanted the Autonomia groups to maintain total independence, even though it involved occasional, temporary joint coordination for some specific objective. There were also various tendencies in Autonomia Operaia that produced a reading of a new working class, especially the marginal strata of the proletariat, consisting of those who had no occupation in terms of work or student activity. They made up a large part of the generation of young Italians who, in the context of a relative weakness in the power of the state at that time in Italy, came to associate the position of forced unemployment with an accepted rejection of work.[20] But at the same time, there were dogmatic, sectarian group tendencies that continued to restrain, control, and animate the political life of the organized autonomies in the workers' movement. This made the construction of a genuinely new organization impossible.

The fact that these trends in Europe in general, in the United States, in Japan, and more or less everywhere in the world, only succeeded in affirming themselves in small groups and very fragile forms of expression, and the fact that these movements did not lead to a real relation of power in the overall social and political field, left the terrain free for reactionary counteroffensives, and for all kinds of modes of cooptation. From advertising's cooptation of hippie fashion to the system of collective facilities and the control grid applied to all new ways of thinking and feeling, what this brought about was a kind of generalized phenomenon of implosion in the molecular revolutions. A great many friends from the events of 1968 in France committed suicide, were drawn into drug use, ended up in prison or psychiatric hospitals, or fell prey to life in sectarian groups (perhaps less cruel, but just as demoralizing). One must see that the attempts to "organize the movement," as people said in France at the time, were made after May 1968, at a time when the movement had already been crushed by Gaullism and was falling into the clutches of repression. Thus, overnight, the members of minorities in general, people who were spontaneists, began to invent parties like Gauche Prolétarienne (Proletarian Left), sectarian groups with dogmatic conceptions, which introduced a new kind of bureaucratic efficiency into their operation, losing any kind of contact with the reality of the movements, and sterilizing everything that was of the nature of action committees, feminist movements, movements struggling for alternatives to psychiatry, and so on.

Here we could also make an analysis that is a little different, although similar in some points, about what happened in Italy. Despite the fact that Autonomia Operaia in Italy wanted to establish itself as an extremely fruitful social movement, it reproduced such a strongly sectarian way of operating that there was no possibility of articulation, and its sectarianism eventually left the door open for things like the Red Brigades—in other words, totally suicidal movements.

During this period of ebbing spirits and demoralization, at the same time there also began to be an effervescence of all kinds of theorization that set out to show that all those perspectives were, if not crazy or idiotic, at any rate utterly insignificant. And then a considerable portion of the French intelligentsia, which still professed to belong to the left (the chic, well-behaved left), began to proliferate everywhere and all the time, and not just in the mass media. Their slogan was: "We're cured of all that. Politics and militancy are out. We're entering a new age," (and here's a suggestion, notice this expression if you don't already know it, because it's worthwhile, it was very fashionable in Europe) "the *postpolitical age.*" There were also theorists that went much farther and considered we were in an *age of social implosion.* And there were also others who alerted us to the existence of serious things, which we should always take as a reference, and which should never be abandoned: the transcendental values, starting with those of religion. Then there was a kind of collective sermon, in which there was an attempt to say that everything that seeks to act in terms of social issues and class struggle is absolutely synonymous with a course that leads to the "gulag." Therefore, according to those theorists, the only thing to do is to let the elites control production: we are led to this massive, inevitable choice. The next step was, not to make a specific eulogy of capitalism, but to say things like "it must be said that capitalism is the lesser evil," or "if we have to choose between the well-known freedom that prevails in the United States and the not very clear attempt involved in the taking of power by the Socialists in France, it's obvious that American capitalism is much better." This led to a whole series of rationalizations about neoliberalism, and the marvels of the freedom of the US market. Those theorists made their choice: they were incontrovertibly on the side of US imperialism. They included Baudrillard, for example, and also the intellectuals who became known as the "New Philosophers," such as Bernard-Henri Lévy.

This leads us to a curious paradox: a leftist coalition took power in France, and all of a sudden the whole leftist press took on a right-wing tone. I associate this with a kind of counter-wave that has fallen over all French and European culture in recent years, a consequence of the failure of what I call the new culture. Perhaps, as I said at the beginning, this failure may be precisely the kind of lesson that we could take as a starting point for the question that you raised about the relation of movements, in their autonomy, with parties.

What seems to me exciting in what I understand of Brazil now is that these problematics—which globally we could call counter-cultural or having to do with molecular revolution—are being reconsidered on very different bases than those that appeared in Europe in the 1960s and 1970s. We are witnessing a renaissance of all these processes of singularization in the field of desire, a renaissance that is nevertheless accompanied by an attempt also to consider political and social problems on a global scale. Perhaps this will help to prevent the kind of failure that we experienced in Europe. However, in the end, what guarantee is there that this awakening of the minorities, marginalities, and molecular revolutions here in Brazil now is not a wave that runs the risk of exposing itself to the same counterflow? What guarantee is there that in a few years we won't be saying "No, that whole business was a sort of fashion, a retro fashion," "Actually, Brazil is quite a long way from Europe, so the fashion took a while to arrive," and so on. Perhaps I'm utterly retro, but I've never changed my point of view since that period in 1968, which was a very rich period culturally. I don't believe for one moment that it involves a problem connected with some kind of "fashion." On the contrary, I believe that it's something basic, something that must be taken into account by all liberation movements. Otherwise, all the liberation movements will automatically succumb to all those perspectives of ebbing spirits and demoralization that I described.

What I think is important in Brazil, therefore, is the fact that the question of an organization capable of confronting political and social issues on a large scale is not going to be raised after some great movement of emancipation of minorities and sensibilities, because it's being raised now, at the same time. It is clear that it isn't a question of creating some kind of collective union in defense of the marginal, a common program, or some kind of reductive unifying front. That would be utterly stupid, because it certainly isn't a question of the minorities and marginal groups making an agreement or adopting the same program, the same theory, or the same attitudes. That would take us back to the old mass movement conceptions of the socialists and the communists. *It's not a question of adopting a programmatic logic, but a "situational logic."*

On the other hand, it also doesn't mean that tendencies seeking to affirm their singularity should abandon machines such as that of the PT. If that happened, gradually we would find only one kind of singularity in the PT: that of the "hard line" professional militants, the people who are capable of traversing all ages and all sensibilities with some kind of impermeability. That's where the problem lies.

Of course, I'm not trying to outline a philosophy of this issue. But it seems to me that it's necessary to invent a means that allows the coexistence of these two dimensions. Not just a practical means, a means of real intervention in the field, but also a new kind of sensibility, a new kind of reasoning, a new kind of theory. Perhaps even, as I never tire of saying, it's also necessary to invent a new kind of logic that no longer functions with the logic of the principle of contradiction, and that is capable of articulating these antagonistic dimensions, because they have to remain antagonistic and yet function together.

I don't believe that either you or I have resolved this issue. But it's important to raise it, and to do so collectively. *It's important to question political organizations about the issues of desire; but it's also important—and very much so—to question the economy of desire about the machines of the state.*

Round-table discussion at the ICBA, Salvador, September 14, 1982:

Marcus do Rio: As far as autonomy is concerned, it seems to me that what's required is not a reflection about the notion of political representation and party organization, with a program directing everything toward a final conclusion, but one that might point to a different kind of organization and of contact between the various groups.

I have a metaphor for this—daily life in contemporary societies is like a desert, an enormous, arid, inhospitable desert, which each person crosses as best he can, with the conditions available to him. Molecular movements are like the old Tuaregs who crossed the Sahara with their caravans, establishing contact between distant peoples and seeking shelter at the oases. They are the *new Tuaregs,* crossing the desert in search of new oases of pleasure, making contact with other caravans. The political parties are like the big capitalist companies, with their plans to build huge dams to irrigate the desert and transform everything. I particularly like this metaphor because I recently found out that ecologists have discovered that the common view that people generally have of the desert as a dead, lifeless place is utterly false. The desert has a complete environment of its own, with its own forms of life. Therefore, irrigating the desert is also a kind of ecological disaster. Perhaps the minority groups are more correct, crossing the desert of daily life in their caravans, like new Tuaregs, without worrying about irrigation projects and dams.

Debate held by a branch of the PT in São Paulo, August 29, 1982:

Question: There's something that I wanted to ask everyone here: if we created a relation between autonomy, processes of singularization, and the PT, how would people consider Lula's declarations about irrelevant matters? For example, when he says that transvestites can't stay in the street, or prostitutes; when he talks about drugs, when he praises labor, when he emphasizes on Christianity, when he talks about Christian education?

Question: In a certain debate about violence, a metalworker said that, for him, homosexuality had nothing to do with problems of violence, because fags *should* get beaten. Clearly, one can't expect any other attitude from that fellow, and perhaps one can't expect any other attitude from Lula. On the other hand, I'm wondering how we could take these issues to the PT in a more worked-out form, without expecting people with a life process that is entirely different than ours, people full of preconceptions, suddenly to come and defend things that have never even crossed their minds?

Maria Tereza Aaron: There's a big problem behind the PT—the Catholic Church. In São Paulo, its influence on the PT is considerable, but it seems that in the rest of Brazil—and it has a parish in every town in the country—it completely dominates the party organization. So the problem is not whether Lula said this or that, because he has a very straight outlook, as everyone knows. What's more, I don't agree that all metalworkers are straight, precisely because I have a number of gay friends who meet lots of metalworkers in places where they go to have sex with men. So I think that the PT's big problem is the Church, and perhaps also the intolerance of people from the traditional political organizations, with their old methods, who don't want to deal with the multiplicity of desire and the need to dilute power.

Néstor Perlongher: I think that not enough importance is being given here to the problem of political statements, in the following sense: the big problem of the connection of these small micropolitical movements—which existed in Peronism, in Argentina, as we can't deny, and which also exist in the PT, as we can't deny—is the statement with which those micropolitical movements are articulated. If this is true, I think that the power of those declarations is being underestimated. The conventional guy, whether he's a worker or not, becomes totally unglued when a pretty, intellectual fag appears, speaking on behalf of the PT. A guy like that isn't going to connect with this kind of statement. So the ones who wind up taking over the leadership of those movements are not the ones who are able to think, and they're not us, the freaks; they're the bureaucrats, the ones involved in the daily administration, people who say things like "now it behooves us to support democratic censorship" (this took place the other day in a meeting of the assembly against censorship). So what I ask is: up to what point are we from the micropolitical, minority, molecular movements going to defend these archaic statements like democratic censorship, or the reduction of the idea of revolution to a modification of the economy, which leads, as has been seen, to overexploitation and superdictatorship?

Guattari: I don't suppose you're going to prepare a notebook of complaints for Lula, asking him for proof that he has an accurate conception of what the fate of homosexuals, blacks, women, the psychiatrized, and so on is going to be. What Lula has to be asked is to contribute to the overthrow of all molar stratifications as they exist now. As for everything else, each person has to assume his responsibilities in the position he's assembled socially. I don't think that Lula is the "Father of the Oppressed," or the "Father of the Poor," but I do think that he's performing a fundamental role in the media, and that's essential at this point in the electoral campaign. He's the vehicle of an extremely important vector of dynamics in the current situation, such as the well-known power that he has to mobilize people who are totally apolitical. In this respect, Lula is not identifiable with the PT. The role that Lula is performing in the media is very important, because nowadays one can't consider the struggles at all the levels without considering this factor of the production of subjectivity by the media. So what can be said is that, at present, as "Mr. Media," Lula seems to be performing a role in a positive dynamic. What's going to happen a year from now, after the elections, we shall have to wait and see. I simply allowed myself to point out that the inherent logic of the current movement in Brazil is leading it to consider a new political approach. Its intelligence consists, precisely, in its ability to assemble the situation that's being considered here now. Which doesn't mean resolving it, or embodying it, or considering it consciously.

Informal conversation, São Paulo, September 19, 1982:

Suely Rolnik: We seem to be experiencing a double becoming in this process of the democratization of Brazilian society: on the one hand, the more obvious facet, a "becoming-citizen"; but on the other hand a "becoming-autonomous," which involves a becoming-woman, a becoming-Indian, and so on.

Guattari: And there's a becoming-black, which is extremely important and has been asserting itself in recent years. And also a becoming that I don't know how to describe because the words are so stupid, a becoming-environment, a becoming-raised-consciousness about the faces of Brazil, its landscapes, its plant and animal realities. I have an impression that this could transform modes of subjectivation profoundly.

Question: What would an outline of the cartography of these various becomings be like, including a "becoming-citizen," to use Suely's expression?

Guattari: In my opinion, between these becomings of a molecular nature in the field of desire, on the one hand, and these engagements, these pragmatics of social work, on the other, there is an inevitable rupture, which I believe should be accepted as such. And it clearly isn't a question of making a paranoid rejection of both sides: the militants rejecting those on the "desiring" side, saying that they're a drag and that they'll never be able to do anything together, or, inversely, the desiring accusing the militants of wanting to take them over. On the contrary, I believe that it's necessary to grasp the dimension of this radical heterogeneity in order to be able to find practices that will make an affirmation possible in both fields. But I also think that one shouldn't imagine that one fine day we're going to have an idyllic political party that isn't phallocratic, racist, and so on. That vision could even be dangerous. As soon as you set foot in the media, in this social affirmation, in this specific mode of representation, you're entering structures that inevitably contaminate you, that mark you subjectively, that set traps for you, that make you risk being dragged along by microfascist processes despite yourself. And as that's the way it is, it's best to know what's happening and at least be alert to it, instead of going on saying that you accept responsibility at this level of the social work and, at the same time, the molecular becomings. It's never true and it's best to recognize it openly, not to keep blaming oneself but to maintain a questioning attitude, to induce the analytic process.

The term "militant" is highly tainted. It acquires an extraordinary capital of devotion, courage, and involvement on the part of people, but at the same time it evokes meanings such as "military," and "regimentation," which are marked by negative, unpleasant, deadly connotations for the economy of desire. In any case, it seems to me that there's no easy way of getting away from it. But in the final analysis, it doesn't bother me that in the PT there are traditional militants, sectarian groups, and the like. They're minorities, too. Admittedly, they're a drag, but they're not the only ones. There are people who are a drag everywhere, and if we had to eliminate the people who are a drag from our whole field of existence, I don't know what things would come to.

It's true that I've been insisting on the importance of the PT throughout the trip, hazarding a thousand hypotheses. But I don't see why one shouldn't risk making an affirmation, even if one is French and has come to Brazil for only a month. So what? After all, it's by risking making affirmations of this kind that there's a possibility of experimenting with reality. If not, if we play the part of cautious, well-informed journalists all the time, we'll end up not connecting with anything.

Correspondence, May 1983:

Suely Rolnik: I've been thinking about how the book should deal with the considerable space that the discussions about the PT took up during the trip. Perhaps it isn't appropriate to reproduce the "electoral campaign" facet, for the simple reason that it's no longer a topical issue. But at the same time, it could be important to do so as long as it's in a way that reveals, and even emphasizes, what in my view was central in your investment in the PT: not to focus on the PT itself, as something sacred, but on the kind of device that the PT represented at that time. A device that made possible the expression of issues concerning formations of desire in the social field; and, above all, a device that made possible the articulation of that plane of reality with the plane of the struggles that require broad social and political agglutinations. I would even say that the agglutination of these two planes was the leading figure in your campaign for the PT. What was unusual about your position was precisely the fact that you called attention to the need and possibility for that articulation to take place. And throughout the trip you never stopped recalling the fact that, recently, this tendency to downplay the broader social struggles has caused damage at least as serious as the disregard for the problematics related to desire.

In addition to having made it possible to highlight this kind of issue, the discussions about the campaign also helped us to tune in to the frequency of a completely deterritorialized official political voice in the voice of Lula (a kind of free radio station, but with the peculiarity of broadcasting directly from within the official media). Those discussions also helped to make it possible to see, in the PT at that time, a collective assemblage that was drawing the political scene outside its traditional domain. In short, a "war machine."

But now things are different. In addition to the fact that we are no longer in the electoral campaign, there's no guarantee that the PT still is and is still going to be that device, which makes the presence of this element in the book questionable, at least with that emphasis. That's why I was saying that it would only be interesting to preserve it in order to share the understanding that the existence of this kind of device is essential in order to make the processes of singularization less vulnerable. Therefore it's necessary to be sensitive to its emergence in a great variety of social fields—not only in political parties, of course, and not only in the PT. I'd like to know what do you think about this, because, if I take option to abridge it, that will dilute much of the aspect of the factual historical document which might be important to preserve. I'm thinking here particularly about the fervor of the first campaign for direct elections after the dictatorship, particularly in connection with the PT candidates and the formation of the party in that process. What would remain would be more a record of the theoretical discussion.

Guattari: It seems to me important that the problems of the organization and the constitution of a new kind of machine for struggle should be concealed as little as possible. Even as a failure—which, after all, may not be the case—it seems to me that the experience of the PT is primordial. *How can we make the new components of subjectivity emerge on a national scale (in terms of the media)?* What is important here is not the result, but the emergence of the problematics.

There is no scope for futurology; history will decide. There are two possibilities: either the PT will be completely contaminated by the virus of sectarianism, in which case each autonomous component will "make tracks," and the PT can go to hell; or else the process that seems to be being triggered off in some places will tend to neutralize these sectarian-style components, and it may even happen, according to Lula's hypothesis, that, depending on the strength of the movements, those components may eventually dissolve. Everything will depend on the local circumstances and the usefulness or not of the instrument of the PT.

If all this goes "down the drain," if the PT becomes another PMDB and Lula becomes a leader of heaven knows what, then that's it, it's over. It would only mean that the consistency of the process didn't take hold in this kind of assemblage, and that the struggles of molecular revolution will continue through other paths. Whether we are optimistic or pessimistic, the problem will arise again one way or another.

Letter from Guattari to Suely Rolnik, Paris, May 24, 1983:

How's the PT coming along? Can we still expect anything from it?

Democratic centralism or spontaneism

If we insist on dealing with the problems of a political practice from a classical viewpoint—a tendency, a group, or a method of organization versus autonomous groups that do not want to know about leaders, or to articulate themselves—we shall find ourselves in a total impasse, because we shall be revolving around an eternal debate that sets modes of apprehension of the domain of centralism against "spontaneism" or anarchism, considered as sources of generosity and creativity, but also of disorder, incapable of leading to true transformations. It does not seem to me that the opposition is this—between a supremely efficient, centralized, functional device on the one hand, and autonomy on the other.

The dimension of organization is not on the same plane as the issue of autonomy. The issue of autonomy belongs to the domain of what I would call a "function of autonomy," a function that can be embodied effectively in feminist, ecological, homosexual, and other groups, but also—and why not?—in machines for large-scale struggle, such as the PT. Organizations such as parties or unions are also terrains for the exercise of a "function of autonomy." Let me explain: the fact that one acts as a militant in a movement allows one to acquire a certain security and no longer feel inhibition and guilt, with the result that sometimes, without realizing it, in our actions we convey traditional models (hierarchical models, social welfare models, models that give primacy to a certain kind of knowledge, professional training, etc.). That is one of the lessons of the 1960s, a period when, even in supposedly liberating actions, old clichés were unconsciously reproduced. And it is an important aspect for consideration, because conservative conceptions are utterly unsuitable for developing processes of emancipation.

The question, therefore, is not whether we should organize or not, but whether or not we are reproducing the modes of dominant subjectivation in any of our daily activities, including militancy in organizations. It is in these terms that the "function of autonomy" must be considered. It is expressed on a micropolitical level, which has nothing to do with anarchy, or with democratic centralism. Micropolitics has to do with the possibility that social assemblages may take the productions of subjectivity in capitalism into consideration, problematics that are generally set aside in the militant movement.

In my view, it is necessary to try to construct a new kind of representation, something that I call a new cartography. It is not just about a simple coexistence of centralized apparatuses and processes of singu-larization, because, at the end of the day, the Leninists always had the very same discourse: on one side the Party, the Central Committee, and the Politburo, and on the other, the mass organizations, where everyone does his own little job, everyone cultivates his garden. And between them are the "transmission belts": a hierarchy of tasks, a hier-archy of instruments of struggle, and, in fact, an order of priority that always leads to manipulation and control of the struggles of molec-ular revolution by the central apparatuses.

The construction of machines for struggle, war machines, which we need in order to overthrow the situations of capitalism and impe-rialism, cannot have only political and social objectives that form part of a program embodied by certain leaders and representatives. The function of autonomy is not that of a simple degree of tolerance in order to sweeten centralism with a pinch of autonomy. Its func-tion is what will make it possible to capture all impulses of desire and all intelligences, not in order to make them converge on a single arborescent central point, but to place them in a huge rhizome that will traverse all social problematics, both at a local or regional level and at a national or international level. For example, at the level of how children who have not read the great theorists feel, or people who are victims of racism or sexism. Not just in abstract proclama-tions, but on an immediate, practical, concrete level.

Everything that can be said, written, or practiced in connection with the issue of democratic centralism—at a conscious level, at the level of daily practice—is configured as a tracing of models that exist in other places, such as industries, administrative powers, or state powers.

I am far from any idea of spontaneism in the field of the economy of desire: something undifferentiated that would need to pass through the meshes of the network of some democratic centralism. I have never thought and have never said that it would be necessary to channel the energies of the various autonomies; precisely because, in my opinion, it is necessary to reject that notion of energy completely, in the whole field of human sciences. Desire, on the other hand, corresponds to a certain kind of production. Desire has infinite possibilities of assemblage and creativity, but it can also enter into processes of implosion. *I have nothing to do with any liberating mythology of desire for desire's sake.*

Interview by Néstor Perlongher: [21]

Néstor Perlongher: How could one connect the molecular revolution that you propose with classical anarchism, or with Trotskyite, Leninist, or some other kind of revolutionaryism?

Guattari: In principle, there's no connection at all. They belong to completely different phenomena. So much so that the processes of singularization and of collective assemblages of desire also take place within Marxist formations, as in the case of Poland. It's true that the anarchists made some attempts, especially during the Spanish Civil War: but those anarchistic, spontaneist attempts generally lead to failure and sterility.

I would call on the anarchists to be more singularizing, more libertarian. And on the Marxists to be more centralist, not to stray into some kind of bureaucratic libido.

A CERTAIN CONCEPTION OF HISTORY

Meeting with philosophers and psychoanalysts, Sao Paulo,
August 23, 1982:

Miriam Chnaiderman: I was thinking that one could imagine a conception of history based on the notions of micropolitics and the molecular.

Guattari: I very much like Braudel's way of thinking, particularly his notion of "world-cities." It seems to me that there is the idea of a production of universes of possibles that suddenly unfold. When he makes this kind of genealogy of world-cities, starting with Venice, Antwerp, Amsterdam, London, etc., in a way he's showing that there's a development of multiple "machinic phyla": at an economic level, at the level of demographic flows, at the level of the establishment of markets, of an area of concentric exchanges, and so on. But at the same time, these machinic phyla are only understandable if we refer to the notion of a "constellation of universes." The development of material civilizations such as that of Venice can't be separated from mutations in the order of musical creation, architecture, and philosophical conceptions without lapsing into an idealistic causality, a pseudo-materialistic causality. There's a "reciprocal presumption" of the mutations of machinic processes. When a world-city assemblage such as Venice is established, what changes is a principle of reciprocal presumption, a certain kind of logic, a certain kind of apprehension of religious problems, of apprehension of what the Mediterranean basin is, of artistic views, and so on. In other words, there is no order for the entry of these mutations. It's not a case where one can say that first there was the creation of new types of boats, a technological invention, for example, and those creations brought about the concentration of a certain commercial flow. It's well-known that a technological discovery in the domain of boat design, which makes it possible to cross the Atlantic, may very well exist during an entire historical period without entering a constellation of universes, and two centuries may go by before this takes place. For example, the system of retirement payments or the system of monetary circulation have existed since ancient times—since the Roman Empire—but why did they only acquire momentum with the constitution of world-cities such as Genoa, Venice, and Pisa? Another example is capitalistic flows. They've existed since the pharaohs, if we want to date capitalism. Actually, the dates of the birth of capitalistic assemblages vary according to commercial capitalism, and according to areas of territorial expansion...

Domingos Infante: In *A Thousand Plateaus* there's an example of a war machine which is a quotation from Jorge Amado's *Capitães de Areia*.[22] I'd like you to talk about that a little.

Guattari: Deleuze and I tried to consider that the systems of over-coding of "archaic," "primitive" territorialities developed in relations of segmentarity, and that this "relatively supple segmentarity"[23] in archaic societies leads to a "rigid segmentarity" in state systems. But this doesn't mean that there are linear dialectics here. The state already exists potentially in any kind of molecular segmentarity. However, this opposition seemed to me too simple to account for the phenomena of irreversibility that, in a way, constitute the profile of history. I actually believe that there is no repetition of history, whatever the constancy of the systems of overcoding. We marked this specificity at the level of machinic phyla. The war machine is one of these phyla which crosses all structures.

In other words, the war machine is something that places factors of irreversibility at the level of phyla inside structures (if one can talk about an "inside"), in coexistence with them, in coassemblage with them, and in this there is no ordering at all. At the same time, there is always the possibility of a dispersal, a resegmentation, a return to segmentary systems. That is what one sees, time after time, in the histories of empires: at certain points there are great concentrations of state powers, which at other moments disperse. What is irreversible, however, is the phyla, the phyla of the war machines, the phyla of the semiotic machines—for example, the fact that once a certain kind of writing is discovered, it is never lost. Whatever alternatives there may be between segmentary machines and state machines, the war machine continues its phylogenetic evolution, an evolution that in a way is completely heterogeneous to the oppositions of history, to its structural to-and-fro.

That's why I would place the war machine at the level of these three articulations. There's always a concrete war machine, which is military technology, technological mutations. There are always potentialities, ways in which war machines are articulated to the totality of machinic orders, the totality of positions of social structures. There are always ways of placing them in what I dare not call the phyla of history, because it's a certain kind of history that runs throughout history. This kind of history can remain suspended for a long time. For example, we can go on using the iron sword, or the horse, for a long time. Then, suddenly, there's a machinic mutation, and it's as if history is suddenly made as a result of this mutation, although meanwhile, on other levels, centuries of institutional history have passed. It's as if there were abrupt breaks in machinic history, which, in a way, is what punctuates history, giving it its character of irreversibility.

We could go back to Braudel's examples: there's a machine of semiotic economy that can remain like a virus in a latent state until, one fine day, it enters into conjunction with a technological discovery—the discovery of gold mines in Peru, or of silver mines in some other country—which overthrows the structures of machinic phyla, particularly the structures of war machines, this time irreversibly. That vast structural history may be occurring during the same period, creating great empires, great conglomerations.

Olgaria C. F. Matos: What I have difficulty in understanding is how one could reconcile the creation or transformation of history with a framework that is completely established. Where can silence be inscribed? How does the irruption of the new take place?

Guattari: That's the aporia: in the first place, nothing is possible in the domain of creation that does not start from the phyla that are *déjà là*. Nothing escapes from the stratifications. Secondly, that which is not *déjà là*—the constellation of possibles of universe— emerges fully fashioned, just as in mythology, Dionysus emerges from Zeus' thigh fully fashioned, sweeping away the complex of coordinates that are *déjà là*. It's then that a "threshold" creativity takes place.

Let's take the example of Leninism. When Lenin invented the Leninist war machine, he invented something relatively mutant. It's clear that one can always say things like "Yes, but the Jesuits had already invented it." Even so, there's a rupture, a "Leninist cut," that is, something that appears in the way of considering militant action, theoretical writing, or the relation between social classes, nationalities, and so on. At the same time, the Leninist universe projects itself on the totality of what exists in the domain of the workers' movement, social democracy, trends in the field of peasant organizations, and things like that. Then one sees that the emergence of a historical novelty—and this is something also described by Sartre— rewrites and reinterprets the totality of potentials that already existed in stratified form.

Something else that illustrates this is the invention of a musical universe, such as that of Debussy, or of John Cage, universes that rewrite the totality of music with a single stroke, reprojecting a possible. Debussy, for example, completely rewrote Bach, inventing another possible listening, another way of hearing and perceiving, and even a way of rethinking, rewriting, and recomposing Bach's own scores.

Olgaria C. F. Matos: That's precisely why I don't understand the business of Lenin very well. He understood the Russian Revolution as a French Revolution recommenced, that is, as a continuation of Jacobinism. All metaphors and all historical analogies were there to be placed in a scenario that had already been lived, done, and thought. It's no accident that the Russian revolutionaries from before and after the revolution didn't revert to using their real names, but kept their names from the time of their clandestine activity. That's what makes me think that it actually takes place in the framework of a "repetition" in the sense of tragedy.

Guattari: I think that in the final analysis our problem is one of terminology. I'm not making a value judgment. It's clear that Lenin invented something, because it ran through the world like a mutation, like a Japanese flu virus, which perhaps may not be completely invented, but one way or another it takes hold of the whole world. That's what happened, the whole workers' movement caught the Leninist flu. So, all right, we ask ourselves to what extent it's an old flu, from an old source. But in one way or another we have to recognize that a machine, the Leninist machine, was effectuated as an uncircumventable phenomenon. One can no longer continue to write history in the same way after the Leninist invention, despite all the phenomena of repetition that you quite rightly pointed out.

Laymert G. dos Santos: The revolutionaries may be representing all this as repetition, but on another level, without knowing it, they may be engaged in something else.

Guattari: That's right, there's no immunity against molecular revolutions. Even if one has to act like Lenin, who said he was a faithful Marxist and nevertheless did things that had nothing to do with Marxism, in the same way that what Lacan did had nothing to do with Freudism.

Olgaria C. F. Matos: I think I didn't explain myself properly. It's clear that there's a lack of synchronization between what people represent to themselves and what they do. That's precisely where the problem lies for Lenin: he had a "surplus of signifier," we might say, on the revolutionary side, that is, he was a vehicle of the new. But when he began to represent the new in the form of repetition, then there was terror. In other words, he didn't recognize the new as such: when the movements exploded like something unexpected, he rejected them, because they were unthinkable, they went beyond the possibility of control of historical time. So I don't know how that surplus of signifier, which always exists in history, can be understood in a conceptual framework.

Guattari: In the case of Lenin, actually, and also in the case of Hitler, whatever their archaic references may have been (references even clearer in Hitlerism, with all the business of race, and so on), nothing prevents there being a new phenomenon there, a phenomenon of rupture, in the sense that one can't write or conceive the development of history, the before and the after, in a continuous way. It's incontrovertible that there's some kind of novelty there, despite all the signifying redundancies. That novelty must be placed precisely in the order of machinic ruptures. What happens, in my view, is that the more unbearable it would be to accept those ruptures, inasmuch as they represent a kind of death, a kind of irreversibility in earlier systems or processes, the less they are represented in affects and in manifest discourse. It's quite common for discoveries to be treated within the references of earlier systems of coordinates—the revolution of quantum physics comes to mind. There are often considerable mutations that appear in the order of a scientific and aesthetic phylum, and that later… Stravinsky is a good example: to the same extent that he introduced ruptures in the real phyla of the history of music, he was converted to classicism.

Olgaria C. F. Matos: What I was thinking is that, clearly, there was the new, there was change. One could no longer write history in the same way as before, after the Russian Revolution. The same thing happened with the French Revolution. But I really wonder how it is that Lenin could reestablish the most grotesque forms of capital and endow them with a socialist conception. I'm referring to the time when he went back to Taylorism and used it in the Soviet Union, or when he read the three volumes of *Capital* as if it was the civilizing character of capital, when *Capital* is actually the history of capitalist barbarity. Where could he have got that perverse interpretation?

Guattari: What difficulties do you see on that level? I don't see any difficulty.

Domingos Infante: I think that you're raising a question of will—in other words, the fact that we understand all this doesn't prevent us from wishing that this kind of thing hadn't happened.

Laymert G. dos Santos: That it hadn't happened in that way.

Olgaria C. F. Matos: It's not that. I wanted to try to understand why it happened like that, not on a historical level, or an economic level, or a militant level, but precisely on the level of signifiers. Otherwise, what theory of history underlies this explanation?

Guattari: This leads us to the ambiguity of capitalistic flows that function in two senses: in the sense of an appropriation of machinic processes—each machinic mutation has to become compatible with the structures of representation, social structures, personological poles, hierarchies, territories, and so on—and, in addition to that, in the sense of there being a structure of reterritorialization. It's necessary that there should be, at the same time, this appropriation and this redundancy, this support for an order, a system, or a representation: perhaps that's precisely what characterizes the economy of capitalistic flows.

We could take this back to the birth of Christianity. Christianity may have been the first great capitalist religion, because it captured all the factors, all the flows of deterritorialization that threatened to break up the Roman Empire from all sides, and at the same time it also gave the image of a possible subjectivity that traversed the various status levels, an image that perhaps could even include slaves. We know very little about it. One would have to look at it closely, but in any case, that image could certainly include barbarians. It was a deterritorialized religion, and, furthermore, it created a factor of deterritorialization—in the sense that it was a religion of salvation—while at the same time it totally reterritorialized—in the crucifixion, the Father, the Trinity, the Church, and so on. So we always have this kind of double movement: the capture of deterritorialized flows, the organization of an order by means of these mutant machines, but, immediately afterwards, the recomposition of an order even more rigorous than the old order could ever have been in the field of territorialities. In other words, Christianity is the capturing of deterritorialized flows and, at the same time, the establishment of an overcoding more powerful than ever before.

And that may be why it's not appropriate to separate Stalinism from Leninism, as Trotskyite idealisms seek to do, because even in Trotskyism there's a Stalinist perspective of reterritorialization, starting with what you pointed out about Taylorism, military hierarchies, and so on. The militarization of the unions is also a Trotskyite idea, we mustn't forget that. We shouldn't put everything on Lenin's shoulders.

Interview by Pepe Escobar for the "Folhetim" section of the Folha de São Paulo, *September 5, 1982:*

Pepe Escobar: The dominant culture is very serious. After the crisis of ideologies, the advent of postutopian society, the frustrated revolutions, can one still say that history exists? Isn't everything a parody, a repetition in a tragicomic key?

Guattari: No, I don't think so. It would be a mistake to think that history repeats itself, especially at present. All the "retro" fashions, the attempts in the media, are minor drugs. The crisis that the world has been going through since the war of 1914 has nothing to do with earlier crises. There's a prodigious acceleration of history, which is visible in the realm of biology, and of computer technology. In the past twenty years it's also been visible in the evolution of microphysics and astrophysics. But all these disturbances don't register on the usual seismographs. They don't enter the heads of theorists, practitioners, and journalists. They're like X-rays. What are Mr. Reagan, Mr. Brezhnev, or Mr. Hua Guofeng thinking? That everything will continue as it is? That one day we'll wake up and find eight or ten billion inhabitants on the earth, in Brazil perhaps 400 million in the year 2000, and that everything will be OK, without any problems? Don't make me laugh. There's a tremendous acceleration of history, but on the other hand the people with responsibility, the people who could take some initiative, seem to be stunned.

There was a time in the eighteenth century when there was a process of transformation of productive forces, science, and the arts, and at the same time of social forces: revolutions in England, France, and the Americas. The transformations have multiplied a thousand-fold, and yet we're still going on with the same system as in 1945, with the same kind of utterly ossified political party, constitution, and organization of pseudodemocracy, and the same inability to find a new mode of life and of production. History, which is constantly on the boil, always has to fit into the same saucepan. From time to time there's a city that explodes. Beirut, for example. Or a country that enters a black hole, such as Cambodia. We have to stay alert. Those are accidents. Always marginal. They're the negative, crazy side. On the positive side there's 1968, for example, and other questioning movements that shook the torpor of the time. The Polish 1968 was different. It wasn't a picnic that lasted two months, but ten million people who for a year and a half or two years torpedoed the whole way of looking at life in the Eastern European states. *We are definitely not immersed in a situation of an absence of history.*

REVOLUTION?

We have to try and think a little about the meaning of *revolution*. This term is now so broken and worn out, and has been dragged through so many places, that it's necessary to go back to a basic, albeit elementary, definition. A revolution is something of the nature of a process, a change that makes it impossible to go back to the same point. This, incidentally, goes against the meaning of the term "revolution" when used to refer to the movement of one star around another. *Revolution is, rather, a repetition that changes something, a repetition that brings about the irreversible.* A process that produces history, taking us away from a repetition of the same attitudes and the same significances. Therefore, by definition, a revolution cannot be programmed, because what is programmed is always the *déjà-là*. Revolutions, like history, always bring surprises. By nature, they are always unpredictable. That doesn't prevent one from working for revolution, as long as one understands *"working for revolution" as working for the unpredictable.*

What I am saying is not all that absurd: a poet or musician involved in a productive process—if he isn't completely tied to a university or a conservatory—will never know what he's producing until he produces it. It's his process of production that transports him, even going beyond what he expected. We could make an incredible list of all the creators that were overcome in their production, to the point of arriving at suicide or madness.

Getting back to the subject, as I see it the idea of revolution is identified with the idea of process. Producing something that doesn't exist, producing a singularity in the very existence of things, thoughts, and sensibilities. *It's a process that brings about mutations in the unconscious social field, at a level beyond discourse.* We could call it a process of existential singularization. The question is how to ensure that the singular processes—which almost swerve into the incommunicable—are maintained by articulating them in a work, a text, a way of living with oneself or with others, or the invention of areas of life and freedom to create.

It is not just nowadays that one hears the term "revolutionary" used to describe certain situations or projects. What does revolutionary mean? Is it possible for a project to be permanently revolutionary, as in the Trotskyite conception, for example? This is clearly an automatic play on words, because revolution, by definition, cannot be permanent: it is a certain moment of transformation, which we might describe as a moment of irreversibility in a process. It's not my place to lecture about this, but the study of irreversible processes is an important theoretical problem in science, especially in the field of thermodynamics. So we could call a process revolutionary if it takes an irreversible course and therefore, we might add, writes history in a way that is without precedent.

What I have just said seems very banal, but, if we apply it to certain clichés, things become more complicated. Is it possible for a class to be inherently revolutionary? The fact that a social, political formation—the unions, for example—claimed to be revolutionary over a period of fifty years, as in the case of the Soviet Union, is obviously a contradiction: *revolution is either processual or it isn't revolution.* When the French Revolution stopped, signs were put up in all the town halls, and school children had to learn the declaration of human rights by heart: it was a revolution that no longer had a processual character.

Revolutionary microprocesses involve more than just social relations. For example, Modigliani saw faces in a way that perhaps nobody had dared to do before then. For example, at a certain moment he painted a particular kind of blue eye that completely changed what we might call the "faciality machine" that was in circulation at the time. This microprocess of transformation, in terms of perception and practice, was taken up by people who perceived that something had changed, that Modigliani had changed not only his own way of seeing a face, but also the collective way of seeing a face. This process preserved its vitality, its revolutionary character, in a certain social field, at a certain point in time, and for a certain period. Later, the history of painting processes happened somewhere else; other processes and other revolutionary mutations appeared, and, in some way, located new microprocesses in a nascent state. Well, the problematics of revolution involve this kind of thing, too.

I don't believe in revolutionary transformation, whatever the regime may be, if there is not also a cultural revolution, a kind of mutation among people, without which we lapse into the reproduction of an earlier society. It is the whole range of possibilities of specific practices of change in the way of life, with their creative potential, that constitutes what I call molecular revolution, which is a condition for any social transformation. And there is nothing utopian or idealistic in this.

Nowadays one no longer even dares to utter the word "revolutionary." Admittedly, it's rather silly to imagine that there could still be a "genuine" revolution. In France today, to speak of revolution is not at all cool. Many French intellectuals exclude the problematics of class struggle, but that does not mean that they have ceased to be an issue in history. What is happening is simply that at present they are at a well-known impasse. All the systems of modelization that claim to be revolutionary really function much more like something that brings about the rejection that I mentioned, something that blocks revolutionary processes. However, *despite all the bureaucratism with which it is conducted, this struggle is necessary: the whole point is not to confuse it with a revolutionary process.* But the fact that it is not revolutionary does not make it less important. Let's take as an example the problem of shoring up a roof: the question that arises does not have to do with knowing whether shoring it up is revolutionary or not, but knowing whether we are running the risk that it will fall down on our heads. One can say the same about social relations. It's perfectly legitimate that the working classes and various interest groups use whatever means they can to resist oppressive systems. That's one thing; but articulating a politics of revolutions (in the plural), molecular revolutions, is quite a different thing. It's important to avoid the dualist, binary logic that sets Marxism/social struggle/union struggle against molecular revolutions, as exclusive alternatives.

INTEGRATED WORLD CAPITALISM
The "nonguaranteed"

In Italy, various tendencies within Autonomia Operaia produced a reading of an undeniable fact: the emergence of a new kind of working class, especially in its marginal strata, the irreversible development of a considerable quantity of the population that, by definition, did not fit into the processes of guaranteed work. They were what those tendencies called the "nonguaranteed," "precarious workers," "black workers," "student workers." They were the *marginati*, those who had no occupation in terms of work or student activity, who rejected the legitimation of the prevailing processes of production, the system of exchange as it existed. They developed a different kind of relation with society and daily life, a different kind of investment of everything that we call production of personal and collective life, a different kind of relation with work, associating the position of involuntary unemployment with a deliberate rejection of work in the form in which it was presented to them.

The categorization of classes—working class, lower middle class, bourgeois or middle class, peasant, and so on—does not help us in the slightest to clarify the issue of molecular revolutions. It seems to me that the modes of structuration of social subjectivities now do not consist in separating the various categories of the population into these types of entities with mutually antagonistic social relations. Or rather, to be more precise, it is clear that these separations and segmentarities continue to exist, but they coexist with a different mode of subjectivation, which runs through this whole range of social segmentarity.

So let's keep these categorizations of class, but cross them with another mode of categorization. I would propose three categories: the *capitalistic elites*, the *guaranteed workers*, and the *nonguaranteed*. These three categories all participate in the same way of arranging the social order, the same productive and mental disciplinarization—with highly accentuated relations of internalization of the position that each person occupies in relation to others. For example, in the subjectivity of the "nonguaranteed" there is a double internalization of the superego: "I'm not guaranteed, so I'm shit," "if I was worthwhile, I'd be in pictures, in films or advertising"; in other words, in the standard of living ideals incessantly conveyed by the media of the elites. But if we observe the subjectivity of the elite, we see that it also internalizes the subjective dimensions of the guaranteed and the nonguaranteed: "I form part of the elite because I occupy an executive position, or I'm a university lecturer, or something of the sort. But in a way, I need to keep alert, because if I don't kowtow to the dominant etiquettes and rules, from one day to the next I, too, can fall into the category of the nonguaranteed, because I don't have the position of the financial aristocracies or the ancient nobility."

The category of the guaranteed is constantly taken up with this oscillation between guaranteeing their place and aspiring to be the capitalistic elite, knowing full well that this is utterly impossible. There are determinations of semiotic formation, or determinations of cultural formation, that make it impossible for someone to be legitimated to join the capitalistic elites, no matter how brilliant he is, no matter whether he studies all the books in the world, no matter how extraordinary his work is, if he's from a certain social milieu. So, in order to make up for this, he'll try to occupy a certain kind of intermediary position, but there is no way that he will ever have access to full recognition by the system of the current elites. This is something that exists in the "developed" capitalist countries, also, obviously, in countries such as Brazil, and increasingly in countries beyond the Iron Curtain: *there are very strong unconscious barriers that define the elites.*

The capitalistic mode of production of subjectivity intervenes in a very wide variety of milieus. Therefore, the question that arises is not one of knowing whether you are in a lower middle-class milieu or in a lecturers' milieu. What you need to know is what your position is in relation to the unconscious categorizations of subjectivity: "Do you have the desire—and the possibility—to be integrated into the capitalistic elites?" "Are you going to behave in such a way as to survive in the system of 'guaranteeism'?" This category of the guaranteed exists in the working class, in the milieu of the intellectuals, and among the military—it exists everywhere. So the problem that arises now has to do with the fact that, in the field of the nonguaranteed, we find not only people excluded from society but also components that convey a contestation of the processes of subjectivation in their totality. Components that even convey a questioning of what can happen on the level of the capitalistic elites.

Marx said at some point that the working class was the vehicle of an aspiration that concerned all strata of society, and it was this that gave it its revolutionary potential, a potential which, for that very reason, had to do not only with its own destiny but with that of all social relations. But *it is obvious that the guaranteed working class no longer has this revolutionary potential at all,* because it lives in a state of dependence and counterdependence on the elite systems that are literally tearing it apart. It is the nonguaranteed working class, or the guaranteed working class that rejects the system of guarantees, that is the vehicle of the revolutionary aspirations that concern all these modes of subjectivation. That is how I would put the problem, to enable us to conceive of alliances and systems of transversality that are able to pass between any social categories, because what unites is the subjective position, the position of desire in relation to the tendency of Integrated World Capitalism to take control of all modes of subjectivation.

As for the sociological divisions of class, capitalism knows very well how to deal with them. Nowadays, however, the real terrain of their vulnerability has become the capacity to survive and create, a capacity directly threatened by capitalistic subjectivity. During the counterculture period we saw fully guaranteed people from the elites with high salaries feeling terribly unhappy and barely able to put up with their mode of existence, and preferring to give up their social status in order to feel good with themselves and in their social relations.

It's something of this nature that is at issue here: the welfare state and the system of guarantees are, in a way, radically alienating. But this brings potentials of enormous contestation, which cut across everything.

It seems that the old dichotomy between guaranteed and nonguaranteed workers is now being overcome both in the PT, in Brazil, and in Solidarity, in Poland. A new kind of alliance is being established, an alliance that brings together a very wide variety of the nonguaranteed and the guaranteed who reject the system of guarantees.

This crisis (which is not just economic)

The world crisis in which we are immersed is, in my view, a *crisis of modes of semiotization of capitalism*, not only on the level of economic semiotics but also on the level of all of the semiotics of social control and modelization of the production of subjectivity.

The emergence of this enormous reactionary wave that has submerged the planet is largely the result of the development of the economic crisis that appeared in 1974. But actually, it's not really an economic crises. More precisely, this economic crisis is only one of a whole series of crises. Incidentally, it's precisely because the traditional leftist union movements experienced this situation solely in terms of economic crisis that the whole complex of social resistance movements were totally disarmed. And, in the absence of responses, it was the most reactionary formations that took control of the situation.

There is reason to consider that the essence of the world crisis (which at the same time is a kind of social world war) is the expression of the enormous emergence of a whole series of marginalized strata all over the planet. There are hundreds of thousands of people who live with hunger, and there are also hundreds of thousands of people who cannot recognize themselves in the social frameworks that are presented to them. This crisis of models of life, models of sensibility, and models of social relations does not exist only in the poorest "underdeveloped" countries. It also exists in broad sectors of the masses in "developed" countries.

It is no longer a matter of what traditionally used to be called "cyclic crises of capitalism." It is a crisis of modes of relation between, on the one hand, the new facts of production, the new facts of distribution, the new revolutions in the mass media, and, on the other hand, the social structures, which have remained in their ancient forms, totally crystallized and ossified. The powers of the state become more and more reactionary as they become increasingly aware that they are sitting on top of a veritable pressure cooker that they are no longer able to control. Is it possible to believe that the conceptions of neoliberal US economists will allow the continuance of a world order that can contemplate this tremendous rise in poverty? That can contemplate this devastation of entire continents, not only from an economic viewpoint but also from the viewpoint of a minimum expectation of life? I do not feel any blissful, starry-eyed optimism about the current situation. On the contrary, I believe that there will be utterly atrocious challenges that will be expressed in massacres like those that took place in Cambodia, Iran, and Lebanon. Imperialism, in all its versions, is preparing highly violent forms of intervention, and its experts—at any rate, the Americans—are actually thinking of the possibility of using miniature atomic weapons to intervene locally in these conflicts.

It can't be said that I am predicting a linear evolution toward a new kind of revolution. But it is not starry-eyed optimism to believe that substantial historical upheavals are on the agenda for the coming years. This further increases the urgency of the need to create new instruments of struggle, new types of conceptual references to understand the evolution of these unaccustomed situations.

One of the characteristics of the crisis we are experiencing is that it is not situated only on the level of explicit social relations but also involves formations of the unconscious, religious, mythical, and aesthetic formations. It has to do with a crisis in the modes of subjectivation, the modes of organization and sociability, and the forms of collective investment in unconscious formations that utterly escape the traditional academic explanations—whether they be sociological, Marxist, or otherwise. The crisis is global, but it is apprehended, semiotized, and mapped in different ways, according to the milieu.

Broadly speaking, there are generally three kinds of attitude in relation to this crisis. The first, which I would call systematic nonrecognition, has two aspects that we know well: on the one hand, the dogmatic Marxist line that, when it is not in power (but aspiring to power), always considers that "the issues of subjectivity and of new needs certainly exist, but they can only be addressed after the taking of power." And when they are in power (which leads to catastrophes like those that we have seen in Cambodia, or in the countries of Eastern Europe), instead of considering the specific character of collective subjective problems, they usually set them down as errors (party errors, manipulations by the enemy, and things of that sort). On the other hand, we have the theories that are in vogue, for example, in the United States (neoliberalism, the libertarian movements, the whole trend that formed around the Chicago School, Milton Friedman, and so on), which do not specifically consider the complex of problems related to the new kind of social movements. For those trends, these movements are residual forms, outdated forms, of modes of subjectivation. It is a kind of social neo-Darwinism, which considers these forms of collective subjective resistance as archaisms which, for that very reason, must be crushed, overcome, coopted, used, or reworked. For these theories, salvation can only come from a kind of selection that is based on an axiomatics founded on property, profit, and social segregation.

The second kind of attitude to contemporary social movements can be placed, broadly speaking, under the heading of a certain kind of social democracy, especially the French variety. In this case there is an attempt to confine the problem to two groups of subjects: on the one hand, it is considered that there should be a reorientation of international relations, shifting from an East-West axis to a North-South axis (that is, to relations between "developed" and "underdeveloped" countries). This is more or less the gist of the theme that Jack Lang developed at the conference held by UNESCO in Mexico. On the other hand, this time on the level of internal relations, it is considered that there is indeed a specific problem for a whole series of social categories that are not inserted in the dominant capitalist processes. This ranges from nationalist or regionalist problems—for example, in France, the problem of Corsica, the Basque region, Brittany, and so on—to the problems of the feminist movement, the homosexual movement, etc., or the problems of change in the relation with the media, as in the case of the free radio movement. But what characterizes this second attitude is the fact that it considers these specific questions only enough to define the problems and take them over. This was the ideology of Kennedyism, which at a certain point tried to set up a series of programs that sought to channel and, at the same time, help to control the black movement, the Puerto Rican movement, the hippie movement, and so on. From this example we might say that the first attitude (nonrecognition), and the second (cooptation) are not opposed to each other but are complementary, and perfectly so. This partial recognition can provide itself with extremely repressive attitudes against elements that are not integrated in these processes of cooptation. Here we can identify an extremely vigilant, precise modulation of cooptation.

I think the best example of this is Federal Germany, where there are highly developed and highly structured alternative sectors in the main cities, where a process of collective subjective autonomization is developed, and this process coexists with systems of social control based on computer surveillance to such an extent that it is now estimated that four or five million people are totally classified and monitored by computers. France oscillates between adopting a solution of the German type, with general computerization, etc., in view of terrorist threats, or creating state functions—such as a Mr. Prisons, Mr. Corsica, Mr. Women, Mr. Free Radio—to establish a dialogue that will make it possible to find methods of negotiation and funding.

We find the same kind of ambiguity in Poland, but in a much more catastrophic context. On the one hand, the Jaruzelski government would like to try to invent a union structure that would have a real connection with the social movement and that would make it possible to get away from the kind of permanent general strike that exists in Poland. On the other hand, however, it utterly rejects all the political consequences of the genuine revolution that took place with the Solidarity movement.

Therefore, the attitude of cooptation is complementary not only to the attitude of nonrecognition but also to the forms of extremely strict, violent repression through the application of a social control grid. Equally complementary, in fact, on the level of international relations, are the attitudes of the two great dominant powers, the United States and its allies and the Soviet Union. We can see it in operations such as the British aggression in the Falklands or, more recently, in the total passivity of the great powers, their complicity, in the Israeli aggression against the Lebanese and the Palestinians. Regardless of the modality, there is a kind of complementary approach to what I call the North-South focus, in the sense that in every country there are North-South axes: in the "developed" countries there are Third World or Fourth World areas, and in the so-called "underdeveloped countries" there are areas of the North, in other words, areas of Integrated World Capitalism. So we can say, schematically, that there is a kind of vectorization of the general issue of these new modes of subjectivation that have to do with relations with the Third World on an international level and also with a kind of Third World that is created within the so-called "developed countries." More specifically, I mean that, in a way, there is a common frontier between two kinds of problematics, despite all the differences in the situations. For example, on the one hand, the problematics that the Italian comrades raised concerning the nonguaranteed, precarious workers, and all the existing marginalities, and the problems of the overexploitation and sometimes even the physical liquidation that takes place in the Third World.

Coming back to the point where I started, it is clear that this does not eliminate the fact that the way in which these problematics are embodied is completely different, depending on the context. For example, the problem of the blacks in Brazil is not directly comparable with that of the *marginati* in Milan or Bologna. However, perhaps we can consider that they both form part of the same kind of general crisis that now pervades every society on the planet. What unites them is something that swoops down on them and comes from outside: a certain politics of Integrated World Capitalism for the restructuring of social relations and the relations of production. We can say that there is a complementarity between the operations of integration and cooptation in the various situations on the planet. Hence the attitude of the leaders and theoreticians of imperialism, about which I was speaking, which considers certain operations as necessary and inevitable: the unification of collective labor power, its integration in new technological mutations, and the internalization by all individuals on the planet of a certain kind of relation with writing, technology, the body, desire, and so on. Seen from this perspective, the crisis is no more than a little upset over nothing, a minor accident on the road, from which, sooner or later, we shall miraculously extricate ourselves.

But this crisis really did explode, incontrovertibly, in 1974, and ever since then the light at the end of the tunnel has been announced each year. Nevertheless, everything leads us to believe that this is a challenge on an international scale, for a whole period of history. A crisis that we could also describe as war—world war—with the difference that it is not an atomic war (although that possibility is not excluded), but a succession of local wars that always have to do with this North-South axis.

And finally, the third kind of attitude. Unlike the two previous attitudes, in this case the subjective mutations are properly considered, in terms of their specific character and their common trait—they are different forms of molecular resistance, cutting across societies and social groups, with which this attempt at social control on a planetary scale clashes.

War, crisis, or life [24]
Félix Guattari

World society has become flabby and shapeless, without any energy
capable of fueling a consistent possible. The continents of the Third
World vegetate in the appalling fermentation of poverty; the oil slicks
of Reaganism and Thatcherism expand at the whim of economic
tides; the scum mark of the dictatorships of Eastern Europe is encrust-
ed more and more deeply in the lives of hundreds of millions of
human beings; dangerous vapors are beginning to emanate from the
"Southern" experiments of European socialism; and once again fascist
sordidness seeks its way among the fauna of the lumpen bourgeoisie.

With a series of violent movements, as if emerging from a state
of coma, we try to dissipate all these fogs of *déjà vu*.

First, war. First, the affirmation that these dimensions of a
planetary supershow—its air of a mechanical ballet of death, its
technical and strategic ploys increasingly detached and out of step
with the geopolitical realities and even the processional chains of
pacifism that it resuscitates—that all this, ultimately, does not interest us. The illusions of the prewar period, such as *The Bridge On the
River Kwai, The Great Cemeteries under the Moon, The Call of Amsterdam Pleyel*—we have already forgotten all that! We are not
credulous enough to think that the great powers are seriously seeking to resolve their differences by launching intercontinental
missiles. It is so clear that their true complementarity, their increasingly accentuated complicity, is leading them to integrate the same
segregationary capitalistic world system. And the war simulacrum—
which they are forever sticking in the media market, playing the
game of great apocalyptic organs—also seems to have as its prime
function the occupation of the space of collective subjectivity, thus
diverting it from consideration of the social urgencies that afflict it:
any impulse of desire, and any transnational, transcultural raising of

consciousness, such as those that worked through the last two decades, is banned. Their war is not ours! The only true world war that affects us is the crumbling, cancerous one, unsustainable to civilized eyes, that has been sweeping the planet in waves for half a century. There is still El Salvador, Nicaragua, Poland, the Boat People, Afghanistan, South Africa—in the end it gets disheartening, it's best to change the channel. Under these conditions—whatever our "solidarities" of the left may be—we don't bar ourselves from rejecting the nuclear options of the French Socialists on the military level. The game of the strategic balance of forces is constitutive of the will of the great powers to subject the oppressed peripheries, and we do not know how to yield to its logic without betraying the emancipation of the people for which we seek to work.

Then there is the crisis. Here, too, there is a vast machination to tighten the degrees of submission and "disciplinarization" of the populations of the world and bring them ever closer to the limit of strangulation. Everything is done to present it as an incontrovertible fact. Unemployment and poverty rain down on humanity like biblical plagues.

As this description of the political economy is the only one conceivable, one is led—with rare exceptions—to think of solutions completely marked by this very conception. However, it is clear that the appearance of self-sufficiency that econometrics now presents is proportionate to the loss of credibility of those reference models! It is certainly irrefutable that many of these indexes or forecasts worked. But to what kind of realities do they refer? Really, to subsets of productive activities and social life that are increasingly limited, detached and alienated from their global potentials. The flabby, self-referenced corpus of economic and monetary scriptures has become a brainless, tyrannical tool of pseudonegotiation and pseudocollective management. (A recent example: the central banks going to save Mexico simply in order to enable it to pay back, in the short term, the interest on the debts that it had contracted with them.) And what if, ultimately, the crisis were simply a crisis of models? A crisis that now, under a regime of psychotic capitalism, is precipitating the social division of labor, the objectives of production, and the combinations of modes of semiotization of exchange and of distribution, all simultaneously? The hope of "light at the end of the tunnel," and the myth of the "great recovery" (but recovery of what and for whom?) hide from us the irreversible character of the situation that was engendered by the continuous acceleration of technical and scientific revolutions. "From now on everything will be different." Great! But there are two possibilities: either these disturbances will be complemented by mutations of social subjectivity capable of leading them "far from equilibriums"[25] currently existing, toward emancipative or creative paths; or else, progressing from crisis to crisis, these disturbances will oscillate around a point of conservatism, a state of repressive stratification and depression, with increasingly mutilating, paralyzing effects. Other systems of inscription and regulation of social flows are conceivable on this planet! In all fields of aesthetic and scientific creation, models have been imposed that break away from oppressive hierarchies—nonarborescent, "rhizomatic," "transversalist" models. Why not in the social domain?

Let's go back to the areas of politics and micropolitics, despite the fact that in some intellectual circles it has become fashionable to adopt disenchanted positions, considering oneself outside time, beyond history, describing oneself as "postmodern," "postpolitical," etc. It's true that the overconsumption of information and manufactured culture may lead to indigestion! But is that a reason to consider ourselves the supernumeraries of our age? Our ideal would be, on the contrary, to be able to go where breaches are being made. Not before or after! Precisely at the breaking point, where new languages are developed, new coefficients of liberty are sought, and different ways of seeing, feeling, thinking, and creating are experimented with, beyond messianism and the creeds of spontaneism or dialectics. But why deny it? Certain political issues are fundamental for us, and especially certain refusals that lead us to "commit" ourselves, of our own accord, to certain somewhat hazardous adventures. Our experience with dogmatic forms of engagement and our irrepressible inclination toward processes of singularization make us immune—or so we think—to any overcoding of aesthetic intensities and assemblages of desire, irrespective of political propositions and party ties, however well-intentioned. In fact, one has only to follow the trend: every day new corridors of passage between previously compartmentalized domains of art, technology, ethics, politics, and so on are opening up before our eyes. Unclassifiable objects, "strange attractors"[26]—to paraphrase the physicists once again—incite us to burn the old "cliché languages," to accelerate the high-energy particles of meaning in order to enclose other truths. And we are caught dreaming that many things are possible! In one sense or another.

A FUTURE THAT HAS ALREADY ARRIVED:
Lula and Félix Guattari, a Conversation
(São Paulo, September 1, 1982)[27]

Guattari: In France we don't precisely know what is taking place in Brazil today, this whole effervescence of ideas, of the will to change, which in the upcoming elections of the month of November will probably scuttle the dictatorship to which you've been subjected for eighteen years. We know your name, we know of the existence of the PT, but we do not even suspect the importance this party is acquiring. The last time I came to Brazil, three years ago, the union militants of the left were still subject to severe repression. In Campinas I had a long conversation with Jacó Bittar[28] and other militant workers who, at the time, spoke about plans to shift to large-scale militant action, creating a new party. Today this has been done. And it even seems that the results were quite unanticipated, because an entirely new climate now reigns in Brazil, where a whole range of desires for transformation, arising from the most diverse social categories, appear to have embodied themselves in the movement which the PT has come to articulate. To the point where the right no longer seems capable of playing the game on its own terms, as it did before. The consolidation of workers' rights, the establishment of a minimum of political democracy, the development of new spaces of freedom for the minorities which have been working with you, all this seems close at hand. Do you think that in spite of this, the right still has the means to block the process? What, for example, is the significance of the maneuver it has just carried out, by imposing an electoral procedure that will act to restrict access to the voting booths for certain social classes which have difficulties correctly filling out the ballots? What is one to think, in this regard, of the ambiguous attitude of the PMDB? Can the right still intimidate the electorate by blackmailing it with the threat of a military coup?

Lula: I believe the right is still very strong in Brazil. In fact, it continues to be the sector that disposes of the greatest force in this country, since it exercises control over the states, the vast majority of municipalities and the armed forces. It's true that an atmosphere of expectation exists throughout society, with respect to the changes that can arise through the electoral process. The right remains powerful, and not only in the government. There are a lot of sectors on the right which are now disguised as liberals, and are trying to acquire positions of power inside opposition parties such as the PMDB. What is most serious is that at the moment when the working class begins to protest, seeking to walk on its own two legs, the right, the orthodox left, and the liberals are coming together in an effort to impede the organization of the working class. The electoral process will be tumultuous. And it will be more difficult for the PT than for the other parties, in so far as its candidates will be unable to go on television. And also because of this new type of electoral ballot, adopted yesterday, where the Party's emblem will not appear, and where the voter will have to write the complete name of the chosen candidate, which will greatly complicate the task. It seems that the true objective of the government, in all this, is to undermine the meaning of the elections, striving to obtain the nullification of a great quantity of ballots. We of the PT are very preoccupied with these questions, but we are aware that the struggle of the PT and the struggle of the working class will not stop with the electoral process, which, in reality, for us represents just one more step in the organization of the working class. That is the only reason we accepted to take part in the elections and decided to present our candidates.

Guattari: And the risk of a direct military intervention?

Lula: In a country governed by the army there is always a risk that military repression will increase. As long as the people do not organize, as long as they do not have a political consciousness, this risk will subsist. It's for this reason that we say, in the PT, that the most important thing that we have to do is organize the working class. Then it will be up to the working class to decide its destiny for itself.

Guattari: The PMDB tries to exert a type of blackmail on the electoral body, with its campaign for a supposedly "useful vote," proclaiming that the PT does not have sufficient maturity and that its leaders do not have the real competence to justify its bid to manage the business of the country. Can this type of argument have an impact on public opinion?

Lula: I believe that this argument can have a certain kind of influence on the electorate. In the first place, because the experience of political participation by our people is still very limited. Over the course of our entire lives, that is, since the proclamation of the Republic, we have been treated as a mass to be manipulated. The people have always been induced to believe that there exists no possibility of self-governance and that it is necessary for someone to guide them. In the second place, because of the class prejudice that exists in our country. Many sectors of the middle classes, in particular the upper-middle class, and the whole of the national bourgeoisie, consider that a person's capacity can be measured by the quantity of diplomas or the accumulation of revenue in banks, or by property, commercial paper, etc. One of the great tasks of the PT is, precisely, to demystify this historical error, according to which we only serve to work. And to prove that the administration of a state is not a technical question, but rather a political one.

Guattari: In the march that crossed São Paulo two days ago, for the public presentation of the PT candidates, a large paper banner, carried by four or five persons, read: "We know how to work, we know how to govern."

Lula: The whole question is where the state stands: on the side of economic power or on the side of the workers? We consider this call for a "useful vote" to be a fascist proposition, since it presupposes that the existence of the PMDB's political force depends on the nonexistence of other political forces. And we of the PT, we defend the existence of the PMDB, in the same way as we defend our own existence.

Guattari: This "competence test" seems to me all the more unfounded in that the present leaders have already given ample proof of their incompetence and corruption. In the PT convention, in the month of July, you reaffirmed that your party will not make any agreement or compromise with the PMDB and other formations of the traditional left. Would you maintain this position after the elections? For example, would you reject participation in a "left coalition" to administer the state of São Paulo?

Lula: I don't see how we would be able to reconcile such divergent interests. I don't believe that the progress of a class can depend simply on the fact of some of its members occupying official positions. I was already contacted by a person from the PMDB who explained that one of the great preoccupations of his party was, if they win the elections, to obtain support from the PT, so as to govern tranquilly, without strikes, without social convulsions.

Guattari: The PT was born in the flux of the movement of São Bernardo, after the industrial working class proved it was capable of engaging in extensive political struggles which could bring together members of the entire working class, but also of the middle classes, intellectuals, etc. I know that the PT is concerned with the interests of peasants as well: it has even formulated the first real agrarian reform program for Brazil. But does the PT not essentially remain, even today, what I would call a "party of the cities"? What support does it have in the countryside?

Lula: I would say that, proportionally, the PT is stronger in the countryside than in the cities, principally in the North and in the Northeast of the country. The accusation that we are only a party of the cities has lost its substance, insofar as our work in the countryside has developed considerably. But it's difficult work, which takes place under terrible financial conditions. There is, for example, a great lack of means of transportation, which is a serious problem in a country as large as ours. I believe nevertheless that for the first time in the history of this country, we have concretized the old dream that the Brazilian left never realized: the union of the workers in the countryside with those in the city.

Guattari: There are a lot of Catholics in the PT. It's said that they even have the support of the episcopate. What type of relation has the church established with your party? Would it be anything comparable to what exists in Poland between the religious hierarchy and part of the Solidarity union leadership: regular consultations, the church as an intermediary with the established powers, and so forth?

Lula: No. That type of relation with the church does not exist here. What does exist is that, since Puebla,[29] the Brazilian church, or better yet, a part of the Brazilian church, decided to make a decision on the question of the organization of oppressed peoples. It was from that moment that the grassroots communities and the "progressive" bishops began to appear. And what happens is that the forms of organization they propose coincide with those of the PT. No bishop leads Christians to sign up for the PT. But I believe that all of the bishops—or at least a large number—lead Christians to adopt criteria for their choice of parties and candidates, and this too coincides with the political proposals of the PT. Now, any other party could adopt forms of organization similar to those we suggest, such that the current orientation of the church could benefit all.

Guattari: The economic program of the PT foresees a collective reappropriation of the major economic structures, such as banks and industrial complexes, to liberate them from the dominion of national monopolies and multinationals. Would this not imply a certain underlying conception of future relations between the state, the economy, and society? What form, according to you, should this collectivization take? A nationalization with state-centered characteristics, or a more self-managed process?

Lula: If I had to respond immediately to such a question, I would say that things are oriented more toward conversion to a state-run system (*estatização*). However, it's necessary to remain with our feet on the ground, and realize that processes of transformation do not take place because we want them to, but rather by virtue of the political forces that support them. If, in the first stage, we could engage in a nationalization,[30] this would be important, although the final objective continues to be a state-run system. But things need to be clear: this state-run system would only have meaning in the framework of a democratic state, where the people can manage and administer their industries and banks for the benefit of the collectivity and not in benefit of the state bureaucracies. We should be realists, the proposals of the PT cannot be dreamy: today we don't even have union delegates, not even factory commissions. If we obtain these, it would already be a decisive step, which could be followed by other steps, taking us closer to a form of comanagement, of access to the accounting of businesses, with a power of decision to discuss projects and investments. Next, we would come to the stage of nationalization, and we would accumulate forces to pass finally to a state-run system. It's as if we were climbing a ladder of 16 rungs: if we do not climb one rung at a time, we risk falling and breaking our legs. We don't want to rush thirsty to the gallows. What we want is to slake our thirst! For this reason, we must be careful.

Guattari: So you don't see an already constituted model at the top of the ladder, a Soviet, Chinese or Cuban type of model?

Lula: No, in no way whatsoever. And not a French or a Swedish one either.

Guattari: You want to forge another type of state, another type of society. But isn't there a contradiction between this creative perspective and the manner in which the PT defines itself today as a centralist organization? I have read the statutes of the PT. They seem a lot like those of any traditional communist or socialist party.

Lula: You speak of the official statutes! Those statutes are the same for all parties. But the practice of the PT is completely different. For example, the statutes of the PT foresee conventions with one delegate for each municipality. The PT invented another "figure": that of the decentralized preconvention, open to the participation of many more delegates. The official conventions would only serve to ratify the decisions of more ample conventions. In spite of all its imperfections, the PT managed to create a system of grassroots groups, guaranteeing that all the decisions pass through a process of discussion at a local level, in such a way that national instances will always have an exact comprehension of what the whole of the party thinks in reality.

Guattari: I had an opportunity to verify what you just said when I encountered militants of the local committee of the PT in Pinheiros. Diverse groups qualifying themselves as "autonomous" (ecologists, feminists, homosexuals, etc.) were gathered around the committee. This committee upholds positions that seem very much in the minority, or marginal in relation to the whole of the party. Certain hierarchical aspects of the PT tried to prohibit the candidacy in the next elections of Caty Koltai, who is presenting a "situationist"-type program under the party's name. Finally, there was a convention of the kind you referred to, which resolved the question by approving the candidacy of Caterine Koltai after a public reading of the program in question.

We have an expression in France to describe the rigid, dogmatic language of many militants: we say they speak a "wooden tongue" (*langue de bois*). With relative success, a certain number of experiments with free radios, in Italy and in France, have tried to replace this "wooden tongue" with means of expression better adapted to real social groups, minorities, different sensibilities. Do you also have in mind the creation of free radios, which are neither under the control of the state, nor that of parties or commercial groups?

Lula: We are not yet at the point of creating alternative media! But I think we will get there. You just need to understand that we are in Brazil, not in Europe. It's another universe, another political culture, another experience of struggle. But I believe that we will get there, since it's the only way of liberating ourselves from dependence on the official media.

Guattari: How are intellectuals seen inside the PT? Do relations of a new type exist between them and social movements? I'm thinking, for example, of the kinds of relations that are forming within Solidarity in Poland.

Lula: A very important fact, within the PT, is the demystification of the distance between intellectuals, students, peasants, and workers. The PT has brought people closer together; it has created new relations of fraternity, and here, people feel more equal. I even believe that one of the reasons for the great success of this party is the fact that within it there are no divergences based on the social position and class origin of its members. In truth, this type of prejudice existed less in the working class than in other sectors of society. I sincerely believe that people live freely inside the PT.

Guattari: In the march that crossed São Paulo, there were some banners of solidarity with Solidarity. Does this correspond to the position of the PT as a whole, or is it a minority position?

Lula: It's an official position of the PT, and the banners you saw were those of a current within the PT, called Socialist Convergence/Liberty and Struggle, which was actually born in Paris.

Guattari: You met with Lech Walesa before his imprisonment, when you went to Europe. Did the PT maintain relations with the exiled leaders of Solidarity?

Lula: No, since right after the wave of imprisonments in the month of December, we sent two official letters to the office of Solidarity in London and did not receive a response. (The last one was even sent back.)

Guattari: What was the position of the PT during the Falklands war?

Lula: The PT pronounced itself against the demonstration of force by England, but also against the dictatorship of the Argentine military. In the PT we think that General Galtieri tried to strike a "master's blow" in hopes that the Argentine people would forget their internal problems: the thirty thousand disappeared, 150% inflation, etc. The result: this did not resolve anything on the internal level and Argentina was left completely demoralized. The worst in all of this is that the human lives lost will never be regained. At any rate, this war left one thing clear: developed countries will always prefer to help each other, rather than being in solidarity with underdeveloped countries. And an example of this was the Americans who, despite being Argentina's largest creditors, did not hesitate to abandon the country to support England.

Guattari: Do you approve the slogan, "The Falklands are Argentine"?

Lula: This question was heavily debated inside the PT. We discussed it an entire day. My position is that the Falklands belong to Argentina.

Guattari: At least they belong to the Latin American continent!

Lula: Indeed. But one mustn't forget that the first owners were French. And it's necessary to take into consideration the two thousand English who have lived there for so long. But Latin America and Argentina have a right over those islands.

Guattari: If I understand correctly, you did not approve of the position taken by a great part of the Argentine left on this question.

Lula: No. I was even invited to participate in a meeting in Peru, where diverse sectors of the Argentine left—including the Montoneros—declared their intention to return to Buenos Aires to support General Galtieri. I refused to go. The PT would never support either the Falklands War or General Galtieri. With the left in Latin America—above all the left connected to Argentine and Brazilian communist parties—we never know if we are really on the left or the right!

Guattari: What is the position of the PT with respect to the threats of intervention by the United States in Nicaragua, in El Salvador or in Cuba?

Lula: We are in solidarity with all the oppressed peoples of the world. We think that the Salvadoran people should resolve their problems themselves, without any meddling by the United States. The same holds for the people of Nicaragua and other peoples of Latin America. It would be better if the American government got rid of racism and unemployment in the United States, rather than preoccupying itself with a possible embargo of Cuba or of Nicaragua. In the PT we think that Reagan is only the president of the United States, and not president of the world.

Guattari: Is it not a kind of fate for countries that try to leave the North American zone of influence, to find themselves as though sucked into another form of imperialism, that of the Soviet Union? And this, for all kinds of reasons: economic, strategic, etc....?

Lula: What is necessary, in reality, is to create conditions that permit a dependence neither on American imperialism nor on Soviet imperialism.

Guattari: Does the PT maintain privileged relations with the Socialist International?

Lula: No. In the PT we do not preoccupy ourselves with establishing agreements with any existing internationals. Besides, while we're in a phase of growth, ideological questions will not be given much consideration inside the PT. It would be premature to get involved on the international level. We hope to establish direct relations with all the democratic forces of the world and this will only be possible if we do not take ideological options at the top, before the grassroots makes its own decisions.

Guattari: I thank you for responding so frankly to my questions.

Lula: From my side, I would like to know your point of view on the present politics of the French Socialist Party. Is it putting into practice what it proposed before the elections?

Guattari: Let's start with international politics. François Mitterrand asserted the will of France—particularly in Cancun—not to give imperialist American policies a free hand in the Third World. But this did not stop him from supporting Margaret Thatcher and Reagan on the question of the Falklands! On the other hand, the

French socialists loudly asserted their solidarity with the resistance of the Polish people. But they don't want to touch the question of commerce with Russia, for example. Business is business! After taking a cynical, ambiguous path in relation to Israeli policy, France decided to offer a certain assistance to the martyred peoples of Lebanon and Palestine. It seems to me that we are always wavering. In certain regions of the world, such as Africa, the politics seem even less clear. It's true that it's easier for France to be antiimperialist in Latin America than in Africa!

Lula: Why easier?

Guattari: Because in Africa the socialist government has to deal with the management of a whole neocolonialist heritage. In spite of this, I believe that there are still certain positive aspects of the international politics of France. For example, the denunciation made by Jack Lang, French cultural minister, in Mexico, before UNESCO, of North American practices with regard to "cultural exportation," above all in the domains of television and cinema. His idea of a new type of cooperation between different components of what he calls Latin cultures could also be interesting. Thus, not everything is negative on this level, far from it! On the other hand, what seems to me to have gotten off to a very poor start is domestic politics. After a period that we can call a "state of grace," because it passed amidst surprise and the hope of great changes, with measures to raise the standard of living of the most underprivileged categories and, above all, measures to safeguard liberties (suppression of emergency tribunals, liberation of political prisoners, abolition of the death penalty, etc.), the government has gradually sunk into the crisis: it is flailing about, unable to solve the problems of inflation, unemployment, capital flight, the paralysis of investment, the decline of exports, etc. And so it gradually begins to manage the country in a way that a conservative government would have done. The bottom line is that the Socialist Party does not have a true politics of social transformation. It preoccupies itself with day-to-day problems and increasingly behaves like a classical party. Now, just a while ago, I asked you about the statutes of the PT, too formal, too rigid for my taste. But with the PS it's another thing! It's not only the statutes that are suffering from sclerosis! In the PT, you try, at the very least, to deal with the question of the autonomy of the diverse social classes and minorities that have associated themselves with the party's actions. Without a doubt, there are still some problems. Rest assured, I'm not idealizing the PT! But in France this type of problem is not even dealt with, or it only appears in campaign periods, when it's raised to lure votes. I know that the question of minorities and the marginalized is dealt with, in Brazil, in very different terms and on a much larger scale, to the point where actual parties confront themselves with the problem. But in France there also exist phenomena of social marginalization, of subjective minorities, with respect to increasingly large groups, and increasingly broad social categories. In the face of these questions, which are, in truth, at the center of the crisis, French society nods off in a dreadful conformism and dreams of its glorious past. In these most recent times, terrorist provocations have served as pretexts for the reappropriation of a worn-out theme, "security above all," and there is again talk of a "network of computerized control" of society, West-German style. I know very well that one cannot expect everything from a party, and that we can ascribe the present impasse, in large measure, to the international dimensions of the crisis. But everything is of a piece, and one cannot indefinitely dilute the responsibilities of a party that does not respond to the aspirations for change that voted it into power. If the socialists do not decide to modify their own mode of functioning as the party in power, their conception of intervention in the social field—or better, the glaring absence of any concrete perspective in this field—then it is clear that a feeling of dejection, an irreversible loss of confidence will eventually set in among the majority that brought them to power. And France would fall once again into the hands of the worst reactionary groups. In spite of the differences of context—which are always considerable, and moreover, obvious—I believe that certain social problems tend increasingly to traverse countries and even continents. For me, Solidarity in Poland, the PT in Brazil, are kinds of experiences on a grand scale that try to invent new instruments of understanding and collective struggle and even of a new sensibility and a new political and micropolitical logic. The conquests and failures of these experiences do not only concern Poland or Brazil, but all of those who, in different social conditions, run into the same kinds of organizational and bureaucratic dead ends, the same sclerosis… In truth, this is happening all over the surface of the planet on all social and individual levels, beginning with the most immediate level of language. I was sincerely fascinated when reading a collection of your interviews and speeches,[31] by the freedom of your tone, by your way, for example, of speaking of Ghandi, of Mao, of Castro or of Hitler, without any of the customary precautions, without clichés, and even risking some untimely considerations in what might be called an "imprudent" way. You don't seem to take into account that at times your proposals could be used against you, you seem to have an a priori confidence in the good faith of your interlocutors.

Lula: The great force, the best arm of the PT is precisely this: nondogmatism. Because dogmatism is the same throughout the world. For example, when I went to Italy, I participated in a meeting with the *Manifesto* group, and even there we could clearly perceive that the people are indoctrinated by their manuals. It's only subsequently that they get to practice. But we believe that practice should be strictly tied to theory. If not, it makes no sense. We are not interested in discussing theory if the people themselves are not disposed to discussing it. It's necessary to awaken their interest beforehand. It's obvious!

Guattari: In this respect, don't you have the impression that there are also a lot of militant, traditional, dogmatic components coexisting inside the PT? Could it be that the old sectarian groups that also invest in the PT are evolving toward your side?

Lula: The tendency is, above all, toward "dilution" inside the PT, without there being any "ideology police." The more numerous the workers are inside the PT, the less there will be a need for the survival of such tendencies.

Suely Rolnik: Certain worker candidates of the PT have great difficulties in mounting their campaigns, since they have less time and fewer material resources.

Lula: This is a very serious problem inside the Party. We have every interest in electing a maximum of worker candidates. But we have difficulties creating conditions that permit worker candidates to pursue a campaign similar to others. To this, you must add the fact that a lot of worker leaders, who could easily be elected deputies to the Parliament or state assemblies, were obliged to present their candidacies for senate and state gubernatorial offices. But in order to consolidate the legalization of the Party, it would be necessary to have the broadest possible base of candidates.

4

DESIRE AND HISTORY

PSYCHOANALYSIS AND ANALYSTS' ASSOCIATIONS

It seems to me that, at least for a considerable part of his life, Freud tried to avoid becoming a professional of psychoanalysis. Later, everything eventually declined into institutionalization and reductionist systems.

There are surprising things in Freud's thinking, full of a youthfulness and vitality that give off great whiffs of oxygen. But the way that psychoanalysts use his thinking makes one want to flee.

I am constantly repeating the same refrain: the practices of subjective production and the references to the cartographies related to those productions belong to the purview of assemblages that are always in the course of being destroyed and rebuilt, unmade and restored to operation. They do not belong to the purview of universal processes, which are those of a general mathematics of the unconscious, or to that of a specialized association of interpreters of the unconscious. The reappropriation of the processes of subjective singularization, the molecular revolutions against the production of capitalist subjectivity, on a certain level, also involve a questioning of such an association of psychoanalysts, in the same way as they involve a questioning of a certain kind of university training.

Meeting at the Freudian School of São Paulo, August 26, 1982:

Guattari: Before beginning, I'd like to know something about how the people in this group work—whether there are private consultations, whether it's institutional work—so that I can get my bearings to some extent.

Comment: Our work is specifically clinical. We are questioning what the effect of the transmission in psychoanalysis would be in clinical practice. Is it possible to operate psychoanalytically within an institution? If so, what kind of a group would institutionalize psychoanalysis? In fact, is it necessary to institutionalize psychoanalysis? Could the group assume the characteristics of a supposedly subject group in order, in its practice, to provoke some kind of questioning of the normal situations that perpetuate themselves in clinical practice (that is, bipersonal clinical practice)?

Guattari: This issue has been present ever since the creation of the Freudian School. For Lacan, it was a matter of placing the issue of analysis beyond any and every institutional phenomenon stratified in hierarchical modes, in modes of training and promotion. The ambiguity of this issue soon crystallized in an institutional form in the Freudian School. From the outset it was clear that there were two tendencies: those who considered that the teaching sector should be a specific sector of analysis, and those who wanted—at least formally and, incidentally, quite effectively—to create a section for the practical application of analysis in the field of institutions. It was soon realized that there was really no genuine communication, no true collective collaboration, between the different components of the school. Briefly, they constituted not so much two tendencies as three groups: a group of teaching analysts who had done their entire training and worked, until then, in the context of the old psychoanalytic institutions; a second group, for whom analysis was only one element in their practice and training, because they were also working in institutional sectors; and a third—academic—component, which in my view acquired undue importance over the course of time. The debate focused on the problem of teaching, which was extremely difficult to elucidate in terms of its real implications. The first axiom, which was that the analyst constituted his own authority to regard himself as an analyst, led to strange categorizations of the analysts in the school: members, practitioners, and after them, at the end of the line, the anonymous mass of those who were authorized by no one but themselves.

This wouldn't have had the slightest importance if it hadn't actually corresponded to a way of bringing about the persistence of a certain kind of conception of psychoanalysis, a certain kind of conception of training, a certain kind of intervention, especially in the field of schools, universities, and institutions. What may be even more important is the fact that this way of working has completely sterilized analytic research, basic theoretical research. The ideal system that Lacan had proposed (the "cartels") never functioned in this way, but in the way generally adopted by sectarian groups. The cartels were set up around one leader or another, and they debated power relations, which created a hierarchy, albeit a tacit one. It thus progressed from a formula that should have been one of a creative openness of analysis to a formula that we might call radical-socialist: everyone fending for himself, everyone doing what he wants in his own little corner. Positions as heterogeneous as those of Dolto, Mannoni, Leclaire, Oury, and others coexisted—at least twenty radically different positions could be instanced.

So, Lacan went on with his attempt at theoretical elaboration without, in my view, having considered the issue of analysis in fields that were not those of the original Freudian practice. No progress was made in the sense of understanding what the issue of analysis might be in analytic, university, or psychiatric institutions, in establishments for children, in social formations such as grassroots movements, political movements, and so on. The result of this inability to create new conditions of production is that the issue of analysis has now come to a very serious impasse. And yet the importance of this issue goes beyond the traditional field of psychoanalysis and even that of clinical practice. *The issue of the analysis of the formations of the unconscious has to do with basic questions such as the future of movements for social transformation.*

Debate at the Psychoanalysis School of the Sedes Sapientiae Institute, São Paulo, August 31, 1982:

Miriam Chnaiderman: I agree with the view that you have of psychoanalysis, provided that one thinks of it in terms of the historical process, the process of the foundation and the history of psychoanalysis—and not only psychoanalysis but also the world in which it takes its place. This is one of the many issues that we are considering. I know that in France you are also exploring this issue, but perhaps here things are less frozen than in Europe, perhaps they have a different aspect than there. I agree with what you say is happening in the history of psychoanalysis, but I believe that, basically, it's happening because of the power structures that have governed psychoanalysis. One of the questions that I ask myself, and that we consider here in the school, is: in what way can psychoanalysis be transmitted without once again succumbing to the same power structures that have characterized its history? Another question that

I ask myself is whether it might not be possible for psychoanalysis to become precisely that production of singularity and multiplicity of which you speak. Even to follow your proposal in *Anti-Oedipus* and go back to the conception of energy as it exists in Freud—and also to consider how much can be learned with novels, and with art and its processes of production.

Guattari: A word with regard to your point about the fact that, ultimately, all evil comes from the institutions, although everything is possible in terms of psychoanalysts as they are. I don't see any problem in the fact that there are social professions that consist in talking to someone, even for quite a long time, lying down on a couch, paying, and so on. There are many other professions just as surprising as this one. After all, this kind of profession, which consists in taking an interest in the discourse of another, permeates the social field as a whole. The way things are going, I don't see how one could imagine suppressing, overnight, the whole apparatus of what they conventionally call "social workers," all the people who work in the social production of subjectivity in one way or another—in fact, who doesn't work in it? Moreover, I have nothing against the fact that these people organize themselves to create unions, defend their standard of living, hold seminars, and exchange information about their practice. Fine. Or, rather, it's not "fine," but there's no other way. Nevertheless, this is precisely one more reason for questioning the particular position of these psychoanalysts, and of all these people who work with the production of subjectivity.

Currently, in establishments for children in France, we often find a paradoxical partnership consisting of an instructor and an analyst. The instructor, who spends all day on the front line with the children, working, playing, and discussing, is completely committed and yet is totally inhibited, and this is because he is under the imaginary tutelage of a psychoanalyst who, in turn, is hermetically sealed up in his consultation room. The psychoanalyst sees the children for half an hour a week at most, but even so he assumes the right to intervene in the group of instructors and say things like: "Be careful, you're upsetting the transference, it's best for you not to interfere with suggestions about these subjective issues." It's so effective that sometimes he doesn't even need to speak, because the instructors, the families, and everyone involved in this social reality become totally paralyzed as a result of the anguish and terror produced in them by the mere presence of the psychoanalyst, with his supposed knowledge. They say to themselves: "I haven't been psychoanalyzed, I don't know about psychoanalytic theory; if I dare to say or do anything, it may be really stupid!" On the basis of this mythical position embodied by the psychoanalyst, a complete hierarchy of knowledge and power is established, a kind of pyramid of modelization. It's obvious that I don't need to make a point of drawing your attention to the fact that this same pyramid exists in other forms throughout the social field.

What is important is not that psychoanalysts should make a break with their conception of practice, but that they should make a break with their conception of neutrality, their conception of the relation with the other, when the other is really someone who brings them something that is of the order of a certain contextualized set of problems. I'm referring to the fact that psychoanalysts say that they don't have to get involved with micropolitics, that they don't have to dirty their hands with the realities that confront them, that all they need is themselves. They're depositories of a science of the mathemes of the unconscious, which gives them quite enough work in their armchair, with the result that they leave the rest of the administration of the problems to the social workers, prison wardens, psychiatric nurses, and so on. In my view, they're simply reactionaries: they work systematically toward the consolidation of a certain production of subjectivity, and the more effective they are—they really are very effective—the scarier they are. They monopolize the field of the analysis of unconscious formations, when that issue is precisely one of the fundamental things that the whole social field should reappropriate.

In my view, cartographies made in attempts at collective expression, such as *candomblé*, or in poetic or literary expression should be considered as analytic cartographies in their own right. They have the good fortune that they can take their place outside the control grid of collective facilities. Analysts, for me, are people like Lautréamont, Kafka, Artaud, Joyce, Proust, and Borges.

Question: If we set out from this conception, we can no longer say that psychoanalysis or clinical practice in general are privileged places of analytic thought and practice.

Guattari: Of course not. Which is not synonymous with a condemnation of the métier of the psychotherapist or any other function of the social worker. It's as if I were asked whether we could consider poetry to be intrinsically linked to the profession of the literature teacher. I would say no. There might happen to be a literature teacher who is also a poet, but the relation is totally circumstantial. This doesn't condemn the profession of the literature teacher, but it totally separates the notion of poetry from that kind of profession and from the academic reference. It's the same with psychoanalysis.

Another approach to this question is to recognize that the "psy" professionals are in a position of strength to impede analytic processes. The analysts are the ones who "resist," in the sense that we might speak of the resistance during the war; it's a Society of Friends of the Resistance, a unionism of antianalytic resistance. I mean that if Freud discovered something of the nature of the unconscious in the individual and social field, he didn't simply find it in his head; it's clear that it was raised as an issue somewhere. And since then the unconscious problematics of subjectivity have not ceased to assert themselves in the political and social fields as a whole. In this context, it's terrifying to see the extent to which the analysts' associations participate in modes of cooptation. But not only them. Analysis has to do with a social arena that goes far beyond psychoanalysis itself. In this sense, for me, analysts are like journalists, like the media, like university teaching, which prevent analysis from taking place. In saying this, I think that I'm not far from some of Lacan's more violent formulations, in certain periods of his life (not in all periods, unfortunately), especially when he was founding and refounding schools and all that business.

Debate held by a branch of the PT in Rio de Janeiro, September 11, 1982:

Guattari: What is at work in psychoanalysis is really not restricted to the confines of the couch but also has to do with its existence as a very specific reference of elitist initiation. Psychoanalysis functions as a kind of religious or ideological reference that is present in the attempt to redefine social relations on all levels. I had constant discussions about precisely this aspect of psychoanalysis with a great friend, now no longer with us, Franco Basaglia. For him, in the Italian context, psychoanalysis was not of the slightest interest, and it wasn't even worth talking about. He would say: "Well, if certain idiots have money and time and want to get into it, that's their problem!" In my view, however, it's very important not only to discuss it, but also to observe how it's developing, because it is one of the elements—and not an insignificant one—of the apparatus of capitalist subjectivation, which does not function only in visible relations. Both the schools of psychoanalysis and the kind of relation established in psychoanalytic work bring into play models, abstract machines, and systems that go beyond the field of production of capitalistic subjectivity as a whole.

Question: Does psychoanalysis have this impact on all social classes?

Guattari: Yes. Of course I'm adopting a paradoxical position in order to be provocative. I know very well that people in *favelas* couldn't care less about psychoanalysis, Freud, or Lacan. But the abstract machines of subjectivation produced by psychoanalysis through the media, magazines, films, and so on are certainly also present in what takes place in the *favelas*.

PSYCHOANALYSIS AND REDUCTIONISM[1]

From what I have sensed of what is happening in Brazil, if I had the opportunity to propose that something should be added to the programs of transformation—a footnote, a supplementary topic in the PT's program, for example—I would suggest the *freedom of construction of new types of models relating to the analysis of the unconscious.*

The methodologies of modelization in the analytic field are an interesting theme for debate, and deserve some comment. The title for a debate on this theme might be "Psychoanalysis and Reductionism." We can try to trace, not the history of psychoanalysis, but its trajectory, as the trajectory of a long attempt at reduction. Familialism, that is, the reduction of the representation of the unconscious to a certain family triangle, is only one of the steps in this trajectory—the one on which most attention is generally focused. I think that the problem of reduction has been present since the birth of psychoanalysis, in what might be called the "first Freudian miracle," Freud's stroke of genius, which at the same time was a stroke of madness. It really does seem to be a kind of miracle, in the sense of the miracle of creation: a person utterly steeped in scientific, not to say scientistic, conceptions, who all of a sudden literally invented a new reading of subjective effects. While he was pursuing the steps of his training as a scientist, with a career basically focused on research in neurology, biology, and physiology, Freud abruptly entered a different kind of logic for dealing with psychic events, which until then had not been taken into account by the dominant means of representation. This paradox persisted in all his work: he never allowed his new method of reading entirely to take the place of his old concern, which I would describe succinctly as scientific reductionism. The two investigations went on in parallel throughout his whole life, but without maintaining the same relative importance.

For many years there was quite a radical dissociation. On the one hand, Freud carried out an entirely new reading of subjective phenomena: this is the case with his way of listening to hysteria, dreams, jokes, slips of the tongue, fantasies, and all the symptoms of the psychopathology of daily life. And he performed this listening in the spirit of a systemic collection of data, like an absolutely passionate exploration of new continents. On the other hand, he constructed a reference machine, a psychology, that he claimed to be scientific, and that he developed feverishly, especially in his dialogue with Fliess.

In all the works of this period—*The Interpretation of Dreams, Psychopathology of Everyday Life, Moses and Monotheism*, etc.—it can be seen that the work of capturing, collecting, and classifying the singularities of the unconscious is much more important than the work of theoretical elaboration. This does not mean that there were two velocities, with the theoretical maturation being slower. We could almost say that Freud's work consists of just a single piece, like Dionysus, born fully fashioned from Zeus's thigh.

We find these two tendencies in an extraordinarily elaborate text that you are certainly familiar with, "The Project for a Scientific Psychology." Firstly, there is an extremely ambitious claim to neurophysiological scientific status, with a theoretical schema not supported by any experimental investigation but based on the formulation of various promising, original hypotheses, which were later confirmed by neurology. Secondly, there is the construction of a psychic device, a highly elaborate representation of the psyche. This essay is one of the texts that Freud submitted to Fliess, who left them in a desk drawer, so that for many decades they were not known. In fact, that drawer probably contained the most essential aspects of Freud's work, which we see projected in his later theories. It's also likely that the problem of reductionism and familialism resides precisely in the distance that lies between the manuscript in the drawer and the exercise of a sensitivity, an openness, to the singularities in the fields that Freud considered.

How do psychoanalysts and psychologists deal with this distance between the theory in the drawer and the singularities that they encounter? Obviously, I don't mean that the theory should be thrown in the garbage. It is undoubtedly important that it is in the drawer—at any rate, the one place where it should not be is at the center of the analytic device. *I believe that theoretical elaborations in the field of psychoanalysis are ways of mapping the formations of the unconscious or the situations that render them present, from which one cannot make a schematic outline or a general theory.* We must always be ready to store our own cartographies in a drawer and invent new cartographies in the situation where we find ourselves. Basically, isn't that precisely what Freud did during the creative period that gave rise to psychoanalysis?

Thus, we can consider as the first figure of modelization the presence of an activity of creative interpretation of subjective facts, viewed from an entirely new angle, and, concomitantly, an attempt to control everything in a schema of interpretation that claims to be strict and rigorously scientific.

In what he called his "first topography," Freud organized the world of significances by assigning them to one of two containers: on the one hand, the Unconscious, and on the other, the Preconscious and the Conscious. Within the Unconscious we find a highly differentiated world of meanings, statements, images, and latent representations that simply depend on a particular logic: this is the so-called "primary process," which has a logic that is neither poorer nor richer than that of the secondary process, but simply different. For example, it conveys object representations that the logic of the secondary process cannot convey—at least, not in the same form; it has a way of staging negation that is utterly different than the logic of the secondary process, which is conscious and socialized—or rather, it does not know the negation that is operated by the dominant significances. It proceeds by displacement, condensation, overdetermination, hallucination, and so on.

On this level, Freud represents the diversity of all these nonsense items as being taken from a conflicting system that bars their access to consciousness and complete significance. Everything that tends to be sucked up by this vortex of nonsense, which Freud places in a general theory of sexual drives, begins to be described as a defensive conflict. As the nonsense world attempts to find its own consistency, it clashes with the representations of the Conscious, which constitute the dominant everyday significances. One agency, the one that represses, seeks to unbalance and restrain the mechanisms of this new logic. Analysis thus consists solely in a process of interpretation that will distinguish the latent meaning of the statements with which it is dealing, in order to remove the defensive conflicts that impede their access to consciousness. It essentially involves providing a status for producing the interpretation of facts that really only have a nonsense value for the dominant significance. It is as if

Freud needed to justify his way of creating meaning from nonsense effects, on the basis of his first theory of repression. But what is especially important is that it is a very rich and highly differentiated world. This period of Freud's theoretical elaboration is like a kind of discovery of a number of new worlds. The unconscious is still a teeming universe, a producer of new meanings and fantasmatic scripts that can be found in religion, art, childhood, ancient societies, and so on.

In Freud's "second topography," the unconscious-preconscious-conscious triad is replaced by the id-ego-superego triad, and the demarcation between these three specific modes of semiotization, these three processes, is no longer the same. *It is precisely the specificity of the primary processes that tends to be lost*: they now inhabit not only the id but also the ego, the superego, or the ego ideal. The dissolution of the unconscious is much more accentuated here. *The logic of the unconscious is dragged toward a kind of undifferentiated matter*, something that at the end of Freud's life was related purely and simply to chaos, a drive disorder, reified in the form of a death drive. A genetic perspective—the oral, anal, phallic, and other phases—gradually replaced the relation between the psychic agencies as different logical containers, different ways of semiotizing those realities. According to this new viewpoint, the psychic agencies are generated from one another in a general process of maturing and—why not say so?—of normalization. In other words, we have a kind of obstacle course that makes it possible to integrate the logic of the primary process, by successive steps, to the norms of the Ego, the norms of social values, the dominant norms. And this genetics of entry to the dominant significances—which, if all goes well, will lead to sublimation—participates in the actual assembly of the psyche. *What is the trajectory of psychoanalytic practices—the story of the institutionalization of psychoanalysis—if not this gradual reduction in the perception of the unconscious?*

The initial point of departure had been a logic of repression, which translated the expression of a conflict between heterogeneous modes of semiotics. Gradually a different mode of referencing became increasingly dominant, the mode of identification, where the same kind of drive modality is no longer at work. What establishes law, what establishes order, is no longer a conflicting relation between separate containers but a process of integration that, in the course of the history of psychoanalysis, uses different types of modelizing instruments.

The modelization that was to become increasingly dominant was that of the genetic reading, which made the nonsense of the unconscious enter a perspective of phases of integration to the social, a perspective of systems of imaginary identification known as "personological poles." Each phase was associated with a particular personological figure: a certain figure of the mother for the oral phase, a certain figure of domestic social control for the anal phase, a certain figure of integration to the world of paternal values with the Oedipal triangulation, a certain figure of submission to the dominant values with the castration complex and the period of latency. It is on the basis of this modelization that one sees the ability of the ego, the superego, and the ego ideal to give their supposedly truthful meaning to the primary processes, which, incidentally, gradually lose their consistency. And this does not take into account the phenomena of singularity of the unconscious, the raw material of psychoanalytic experience, which nevertheless remains highly differentiated.

But in this intermediate step there are still complete persons in a familial game, that is, in a real social game. Later, this modelization based on images (imagoes) is transformed. The poles of reference are no longer complete persons but the notion of an object, an object of desire, which replaces the notion of the object as developed in the first drive-based model. With the primacy of the

Oedipal triangle and the fact that all the basic issues revolve around the phallus and castration, the objects lose their imaginary dimensions in favor of a proto-structuralist conception of object relations. Everyone here knows Lacan's reaction to the orientation of psychoanalysis in the English-speaking world: it consisted in proposing a conception of the object as a function of a symbolic order, the so-called object "a." One is no longer dealing with real mothers and fathers on a fantasmatic stage, but with paternal functions, maternal functions, and so on, completely detached from the realities of the family. From the logic of the partial object, all that is highlighted is the kind of family and social relations implied in it. The primordial thing in the unconscious is not the relation with the father and the mother in specific situations, but the way in which prototypical relations are organized around these objects. This movement of "structuralization" of the unconscious does not stop here: soon we come to a general interpretive reference that, in principle, should allow a reading of all subjective phenomena, based on fixations on the mother's breast, based on a certain economy of the anal object present in the entire social field, based on a certain logic of the phallic object present in all the power relations that can be interpreted in the social field, and based on an ascetic submission to the logic of social modelizations. This general interpretive reference became a kind of mathematics of the unconscious. This phase was pretentiously surpassed by the movement of modern psychoanalysts, the contemporaries of Lacan. This time, the world of representations was itself to become only a world of signifiers, conceived in accordance with linguistic theories that reduce language to systems of distinctive oppositions. *The concept of libidinal energy was almost definitively eliminated.* Any reading of facts in the unconscious was referred back to a universal mathematics—what Lacan called "mathemes of the unconscious"—that constructed and produced all kinds of subjectivity.

Let's go back over this trajectory with the question of drive. The first topography begins to be simplified and undergo a reductionist treatment with the consolidation of the theory of drives, around 1905, with the publication of the *Three Contributions to the Theory of Sexuality*. The theory of drives considers that the different representations of the unconscious—of the multiplicity making up the unconscious—are under the control of a system of drives that is neither instinct nor representation in the sense of the psychologies of conscious perception. The drive system is an instrument that Freud invented in order to understand what happens in the unconscious. The system partly depends on the organism, through organic "sources" that exercise a "pressure" of energy. Freud maintained that this energy was of a particular nature, the "libido," which he distinguished from biological energy or from general psychic energy. It was in connection with this issue, incidentally, that the rift with Jung developed. The "goal" of a drive—its satisfaction—was sought by means of an "object."

I will not go on about the different stages of the system, but I would like to call attention to the fact that, when Freud transported this model of drives to the unconscious, and when he considered that behind the text of the dream, or symptom, or bungled action there was a drive-based conflict, a twofold operation took place: on the one hand, a category of biological, drive-based undifferentiation was introduced as a pure quantity of affect, and, on the other, the differentiation of meaning was transferred from the unconscious to the conscious and the preconscious. This operation has had a continuous development throughout the history of psychoanalysis. This history thus consists in increasingly setting aside the biological dimension of the source and pressure of a drive, utterly losing the notion of a goal, in favor of the notion of an object.

Now that the ground has been prepared, I feel ready to venture my own conjectures.

The reductionist problematics in all these processes should not be considered as totally aberrant or false, in my view. After all, all these modes of semiotization are supported by subjective stratifications: various figures of modelization produced both in psychoanalysis and in subjectivity in general. So, considering the process that led from the modelizations of the pioneers of psychoanalysis—the craziness and brilliance of Freud, Jung, and so on—to the current modelizations of psychoanalysis, with their alienating realities, the question I ask is this: if we want to understand this process, don't we have to carry out a reading of what the mutations of subjectivity were during that very period (given that considerable attempts at the modelization of subjectivity also took place in the social field during that period)? In other words, the perspective that I would like to suggest is that, instead of limiting our analysis to differences in doctrine, why don't we consider that we are dealing with different modes of cartography of the unconscious? *Instead of contrasting these different modes of cartography in terms of a certain coefficient of scientific quality, why not distinguish them in terms of their apprehension of a certain reality of semiotization—the reality that these modes of cartography confront?* For example, the way in which Aristotle read the political field, or Montesquieu read political and social realities, or Marx read the same realities—which, of course, were not the same—cannot be contrasted in the sense that some contain more truth or more reality than others. The ways in which Homer read the reality around him, or Dante, or Goethe, or Proust, cannot be set against each other as being marked by different coefficients of truth. All of these readings are absolutely true, because they correspond to a semiotization of realities that are themselves heterogeneous. Once psychoanalytic modelizations are considered as being of this nature, and not of the order of a supposed scientific reality that is present in all times and spaces, the question that arises has to do with trying to capture their articulation and the kind of mutation that their reference involves, assuming, also, that the problems of modelization remain completely open.

It is necessary to try to return to an original view, not of Freudism but of Freud's craziness and genius, a view that has more to do with President Schreber than with the virtuosity of contemporary psychoanalysis. It is necessary to propose a model of the unconscious that will enable us to apprehend better the articulation between these different modes of semiotization. This means an unconscious that is not reductionist, unlike the unconscious of the familialist conceptions of the early Freudian models of the unconscious, or the structuralist unconsciouses, which reduce everything to the semiotization of the signifier, or even the various formulas connected with the systemism in vogue in family therapy.

On another occasion I dared to propose a modelization, which this is not the appropriate place to set out in detail, a general cartography of the formations of the unconscious, a model of the unconscious, in which the various modes of semiotization could form connections between themselves. For example: possibly a topography could be proposed that, instead of functioning in accordance with a system that always comes down to a binary economy of subjective production, would have nine types of input at once, associating:

1) A certain conception of the first Freudian model of drives: the conceptions of drive energetics before they were drained of the problematics of the body and nonverbal energies.

2) A conception of modelization of an iconic nature. I think that there is a specificity in iconic components, despite what Barthes or the semioticians say. They always arrive at a conception that startles me: the economy of iconic semiotics is supposed to be dependent on the semiotics of language, because language can interpret them. This reasoning seems to be sheer sophistry. It is obvious that in animal ethology, for example, there is no economy of language, there is no linguistic discursiveness, and yet one finds the

presence of perfectly worked-out iconic semiotics, with their own way of functioning, without involving the discursiveness of the signifier at all. It is this same reasoning that informs the operation of the evacuation of the imaginary in Lacan, an imaginary that is preserved in Freud, with his distinction between word-presentation and thing-presentation.

3) A component of the order of what Pierre Janet called "automatisms of repetition."

4) A perception of the unconscious like that of Sartre, in his attempts to develop an existential psychoanalysis. It is the unconscious of *Nausea*: Sartre spoke about it a great deal, while constantly asserting, intrinsically, that nothing could be said about it with precision. One might consider that in this dimension there is a pure, nondiscursive memory of being: here, discursiveness turns back upon itself.

Of the same nature as this perception are the metaphors taken from Freud by Lacan, concerning the *fort-da*, the threshold of pure repetition, in the same way as Blanchot's "world of the unnamable" and Bonnefois's *arrière-pays*.

5) A much more structuralist conception of the unconscious, accentuating the signifier.

6) Productions of the unconscious that depend on more collective formations, as in the case of Jung's concept of "imago," or components of the unconscious having a systemic inscription, inherited from Bertalanfy,[2] which are currently being elucidated in the field of family therapy.

7) A modelization of the unconscious according to what I would call anagogical semiotics, in accordance with Sylberer's conception.[3] This conception corresponds in many respects to Jung's understanding of the unconscious. It is also a model that should restore specificity to the semiotic productions of archaic societies and to the mythological conceptions of subjective productions. In

such conceptions there is a whole economy of souls, of spirits, a whole apprehension by affect that does not involve discourse on a signifying level, yielding a knowledge of the universe that precedes any discursive process. Let's take the example of music: in a certain period of the history of music we have the semantics of oral music, the semantics of writing of all kinds, and the conjunction of the two universes: a machinic complex that associates a writing machine with machines of oral, instrumental, and melodic music. Even before any effective musical production is created, there is the delineation of a potentiality of polyphonic or harmonic universes. Even before two notes have been articulated, this universe is apprehended precisely with this character of affect, this character of perturbation that may even lead to madness, or else to inspiration, or simply to discovery. In other words, a universe emerges even before there is discursiveness.

8) A component that Deleuze and I call "capitalistic unconscious," which we might attribute to Metro Goldwin Mayer, for example, or to Sony—why not? It corresponds to the subjectivity produced by the media and by collective facilities in a general way, that is, the production of capitalistic subjectivity.

9) Lastly, for the time being, what Deleuze and I call "machinic unconscious," which raises the issue of the articulation of these other components, but does not treat it as a process of closure, of control of unconscious formations. On the contrary, it is a means of reading the unconscious—at least, when its production is possible. In other words, *the machinic unconscious corresponds to the assemblage of the productions of desire and, at the same time, to a way of mapping them.* The machinic unconscious is what seeks to produce subjective singularities. This means that *the formations of the unconscious do not derive from a* déjà-là *but are constructed, produced, and invented in processes of singularization.* Because these processes are found in a breach with the dominant

significances, they lead to micropolitical problematics: a way of trying to change the world and the dominant coordinates.

The fact that these nine components are associated with names of people is a touch of humor, but perhaps it is not so absurd. These people, these great fantasists, embody characters *bound up* with the specificity of something. Their error lay in having constructed a reductionist system, probably to prevent the coexistence of these various dimensions, and certainly to prevent that of many others which do not form part of this schema. At any rate, this schema is no more than a procedure for work and reflection. It serves as a support system, a system of questioning in order to know what we are dealing with. Take the example of an obsessive syndrome: very probably it is something that participates in two, three, four, or even nine of these dimensions, and not just in the conflict that operates in the personological registers. An obsessive syndrome is something that clearly operates on the level of a persistent repetition, that is, a desire for appropriation, a kind of eternal going back to apprehend the inapprehensible. I wash my hands in order to try to capture a sense of cleanliness, and I remain in an absolute *almost*. It is something that undoubtedly also brings into play a repetition compulsion, totally heterogeneous in relation to the behavior of washing one's hands. It is something that brings iconic representations into play. If I wash my hands in order to combat microbes it is because I have a representation of microbes, and because I believe that there really are microbes there, and not anything else. It is also something that can bring micropolitical strategies into play, involving familial or imaginary triangulations, and so on. It may also be something that brings factors of an objective unconscious into play on the level of abstract machines—for example, there is a threat from the world hanging over me that causes me to yield to this kind of symptom. There may be many other components in the consistency of an obsessive syndrome. In all this, what is important is to know at what point there are coefficients of semiotic efficiency; when something happens, at what points can we consider what happens as being linked to a particular praxis of assemblage.

I mentioned nine components of assemblage; others may rearrange them and produce eighteen, or thirty-six—or heaven knows how many dimensions—simply because the more complex the models become, the less risk they run of using systems of reference that crush the sensibility to what happens. Consider the Freudian models, for example: as they were gradually simplified in order to arrive at an Eros-Thanatos opposition, in some way they corresponded to a certain kind of reductionist practice. Or when we found ourselves thinking in terms of only one dimension—for example, that of the signifier/signified. It can even happen that one component in an assemblage may be in a position of primacy, but the schema requires us to be alert to the emergence of a question: what becomes of the other components?

I have no other ambition with the proposal of this general cartography of the formations of the unconscious.

THE INFRASTRUCTURE COMPLEX

Excerpts from Guattari's talk on "Semiotic Energetics" at the Cerisy Colloquium in France, June 1983:[4]

I am going to examine briefly certain effects that invalidate the importation of notions of thermodynamics by the human and social sciences.

Marx wished to undergird social relations with the flows of work, and Freud wished to undergird psychic life with the flows of sexual libido. (I shall leave aside the characterization that Freud makes of certain drives as nonsexual—the drives of self-preservation, or, in his last theoretical analysis, the death drive—because they are always, and essentially, instituted in a bipolarity relative to the sexual drives, by a kind of dualist energetics). Certainly, neither of them intended to establish a mechanistic causality between an energy base and social or mental superstructures. We know, however, that their theories provided a reinforcement for highly reductionist conceptions and practices! It is obvious that any comparison between their methods would be arbitrary, and more arbitrary still would be any conjecture about a possible influence of the former on the latter. However, perhaps we might wonder about a certain parallelism between the two, which I shall relate, on my own responsibility, to an "Infrastructure Complex," the evils of which were exercised in the social and human sciences as those sciences gradually established themselves in industrial societies. "Whatever field is considered, give us a base that can be described in terms of energy, and with it we shall construct a genuine science." It is on the basis of this kind of paradigm that an "entropic superego" was established, the main effect of which was to make those who were concerned about it incapable of perceiving a movement, a transformation, an alteration, or anything that could be experienced, without linking it to a common economy of energy, based on the two sacrosanct principles of thermodynamics.

We can represent this parasitic agency as a kind of epistemological crab stripping out the data on which it feeds, always following the same ceremony:

1) with one of its claws it sets aside, as a single, scientifically consumable reality, what it determines as being of the order of the energy capital in question; then it minces up this energy data to free it of any specific trait and give it a uniformly convertible character;

2) while with the other claw it reduces the data that resists its attempt at energization to a state of abstract equivalent, which results in Capital, Libido, Music, or Scientificity, for example; and then it produces a super-equivalent (or "capitalistic stew"), based on all these regional equivalents, so that all the intrinsic singularities and structures, all the representations and affects related to them, and, in extreme cases, all the energy processes themselves are totally dissolved and assimilated.

In its terminal phase—I am referring to structuralisms and systemisms—the disease of entropism can appear to evolve toward a remission by the spontaneous withdrawal of the Infrastructure Complex. Indeed, the traditional matter-form dualisms then seem to be superseded by the occurrence of a transfer of formalism, supposedly of the order of superstructures, toward infrastructural levels. Examples of these transfers: capital, in the labor process; the semiotic substance of drive—Freud's *Vorstellungsrepräsentanz*, reduced by Lacan to the state of a signifier—in the libido; or binary digits in computer flows. Note that the Marxists never really attempted to quantify capital in the economic sphere, and that the Freudians quickly placed the libido in the closet of religious relics, or, in various ways, "miraculated" it. Unfortunately, it is nothing like that: the focal point of the reductionism merely shifts toward a matter even more radically purged of its last specific traits for the benefit of an energetic *hyle*[5] assimilated to a flow of binary alternatives.

By postulating a radical separation between the production of subjectivity and semiotic efficiency, the monotheisms of energy, converted to the cult of information or the signifier, led to the risk of failing to consider the dimensions of singularity, "irreversibility,"[6] and "bifurcation"[7] of cognitive assemblages and, more generally, the relations of interdependence between the systemic givens and the structures of expression. This is probably what gives them the prominent position that they occupy in the megamachine of the production of culture, science, and subjectivity that now constitutes Integrated World Capitalism, which has the intention of only allowing the survival on this planet of those modes of expression and value that it can normalize and place at its own service.

What I do not like in the notion of energy as it is used by the social sciences is not, of course, energy as intensity. It is the way in which this notion is taken up, especially the metaphorical application of the second principle of thermodynamics, and of everything that revolves around the notion of entropy. This idea is present in psychoanalysis and in other fields, especially in information theory: it is an idea of a kind of undifferentiated infrastructure, an energy base that gradually creates disorder in the system. From this viewpoint, all operations that concern social life and the communication of affects consist in putting this disorder in order. Energy, drive, instinct, and desire are a kind of suspect, dangerous, terrifying world, which one should deal with like a lion tamer who enters a circus cage full of wild beasts.

Desire as chaos

It does not matter whether drives are directly related to instincts of an ethological type, or defined as drives developed much more from a semiotic viewpoint within the Freudian perspective, or determined in structuralist systems that situate the imaginary in relation to the symbolic, or even situated in relation to systems of coercion in systemism. In any of these cases, we always return to the same idea: necessarily setting this *raw* world of desire against a universe of social order, a universe of reason, judgment, ego, and so on. It is precisely this kind of opposition that we must reject, once we decide to consider the true components that create subjectivity. If there is something fundamentally new or fundamentally valid in Freudian phenomenology, at its origin, it is precisely the fact of having discovered that on the level of the supposed primary processes—whatever theories may have come later, in which Freud used energy categories of equivalence, like that of libido—we are always dealing with highly differentiated processes. The world of dreams, the world of madness, the semiotics of childhood, and the semiotics of so-called primitive societies have absolutely nothing that is undifferentiated. On the contrary, those worlds involve highly elaborate operations of assemblage, syntax, and modes of semiotization that do not necessarily imply the existence of meta-languages and overcoding in order to interpret, direct, normalize, and order them.

This area has immediate political and micropolitical impacts. In social emancipation movements, outside the traditional frameworks of organization, we find these Manichean models imported almost systematically (for example, the opposition between democratic centralism and spontaneism). I think there is a homeostasis between this debate on a political and social level and all the other theoretical references that exist in psychology, social psychology, psychoanalysis, etc. We always come back to the idea that there is necessarily a symbolic modelization, a primacy of well-ordered languages, well-differentiated modes of structure, which must necessarily assume and overcode a supposedly undifferentiated economy of desire and spontaneity.

Desire seems to be something fuzzy, rather nebulous and disorganized, a kind of raw force that needs to pass through the meshes of the symbolic and of castration according to psychoanalysis, or through the meshes of some kind of organization of democratic centralism according to other views—for example, people speak of "channeling" the energies of various social movements. One could enumerate an infinity of types of modelization, each proposing to discipline desire in its own field.

This notion of chaos always leaves me feeling constrained, because every time it is mentioned one is adopting the way of seeing of the dominant modelization. Even US sociologists who analyzed the reality of communication between the media and individuals perceived that it is definitely not a direct communication. It takes place through a whole network of what they call primary groups, with thoroughly grassroots filters of leadership, that can function either to accelerate the dominant system of modelization or to inhibit it. So the idea that there are central organs projecting over a chaos, an idea parallel to the various modes of theorization of drives, does not seem to me to be a good interpretive "grid." The fact that assemblages of enunciation do not have access to microphones, television, or newspapers does not automatically transform them into chaos.

In other words, the issue of the singular assemblages of enunciation does not emerge *ex nihilo* from a chaotic reality: there are thousands of outlines, thousands of catalyzing elements, highly differentiated and capable of being articulated to one another or being engaged in a creative process, or entering into phenomena of implosion, self-destruction, or microfascism—which, even then, does not transform them into chaos.

When I try to consider the problem of desire as a collective formation, it soon becomes clear that desire is not necessarily a secret or shameful affair as all the dominant psychology and morality maintain. Desire permeates the social field, both in immediate practice and in very ambitious projects. Because I do not wish to get caught up in complicated definitions, *I propose to denominate as desire all forms of the will to live, the will to create, the will to love, the will to invent another society, another perception of the world, and other value systems.* For the dominant modelization—what I call "capitalistic subjectivity"—this conception of desire is utterly utopian and anarchic. For this mode of dominant thinking it is OK to recognize that "life is very difficult, that there is a series of contradictions and difficulties," but its basic axiom is that desire can only be radically cut off from reality, and that there is always an inevitable choice between, on the one hand, a pleasure principle, a principle of desire, and, on the other, a reality principle, a principle of efficiency in the real. The problem is to find out whether there is not another way of seeing and practicing things, whether there are not ways of fabricating other realities, other references, which do not have this castrating position in relation to desire, which attributes a whole aura of shame to it, a whole kind of climate of culpabilization that creates a situation where desire can only insinuate and infiltrate itself secretly, always experienced clandestinely, in impotence and repression.

There is a theoretical issue that seems to me an important matter for reflection for all those who work in psychology, psychoanalysis, or social work in general. How do we consider desire? All the modes of elaboration of desire, and especially all the specific pragmatic modes of desire identify this subjective dimension as something of the order of an animal instinct, or a drive functioning according to semiotic modes that are totally heterogeneous in relation to those of social practice. We can refer both to the classical theories of psychoanalysis and to the structuralist theories—on this point, at least, it makes no difference. For any of these theories, "desire is OK, fine, it's very useful," but it has to fit into frameworks—ego frameworks, family frameworks, social frameworks, symbolic frameworks (it doesn't matter what we call them). And in order to achieve this there have to be certain procedures of initiation, castration, and ordering of drives.

For me, this is a highly questionable theory. In any dimension in which one considers desire, it is never an undifferentiated energy, it is never a function of disorder. There are no universals, there is no brutish essence of desire. *Desire is always the mode of production of something, desire is always the mode of construction of something.* That is why I think it is very important to dismantle this kind of theory. I am convinced that there is no process of genetic formation in children that leads to a maturation of a desiring economy. A child, however young, experiences a relation with the world and a relation with others in an extremely productive, creative manner. It is the modelization of the child's semiotics by the school that leads it to a kind of process of undifferentiation.

The dominant conception of social order implies a definition of desire (of collective formations of desire) that is fairly disastrous: as a flow that has to be disciplined, so that a law can be created to establish control over it. Even the sophisticated structuralist theories develop the premise that one must accept symbolic castration so that not only society but also speech itself and even the subject may be possible. I think that this conception of desire corresponds very well to a certain reality: it is desire as it is constructed and produced by Integrated World Capitalism. *It is IWC in its deterritorialization that produces this brutish figure of desire.* In any case, this image is not appropriate, because the animal economy of desire also does not correspond to this model. One has only to read a little of what the ethologists have said to see that instinct, drive, or desire—the name is not important—in the animal kingdom has nothing to do with a raw drive. On the contrary, it corresponds to highly elaborate modes of semiotization, forms of micropolitics of space and interrelations between animals, involving a whole strategy and even, according to the ethologists, a certain aesthetic economy.

In which case, this opposition—on the one hand, desire-drive, desire-disorder, desire-death, desire-aggression, and, on the other, symbolic interaction, power centralized in state functions—seems to me an utterly reactionary reference. It is quite conceivable that a different kind of society could be organized, one that would preserve processes of singularization in the order of desire, without entailing total confusion at the scale of production and society, and without entailing generalized violence and an inability on the part of humanity to manage life. Rather, it is the production of capitalistic subjectivity—which leads to incredible devastations at an ecological and social level throughout the planet—that constitutes a considerable factor of disorder, and that can lead us to absolutely definitive catastrophes.

Critique of the idea of conflict

Debate at the Psychoanalysis School of the Sedes Sapientiae Institute, São Paulo, August 31, 1982:

Miriam Chnaiderman: If psychoanalysis is considered as being a process of production of subjectivity, I wonder whether it may not also be a producer of singularity and multiplicity, once we reassume the notion of conflict as central.

Guattari: I think not. I believe that Freud's modes of reference, which have to do with psychic conflict, introduce notions of energy that are not compatible with the reality of the semiotic processes in question. Therefore, the need that arises is to articulate models of understanding of this production of subjectivity that broadly get away from all the metaphors of thermodynamics. Those metaphors do nothing but introduce categories of determination, and levels of drive infrastructure and representative superstructure that prevent all understanding of what the processes of singularization are.

How can we approach the occurrences of singularity that we find in neurosis or dreams, in collective formations of the unconscious? How can we propose a mode of cartography that is not committed to these theoretical references and these reductionist practices? The question arises at the very level on which Freud establishes his concept of the unconscious. The unconscious results from a conflict that involves a dynamic opposition: one thing is repelled by another and at the same time attracted, toward the primary system of identification, for example. This dynamic vector, which is associated with every kind of energy metaphor—investments, libido, pressure, and so on—participates in the same subjective entity: it is the individual who has a repressing agency—from the viewpoint of the first or the second topography, or the structuralist viewpoint—and it is the individual who has an unconscious marked by his history, fixations, etc. In the approach that I am suggesting, it is precisely this subjective unity that does not exist. The notion of assemblage that I propose as a replacement for Freud's psychic agencies does not correspond either to an individual entity or to a predetermined social entity.

Meeting at the Freudian School of São Paulo, August 26, 1982:

Guattari: In my view, the phenomena that psychoanalysis treats in terms of conflict cannot be apprehended in that way. Take the example of the notion of repression: it is a procedure of semiotization—of oneiric, fantasmatic, or symptomatic assemblage, of paraphraxis or similar things—in conflict, which creates this dynamic of repression. The conflict may be of a topographical nature (in the first topography, between Unconscious, Preconscious and Consciousness), or of a drive-based nature (oral drive, anal drive, sexual drive, symbolic drive, etc.), or even of the nature of personological conflicts of Oedipal triangulation (identification, etc.). Or none of those things.

An enlightening example is that of the dream. In the experience of dreaming, everyone goes through successive "grids" of reading that are increasingly reductionist. The problem arises in terms of assemblage of enunciation and not of interpretation. There are at least two, three, or four phases in this experience, two, three, or four assemblages taking place. In the first phase, which I call the "phase of oneiric semiotization as such," we have a certain assemblage of enunciation that is characterized by not belonging to the space-time coordinates that we work with in society. Let's call it "assemblage A." Note that this semiotization is not necessarily individuated: in the experience of dreaming we often perceive that we can be many characters at the same time, passing from one to another in a kind of chain. We wake up and go on to the second assemblage, which I shall call "B," in which there is a return to the semiotic material of level A. We note that the transition from one assemblage to another is organized in accordance with a kind of phenomenon of general compression of semiotic coordinates. This infinitely rich and differentiated world, in which we were still immersed just a second ago, this kind of phenomenon of implosion, loses its pseudodiscursive richness with each passing second and is gradually drained of substance. It is as if it were the expanding universe, some fragments of which may be preserved while other elements may be forgotten and afterwards remembered and noted down. A third assemblage takes place here, that of recalling. We are surprised to find that the few elements of the complexity of the dream that we can preserve are revealed to be extremely rich in themselves. It is precisely here that Freud's discovery of the interpretation of dreams is situated: a small semiotic nonsense phenomenon may play the part of a semantic nucleus that will function as a pole of attraction, by association of very diverse lines. On level B we had a phenomenon of expansion and expulsion of meanings, whereas on this third level we have a kind of phenomenon of attraction, contraction and concatenation of meanings. Oral enunciation for an interlocutor in a specific situation—for example, recounting a dream to one's wife at breakfast—constitutes a fourth assemblage. Here, a whole series of affects, feelings, and impressions are left aside. Yet another enunciation, different than this one, might be directed to a psychoanalyst. It is as if it were not the same dream: another assemblage, another material of expression. We could invent further assemblages of enunciation, further constellations of universe, always setting out from the simple element of singularity that is constituted by the semiotic production of a dream. For example, we can use it in the writing of a novel, or even in another dream, in which we might have a feeling of *déjà rêvé*, of having had the same dream before, and so on. However, it is not a question of interpretation here: these different modes of semiotization are not arranged in a relation of conflict or repression between a supposed latent meaning and a manifest meaning. *There is no deformed latent meaning, no true meaning awaiting an interpretation that will lay it bare. No system of significance has primacy over the others.* Assemblage A is just as true as B, or C, or D. They are simply not of the nature of a single system of semiotization. In the transition from one to another, what takes place is a rupture of assemblage. It is a matter of discovering the differences at work in the various systems of semiotization, and not reducing one to another—for example, not considering assemblage E, the enunciation to the psychoanalyst, as being the one that illuminates the truth in all the others. I would say that *the truth, here, becomes merely functional.* What purpose does dreaming serve on level A? What is the point of telling my dream at breakfast? What does telling the dream to the psychoanalyst generate in terms of productivity or nonproductivity?

Without wishing to go on with this example, I would nevertheless like to emphasize the fact that the perspective that situates the issue of the unconscious in the enunciations and not in the statements—or, to be more precise, in the assemblages of enunciation—is something that, at the very least, enables us to economize on dualisms, of the "manifest and latent content" type, and also of the "taking control of significances" type, whether by the ego or by an interpreting psychoanalyst.

This problem, which is already quite complicated in the example of the dream, becomes even more complicated in the case of other psychic objects, such as contexts of social reality, or artistic productivity. In these cases, the differentiation between assemblages is even more blatant. In the example of the dream we have only three characters: the ego of awakening, the interlocutor at breakfast, and perhaps the psychoanalyst. In other systems of assemblages we have complex institutions, work facilities, facilities for the modelization of meanings, and machine systems. Significations—speech or writing—are less and less restricted to the space of the relation between individuals, and more and more mediated by machinic systems, not only explicit (a tape recorder, for example), but also invisible (behavior patterns, references, identification machines—in other words, a whole series of elements of social significance that direct ideas and attitudes literally by remote control). In other words, all modes of production of subjectivity are involved in an assemblage of enunciation, whatever level we may be on: small groups, institutions, or vast national linguistic sectors. The unconscious is considered here as a singular production of statements, affects, and sensibility, always resulting from the intersection of different assemblages. An example of this is the nucleus of intensive singularity that emerged in the dream just now, and that took shape in various registers of expression: assemblages A, B, C, and D.

Renato Mezan: You say that it is not a question of conflict but of a rupture of assemblage. What if we fantasized a bit and suggested, in very Freudian fashion, that there is a conflict at each level of rupture of assemblage? For example, you wake up and write down your dream; a little later, it reappears in another register—for example, speech. You tell the dream to your wife—which, of course, does not happen without arousing effects and affects—and you have the impression that you have lost an important part of the dream. Then you tell it to your psychoanalyst, and so on. I don't see the point of treating these situations in terms of transformations as you do.

Guattari: Of course, and I have nothing against it working in that way… but with one proviso: thinking in terms of conflict implies problematics of energy transfer, dynamics, etc. My idea is this: when I apparently replace one symptom with another—I have a stomachache and later, finally, it goes away, and I travel, and I fall in love, and so on—there is no continuum of the order of displacements of affect as a quantity of energy of a Freudian type. *What happens is that there are blocks of possible that replace one another as such: each new constellation of universes creates a new block of possible, without any character of continuity.* That is why I reject the issue of conflict: there is no conflict, and there is no continuum; there is simply the mutation of a kind of possible which does not take place gradually, progressively—by induction, transfer, displacement, or multiple determination, that is, by an economy of primary processes. Really, another constellation of possibles is created at one fell swoop. From a phenomenological viewpoint, it seems to me that this is a better way of apprehending these phenomena of rupture. These phenomena are the creation of new fields of the possible, and this does not take place dialectically in relation to other fields of the possible: they coexist. There is always the possibility of somatization, there is always the possibility of falling into the same black holes: *one is never cured of anything*; there are no dialectical displacements. We are always everything all at the same time: awake, conscious, in love, ambivalent, and so on. And it is not a question of a conflictive ambivalence, but of the fact that all these constellations take shape simultaneously on this level. This is the only important aspect in what I'm saying. It seems to me that the dynamic, economic treatment of subjective problematics doesn't allow us to apprehend the character of rupture and overall unfolding of a whole field of possibilities. In this context, the notion of sublimation becomes absolutely incomprehensible—and anyway, no one talks about it any longer. Nevertheless, we are well aware of the phenomenological reality to which it refers: phenomena of abrupt rupture that are not merely of the order of Freudian sublimation, but of the order of a change of constellation of universes (a state of watchfulness, a state of sleep, a state of delirium, a drugged state), or simply of the order of a change of subjectivation (talking in a group, talking on one's own, typing, driving a car). It's clear that it isn't the same kind of affect, the same kind of articulation of substance of expression, or form of expression, that we bring into play each time. There is no principle of constancy: each time, a different assemblage is created.

Well, if I insist so much on the difference between these conceptions of how the relation between assemblages functions, it is because they also imply a difference of position with regard to capitalistic flows. What I mean is that the idea of conflict is inseparable from the establishment of capitalistic flows as a general translatability of all possible, imaginable languages, as a general equivalent for economic, libidinal, or semiotic orders, and so on. However, it's obvious that thinking that the relation between assemblages might be of another nature doesn't make what is implicit in the idea of conflict disappear. But at the same time—and this is what is important—the existential semiotics retain their potential. We go on in the same archaic societies. We go on with the same kinds of problematics.

Interpretation: the analyst and the pianist

We saw how the expressive singularity that emerges in the dream occurs in various registers of expression. And I suggested that, in my view, none of them is an interpreter of the others. It's just like a musical note in symphonic expression: it can exist simultaneously in the registers of rhythm, melodic construction, harmonic construction and counterpoint, and in a wide variety of instrumental registers. In the case of music, it's clear that it doesn't make sense to say that certain singular concatenations of notes, which specifically pertain to one of these levels, provide a general interpretation of the other levels. The musical notes do not belong to the piano, even if they are played on the piano, but to the melody, and to the intention of the musical universe that is proposed. Musicians nowadays understand that music does not consist in simply repeating notes, that the referent does not just reside in the musical text, but resides in the production of a movement of expression, which is called interpretation. If psychoanalysts' interpretation took on the same meaning that the word has for musicians, I would stop ragging on interpretation—and I would stop ragging on psychoanalysts.

With a dream, the problem that arises is not the interpretation that is made of it, whether by a qualified psychoanalyst or not. *The problem is how the dream will be interpreted in the assemblages that are triggered off.* These assemblages do not necessarily involve two people—one on the couch and the other in the armchair. The assemblages that are triggered off may belong to the sphere of the family or household, or to a relation with space, an ethological relation, or even a power relation conveyed by a whole series of micropolitical problematics. The statement that appears in it may find its concatenation in the power relation between the wife and the place where she works, for example, or the system of values in which she participates.

Interpretation, for me, is not the manipulation of a signifier-key that solves some kind of matheme of the unconscious. *It is primarily work that consists in situating the various systems of reference of the person before us, with his family problem, his conjugal, professional, or aesthetic problem, or whatever.* I say "work" because these systems are present, but not in an ordered collection. They lack functional articulations—what I call the "elements of passage"—which suddenly cause other coordinates of existence to emerge, making it possible to find a way out. *Slips of the tongue, bungled actions, and symptoms are like birds that come and tap their beaks on the window. It is not a question of "interpreting" them. It is a question of situating their trajectory to see whether they are in a position to serve as indicators of new universes of reference that could acquire sufficient consistency to bring about a radical change in the situation.*

I will give a personal example: I consider poetry to be one of the most important components of human existence, not so much in terms of value, but rather as a functional element. *We should prescribe poetry in the same way that vitamins are prescribed.* "Be careful, buddy, at your age, if you don't take poetry, you won't find things easy." Nevertheless, although poetry is very important for me, it only rarely happens that I read or write a poem. Not because I lack the opportunity to do so, but because the opportunity slips through my fingers, and then I say to myself: this time it didn't work out. With music, it's the same thing: it's also fundamental, but I can go for weeks and forget that it exists.

It's partly on this basis that I manage my strategies. What is one to do, in a particular context, with a particular person or group, in order to have the most creative relation possible with the situation that one is experiencing—like a musician with his music, or a painter with his painting? A cure would be like constructing a work of art, with the difference that each time it would be necessary to reinvent the form of art that one uses.

A little prescription, in passing. Someone who really "shook me up" when I was twenty years old and was fairly lost was Oury. I had explained my crises of anguish to him in detail on various occasions, without appearing to have moved him. Until one day he gave me this Zen response. "Does it happen at night before you go to sleep? What side do you sleep on? The right side? Good, then just turn over onto the other side!" Analysis is like that sometimes: just turn over. One needs to rediscover the humility of the early days of the Church and say to oneself: "Be patient, it doesn't matter. Inshallah!" It's a bit elementary. Obviously one can't say this just any old how. It's also important to have the right semiotic tablets at hand. It's precisely these small indicators that cause significances to break down, giving them an asignifying scope, and also making it possible for all this to function with humor and surprise. A drugged guy with a gun in his hand, and you ask him: "Do you have a light?" Then the moment merges with the world. It's in this register that one can find the poetic category of performances, the music of John Cage, Zen ruptures, or whatever one calls them. The acquisition is never definitive. It's necessary to learn to juggle, to play scales: a certain control is acquired in relation to some situations but not others, and then it changes with age, and so on. One of the biggest pieces of nonsense in the psychoanalytic myth is thinking that, just because you spent ten years on the couch, you're stronger than other people! It's not true at all. *Analysis should simply give you a "plus" of virtuosity, like a pianist, for certain difficulties. That is, being more prepared, having more humor, being more open to jump from one frame of reference to another.*

Debate at the Psychoanalysis School of the Sedes Sapientiae Institute, São Paulo, August 31, 1982

Antonio Lancetti: You make it clear that psychoanalysis, with its interpretation that makes the symbolic order absolute, functions as a reactionary, overcoding practice. I agree. If I understand correctly, you also say that it isn't a question of interpreting desire. Here, I have two questions. Doesn't that also constitute a kind of absolutism? And is it no longer possible to intervene in an analytic sense—in other words, is the work of transformation in the field of desire no longer possible?

Guattari: We're always revolving around the same difficulty. It isn't possible to try to make a general criticism of models without running the risk of lapsing into another kind of modelization, with the same oppressive function. Let's take a specific example, which may allow us to advance in terms of the issue that you raise: the contemporary concept of interpretation in psychoanalysis. I imagine that there are no virulent Lacanians in this room, or else they would already have stood up to remind me that Lacanian concepts and the current psychoanalytic practice of interpretation are not at all modelizing. In a way, they would be right: for the structuralists the essence of interpretation comes down, purely and simply, to compressing all productions of statement with an area of silence. Their theoretical conception and their practice consist in systematically conducting a kind of draining of every phenomenon of meaning. With the shameful practice of short sessions, and with the shameful practice of maintaining a silence that can go on for years or even decades, we are faced with a kind of paradox of semiotic communication: in the input, a multiplicity of statements, and in the output, those statements have been completely drained of their semantic and pragmatic implications.

This interpretation by reducing statements to nonsense does not mean an absence of modelization; on the contrary, it is the height of modelization, and specifically of capitalistic modelization. For isn't that what the capitalistic mode of production does in relation to everything that is of the nature of a system of meaning? Every phenomenon of production of sense or meaning is related to a general equivalent of non-sense, a generalized exchange value. This drains away the content of all values of desire, all use values, and then reappropriates subjective productions, or reterritorializes them in a well-controlled grid of production relations. Seen from this viewpoint, psychoanalysis produced an unprecedented model of power. A power not expressed, from outside to inside, by material means of coercion, nor by the imposition or suggestion of a content of significances, but by the mere creation of the kind of sado-masochistic situation that I have just described.

So, for me, it's inconceivable, incomprehensible, inadmissible or whatever to claim to give scientific value to a practice of this kind. On the contrary, it's something that corresponds to a basic micropolitical act: an attempted neutralization of subjective potentials, of which one might say that it only concerns those who submit to this kind of practice, or those who can afford to pay for this kind of practice, or even those who implicitly postulate the dominion of this kind of practice. But it's not true. This kind of production of interpretation through nonsense does not merely concern specialized milieus, at least in European countries. It is an attempted modelization that tends to be highly valued by a system of social promotion in various fields (psychiatry, mental health, the university, and so on). Psychoanalysis is, in a way, a kind of education for the elite, just as learning to play the piano used to be for young girls from good families. There was also a time when leaders had to go through the National School of Administration (ENA), but now we are entering an era in which anyone in a position of leadership, in a position to become a business director or an executive in any social field, has to be capable of being at the entryway of multiple, highly differentiated processes of semiotization, involving infernal micropolitical problematics; and at the same time he has to be capable of constantly responding to this kind of generalized but microscopic and inapprehensible distance. In this kind of practice, psychoanalysis, in a way, trains the eye of the bureaucrats, the eye of the technocrats—in other words, the eye of all the hierarchies that do not claim to have their pragmatic point of support limited to the register of effectiveness, and whose own subjectivity tends to be reduced tangentially to zero. Psychoanalytic neutrality corresponds to an ideal in the social field of the dominant classes. In a certain sense, paradoxically for this ideology of draining by means of nonsense—which generates theoretical formulations that are sometimes highly sophisticated and virtually inaccessible—psychoanalysis constitutes a kind of laboratory of the more sophisticated forms of subjectivity, a laboratory of a certain conception of the social field.

What all this comes down to is that everything that is of the nature of interpretation, neutrality, and transference, as practiced today by psychoanalysis, really constitutes major micropolitical interventions.

It is clear that one must use the concept of the signifier, as long as it is perfectly placed in relation to other modes of semiotization, other semiotic components. However, everything that has been built up around the Freudian unconscious—especially as redefined in structuralism by Lacan—consists precisely in not considering other modes of semiotic efficiency, and placing them, a priori, outside the field of psychoanalysis. I consider this position to be completely reductionist. Who was it who said that, from a Freudian viewpoint, the notion of the interpretation of the domain of verbal intervention is very separate from other modes of intervention? It seems to me utterly fictitious to think that there may be an effectiveness of signifying interpretation that is not linked to other levels of semiotic efficiency. We can find a functioning of relations on levels of iconic, spatial, or economic semiotics—in other words, on a whole series of qualitative levels that are not directly within the scope of discursive systems of the signifier. This means that the issues that are raised specifically in connection with interpretation, whatever it may be, are always the following: Is it effective or not? What was effective and what was not? In other words, what actually intervened to change a mode of subjectivation or not change it?

This leads me directly to consideration of the practice of analysis. I think it is necessary to disassociate the theoretical differences of analysts completely from an appreciation of the assemblages that they put into operation in their practice. This observation is of a very general nature: it applies equally to family therapists or to those who have other theoretical references. Through these practices, some components operate that are not within the competence of signifying semiotics. And precisely because these components are not recognized in that other status of semiotic functioning of "encoding," they acquire even greater importance. One has only to think of the rituals, the session etiquette, the rationalizations about the problematics of money, the refusal to consider family and social interactions—all the very elements that operate as pragmatic components, defining the status of the statements produced in a session. In other words, there are really some inputs of vectors (political, social, machinic, cultural—although one would have to redefine the term "culture") that are intrinsically bound up with the processes of analysis.

Informal conversation in Recife, September 16, 1982

Question: In your view, could we consider the analytic as an expression of a process of singularization?

Guattari: I agree, but with a small difference in terminology. I don't think that we should confuse an analytic process with its expression, if we want to avoid repeating precisely what separated Freudism from Freud's initial intuition, which was that of the primary process as a bottomless abyss from the viewpoint of the understanding that one can gather from it. In Freud, there is an almost schizophrenic investigation of what Dora's discourse signifies; at the same time, what he might say or explain about it, for himself or for Fliess, collapses. What he managed to say was: "Well, let's put all this on one side for now, and come back to it if need be." So I don't think that there is a problem of expression here. The processes of expression, if they can be described thus, are already the expression of the process, whereas, from an immanent viewpoint, the processes are, in themselves, creativity, machinic mutation, always capable either of reincorporating the process of expression, or of being crushed in it, becoming stratified in it, being captured by systems of redundancy.

Question: So the analytic is the actual process of mutation, the exercise of the process.

Guattari: For me, the analytic is the process, the machinic process as such. On the other hand, the articulation of a process with systems of expression can be of the greatest importance. That's what distinguishes my ideas completely from any kind of spontaneism, from all Reichian reductions in relation to expression of desire.

Question: Do you mean that the articulation of these processes of singularization with the dominant system of expression can involve the mutation of the system?

Guattari: That's one of the possible figures, in the sense that there is no absolute level of singularity, no absolute level of process, of stratification. Nowadays, what constitutes a process can be transformed into a reified stratum in the twinkling of an eye; what constitutes a reified structure can change and engender a process of mutation of history; it's necessary to exercise a logic that gets away from sociological categories, from divisions between the individual, the microsocial, and the macrosocial.

Question: Doesn't the idea of an "analytic act" clash with your definition of the analytic in terms of its processual character?

Guattari: Yes. However, I'm very mistrustful of the notion of an act, because it introduces a cut between a field of the act and a field of non-act, an undifferentiated field, which an act comes and animates, overcodes, organizes, and orders. So I prefer the notion of assemblage, instead of the notion of an act. The notion of assemblage can comprise:

> 1) movements of flows of any kind, which are not of the nature of an act (demographic flows, flows of blood, milk, hormones, electricity, or whatever);
> 2) territorial dimensions, which are even a certain kind of act, but an act of protection, circumscription, or subjectivation that seeks to situate itself as such;
> 3) processual dimensions, machinic dimensions, which do indeed belong to the register of an act;
> 4) dimensions of universes that, on the contrary, are absolutely not of the nature of some kind of will—a processual will,

or a will for territorialization—but are a kind of encounter with other dimensions of existence. The discovery of love, aesthetic discovery, or the discovery of new fields of the possible don't belong to the register of an act. Here we might also refer to Kierkegaard or Pascal: it has to do with the givens, whether something happens or not. It belongs to the domain of grace: you can cling as much as you want to your prayers, or your voluntarism of transformation—and in this the analysts, like everyone else, must be utterly modest—either it happens or it doesn't. At the end of his life, Freud perceived this perfectly. In "Analysis Terminable and Interminable,"[8] we feel that he's questioning what happens, after all, at the end of an analysis.

Question: From this viewpoint, the term "analytic intervention" also becomes problematic.

Guattari: You have to understand that these words were very worn and spent. It was I who carelessly launched the term "institutional analysis," and also "analyzer," "transversality," and so on, which became dainty tidbits for many university professors, psychiatrists, and psychosociologists. They swiftly coopted it all, translating it in terms of psychosociological intervention: there are Institutional Analysis groups that are contracted by big companies to carry out something equivalent to a Japanization of the working class. So it ended up leading to doctrines of intervention, specialists, and specialized institutional bodies.

When I speak of assemblage, it's not exactly an act, and it's not exactly an intervention, which doesn't mean that it may not involve them. It may involve them or not. As I see it, analysis has to assess relations of pure semiotic discernment—without an act, without an intervention—a relation with the quality of things, with the rhythms of time; and then we can also include the relation with voluntary acts, with interventions that are based on complex apparatuses. Analysis also has to assess the relation with the arrival of abstract machinisms, mutations of universes that completely alter the conditions of any perception, any act, or any intervention. For example, the mutation that is now pervading the whole of Poland does not come merely from a sum total of acts, interventions, or religious relations. It's really a change of coordinates of universe. It's a different Poland. This is what causes the same acts, the same words, and the same phrases to change their meaning and pragmatic scope completely, because we are simply no longer in the same world.

Basically, there are generally two attitudes in relation to other levels of semiotic efficiency. The first considers that they are outside the field, constituting a supposedly "extraanalytic" field, and that, to that extent, they do not make any kind of break with the specificity of the transference and the psychoanalytic interpretation. That is the traditional analytic position. The second attitude considers that these other levels can only be articulated by means of a theory of the signifier that would embrace them all. In the first case we have a stratified segmentary conception of practice and the analytic system of reference. In the second case we have a general reductionist conception, with what I believe to be deeply reactionary implications.

The question with dissident or minority discourses is not whether or not they are the basis of an unrevealed truth. We can imagine minority groups—for example, feminist or homosexual groups—which, in a certain context, present a thoroughly ossified discourse, a distant discourse, based on a truth that is only constructed on the level of Logos; and they may even use psychoanalysis, which, in such a context, as a result of not obeying the traditional rules, is even more repressive. Let's imagine that they are also producing modes of operation that recall traditional sectarian groups. Well, even so, these groups might be performing a certain function in processes of molecular revolution. What is at work, in this case, is not a position of discourse of the order of the production of an unrevealed truth, but a processual issue that engages mutations in the unconscious social field, at a level before or beyond the discourse of the groups considered.

Consequently, the problem immediately shifts. Even so, we may ask ourselves whether another latent discourse is not being conveyed, but one introduced by groups that are not the ones we are considering. At this point we come to an issue raised by the structuralist movement in psychoanalysis, in particular by Lacanism: is there a metalanguage of language which is basically that of the unconscious?

Is the unconscious structured like a language? Behind the language articulated by individuals and groups, do we have to find another language that is the founder of subjectivity? The fact that one may say that this other language is not really linguistic, when what is being invented is a category of signifier inherited from a certain linguistic period, is quite another question. The fact that, in his last formulations, Lacan spoke of mathemes of the unconscious, in a way that refers much more to a kind of mathematics than a linguistics of the unconscious, does not change much in relation to the issue that I want to consider. Let's go back to the example of a feminist or homosexual group which, despite functioning like a sectarian group, is articulating processes of molecular revolution. Would it be sufficient, in this case, to say that this kind of ossified group is not intervening in the field of language, because it is not introducing structural modifications in the social field? This perspective adapts itself both to sociological structuralism and to linguistic structuralism: the theory of the Lacanian signifier would be sufficient to establish a bridge between the two.

The issue that I am raising is of a totally different nature. It does not allow the establishment of that kind of bridge. It does not seek structural equivalences between different levels, but possibilities of reading the articulations between them. *We are no longer on the level of representation but on the level of production: the level of collective, individuated, or machinic subjective production, which has to do with modes of expression that involve both language and the most varied semiotics.* So, ultimately, what is it about? Certainly not about elaborating a kind of interstructural general referent that reduces all the specific structural levels to a general structure of signifier of the unconscious. It is about performing an operation that is precisely the opposite, one that, despite the systems of structural equivalence and translatability, impacts on the points of singularity and processes of singularization that are the real productive roots of subjectivity in its plurality.

If there is an interpretation to be made based on an analysis of the unconscious, it consists in detecting the outlines, indicators, and crystals of molecular productivity. If there is a micropolitics to be practiced, it consists in ensuring that these molecular levels do not always succumb to systems that coopt them, systems of neutralization, or processes of implosion or self-destruction. It consists in apprehending how other assemblages of the production of life, the production of art, or the production of whatever you want might find their full expansion, so that the problematics of power find a response. This certainly involves modes of response of a new kind.

Basically, there are two possible attitudes to the outbursts of these youngsters against the university.[9] And each of these attitudes illustrates a kind of definition of the unconscious. The first consists in saying that there is something in them, in their past, in some cranny of their complex or wherever, that is creating a kind of knot, a kind of inhibition (one could even invent a name to classify it). In these circumstances, it would then be necessary to bring about an anamnesis in order to see what was happening and treat it as quickly as possible, in other words, to interpret it, which in this case would mean bringing what has been repressed to consciousness. Then the boys would get in line, behave, start producing like rabbits, and manage to get their diplomas and excellent places in society—meaning that they would be declared fit, they would be cured. This could be a first axiomatic of the unconscious.

The second attitude would consist in saying: "They don't have anything in their unconscious; you'll see that they don't even have very much to say in terms of content; what they are doing is really more like a kind of scream, as if they were to shout 'I'm fed up, I can't take it any more,' or something like that. But if they went on doing it for a long time, for two or three hours, it would become unbearable for everyone, including them." In this second formula, these youngsters (and everyone else) are not credited with the existence of an unconscious as something that is inside them. It's considered that what they have to say is precisely what they said, and that's what it's about: *there's nothing to interpret.* But what can one do on the basis of this observation?

Here, too, there are two possible options. The first is to shut the door and say "Well, it's not our problem, let them fend for themselves." The second is to say: "What can one do with a situation like this?" That's precisely the question that I was asking myself: "How am I going to face this situation, if we only have interventions of this kind in a debate that I very much wanted to be an open debate? What is my friend here, who is representing the university on the panel, going to think? What is the President of the university going to think?" Not that it disturbs me or makes me feel guilty; it's more because I think that those friends who spoke are very nice kids, and I have the impression that they must be wild about something, which has to do with the unconscious— obviously not the unconscious of the first definition, but the second one, in other words, something that's happening in the mode of collective subjectivation of this event. In this case it's not a question of interpreting, but of asking whether there's something that can be done, something that would assemble this singular event, so that it would have a different scope, not a scope of significance or interpretation but a pragmatic scope. For the time being, it could only be some kind of talking (in other circumstances one might also think of something like dancing, music, throwing stones at windows, inventing free radio stations, or even venturing to do a poem *à la* Prévert).

I would say that the unconscious in the second definition is constituted precisely in the field of possible of which this kind of collective assemblage is a vehicle, thus having to do with the future and not the past. Bearing in mind that this assemblage is not necessarily logocentric, because it can bring into play all kinds of modes of semiotic expression, all kinds of problematics of a political nature, or ecological, or technical and scientific, or whatever.

Meeting with groups working with communities on the outskirts of the city, Olinda, September 16, 1982:

Question: I have a seven-year-old daughter. She had a reasonable relation on our street, which is a small, middle-class street. But gradually she became completely isolated, without any friends. Now, when she looks for other children, the parents or maids always say that the children are not at home. And, according to what the maids say (because they talk to each other), the parents really don't want their children to be with my daughter because she uses bad words. So she's becoming very insecure, and feeling guilty. I feel that in order to deal with this kind of thing it's necessary to have a process of collectivization.

Guattari: I don't in any way want to make a diagnosis, but this reminds me of a rereading that I did of Freud's case of Little Hans,[10] which I shall talk about briefly. I don't know if you remember the beginning of the case: it's exactly like the story of your daughter. Hans couldn't cross the street to visit his little friend Marielda. Every time he wanted to visit her, the family stopped him, explaining that they weren't from the same background. But it didn't stop there: the restriction imposed by the family wasn't limited to contact with his little friend. One after another, all of Little Hans's territories were blocked, all his assemblages were disrupted (with the indirect but active help of Dr. Freud), when what the boy was really missing was precisely assemblages that would allow him to assert himself among children of his age, allowing all the differentiations to function, including sexual differentiation.

My ideas about psychoanalysis don't interest me if they don't help me to understand what kind of shit we're dealing with, not only in personal life, but also in institutions and sectarian groups—I mean, in power relations and all that sort of thing. On the other hand, I believe that, *if we are not able to understand someone's personal difficulties in the light of his social investments and the collective subjectivity in which he participates, then we don't get anywhere.*

SCHIZOANALYSIS

Desire as production

The conception of desire in the social field that Gilles Deleuze and I have tried to develop seeks to question the idea that desire and subjectivity are focused on individuals and result from the interaction of individual facts on the collective level. We set out more from the idea of a collective economy, collective assemblages of desire and of subjectivity that can be individualized in some circumstances or some social contexts.

I want to talk about a rather classical conception of desire as something individual, and of the social domain as something that is constructed on the basis of this individual desire, in a series of successive stages. Of course one can always try to make the cartographic representation of a situation based on these notions. In my view, there are no universal scientific models with which to try to understand a situation; moreover, those very scientific models repel one other, or change places with one another, or combine. Nevertheless, this classical conception of desire underlies a series of phenomena, especially one that seems to me very important, that of the production of subjectivity—rather than its modelization—on a social and even world scale.

Debate held by a branch of the PT in Rio de Janeiro, September 11, 1982:

Question: I would like you to say something about the problematics of political action and individual action. Don't you think that political action necessarily crushes individual desire?

Guattari: In my view, one cannot speak of individual desire. *It is the production of capitalistic subjectivity that tends to individualize desire,* and when it is victorious in this operation, no further processual accumulation is possible. A phenomenon of serialization or identification is established, which lends itself to all kinds of manipulation by the capitalistic facilities. *The question, therefore, is not situated at the level of the grouping of individuals but at that of a pragmatics of processes of production of desire that have nothing to do with this kind of individuation.* When this pragmatics is crushing, it can affect both the individual and the group.

Debate at the Psychoanalysis School of the Sedes Sapientiae Institute, São Paulo, August 31, 1982:

Antonio Lancetti: I think that I've understood your insistence on criticizing what we know as the "analytic movement." The analytic institution, or at least some of its predominant forms, seems to set out, and actually manage, to refer all desiring determination to the symbolic order (the Oedipus complex, etc.). The idea that in this case there is also a possibility of other assemblages and other processes of semiotization is also clear. What is not clear to me, in terms of other processes, is the disengaging of desire from the constituted order, for example in the class struggle as it is traditionally understood by Marxism. My question is this: are these processes also necessarily absorbed, as in psychoanalysis, by overcodings?

Guattari: It's precisely in the problem of the stratifications of the workers' movement that we see the damage brought about by the absence of analytic devices referring to the formations of the unconscious. Really, considerable molecular mutations are taking place in the field of work structures. They are completely ignored and even actively combated by the organizations of the workers' movement, both in their theoretical references and in their practical interventions. We have only to look at the example of Italy, where these mutations led to social movements of what one might call a more "complete" expression: a mode of subjectivation that involved questioning the prevailing processes of production, that is, the whole problematic studied by people like Toni Negri. The fact that this approach was totally rejected and combated led to a considerable impasse: Italy now has four thousand political prisoners—some of the very people who embody this subjective mutation. All the political and social transformations of which the Italian situation was a vehicle in 1977 turned turtle... and that was why.

If we don't want to see situations like those of Poland and Italy, which show us that a certain formation of desire on a collective scale ultimately reinvests in traditional formations such as the Church, then the workers' movement will have to incorporate the analytic problematic—with or without psychoanalysts, but that's another story. And so we'll see the creation of another kind of workers' movement, capable of articulating, on the one hand, the struggles of power relations in society, and, on the other, all the mutations that are causing a new kind of subjectivation to originate in extensive strata of the population. A workers' movement capable of mobilizing the immense force that all this represents.

———

Another approach to the issue of the collective formations of desire becomes necessary in order to understand questions such as those of the feeling of love and its world- and universe-creating complexity, and also questions such as that of the child, in the crucial phase of its incorporation in school systems, the consequences of which are often disastrous. Also in order to understand broader social phenomena—in my view, one cannot comprehend large historical dimensions such as what is happening in Poland now without tackling the issue of the collective formations of desire in a different way.

The issue of an analysis of the formations of the unconscious arises in widely varied contexts. A first example could be an analysis of our own semiotic productions—our own dream when we wake up (in a kind of self-analysis), a poetic production, or any kind of creative production. A second example is that of a dual situation with the establishment of a language constituted as a metalanguage in relation to the levels of primary production. These different semiotic productions are in turn taken into meshes of reading, interpretation, or communication, which direct them into different systems of redundancy. Thus they are codified in different ways in an analytic situation, in the situation of a married couple, or in the situation of a mother-child relation. For example, symptoms of the nature of corporified semiotic productions will be related by the mother to a particular mesh of interpretation, which will not coincide with the mesh of the teacher or the social worker. If we take yet another level of reading, the institutional level, all the levels previously mentioned once again enter a system of interpretation and decoding, which involves elements of laws, rules, and regulations, and some dominant redundancies. These elements are not situated merely as references external to the first levels of production: there will constantly be effects of retroaction. The law, as articulated in a school, for example, or a psychiatric hospital, will reintervene directly at the level of the supposed primary process. This is what we constantly see in the analysis of dreams, in which determinations of a distinctly institutional, political, or geopolitical order appear.

These determinations of laws, determinations of the third, fourth, or nth level of metalanguage, do not take their place as metalanguage, but intervene directly in the syntagmatics of elaboration. And because these other levels do not respond to a single logic of the signifier, we could say that in what seem to be the most primary articulations (displacement and condensation, for example), all kinds of elements intervene with full effectiveness, functioning completely outside the register of the signifier or the register of the famous mathemes of the unconscious. This does not mean that there is an "internalization," or a phenomenon of sublimation of elements that remain essentially external. I repeat: *these other levels intervene in the actual syntagmatics of the elaboration of unconscious subjectivation.* There is a certain way of being articulated with the collective mode of semiotization, particularly that of the media, which intervenes in direct connection with the formations of the unconscious.

In other words, when a political leader or a feeling of racial segregation appears in a dream, it is not suitable to read it with a syntax consisting solely of elements that bring into play the polar oppositions of familialist systems (as in the first modes of reading of psychoanalysis), or a syntax consisting of elements that bring a dialectic of partial objects into play (the phallus, and so on). These are reductionist modes of reading of such phenomena. Because, although it is true that it is always possible to find binary oppositions (for example, Manicheanisms in connection with the phallus and castration), nevertheless, to reduce them in that way is not of the slightest interest. Phenomena such as those of hierarchical suggestion, or the power relation signifying through language or through writing, have different modes of operating, depending on the social register in which the individual being considered is situated. The economy of castration, the Oedipal economy, does not function in the same way, it does not convey the same universes of possibility in every kind of situation. In which case, *what matters is not to establish some kind of little system with a universal signifier key, but on the contrary, always to preserve these capitals of possibility, which are conveyed by each of the different universes being considered.*

There is no recipe that guarantees the development of a genuine process of autonomy, or of desire, or whatever we like to call it. Although it is true that desire can reorient itself for the construction of other territories, other ways of feeling things, it is equally true that, on the other hand, it can be oriented within each of us in a microfascist direction.

The traditional political formations coopt everything that is felt as a need or demand of a social stratum. This functions through the phenomena of advertising and all the balancing that consists in putting forward programs based on consensus. But this approach obviously has many limits: historical mutations in the order of the collective formations of desire break these programs, and pass through them. We could even say that *what is essential in the outstanding historical events in the current period corresponds to collective expressions of desire, which do not in any way fit into these traditional frameworks of modelization.*

What is happening in Iran, Poland, or many Arab countries (we could extend the list *ad infinitum*) are different movements of sensibility and reaction, which are only conceived as irrational from the viewpoint of the dominant practices or organizations. In fact, these movements are bearers of a different rationality.

In order to understand the proliferation of a phenomenon such as free radio stations, it is necessary to situate it as an intervention that takes place precisely at the level of the social unconscious. Perhaps the term "unconscious" is not very appropriate. I use it for convenience, because it would be more accurate to say a questioning of the mode of collective semiotization in its relation with speech, information, and the "media" interlocutor.

What is being experienced in the very specific conditions of Brazil will not fail to have effects on entirely different situations. I believe profoundly in a kind of system of interaction, which I would venture to describe as unconscious at the social level, provided, of course, that the concept of the unconscious is elaborated differently. What is taking place in Brazil interacts with what is happening in Poland, or Lebanon, and—why not?—in Europe too.

For me, the unconscious in history, for example in the present history of Brazil, is the way in which a whole series of minorities experience their problematics of subjectivity, whether resisting the productions of dominant subjectivity, or depending or counterdepending on them.

Round-table discussion at the Folha de Sao Paulo, *September 3, 1982:*

Modesto Carone: I am going to try to reproduce an experience that came from my singularity as a writer of fiction. It may be of some interest here insofar as Professor Guattari spoke, in his presentation, not only of the processes of social control of subjectivity, but also of the "chinks" through which this subjectivity sometimes passes. That is to say, I am going to refer to something personal and singular that attained generalization through language. The experience has to do with my first text of fiction. It was in 1975, a really rough time here in Brazil; shortly before writing this text I experienced the collective trauma of the death of Vlado.[11] In other words, I knew that a person called Vladimir Herzog had been arrested and killed, and I went, feeling very upset, to the place where the funeral procession was going to start. It was only there, at the Albert Einstein Hospital, that I realized that Vlado was an old acquaintance of mine from twenty years before, from the time when I used to go to the Municipal Library. And so it was at that painful moment of recognition that the act of political solidarity also became an act of personal solidarity. Around that time I went through another difficult experience, of an institutional nature, which was the competitive examination for a place as a lecturer at the University of São Paulo. As I see it, it was as a result of these two experiences, together with my grief at the death of my father, which also took place in that period, that one night—almost without *directing* what I was doing—I wrote a story that I called "As Faces do Inimigo" ("The Faces of the Enemy"). It's a story written in the first person, in which the narrator relentlessly observes the growth of the hair on his body. He devotes all his afternoons and part of his nights to the task of verifying whether the hairs are growing straight; when they don't, he removes them without leaving roots or scars, because rebel hairs don't fit in with the geometrical strictness that he demands of himself. At the same time, the narrator is scared of losing the sensitivity of his fingers which makes this task possible. Finally, after a really exhausting session of watching, when dawn is breaking, an unexpected question occurs to him: what do the hairs think about it? He's so startled by this question that he goes to the mirror to look at himself from the outside, and at that moment he discovers, in his own stunned face, that it is impossible to control *spontaneous manifestations*—in this case, the hairs that grow without the consent of their own bearer.

When I think back on what I did, I realize that I wrote the story from the end to the beginning. In other words, I started with the expression "spontaneous manifestations," which was circulating in the country at the time to describe the social phenomenon of rioting and looting. One part of the political opposition to the dictatorship imagined that, through the chink of "spontaneous demonstrations" like these, there was a possibility of disarticulating the repressive control over the people who were demanding freedom. The expression was a catalyst because, in a single verbal instant, it summed up many things that were happening in the country. In a way, it was that historical fact, together with my personal circumstances, that released the energy in me to write "As Faces do Inimigo." The text emerged as a kind of unburdening; thinking back, I feel that at that moment something was formed in me that I might call "my singularity." Without being very aware of it, in a way I was turning away from the social control over people's lives and over intellectual production that was dominant at the time.

I think that this experience is interesting because I didn't believe—and I still have doubts about it—that it was possible to arrive at a "spontaneous manifestation" with so much repression that was not only objective but also internalized. The curious thing is that, by narrating the story in the first person, in a way I inserted myself into an "alienated consciousness" and invested in it. In other words, instead of remaining outside, *pointing at* an alienated consciousness (such as that of the narrator of the text), I entered it, and in so doing—I'm not talking about the aesthetic result, but the process—I realized that, even within a repressive personality, there is some kind of conflict that objectifies itself precisely in this "spontaneous manifestation." In other words, it seems that even in an alienated consciousness a contradictory element acts energetically. On the basis of this observation, and considering the genesis of this story, perhaps it would be possible to generalize a little and imagine that art is not limited to saying what exists: it can also gainsay it. It is to that extent that art is free and demands freedom as a condition for its existence—even because it is regulated by laws that are no longer those that regulate oppression in the realm of social need. In a work of art—and in the human impulse that leads to it—there is a liberating gesture that demolishes the control that is articulated inside and outside every one of us.

Guattari: Your intervention seems to me to be crucial, because it shows that a cartography or a mode of singular construction can introduce itself into a context of terrible repression and, at the same time, into an infrapersonal context that is completely singular. It is in this aspect that your intervention is not situated on a level of metalanguage in relation to the processes of singularization, a level that is nearly always inevitable. The only observation that I would make, but one that would call for a debate that is impossible just now, is that it doesn't seem to me that describing the processes of expression that you speak of as "spontaneous" (relating them to the automatic writing of Surrealism, for example) is the most advantageous way of treating them. On the contrary, I think that they are highly elaborate processes. This elaboration could be something like what Freud, in his first topography, situated as belonging to the nature of primary processes. Incidentally, it is precisely this kind of elaboration that gradually diminished in all the movements of psychoanalysis. From the initial reduction of the primary process to an undifferentiated drive-based mass, we come to a formula of disorder or death drive, or even, in the case of the structuralists, a universalizing theory of the signifier. Everyone here must have had the experience—I, at any rate, have it frequently—of the contrast between the discovery of the complexity, richness, and differentiation that one can have in a dream experience and the poverty of resources that one has when one wakes up, when one tries to express that oneiric expression by recalling it, by writing it down or by drawing. Here I will take the liberty of *questioning all references to undifferentiation, all references to spontaneist mythologies*: every time we succeed in assembling devices of expression that escape from the despotism of the dominant system of significances, and that escape from the articulation of all the dominant syntaxizations, we are actually dealing with highly elaborate machinisms.

Machinic unconscious

I think it is much more useful to aim for a theory of desire that considers it as belonging rightfully to highly differentiated and elaborated machinic systems. When I say "machinic," I am not referring to the mechanical, or even necessarily to technological machines. Technological machines exist, of course, but there are also social machines, aesthetic machines, theoretical machines, and so on. In other words, there are territorialized machines (in metal, electricity, etc.), just as there are also deterritorialized machines that operate on a completely different level of semiotization.

The issue of production, in my view, is inseparable from the issue of desire. Many people don't consider things in this way; there are even those who make a radical cut between the field of work and the field of desire. For them, the field of work is something that should be disciplined, taken over by control structures and hierarchical structures, whereas desire appears as something undifferentiated that, according to the theories, could be attributed to an instinct, a drive, or a raw force, and so on. I think that's completely false.

Gilles Deleuze and I created an expression that may seem paradoxical, but it was very useful in our reflections: it is the concept of the "desiring-machine." It is the idea that desire corresponds to a certain kind of production, and that it is definitely not something undifferentiated. Desire is not an organic drive, or something that is operated by the second law of thermodynamics, for example, dragged along inexorably by some kind of death drive. On the contrary, desire has infinite possibilities of assembly. The desire of a child, for example, cannot, as we see it, be reduced to the schemas of psychoanalysis—its imagoes of triangulations, for example. If we observe things simply from a phenomenological viewpoint, desire reveals itself in direct connection with the most differentiated elements of its surroundings, which range from the family to the cosmos. The child has an extraordinary capacity for taking an interest in abstract processes. All the people who have carried out studies on the psychology of children have had tremendous difficulty in understanding this, because they study the child using a reductionist method, which does not give them access to that particular nucleus of semiotic creativity which allows one to characterize the desire of the child as a machinic desire. This does not mean that desire is a force which, by itself, constructs a whole coordinated universe. Gilles Deleuze and I are very far from any idea of spontaneism in this field. Desire, for us, is not the new formula of Jean-Jacques Rousseau's noble savage. Like any other machine worthy of the name, it can also become jammed or blocked (and even much more so than any technological machine); it runs the risk of going into processes of implosion or self-destruction, which in the social field may be manifested through phenomena that Deleuze and I call "microfascisms." For us, therefore, it is a question of trying to assess what the economy of desire really is, on a pre-personal level, on the level of identity relations or intrafamilial relations, and on all levels of the social field.

Meeting at the Freudian School of São Paulo, August 26, 1982:

Question: So this system of schizoanalysis of yours goes against all psychoanalysis? How do you replace the Oedipal triangle?

Guattari: I wasn't the one who replaced the triangle. The triangle replaced itself. The family itself is transformed as a collective facility, in relation to all the other collective facilities that receive the child, from its education to its entry into collective labor power. All of this is programmed now. There is no natural relation with the mother or the father, or with anyone. Television, for example, plays a role that partly replaces the mother.

Question: And these desiring-machines are in operation from the very first months of life?

Guattari: More than ever.

Debate at the Psychoanalysis School of the Sedes Sapientiae Institute, São Paulo, August 31, 1982:

Question: How can we assemble and link the models formed so far, if they are very often exclusive? How do you deal with the exclusion of one model by another?

Guattari: I have my conception of the articulation of the various registers of these components, but that doesn't mean that I intend to propose them as a new system of modelization. It's something that I worked out in relation to a certain conception of the analytic process, which I called the "molecular revolution." I definitely do not set out from the kind of reference used in the psychoanalytic schools or the universities. But it doesn't seem to me to be legitimate to formulate a different kind of modelization, unless it's required by the experience of a certain problematic. In this case, one could go back to the problematic in a more precise way, trying to show what corporal, iconic, or linguistic semiotics, and what machinic codifications, or representations of the value system are assembled to engender a subjective fact. The relation between them is established through a certain kind of "element of passage," which can acquire both a capacity of intersemiotic efficiency and also an inefficiency of passage, depending precisely on the systems that assemble them.

Meeting with philosophers in São Paulo, August 23, 1982

Question: What changed in *A Thousand Plateaus* in relation to what you had been writing before was, if I understand correctly, a glimpse of something beyond capital?

Guattari: Yes, that's right.

Comment: Which hadn't appeared before.

Guattari: Perhaps it had appeared a little.

Comment: Yes, but maybe not very clearly.

Guattari: Yes, it was really the issue of molecular revolutions, with the notion of "machinic unconscious" which in a way legitimates a treatment of what is generally, and abusively, called utopia.

Schizoanalytic cases

I'm going to tell you about the case of a young schizophrenic (not all that young, actually, because he's about 30 or 35 years old, but he doesn't look it) that I have been "following" (what an unfortunate expression!)[12] for about ten years. This person was classified as schizophrenic some time ago, and he's been committed several times. Since childhood he's lived in a family environment in relative equilibrium, with a lot of conflict, in a relation of extreme dependence on his parents, who are elderly. In the situation preceding the one that I'm going to talk about, he moved basically in three or four kinds of territory, apart from the psychiatric hospital, when he was interned. A family territory completely closed in upon itself, where he lived in a kind of total apraxia, with interpretive and conflictive relations that sometimes led to acts of violence. The only openings, which were actually quite restricted, were a sports club, a ping-pong club or something like that, and a session with me once a week.

The work with me began after he'd been through the La Borde Clinic. That was soon after he'd finished one of his psychiatric hospitalizations. Since then he's never gone back to the hospital. What does the analysis consist of? What does the analysis of a schizophrenic consist of? The session generally begins with him giving me a piece of gum, which I sometimes refuse (because the gum has been in his pocket and it's filthy) and I ask for another; he usually also brings me any administrative papers that he may have received, a few newspaper clippings, and sometimes some sheets of paper on which he's written some reflections. He talks, then he gives me ten francs, and sometimes he gets very angry with me and curses me, saying that it's all useless, and that what is important for him is to be able to work, meet some girls, and so on. Not very much more happens. The sessions go on like this until the time comes when the family territory begins to disintegrate completely and lose consistency. He remains permanently locked up in his room, doesn't do anything, and his mother becomes very ill. Sometimes he goes out, like one day, for example, when he went to Paris to try to see a prostitute, and he ended up in a fight with a pimp; he got hit and was taken to the police, where he was threatened with another hospitalization.

In this situation of total impasse, the intervention that I made (and I'll leave it to your judgment to form an evaluation of it, from the viewpoint of a theory of interpretation) consisted essentially in making a proposal to him, based on the hypothesis that it could be effective. The proposal consisted in having him leave his home and find lodgings, and try to establish a minimum of arrangements for living. Clearly, in this kind of situation this sort of attitude isn't so obvious. The fact that he had no kind of opening to the outside meant that we couldn't guarantee that this proposal wouldn't lead to total catastrophe. Especially when the only references we have are various themes connected with regression, or strong identifications with familial poles. It was important at that point that I should be fully aware of the reality of the risk, and that he, whom I shall call Jean-Baptiste, should know that I was unsure. It was important that he should understand very clearly that I wasn't offering a therapeutic prescription or a psychoanalytic interpretation. So, at that point, what were the semiotic registers of my intervention? First, I called the family. I used the institutional power relations in which I'm involved to negotiate a little money for Jean-Baptiste's needs, a truce in the hostilities, and the suspension of the threats of hospitalization in order to give the experiment a chance.

What was coming into play in the consistency of this assemblage was not only my authority, but also a series of flows that were completely external to me. The first kind of element: whether the parents could give Jean-Baptiste a little money; whether it was possible to capitalize a few things such as social security and disability benefits; and whether the procedures for renting an apartment in a housing project could reasonably be taken on. The second kind of element (which is no longer microsocial or microeconomic, but infraindividual, of the nature of what I would call "components of assemblage," which are, we might say, components of an existential syntagmatics): would these components have sufficient consistency—which I would call "transistence"? Which, specifically, means the following: when he's in a room, more alone than ever, will his mode of perception of space, social relations, and relations of significance be totally destroyed, or, on the contrary, will they embark on a new process?

So, Jean-Baptiste was in an apartment. He began, of course, to interpret the noises of the neighbors, and had a series of problems of that sort. But his relation with the session rapidly began to change its way of functioning: the gum was still there, but, instead of simply telling stories about the family, he began making drawings, describing what happened to him when he heard noises in the block, interpreting all kinds of things, watching television, making various attempts at very fragile social contacts, writing daily texts that were much more coherent, more important. A series of interventions even led him to enroll at a judo club, which didn't work out. He managed to get hired by a company to sell insurance door-to-door. It was terrible work, because, in addition to not paying at all, it consisted in knocking on the doors of unknown people and offering them things that they weren't interested in. It led to terrible conflicts, and eventually it fell apart. A little later he enrolled in law school, and I was surprised at the fact that he kept going to class, although everything seemed to indicate that he made no contacts at all. He was quite shocked that he didn't manage to pass any of the exams, but he continued going just the same. I'm not going to describe the other stages; what's interesting is that through this new kind of assemblage his relations with the family altered, there were certain openings, a considerable change in behavior, a stabilization;

in fact, quite a satisfactory result. *In this new solitary assemblage, he begun to create a mode of expression and develop it, creating a kind of cartography of his own universe*, something that he couldn't develop in the family territory, nor, of course, in the territory of a psychiatric hospital, nor even in his therapeutic relation with me.

What kind of judgment might a psychoanalyst make about this kind of intervention? He'd say, "Fine, you've done an excellent job as a social worker, but obviously it has nothing to do with an analysis of the psychosis." I do actually believe that I can take no credit for having discovered something that might be a latent meaning and that could change his modes of subjectivation like a piece of magic. But the point is precisely that in this case analysis lost its magic qualities, its fascinating qualities. The analysis simply consisted in trying to assess, as accurately one could, the different possible modes of consistency of territories or different kinds of processes—which I call "machinic processes"—that could be set into operation. It also consisted in never encouraging anything, on my authority and at my risk, that might lead him to a total impasse; in trying to assess the possible mutation of what I call a "constellation of universes," which would enable Jean-Baptiste to accept his different modes of semiotization in his situation. It's an ordinary example, of a kind that you must be very familiar with in your practice.

In order to be able to run risks of this nature, it may be useful to have some theoretical references, which, I repeat, have no merit other than that of enabling us gradually to remove those things that act as blinders, as ignorance of these different fields of the possible. That's why I think it's extremely important to realize that the semiotic intervention must be evaluated as precisely as possible in terms of its potential degree of effectiveness. It would be utterly idiotic to think that a phenomenon of transference or symbolic interpretation could have transformed anything about this kind of black-hole libidinal economy that was operating on the family terrain. It was also necessary to try to assess where his own machines of self-elaboration might find sufficient consistency, because the phenomena of writing or new kinds of social connection might not have appeared, or might have appeared with insufficient consistency, which would have implied a need for immediate reorientation.

So, what are the "formations of unconscious" on this level? It's certainly not a question of anything that can only focus on the way in which a signifier represents the subject for another signifier—as Lacan puts it—or anything focused on a process referring only to this particular individual. The unconscious is territorialized on this family field, worked on by a certain kind of social class, for example. The fact that his father was an architect in the city hall was important, because one of Jean-Baptiste's favorite ideas was that he was going to kill the mayor. From this starting point, if we were to set out to reestablish an Oedipus complex, assuming that we were dealing with a displacement of his desire to kill his father, we would not have the slightest difficulty in doing so. But in my view, that's not the most interesting element in this case. We're confronted with a subjective territoriality whose structural elements are disintegrating, irrespective of any interpretive apprehension. Beyond the territory of family and class, other components of this unconscious assemblage are the machinic processes that he chooses as substitutes, which he tries to grasp when he enters the judo club, for example. Yet another component, but on a different level, is the fact that he lives in a situation which has a certain understanding of the problems of mental illness. This constitutes a dimension of the unconscious that is completely external to the familial problems and the infraindividual problems, because it depends on the way in which the social institutions convey and semiotize mental illness. It's true that, despite this, he tried to present himself as a candidate for a job at a notary's office, for example, and that he was received by the mayor (through the mediation of his father, incidentally). But of course he was turned down, and he couldn't accept that. At one point he had the fixed idea of working in a bank, and to crown it all he would only accept the position of manager, which of course didn't work.

There are elements of an objective unconscious in this, but at the same time this unconscious is completely deterritorialized with schemas that are embodied in an attitude, a way of being, a way of coming up against obstacles. Through this we could understand what his political options are, because keeping up with political events is one of his constant concerns. On the one hand he reveals himself to be a conformist, with strong racist tendencies, and on the other he shows a desire to carry out interventions of a terrorist character. This political problematic is definitely not marginal: it's his way of articulating social relations, splendidly embodied in dimensions of economics, class, caste, and so on, and of not simply adjusting to the signifiers of the world.

This example emphasizes the idea that if I were to ignore those other modes of semiotization and encoding, those heterogeneous machinic systems, the effect would be to prevent the revelation of the possibles existing in these various registers. My mere presence or listening would not lead to that discernment.

Comment: I wonder whether what carried most weight in this case wasn't the fact that you admitted your uncertainties to the patient.

Guattari: Yes, that's what I would call the truth factor of a situation. And if there were a possible teaching method for this kind of profession, it would consist precisely in teaching people to be capable of doing a kind of striptease of all their certainties in this field, and doing it right away. Doing it in every situation, so that the elements of singularity and nonsense can be indicators of processes that completely elude us, but that also elude the subject, just as they elude a reasonable description, a well-informed description of the situation.

All of you must have experienced paradoxical phenomena: the fact that returning to a particular place, or taking up the piano again, or simply learning to drive can generate absolutely incalculable fields of possibles. But if we imprint interpretations of a personological nature on this, we risk totally underestimating what these processes represent, leading the person also to underestimate them.

Meeting at the Freudian Psychoanalysis Institute, Rio de Janeiro, September 10, 1982:

Question: How could one resolve or consider the problem of a hypochondriac patient who, after a series of unsuccessful surgical operations, is not even able to recover her physical health in the current medical system? For this person, it doesn't matter that a psychoanalytic interpretation may offer a cure: she wants to sue someone, and she doesn't know who. Her request is strictly social, at least apparently: she wants her health, and not through psychoanalysis but through a system of social medicine that is destined in advance to fail.

Guattari: It's obvious that one can't speak in depth about a case with such general data. We could use your question as a pretext to go back to certain theoretical questions: the symptom of the hypochondriac is a repetition of a certain mode of expression.

Question: I'm not concerned only about the problem of hypochondria, but also about this demand for the medical system to restore her body.

Guattari: A system of somatic expression which causes a symptom, such as hypochondria, to constitute a mode of semiotization that repeats on itself, without being able to enter into connection with processes of individual expression, collective expression, social practices, or pragmatics of various natures—such a system of somatic expression is a kind of narrowing of the possible, which leads to the person being fenced in. This kind of segregation in the register of illness is taken up by the systems of assistance—the doctor, medical semiology, and the collective health facilities that correspond to these practices. This assistance makes it impossible for her to construct her own singularity. Now, might it be possible to treat this question with the theoretical parameters that you used and consider that it would be sufficient to pass from an individual, somatic level to a social level for the problem to be resolved?

That's just one possible example, but it's only an example. It would also be a mechanistic and reductionist view to think that it would be sufficient to transfer an issue of this nature to social expression or social practice for the situation to change. It's the myth that has been conveyed ever since the time of the counter-culture: the social, the collective, corporal, group expression, community life, political militancy, and so on are supposed to bring responses that the other kinds of approach did not provide. This is utterly true for a series of problems, such as problems of neurosis or certain difficulties with children. It's true that, in some cases, changing the register of the reference, moving from the medical context to the family or social context, can have a resolvent effect and trigger off productive processes of subjectivation that transform the practice and conditions of the problem. But I insist on the fact that this is only an example, and that this micropolitical option can only be taken on condition that one doesn't lose sight of the fact that other options are equally possible, and that, above all, we shouldn't have any dogmatic preconception about the choice. The choice doesn't depend on the therapist's knowledge or practice, but on the way in which the situation is assembled. It depends on the choice of cartography that appears in the actual assemblage.

If we go back to the case of Jean-Baptiste as an example, we could say that the alternative that enabled him to avoid hospitalization and constitute at least minimally tolerable behavior did not involve social mediation; on the contrary, paradoxically it involved an accentuation of his isolation. I'm not sure that he would have had the possibility of entering a process of socialization or integration. Perhaps that might even happen in other stages of his existence, but we can't be sure of that either. It might also be that the analytic issue for someone consists in creating a means of expression of his singularities that is entirely outside the systems that are proposed to him: the family, the psychiatric hospital, psychotherapy, and so on.

As a conclusion for the case that you described, I believe that the function of any person in a position of assistance is to mistrust oneself as a therapist, to mistrust one's own theoretical preconceptions. These preconceptions may not only prevent us from seeing, but also cause us to frustrate the possibilities of another processual organization in the existence of the patient, another mode of construction of his subjectivity, his life, his territory, in other words, frustrate the possibility of the constitution of singular, dissident modes. This means that it's necessary to preserve channels outside the norms, not only the norms of dominant behavior, but also the psychoanalytic or psychological norms, however open one may consider them to be.

Interview by Sonia Goldfeder, São Paulo, August 31, 1982:

Sonia Goldfeder: What is mental illness for you?

Guattari: Mental illness, in my view, can't be defined in terms of just a single aspect. It always involves elements of a personal nature, conflicts of the functioning of the personality, relations of a sexual nature, relations of couples, relations in the family, problems of a microsocial nature, institutional dimensions, work problems, neighborhood problems, lifestyle problems. It even involves economic dimensions and dimensions of a moral, aesthetic, and religious order. Mental illness is something that is assembled on all these levels, even if what appears is just a symptom of the body. Let's take as an example a hysterical pain, or psychological behavior that seems to concentrate all these problems, which we call a "symptom" or "syndrome." We can only really understand how the person comes to present the symptom if we understand all the articulations that have led to it. It's not at all mysterious, there are many phenomena of this very nature. Pollution is an example: it can be measured by instruments for chemical analysis, but that doesn't mean that pollution is only caused by a chain of chemical combinations. Pollution is also a way of conceptualizing life, production, and all the systems of human values; and all this can very well be embodied in a particular symptom. The "disease of pollution" is a symptom, but if we want to analyze it and treat it simply as a symptom, we are utterly mistaken. Mental illness involves the same thing. We must be careful not to mistake the symptom for the problem itself.

Sonia Goldfeder: Give a specific example in the field of psychiatry.

Guattari: Let's take the example of a child who is wrapped up in his own world, who doesn't speak much, stops eating, and shows indications of a whole series of physical illnesses. The mother takes him to a pediatrician, who gives him vitamins, or else follows all the traditional psychoanalytic information and seeks to understand the child through explanations such as "the child is fixated on the mother," and so on. In either case, the conduct is not correct. In order to understand the reason for this child being closed in upon himself one has to ask: What happens to him in his relations with the neighbors? Does he have friends? Is he interested in doing anything outside the family territory? What happens with his brothers and sisters? How does he come to construct his own production of life or subjectivity in the family structure? How does he decipher the outside world? What does the future mean to him? Does he think it's worthwhile being committed to the future? What happens to him at school? What types of relations does he come up against? What happens when he wants to draw, or dance, or sing? Increasingly we see that it's the totality of a certain possible—predetermined and precoded by various levels of society—that leads him to close up. This doesn't mean that there aren't specific levels: the level of the body, the level of intrapsychic determinations, or the level of intrafamilial systems. But if I were to treat the case with corporal techniques, with psychomotricity, or with techniques of language reeducation, or even with psychodrama or family therapy, each time I would be cutting out bits of that reality. And very likely I wouldn't be able to understand the totality of the articulations or the totality of the assemblage that causes this subjectivity to suffer, that causes this process to revolve around itself, creating this kind of micropolitics of desperation.

Interview with Félix Guattari by Antoinette Chauvenet and Janine Pierrot, published in the magazine Sciences Sociales et Santé, *vol. II, nos. 3-4, October 1984, Erès, Paris:*

Drugs, psychosis, and institution

In places like La Borde or Marmottan[13]—constantly involved with complex problems concerning money, aging, changing generations, social stratification, and the institution—the interesting thing is the contradictions that the problems bring out. After all, the contradictions are proof that something is really there. If we don't talk about it, if the contradictions are squashed and repressed, a total vacuum is created: we don't get beyond circulars and formal structure. That's why I'm not going to talk about the institution but about *processes of institutionalization*, in order to focus on an open issue. I'm going to offer two reflections: one about the conditions of pertinence of an institutional approach to disturbed personalities—to avoid using grandiose words—and another, even less clear, which has to do with the application of this issue to drug addiction. The first point revolves around the question: "What point can there be in 'working in an institution' when one is dealing with the problems of a complex personality?" The second—which is not strictly within my competence, but which I am tackling on my own, as it happens, on the basis of certain psychopathological profiles—is: "How is this issue specified for phenomena of drug addiction?"

1. Two dangers must be avoided, in my opinion: the first consists in considering the institutional factor as extrinsic to the personal problems, as not really involving those problems. Here we have a certain reductionism from the generation of 1968. Political problems, organization problems, and institutional problems are recognized as being very important, but only in order to frustrate the harmful incidents of society. The institution is never a "protective cushion," but always a pathogenic structure that one should get rid of in order to get to the "real questions"—the questions of the individual, his spontaneity, his richness, and his affects (there's no point in developing this virtually mythological and practically Rousseauistic theme, which is so well known). The second danger, symmetrical to the first but opposite in scope, consists in broadening the institutional issue excessively. I am thinking of various movements such as institutional analysis and psychosociology, and militant movements in the field of "alternative" practice, or even various attempts connected with drug addicts. The group becomes a primordial factor here: it's through the group that personalities are changed and existence reoriented. This

sometimes leads to a kind of Boy Scout approach that is rather fearsome, because it does have effects.

On this point, there should be something of a theoretical retreat. What can we expect from a process of institutionalization? Much more than a mere adjustment of microsocial problems, and something utterly different than a "pathoplastic" intervention, which would be sufficient in itself to adapt "cases" as unique as those of drug addicts, psychotics, autistic children, and so on to the dominant norms. The problem, in my view, is this: even if a naïve phenomenological approach leads us to believe the opposite, we are never in the presence of a direct causality based on institutional factors (or, if you prefer, on the discourse in the institution). In general, one should not count on any single action to be effective on subjectivity, whether it's a certain way of life, or a certain circulation of images, or cooperation in the assumption of responsibility in relation to daily problems, or collective management of memory, the past, or projects. Even if one sees effects, sometimes short-lived but intense, of factors of this kind (positive or pathogenic, as in contagious hysteria), they always involve what I call a *mediation of assemblage*. What I'm saying about the institutional components that we know in situations like those of Marmottan or La Borde, I would also say in connection with utterly different factors (psychopharmacological, psychotherapeutic, ecological, etc.). Even when we believe that we are facing a relation of direct efficiency, we are really in the presence of complex systems of interactions, which we must make discernible if we don't want them to turn into some kind of "black box" from which anything could emerge.

Why, in this field, are the facts always out of step with the representations, as if we were dependent on a relation of uncertainty, like the one that Heisenberg indicates with his uncertainty principle? For a reason that, in my view, is insurmountable and unavoidable: the "objects" that we are dealing with are not homogeneous "subjects," entities that we can define, not even in relation to an individual bodily unit. They are subjective-objective assemblages of heterogeneous components whose outline can never be defined reliably. Any apprehension through speech, any framing through "mass-mediatization," or any possible treatment in the framework of an imaginary economy of the identifications—individual transferential identifications, or more social, more collective identifications—of these assemblages, does not make us immune to the fact that they are always likely to slip between our fingers. And that's all right! Any micropolitics of intervention that is unaware of or rejects this potential discrepancy will have alienating effects and oppressive consequences (even though they may sometimes be difficult to perceive). In other words: when we are dealing with a psychotic, with an individual whom we cannot place in the ordinary coordinates, we can always try to normalize him, "behaviorize" him, in relation to the dominant representations. But once we really talk to him, once it is a question of considering significances that are essential to him—not only in his head but also in his life and context—then we perceive intricate components that are constantly out of step with each other. "Why is he here? Why does he come to see me? Is it possible that he is only the visible part of a whole social group that drives him here?" It is always a complex social assemblage that operates a remote control over an individual in the meshes of a collective facility. We cultivate the myth of an a priori individuation of subjectivity; in other words, people are responsible for themselves and aware of themselves. But most of the time it isn't true! In order to see this one has to free oneself from the reductionist approaches of communication: the guy there who talks to me and does certain things "inhabits" his acts, his gestures, and his words only on the surface. Because all this is really inseparable from collective marks, which include the family, social groups, and primary groups of all kinds.

The individual who we see before us is often nothing but the "ter-minal" of a whole group of social assemblages. And if we don't get to the core of those assemblages, we embark upon fictitious attitudes. It's a question not only of locating the assemblage-insertion in which an individual is constituted, but also of finding a tiny point of support that will enable him to gain some supplementary degrees of liberty. Let's add to this that there are not only "visible," interpersonal assemblages; there are also infrapersonal assemblages. Certain crystallizations of subjectivity only operate in accordance with unconscious dimensions. Without using terms such as "fixation" or "partial object," it can be said that there are *partial existential options* that cause this or that personality to function in a sphere of which we might say, for example, that it is an anal or oral sphere. But there are other spheres that are much more subtle and more difficult to detect: artistic choices, musical choices, relations with the world, relations with the body, or with the cosmos. Here there may also be a substantial discrepancy between the person with whom we are speaking and "what is speaking," really. It's very important to consider this aspect, in my view, particularly in problems of drug addiction.

I have concentrated simply on these two aspects—interpersonal and infrapersonal. But behind them there are countless others: economic and social dimensions of all kinds, which intervene not as infrastructural determinations but as a kind of modeling, or remote control. Certain trails are easy to find. For example, to obtain access to hard drugs (which are usually very expensive), it's necessary to become a dealer. It's simple! But there are also more complicated things. I'm thinking of "relapses" into any kind of dependency—homosexual dependency or conjugal dependency, a search for imaginary "crutches"—lapses from which it's sometimes very difficult to recover. And if we don't take all this into account, we no longer know who we're talking to, or what we're talking about. On yet other levels, we're faced with sociocultural incidents whose impact is equally difficult to apprehend, but which play a no less decisive role: ethnic effects, racial effects, effects that Fernand Braudel says are only discernible over a long period. Living in a society that reinforces segregations, and that confers increasingly greater weight to CVs that give access to one standard of living or another, has consequences for individual and intersubjective positions.

To draw a map of the components of a personality, even summarily, and to consider it as a crossroads of heterogeneous components (which imply not only palpable things that weigh on the spirit, but also "incorporeal" ones that weigh on the body) calls for great prudence in relation to the possible impact of institutional interventions such as those that are administered at Marmottan or at La Borde. The interventions can only have a positive effect if they are articulated with one or more of these architectonic components. Thus we have a system of mediations of which much can be expected, at times, but which can also have certain destructuring or perverse effects. The ideal thing here would be to make a complete "calculation of effect." The collective imaginary protective padding (the "protectionism" of the institution) can play the part of transitory parentheses, the possibility of establishing a distance, recovering one's strength, allowing the rearticulation of a personality; but on the other hand, it can also play the part of a factor of "sinking" or quitting, an infantilization of the relation with society and with the environment. There's no univocal response! What I'm saying here can equally be transposed to psychotherapy, medication, and so on. In other words, it's absolutely impossible to be certain that a given intervention will have a certain effect. *All that can be said is that, when an institutional proposition is enunciated, when an effect of meaning in a subjective assemblage is triggered off, a micropolitics of enunciation (or of the therapeutic act) is always implied, and that the corollary of this is that scientific references are always illusory.* Well, with respect to the first point, concerning the necessary mediation, that's all that I have to say.

2. I have the impression that the "profiles" of drug addiction constitute illustrations of these problematics taken to an extreme: in this case, the need not to proceed except from a multireferential or "polyphonic" vision is even greater. There's no example of drug addiction that depends on a single cause. In the popular, family mythology, and sometimes also among social workers, we find the ancient idea that people get into drugs because of "bad influences," or "bad company"; or we hear clichés like "it's because people begin with soft drugs that they end up with hard drugs"; or we hear the blame being laid on "the modern age" and the desperation to which it condemns young people. Clearly, such considerations are not going to help us to understand what happens with particular individuals. Nevertheless, it's undeniable that some of these dimensions, articulated differently, can be taken into consideration. But the articulating element that will bind the components together and perhaps bring about a mutation of personality does not depend (I repeat) on this kind of univocal determination. It's more a question of something that involves a certain kind of probabilistic phenomenon. A single component will never give a singular profile: a social or family environment that secretes a certain "abandonment"; a context of social drift combined with a certain spirit of rejection of the dominant values; a terrain of biological "prematurity"; a certain mode of orality; a predisposition to narcissistic turnabouts; objective impasses. Each of these factors, taken in isolation, could be a setback, but one that would not have a great impact. But an accumulation of all these elements can give consistency to a mutation of personality; they can transform the universes of reference of a subjectivity, producing another subject, another individual. The person before us still has the same name and the same silhouette, but he's no longer the same, he's a different person. Only a contingent, "probabilistic" conjugation of heterogeneous factors can give rise to these crossings of frontiers and bring about rearrangements of

personality. One might even say that, by definition, a multiplicity of factors should be brought into play so that there may be a subjective effect of transformation or invalidation. When we see no more than one factor, we can be sure that we have to look for others and that we're being short-sighted and "reductionist." All this may appear very schematic and very theoretical, but there is, nevertheless, a critical perspective upon which, in my view, the various specialists, the various conveyors of knowledge and techniques and, often, of presumption, would do well to reflect.

I would like to address another point. Just as psychotics (despite themselves) paroxysmally explore "schizo" dimensions present in our "normal" mental coordinates, in the same way drug users explore certain "matrixes" of ordinary subjectivity, certain ways of constituting ego territories where there is no longer a territory of life experience, where "everything is breaking up" (there's no longer a family, a country, professional associations, or specialized workers). So they reconstitute small, intimate terrains for themselves as best they can, sometimes wretched (but sometimes, also, not at all wretched), sometimes relatively inhabitable (or, at any rate, no less inhabitable than what they were experiencing before), and sometimes real hells—all variations are possible. But we can't deny that they experience a certain mastery or a certain attempt to regain mastery of subjectivation. *We can't be content with a "defeatist" view, with an approach to drug abuse as something that only expresses what is lacking. There is also an active micropolitics here, a micropolitics of apprehension of oneself, of the cosmos and of otherness.* That's what I believe I learned, not with drug users but with anorexics. It seems to me, though, that these profiles present some similarities. I even tend to think that a general theory of drug addiction (probably based on endorphins) might give us a "transverse" view of drug addiction, anorexia, sadomasochism, mysticism, paranoia, and so on. It seems to me that in all these profiles we find comparable attempts to create a subjectivity at a level preceding "basic personalities," preceding the delimitation of one's own normalized body: "I have nothing but at least I have this, a world of pain through a singular pleasure." All these refuges, these impediments, where people manage to overcome some of this anguish, where people survive, where people manage to affirm themselves, where people use aberrant procedures to trigger mini-pleasures, are inseparable from other ways of manufacturing subjectivity in our societies. I'm convinced that if we proceeded in this direction, if we had the means to make minute doses of the systems of self-addiction through endorphins as a response to "external" drugs, we would be led to take an interest not only in partial phenomena such as alcoholism, but also in conditioning at work by the use of images from the media, by fantasmatic scenes triggered off in order to "calm one down," to ward off the absurdity of existence—an absurdity even more pronounced as a result of having lost all support from religion and from delimited territory.

Thus the profiles of drug addiction, cases that actually are statistically rare, are only extreme illustrations of things that really exist everywhere. I even think that "we are all drugged"; the only difference is that we are not drugged "to that extent" or "in that way." At the same time—without making any kind of defense of drugs or schizophrenia (that has *never* been among my intentions!)—it's true that often the "best" people have the most catastrophic outcomes, because of a tenacious refusal or a will to affirmation at any price. They're not the most deficient in relation to society, life, and discourse, but they're the ones that smash into the obstacles most violently. What I'm saying is no doubt equally true in relation to delinquency. And I don't think it's entirely irrelevant to stress this point, because *in a relation of assistance (individual or institutional) the consideration of this axiological dimension seems to me crucial: not in order to promote drug users as champions of a new order and "the promise of tomorrow,"* but because they're the bearers of the most intense *problematics*, and because they're the ones who should be thought about more by society, public authorities, and the political class. One of the contributions of the Marmottan team is precisely the fact that it has respected this dimension. I think that *it is very important not to cause things that are primarily existential ruptures to fall into the register of assistance.* As I said before, this ethical and political dimension is not easy to apprehend: it's the least susceptible to becoming the object of a prescription or a strategy of an institutional nature. It calls for the invention of new assemblages of enunciation and analysis.

To sum up, I would say that the processes of institutionalization cannot function as a monody; what is needed is a polyphony, and one that allows utterly unexpected instruments. There is not the slightest doubt that it is absolutely necessary that asylums and refuges should exist—without becoming the abbeys of the modern age. (Perhaps you know how concerned I am about the threats hanging over the right to asylum in France.) But what has to be "orchestrated" in those places of asylum, and in those refuges? This is a considerable and enthralling problem, bringing into play anthropological, social, and ethical dimensions that concern the whole of society.

A discussion of the process of institutionalization has nothing to do with preestablished organization charts and regulations; it has to do with the possibilities for change inherent in collective trajectories—evolutionary attitudes, self-organization, and the assumption of responsibilities. This is true both at the most immediate level of daily life as well as at a broader social level connected with professional, cultural, and ethnic insertion. What is important here is to be able to work out life programs in relation to complex personalities exposed to rearrangements that are sometimes dangerous. It is as if it were necessary to "rewrite" or refound La Borde or Marmottan for each person who comes to them. This means being ready to have very heterogeneous discourses. "At La Borde we live as a group, we encourage people to participate in activities as much as possible." But equally: "Do whatever you want, remain isolated if it helps you." This heterogeneity of attitudes doesn't involve any duplicity of discourse. On the contrary, it's a question of offering a multiplicity of options. It's important, therefore, to have a range of possibles on the basis of which one (we, the institution) can at least *not do damage*, not add even more things, not cement psychopathic personalities. This embryonic possible has to find its place, be articulated, perhaps proliferate, and set out in various directions. This partial process of subjectivation must be given the conditions to operate on its own and arrive at profound rearrangements of personality. *Not to impede a process of mutation; on the contrary, to contribute so that it is offered space, time, and people who will listen.* Places like Marmottan and La Borde are small laboratories, inadequate in many respects, often working in a roundabout way, but allowing this problematic—or at least part of it—to be preserved: how to create a processual subjectivity when everything is blocked, paralyzed, and stratified, in a game played with marked cards?

We find ourselves in a kind of "double bind": if we question the "specialists" about why their knowledge is compartmentalized, and why they engender a subjectivity in counterdependence, we tend to reconstitute a militant attitude. But militant about what? We've been running the risk of lapsing into a devalued discourse since the point when most of the militant ideologies broke down. It seems to me that there is a new genre to be invented here: something that's being sought, or at any rate something that should be sought. It doesn't have to do with being a sterilized social assistant, or a militant boy scout, but with defining a new social function, an analytic function. The ecclesiastics performed this role many centuries ago. It was up to them to assess the possible relations of subjectivation within and between the various castes and social strata. They worked on permanent adjustments through preaching, through confessions, and through a detailed jurisprudence concerning social groups, hierarchies, sexual relations, and so on.

The subject is not very clear, it's not "given," it's not naturally engendered: we have to work on it. Its modelization—in fact, its production—is artificial, and will become even more so. In response to viral attacks, very well organized research is constantly being carried out on an international scale in order to transform immunological systems! Collective subjectivity also needs a practice that is constantly evolving. The time when reason, sensibility, and mentalities could appear as frames of reference fixed once and for all is past.

Meeting at the Freudian School of São Paulo, August 25, 1982:

Question: I would like you to leave clinical examples, such as the case of Jean-Baptiste's psychosis or these discussions about work in psychiatric institutions, because it seems that, for you, the analytic is not restricted to the field of clinical practice.

Guattari: I'll give an example that's neither psychotic nor individual. It's what's been called the "free radio phenomenon" in France. I'm taking this example precisely in order to illustrate the fact that, in my view, the analytic issue should not be limited solely to clinical practice and references. In the context of this kind of generalized failure of the left in France, as we saw during the Giscard period, all the leftist parties, the small groups and sectarian groups of the far left, were reduced to functioning in a completely stereotyped way, cut off from real social practices. In 1977, with a group of friends who were well informed about what was happening in Italy, we had the idea of trying to start something based on a questioning of the monopoly of radio broadcasting. In our heads, the idea was that it should question the use of the media, especially by the Giscard regime, that it should question the absence of democratic expression in the media, and that it should also try to experiment with what might be another way of working for the small groups likely to be interested in it. I'm not going to describe the whole history of free radio stations in France. What's interesting is the simple fact that the introduction of a technological element, a radio station, miniaturized and homemade with a minimal amount of equipment, had a surprising semiotic efficiency. It was a question of actually placing oneself outside the law, deliberately placing oneself in the position of undergoing prosecutions, arrests, jamming, and so on. The initiative seemed to be almost absurd, because it had the state apparatus and the whole legal apparatus against it. Furthermore, all the unions, the leftist parties, and public opinion as a whole had been captured by this phenomenon of monopolization of expression. Nevertheless, within a few months this intervention had the effect of totally paralyzing the system of repression, and gathering elements of the union movement around this illegal terrain of free radio activities (although they maintained their initial positions in favor of the monopolies), and political elements of the left (François Mitterrand himself—a man who very much represents the law, and who was then in the opposition—was even prosecuted). It also had the effect of mobilizing people in power at the time, and sparking off a crisis among radio professionals.

In order to understand the proliferation of such a phenomenon, it's necessary to situate it precisely as an intervention in the register of the social unconscious, the mode of collective semiotization, in its relation with the media interlocutor, with speech, with information, and so on. I have to say that, after a few years, this process was extensively coopted in many ways that I won't go into here. *What's important is: what was the breaking point that operated in a processual manner?* It's a bit like a tiny pebble that makes a microscopic impa14ct on the windshield and nevertheless causes the entire sheet of glass to shatter.

For me this became clear in the first broadcast we made in 1977 (which earned me my first criminal charge, since then I've had many more), which we called "Radio Vert" (Green Radio). It was an ecology radio station, set up in the newsroom of *Matin Paris*, which is a French daily newspaper. We started broadcasting and were surprised to have no jamming, at least until 9 or 10 o'clock in the morning. Later we realized that this was the time when, in accordance with the labor agreements, the people who were able to do the jamming started work. But even in that limited space of time we'd been able to make the first broadcast, which escaped the information control grid. What was this? A symbolic breakthrough? At the end of the broadcast, the four or five of us there were very pleased. Our fellow journalists in the newsroom said it was marvelous. Nevertheless, I was surprised to find that the technician who was doing the broadcasting, and who was an ecologist, turned his nose up and clearly didn't share our enthusiasm, our impression of having performed a small historical act of breakthrough. When we asked him what he thought, he said, "Well, it wasn't bad for a first effort, but if the idea is to do this, to go on saying this kind of nonsense on free radio stations, then there really isn't any point; if we're going to get involved in free radio, it's only worthwhile if we do fantastic programs"—and he gave us a harangue. We looked at one another and wondered whether he wasn't right. But there was an Italian friend with us who had been one of the promoters of free radio in Italy, especially Radio Alice in Bologna. He looked at the technician with an wry expression and said: "You haven't understood anything! Free radio isn't what you think. What's important in free radio, and what works, is when people tune in to a free radio station for the first time, and they hear a noise, a terrible shambles, the microphone falling over, everyone talking at the same time, and they think: oh, so radio can be like this." And this suddenly opens up what I call a universe of utterly different possibles.

You also find this kind of molecular revolution in a certain period in journalism. Célestin Freinet, a great innovator in pedagogy whom you undoubtedly know, made a revolution of this kind by setting up newspapers with children. He showed that written expression in print, or the expression of drawing and painting, could also be something different. This opening up of a different mode of expression, this opening up of other potentialities, is clearly something that changes the modes of collective subjectivation. A way of subjectivating a school class, a union group, or the communicative life of a neighborhood or village can be radically transformed by the mere intrusion of a machinic process of this nature. Even before there is any kind of development, even before history and power relations alter, possibles can arise.

Now, coming back to Freudism. What did Freud do by listening to hysteria? He drew back the curtains to reveal a new kind of universe of possibles, a new mode of semiotization of subjectivity, in which theoretical considerations, groups, movements, practices and so on were subsequently engulfed. But *initially, what Freud brought about was a break with the universes of reference.* For me, the act of analysis is not something that can be centered on the analyst's interpretation in a certain sequence of discourse. It's something that comes from certain elements of singularity and can cause other kinds of possible to arise, fully armed, in a situation where everything seemed to be predetermined, preinscribed in stratified modes of subjectivation, in modes of redundancy of expression, and so on. Analytic revolutions of this nature were introduced by free association and modes of asignifying rupture, which appeared simultaneously in literature, Surrealism, painting, and so on.

Nowadays we can consider that the way out of an impasse, whatever it may be, always implies that a process of singularization may arise, may approach the issue from new angles, and may create fluctuations that produce a different kind of equilibrium, a different kind of order. It's what Ilya Prigogine and Isabelle Stengers call "fluctuations far from equilibrium," "structures far from equilibrium." In other words, *the "formations of the unconscious" appear here as something that may possibly be produced, found, articulated, and assembled, and not something to be sought, rediscovered, or recomposed on the basis of universes of subjectivity.*

Renato Mezan: I agree with you that there are different levels, different dimensions, and that, as far as I can see, psychoanalysis doesn't account for all of them—but I don't think that it has to. I'd like to go back to the case of Jean-Baptiste and ask you this: where does your performance come in? You say that you didn't interpret, you didn't take the matter to an analytic dimension; so how do you see the effect of your presence in this process of singularization that led the boy to escape from his suffering to some extent? Second question: the expression on the technician's face. We can fantasize a bit and—applying a framework of interpretation and analytic conceptualization—think that the fact that the technician said "If you're going to produce garbage, why bother with free radio?" might possibly mean that he was distressed by that situation. And, if there's something in what I'm saying, how would you see the fact that the guy from Radio Alice said to the technician: "What you're saying has no relation with what we're doing: you haven't understood anything!" My question is: what could have been done, specifically, in this case, in terms of schizoanalysis? I'm asking because I have the impression that the fact that the comrade from Italian radio told the technician that he hadn't understood anything doesn't seem to have led to a process of singularization or breakthrough. How could one focus on this situation from a schizoanalytic viewpoint?

Guattari: I'll go back to the second example, because perhaps it may be easier. I think that this Italian friend, Andrea, made an intervention, an analytic interpretation, because the technician's comment ("If you're only going to produce junk on radio, why are you getting involved?"), as you quite rightly pointed out, was tending to make the group feel guilty and inhibit the potential of free radio. But for this Italian friend, who knew from his own experience that the power of free radio lies precisely in this nonsense effect and its repercussions, it was clear that we shouldn't situate the consequences of our intervention in relation to the dominant modes of valorization in the media field. So what he said was a kind of interpretation of the guilty atmosphere. The important thing in all this, and something that for me was very revealing, was not the invention of a new medium of communication but *the invention of a new kind of relation with what is communicated.* It's of the same nature as the revolution carried out by the great theorist and musician John Cage, who showed that music could also be silence, it could also be a violin player banging his violin on his chair. This suddenly opens up totally unforeseeable musical universes, legitimizing the introduction of noise into the aesthetic order. It's of the same nature as certain phenomena of rupture in the plastic arts with the advent of contemporary painting (I'm thinking principally of the work of Pollock, one of the most significant from this viewpoint). These ruptures concern not only the phylum of what painters produce, but also the way in which we perceive artistic relations in totally different situations.

So, in connection with your first question, I would say that *the prime virtue for anyone who intends to get involved in these issues concerning the formations of the unconscious is not to cause damage. The second is to try to discern the moment when an intervention could have a processual pragmatic impact, which is very rare. And, having succeeded in discerning it, to be capable of finding its limits, which brings us back to the first precept, not to cause damage.*

In other words, I think that in the case of Jean-Baptiste I had retained a certain credibility up to the time of the proposal to rent an apartment, a kind of innocent good faith connected with my own powerlessness in relation to that dramatic situation. At any rate, I hadn't presented the traditional bluff of psychologists and psychoanalysts—giving the impression that, in principle, I had power over that mode of subjectivation, and that kind of situation. And when I proposed that diagram, that plan of living and reorganization, perhaps I was able to do so because I retained a tiny quantum of possible intervention. Whereas, if I had intervened earlier and in any other way, if the axiomatics of the earlier situation had implied the impossibility of any kind of intervention of that nature by me (for example, if what had been agreed was that I would be there in a purely neutral situation, simply listening), then probably that quantum of intervention would not have been possible.

Question: I would like to know how you understand the presence of the chewing gum between you and Jean-Baptiste.

Question: I'd like to know what the psychoanalyst's desire addresses, what moves his desire in the situation to which he subjects the analysand? For example, in the case of Jean-Baptiste, the analyst makes a break with the institution of the family—but by virtue of what authority, what plan, if he doesn't place himself within the perspective of an analytic institution?

Question: I would like to add to that question: isn't there a possible problem of value in the analyst's desire?

Question: In this school we tried to work on the problem of psychosis. Thinking along the lines of our parameters, I was wondering whether, in this case, your attitude hadn't corresponded to a kind of "mother function," in other words, the analyst giving options to the subject. But I think, from what I understood of your exposé, that the most important thing was not to fulfill a mother function, but to do so with a certain uncertainty.

Guattari: As you wish. All these questions intersect at a particular point. *I don't think that there are analytic qualifications or functions that can be attributed to individuals.* One thing is an individual being in the position of a listener, providing assistance, social control, and so on; another is the fact that an analytic process is unfolding. For me, the essential thing is to see that the analytic processes are necessarily decentered in relation to people or individuals. The question of the gum is of this order. What kind of oral relation did Jean-Baptiste establish with me? Was it that he was in a dialogue with a part of me, in some unconscious way? And if so, would it be right to regard that "piece of myself" as feminine or maternal? Here we might think in terms of Lacan's object "a" theory. But that reference might be a trap. It's only of interest if it has pragmatic scope for the triggering of an analytic process; if not, it's only a fantasy that, as such, has no scope at all.

It's clear that, once we have an analyst's desire, it's because, for a start, there is an analyst. And there is a kind of "wish for analytic power," as it were, an expectation of a result, a behavioral modelization. That doesn't mean that the question of desire doesn't arise. But for me, it really arises as a question of transference, that is, as a mortal trap. We could say that *whenever a transference occurs, a situation of alienation has been established, which probably functions as an obstacle to the real analytic processes.* During the period when I worked as a traditional analyst, I established a kind of analogy between all the beginnings of analysis; I even confirmed it with other analysts. It seemed to me that at the beginning of the treatments, from the first session until the fifth, sixth, or seventh month, more or less, a certain productivity existed and was maintained. However, from then on there was a kind of global phenomenon of massification or solidification, corresponding to the establishment of transference phenomena, which would operate for years on end as a real phenomenon of implosion of analytic processes.

Suely Rolnik: The transference would function as a kind of black hole.

Guattari: That's right, a kind of black hole that engulfs all the potentialities of semiotic productivity, whatever its nature may be.

Renato Mezan: That means that, in your opinion, the transference is a resistance on the part of the analyst himself to the analytic process? I would like to ask two questions. First: in the story of the technician, was there a transference phenomenon? If so, what was the phenomenon, according to your conceptions? Second: if, in your opinion, Andrea's intervention exonerated the group, do you think that he helped the technician to change in any way?

Question: Continuing Renato's question, isn't what is operating in this situation the division between intellectual and technical labor that is characteristic of our society?

Guattari: I haven't seen that guy again, I don't know what happened to him, but I imagine that he's had lots of offspring: there was a proliferation of a whole movement of free radio along the lines of a certain technical, technocratic conception. That division between technical work and the work of enunciation implies a totally apolitical, nonanalytic conception of that kind of undertaking. That's why, in free radio stations like the one where I work, specialization of technicians is systematically rejected. The person doing the technical part (not "the technician") isn't outside the cubicle but is directly in the situation of the dialogue. Obviously, this is a factor that adds to the confusion.

With regard to the transference, it's clear that something fundamental happens in connection with it. It's a total encirclement of the situation, putting the situation between four walls—like Sartre's four characters, except that here there are only two. It's a phenomenon of overinvestment, a paradoxical kind of semiotization that is established in this context, which generally leads to a situation in which, on the one hand, nothing is said (by the analyst), and on the other, everything that is said is absorbed, in a radical process of devalorization. It's a sort of deterritorialized sadomasochistic situation that conveys a considerable potential of desire: that's precisely what gives this device an implacable efficiency. It's also the reason why psychoanalytic societies and all the problems that get them worked up are not going to come to an end in the immediate future. Those societies really represent a mutation of forms of power: a prototype of power that is not presented in any way as a taking of power, because it doesn't involve any kind of coercive device. For that very reason this prototype of power is much more powerful. It's easy to understand that it functions as an extraordinary ideal for those who seek to establish an internalized power in all spheres of society. It sounds like a joke, but it isn't. In France—I don't know if the same thing happens in Brazil—there are hundreds of institutions for children. In those institutions the real power doesn't belong to the administrative authorities but to the analysts. They exercise an incredible domination, without manipulating any manifest coercive vector—at any rate, not one made manifest by the usual means.

Renato Mezan: I think that an analytic process doesn't begin just because there's one person called an analyst and another person called a patient. There are plenty of people who call themselves analysts and don't have anything to do with analysis as I understand it.

I think that all this is also connected with a very specific situation in France. I'm thinking particularly of the phenomenon of Lacanism and the appalling vanity that it conveys: his belief that the universe is hexagonal (the shape of the map of France), and his transformation of analysis into ontological processes, ethical processes, and so on. I totally agree with your criticism. For me, analysis consists in paying extreme attention to what happens in a situation, and here we could embark on a very complicated discussion. I'm going to state something that may be a heresy: there's a molecular revolution (in the sense that you give to this term) when there is a genuine analysis, and not just a ritualized, pseudoanalytic farce, such as often takes place in the name of analysis.

Guattari: I don't think that's heresy at all.

Renato Mezan: I was joking when I said heresy. I think that you're setting psychoanalysis on the side of the powers that constrain it, and that go against singularization and autonomization. But that doesn't correspond to my own analytic experience. However, that's another story, a long, complicated one, that we can talk about another time.

Guattari: For me there's no problem, as soon as *I don't see a coincidence between the situation that we call analytic and psychoanalysis*. Psychoanalysis is a practical and theoretical institution, it's a social apparatus to which we may possibly refer when we are in this so-called psychotherapeutic situation. Fortunately, many analysts don't practice psychoanalysis, but they don't know it: they have to be told the good news. And it's precisely by not practicing psychoanalysis that perhaps, from time to time, they may find themselves doing analysis, despite themselves. It's precisely for the sake of analysis that I think it's necessary to combat the institution of psychoanalysis, with its multiple dimensions of sclerosis—institutional, theoretical, praxic, and so on.

Question: I entirely agree with your proposal, which I would call the deinstitutionalization of psychoanalysis. But I think that we can even find the answers within psychoanalysis, as I imagine you yourself did. I would understand the analytic act as a nonsense effect. So what I would ask you is, if we consider the repeated creation of psychoanalytic institutions to be a symptom, could we not imagine that an analytic group—in the sense of a "subject-group," as suggested in *Molecular Revolution*—might, in this context illusorily called an analytic institution, produce some effects of the nature of an "analytic act," which would also spread beyond the institution itself?

Guattari: Here it's a matter of adapting vocabulary. I have the impression that we agree about the basic issue, but not about the way of expressing it. A group can be as analytic as an individual, and vice-versa. On the other hand, a device, which is not the same thing as a group (a procedure, a work of assemblage or semiotization), may aim to have an analytic impact, and may even be cut out for it. Except that this implies a verification of its existence as a process, within that process, which is precisely the opposite of a status or function. That's why I would certainly not go back to my earlier formulation of a "subject-group." I would speak of "processes of subjectivation" or "processes of semiotization," which don't coincide either with a group or with an individual, involving elements that are infrapersonal, organic, perceptual, physiological, ideal, and so on, and also processes that are economic, machinic, and extrapersonal. It's this kind of assemblage that may, at a certain point, acquire the dimension of an analytic process.

Domingos Infante: I would like to make the following observation: the discussion is constantly revolving around the words "analysis" and "analytic relation." The use of these terms doesn't seem to me to be appropriate because, if I've understood correctly, the proposal of schizoanalysis is something that moves completely outside the psycho-analytic field as such. It sees psychoanalysis as a "regime of signs"—the regime of the signifier—and proposes the consideration of other semiotic dimensions. Its outlines are defined in *A Thousand Plateaus*.

Guattari: I agree: I don't see the question.

Sandra Schaffa: I would like to add something, because I also feel that we're confusing things in connection with the word "analysis." Essentially, we may actually have points in common—for example, not confusing the position of the analyst with the analyst as such. Up to that point, we could say, things are considered in the same way. But on the other hand, it seems to me that Félix sets out from a flight, a breakdown in the transference situation, in order to define the analytic process. It's precisely at that point, in my view, that he places himself in a direction radically opposed to that of the psy-choanalytic perspective.

Guattari: This is where I would begin the talk that I prepared for today.

————

For me, the importance of the problematics of the analysis of the unconscious does not lie in knowing how a particular fixation or identification occurred at a certain moment of genetic development. These problematics are only of interest insofar as they allow us, in specific situations of particular social relations, to distinguish *how* processes of individual or collective subjectivation are blocked, either spinning round and round, or else developing symptom formations. An example of this kind of symptom in a group is bureaucracy, empty words, what in French we call *langue de bois*, a stereotyped, dogmatic language of clichés. When I speak of the formations of desire in the social field, I'm not attempting to explain history or class struggle with bits of psychology—or of psychoanalysis, for that matter. On the contrary, it's a matter of grasping and apprehending, as precisely as possible, how subjectivity has ended up in total impasses, or why it's absorbed in processes of production of capitalistic subjectivity, or (which comes to the same thing) why it doesn't succeed in entering into processes of singularization. In other words, it's simply a matter of grasping the reason why—when one is unable to live or survive in a certain place, at a certain time.

The analytic process is like an abstract machine that slips between social stratifications, between periods of time, between modes of sensibility, between what I call "universes."

The problems of the analysis of the formations of the unconscious have to do with such basic issues as the future of the movements of social transformation, or of the modes of bureaucratization, or of self-management conceived outside the criteria of a formal democracy that has proven to be sterile. All these issues have been set aside. Analysis has become a sectoral practice, based on a theoretical conception resting, essentially, on semiotic fundamentals with no direct connection to subjective productions as they exist in our societies. That is, if we consider the evolution of forms of social organization, the fact that modern forms of production increasingly imply the manipulation and production of subjectivity as an essential element. Nowadays there are machinic components that have considerable importance in everything that is at work in the field of information machines. These components constitute a kind of raw material for the very texture of our societies. These components cannot be understood at all on the basis of theories like that of the signifier, as elaborated and placed in circulation in the Lacanian and post-Lacanian situation.

BEYOND THE INFRASTRUCTURE COMPLEX

Excerpts from Guattari's talk on "Semiotic Energetics" at the Cerisy Colloquium in France, June 1983.

The Freudian unconscious

I'm going to describe the stroke of genius, not to say the stroke of madness, that led Freud to invent a semiotic energetics, the first theorizations of which, despite their naïvely scientistic character, were basically less reductionist than the ones he was to develop later, in the context of the institutionalization of psychoanalysis.

One of Freud's greatest ambitions was "to discover what form the theory of mental operation assumes when we introduce into it the notion of quantity, a kind of economy of nervous forces."[14] It's paradoxical to see that his first models of the psychic apparatus—totally steeped in the psychophysical vocabulary of Fechner and the "physicalist" conceptions of Helmholtz and Brücke, with things like "physical sexual tension above a certain value arouses psychical libido, which then leads to coitus"[15]—these first models were prepared at a time when he was also embarking on the exploration of the "abysses" of the unconscious. How could his mechanistic suppositions coexist with his new methods of reading the discourse of hysteria, dreams, slips, and jokes, whose audacity—and, often, we have to acknowledge, their gratuitous nature—only had equivalents in Dada and Surrealism? Consider, for example, the following passage from *The Interpretation of Dreams*: "… in analyzing a dream I insist that the whole scale of estimates of certainty shall be abandoned and that the faintest possibility that something of this or that sort may have occurred in the dream shall be treated as complete certainty."[16]

Without a doubt, the scientistic construction from which Freud never freed himself[17] *had the principal function of immunizing him against the excessively brutal breakdowns in meaning to which he was exposed, not only by his way of listening to neurosis, but also by his self-analysis.* However that may be, even though he did not maintain such direct interactions between energy flows and unconscious psychic life in his later models, we continue to find, underlying his various theoretical constructions, devices that interlace energy components and agencies of mental representation in an increasingly metaphorical way, but also in an increasingly insidious manner. The so-called model of the first topography proposes the engendering of the unconscious from a dynamic of repression of representations linked to curious drives, which associate two levels:

1) One, somatic, which brings into play a "pressure" of energy, the nature of which is not very well defined, but which seems to be of a biochemical order. This pressure has its "source" in zones of excitement regarded as erogenous, and its "goal" responds to a principle of constancy that tends to ensure a homeostasis of tensions engendered by these excitements.

2) Another, psychic, which articulates language events, object representations, fantasies, and intersubjective relations with the "object" of this apparatus; in a way, the object constitutes the variable of the apparatus.

Although anchored in physical energetics, unconscious psychic life as Freud conceived it at the time did not succumb to total dependence of a drive-based causality. In exchange for the distortions that the "primary process" causes it to undergo (displacement, condensation, multiple determination, hallucination, and so on), it is capable of imprinting various kinds of inhibition, deviation, or sublimation on the libido. In this stage of the theory it is really quite difficult to grasp precisely the points of coupling between the somatic and psychic stages of the drive. One does not know for sure whether this curious missile is destined to remain planted in the somatic soil, contenting itself with emitting affects and disturbances in the firmament of representations, or whether, on the contrary, it is already an integral part of the psychic world within which it is called upon to evolve. But that is not what was essential for Freud. *What was important for Freud was to establish passageways between sexual libido and effects of meaning.* This is something that he never gave up, even when he began to seek a cosmological foundation for the unconscious—based on dualist paradigms: life-death, love-discord, order-disorder—for his *initial hypothesis of an energy whose effects were simultaneously physical and psychic.*

With Freud's "second topography," the energy metaphors are gradually dispelled in favor of more anthropomorphic models,[18] *and thereafter the psychoanalytic movement never stops submitting the concept of libidinal energy to a wide variety of treatments in order to try to dominate the theoretical scandal of which it is the vehicle.* Here I shall only speak of its final metamorphosis, under the aegis of Lacanian structuralism. It was a matter of nothing more nor less than its virtually total *liquidation* in the form of a chain of signifiers. Even in his first writings, Lacan distanced himself from Freud's metapsychology. First he stated that the libido was nothing more than a system of notation of energy.[19] Later, reducing thermodynamics itself to no more than an action of the signifier,[20] he even went so far as to deny its character of flow, making it an "organ" of the drive,[21] which in turn metamorphosed into a "treasure-trove of signifier."[22] However, this libido, "organ of the incorporeal," compared elsewhere to a lamella that volatilizes,[23] immortal and asexual like amoebas, and which he also describes as an "omelet,"[24] was not completely deprived of its decidedly sacrosanct status of energy. Nevertheless, it seems that it was a rather particular energy, because it was susceptible, as Lacan noted, "to a quantimetry that is as easy to introduce into theory as it is useless, because only a few quanta of constancy are recognized in this energy." And, Lacan adds, "its sexual color, so formally maintained by Freud as inscribed in the most intimate part of its nature, is an empty color: suspended in the light of a gap."[25]

The schizoanalytic unconscious

The term "unconscious" is maintained here only for the sake of convenience. The field of schizoanalysis really goes far beyond the area that psychoanalysts consider to be theirs, which is:

1) An individual oral performance, generally based on a certain familial way of being of subjectivity, in the context of "developed" industrial societies.
2) Affective manifestations limited to the debilitated area of healing.

Schizoanalysis, on the other hand, makes an effort to mobilize the collective and/or individual, objective and/or subjective formations of becomings—human and/or animal, vegetable, cosmic, and so on. It is interested in a diversification of the means of semiotization and refuses any centering of subjectivity on the supposedly neutral and benevolent person of a psychoanalyst. *Therefore, it abandons the terrain of signifying interpretation for that of the exploration of assemblages of enunciation,* which contribute to the production of "subjective affects" and "machinic effects" (I am referring to everything that involves a processual life, an issue that distances itself, however slightly, from stratified redundancies, an *evolutive phylum* of whatever nature—biological, economic, social, religious, aesthetic, etc.).

Does this mean that, in this field, any prospect of evaluation and scientific prescription is definitively discarded? Might it be possible to conceive of the reconstitution of a model of the unconscious that renounces the *hidden* libidinal parameter (which actually eluded any conceivable test of *falsifiability*), without thereby ceasing to confer a status in their own right on "energetics," in the plural—physical, biological, sexual, social, economic, and so on? In itself, the hypothesis of a "discharge" of energy associated with each psychic operation was not totally senseless. It was only legitimate to mistrust it from the point when it led to the exportation of thermodynamic concepts outside their original field of validity, concepts that had been established precisely in order to exclude the "incorporeal objects" and "dissipative processes"[26] that are characteristic of organic and psychic life. The universality of the principles of convertibility and the increase, with the passage of time, in the entropy that is correlative with that universality, are only "sustainable" in the framework of very specific technoscientific assemblages of enunciation. I imagine, incidentally, that no one would doubt that in ordinary life, principally in the life of desire, the "discharges" of energy depend more on a principle of *defense* than on a principle of balance and constancy.

Therefore I propose replacing the conception of an unconscious founded on an economy of quantities of drive and a dynamics of conflicting representations by a transformational modelization such that, in certain conditions, the territories of the "ego," "universes" of otherness, "complexions of material flows," "machines of desire," the semiotic assemblages, iconic assemblages, assemblages of intellection, and so on can be engendered from each other. Here it is no longer a question of clinging to the form of the agencies, but of acceding to the transmutations and the "transductions" of their substance.

Our psychophysics stands apart from the one to which Freud referred in its refusal to consider a single substrate of material and energy. It does not postulate a Manichean dualism between what we might call an undifferentiated "inertia of energy" and a subjective "anima" that creates differentiation. *Before* the establishment of a matter and a distinguishable extension in the energy-space-time dimensions of the physical world, it sets out from transformations that are established simultaneously between the most heterogeneous domains that one could conceive. It presupposes various modalities of "transversality" between those domains.

What also distinguishes our project of cartography, on a methodological level, from the "effects" and "affects" of earlier scientific perspectives in this domain is the fact that its quantification is different both from physical quantimetries and from traditional logical quantifications. It no longer has as its object complexes regarded univocally, that is, complexes in which the elements have been collected exhaustively in advance, so that one can always know, unambiguously, whether a certain element is part of them or not. It is linked to assemblages that may be subject to radical transformations, "schizzes" or concordances that change their configuration, "reordering through fluctuation,"[27] "implosions without appeal,"[28] and so on. This ubiquity and multivalence of schizoanalytic entities—of which we can find an illustration in dreaming, but also in intellection in a nascent state—remain irreducible. "Monads" along the lines of Leibniz, or "myriads" along the lines of Michel Serres, these entities do not depend only on a mere belonging to "fuzzy subsets" capable of being "encircled" by a probabilistic or modal evaluation, but on a general plane of immanence that involves them all in relations of presupposition, which are to be considered as *levels of consistency of energy*. However, it might be preferable to take things in terms of their opposites and suggest that it is the fracture that each of these entities brings about in this "plane of consistency" that makes specific levels of energy manifest. However that may be, these intensive entities, and the energy quanta related to the consistency of their interrelations (actual and virtual) can only be discerned through the complex assemblages that they semiotize.

We may note that the semiotics in question is no longer a large suburb of linguistics, as it was in the Saussurian tradition. We can imagine it, more preferably, from the perspective of its founder, Charles Sanders Peirce, as an encyclopedic science of the phenomena of expression, a "phaneroscopy." It also borrows certain categories from the glossematics of Louis Hjelmslev, who advocated a broader semiotic opening of linguistics, because he conceived it from a fundamentally "immanentist" perspective.[29]

Meeting with philosophers, São Paulo, August 23, 1982

Guattari: I want to make it clear that what I'm presenting is something that has not yet crystallized: it's a working outline that Gilles Deleuze and I are developing. I would like to try to focus more closely on three types of issues, which I would call procedures of semiotic efficiency:

> 1) when and how a semiotic system starts to change something in reality;
> 2) inversely, how a reality may have a semiotic impact, and, correlatively, the processual systems that result from this (a process here identified with a general formula of the machine in a broad sense—not only technical machines, but also semiotic ones);
> 3) modes of semiotization.

So, what I propose to consider is not of the nature of a model of the psychic apparatus (to reuse an old Freudian expression) with its metapsychology, but of the nature of what I call assemblage. An assemblage of enunciation, which is not a return to the physical-psychic dichotomy, an old split that led to all the aporias in a certain era of psychology: the parallelism in Taine's theory between the physiological and the psychological, or the constant oppositions in

Freud between the systems of physical excitation and the systems of psychic representation. It's true that contemporary structuralist theories in psychoanalysis have seemingly attempted to overcome this kind of opposition. Lacan's drive theory, for example, completely sets aside the old quadripartition of the Freudian theory of the drive in connection with libidinal pressure (undifferentiated sexual energy), sources (erogenous zones), goal, and object. In Lacan's theory, all that remains is the notion of the object, and even so it's treated as a matheme of the unconscious, that is, cleansed of everything that gave it a paradoxical, not to say provocative, or provoking character in Freud (the fact that he placed things like the breast, feces, penis, and so on at the heart of psychic operations).

So if we try to go back to this issue of the energetics, the passage to the act, semiotic efficiency, we may ask ourselves what destiny was allotted to it in existing structuralist movements. If we admit that Lacan's theory of the signifier totally eliminates this problematic, it's necessary to go along with all the implications of that elimination. If there's no longer an issue of energetics as such, if the concept of libido totally disappears during the evolution of Lacan's texts (in favor, incidentally, of the signifier, in a kind of synchrony of the affirmation of the concept of the signifier), this means that there's no longer any reason to maintain dynamic concepts, there's no longer any reason to keep the notion of "conflict" at the center of psychoanalysis. But if it's necessary to suppress the notion of conflict, then the notion of interpretation collapses, because interpretation is an unveiling of hidden meanings, which, in principle, are precisely the repressions that are connected with conflictive situations, and that should be unblocked. Gradually the whole psychoanalytic edifice crumbles. It would be no small task to see what kind of balancing-act could be used to arrive at a kind of monistic view of the unconscious based on the notion of the signifier. Everything comes to be of the order of signifier: drive, subject, phallus, the "other"—there's no need to enumerate all the formulas in this respect. But in this case the problem of the legitimacy of all the underlying metaphors implied by an economy of energy necessarily arises.

In these conditions, as I see it, *what is necessary is not to go back to a general theory of psychic energetics but, on the contrary, to try to differentiate the various energetics that are brought into play, which I would call "semiotic energetics."* In this intention of linking the concept of energy to the concept of semiotics there is an aporia, a paradox that I shall try to defend as best I can, that comes from a reflection offered by one of my physicist friends, an Italian famous for other reasons, whose name is Franco Piperno.[30] I asked him whether it's possible to conceive of the existence of movements or transformations that do not involve a problem of energy. With great tenacity he told me that it's inconceivable. Other physicists have also told me the same thing: for physicists it's clear that there is always a problem of energy. If we want to hold on to the consistency of the concept of energy as manipulated by those who are its administrators, it's unthinkable that there might be a movement of any kind, a translation, an ordering, an effect, a distortion, a qualitative change, that does not imply a problem of energy.

Miriam Chnaiderman: Where's the semiotics in all this? Why a "semiotics of energy"?

Guattari: In any system of semiotic transformation there's the notion of movement. In Chomsky's transformational conception, for example, there is the idea of transformation, which means that we can postulate, a priori, that there's a form of energetics to be invented. It's obvious that if we take thermodynamic energetics and every use of its second principle, which must be questioned, we'll end up with a total mess. So I think it's necessary to try to go back to much more anthropological conceptions of energetics. It's necessary to move from a general energetics, which only exists on the scientific conceptual level that physicists deal with, to a consideration that there are as many stratifications of energy, as many bioenergetics, as there are what I shall call universes of ordering, of valorization, or qualitative dimensions. That is to say, the conversion of energy does not in any way imply that there is not a specific level of kinetic energy, potential energy, chemical energy, biological energy, and so on, each with its globality, which precisely defines its sphere of the possible. It's this sphere of the possible that I would link with the notion of "universe."

Therefore, I propose to abolish the concept of general energetic equivalents—such as the concept of "libido." As a counterpart, I propose to try to capture spheres of specific functioning in which there are systems of encoding, semiotic systems, in such a way that, in the passage from one system to another, one proceeds not by a general equivalent but by passageways. The second cut is that of the process, the machinic processes that organize the combination of effects (it's this combination between the various systems of "effecting" that produces concrete machines) and the processes of "affecting," which would be, for example, the affect at a point of subjectivation.

Informal conversation, São Paulo, September 8, 1982:

Question: I have a question, perhaps rather a foolish one, but I'm going to ask it all the same. It's about the increasing space that Hjelmslev's conception of language has been taking up in your work with Deleuze. This conception already had an important place in *Anti-Oedipus*, in *A Thousand Plateaus* it occupied a much larger space, and from what you've been saying here one can see that the notions of content and expression—which, however you take them, are notions of language—are becoming central. My question may be somewhat perverse. If you say in *A Thousand Plateaus* that the unconscious has nothing to do with language—in response to Lacan, who also looked for schemes based on linguistics—then why is all this space being given over to Hjelmslev?

Guattari: I don't see it that way, because Hjelmslev was never really a linguist, either for us or for anyone else. It's more as a philosopher of language that he interested us: Hjelmslev's focus is that of expression. If you think about it, we could transfer your sentence, *ipsis litteris*, to the ideas of Spinoza: why is Spinoza tending to acquire increasing importance in our references? I think that, in a way, Hjelmslev is an extension of Spinoza with respect to the issue of expression, because it was he who raised the question of semiotics in a very open conception. I think that in Hjelmslev, in a way, there's a deeply destructive view of the linguistic systems and semiotics that reduce everything to the signifier. On the other hand, I think that the problematic of expression in Hjelmslev is only one of the terms of articulation, which, moreover, is not only situated in the expression-content pair, because really it's opposed to three orders—matter, substance, and form. And, whereas Hjelmslev's model was tending to free itself from the signified-signifier opposition (by making it more complex, with his six expression-content categories crisscrossed with matter-substance of expression), we've made it more complex still. We've added a multiplying factor to the overall system, with the introduction of the opposition between the modes of encoding—the modes of expression that depend on... I don't know how to put it... coordinates of universe, incorporeal systems/nonsystems, territorial becomings, sensible becomings, qualitative becomings, value becomings.

5

EMOTION, ENERGY, BODY, SEX

I think we have to be very careful with the references to notions of energy—such as life force, emotion, or even energy itself—that have been so fashionable recently, because they are the kinds of notions that always attempt to "pull" the economy of desire toward a kind of instinct or drive infrastructure, and establish a Manichean dichotomy between a supposed undifferentiated and *the* differentiated. *I think it is much more useful to work toward a theory that considers desire as being immediately of the nature of highly differentiated and elaborated machinic systems.*

Informal conversation, São Paulo, September 8, 1982:

Question: In *A Thousand Plateaus* you include many warnings and instructions for caution, and so on, in the sense that there's a kind of journey that one makes step by step in the book, and at the same time one runs the risk of not being able to go on, and of being sucked in by the journey. So I would like to know whether there is a place for caution, even though one risks being sucked in by the journey; or to what extent the warnings might not falsify the journey. I was hoping that the two of you would develop this issue in the text, not in the sense of some kind of user's manual, but as something that would clarify this question of caution.

I'd like to make an observation: the issues that I'm raising are personal, in the sense that it's a kind of trajectory of mine that intersects with yours, or at any rate with your written trajectory, at a certain point in time. And it's on the basis of that intersection that I'm asking questions.

Guattari: The specification that you're making is important, because the journey that we're talking about is certainly not a journey in the American sense of a "trip," with all the quasi-mystical background that the notion of a trip acquired, we might say, in all the counterculture. So, instead of a journey, I would speak more prosaically of a process. In my view, an undifferentiated level of subjectivity does not exist. Subjectivity is always taken in rhizomes, flows, machines, and so on; it's always highly differentiated, always processual. Therefore, what we might call a schizoanalytic undertaking, a creative assemblage that is a producer of meaning, a producer of acts, a producer of new realities, is something that conjugates, associates, neutralizes, and assembles other processes. But the effects are not necessarily cumulative. Processes can support each other to reach dead territories. Unfortunately, that's what tends to happen a great deal, what often happens, in the conjugal economy, in the domestic economy. Two people are involved in a process of love, and that process eventually leads to a closing of territory, which neutralizes each and every possibility of richness (including sexual desire), every opening. The same thing can happen with all other modes of the process of expression.

It's in this sense that we can speak of a kind of caution. Not in order to make some kind of general moral category out of it. The question of caution arises precisely as a reaction to the spontaneist mythologies of a certain era: it has nothing to do with the idea of "anything goes," with improvisation, with "freeing oneself," with "enjoying the body," and so on. It's much more the idea of taking into account both the richness and the precariousness of these processes. We could give many examples. I gave the example of the feminist group in Lotta Continua: a process of singularization—that of feminism—can cause a movement to explode. But we can also cite the example of creative processes connected with drugs. It's true that LSD—or drugs in general—can develop perceptual processes, enriching semiotic processes, when they are assembled with a personality such as Henri Michaux. Unfortunately, the Henri Michaux assemblages are not very common, and we can easily find phenomena of implosion, neutralization, impotentialization, or quite simply phenomena of black holes. Fascism can also be considered, irrespective of all social and political determinations, as the expression of an accumulation or snowball of microfascisms. To say this implies distinguishing fascism from other forms of totalitarianism, from neutral totalitarianisms. Fascism is, on the contrary, a hyperactive totalitarianism.

In short, the economy of desire can also lead to phenomena of catastrophe, to a black hole.

Meeting at the premises of the Grupo de Ação Lésbico-Feminista, São Paulo, September 2, 1982:

Question: Don't you think that the problem nowadays is that no space has been left for emotion?

Guattari: I would like to make two observations about this issue of the reconquest of emotion. On the one hand, it's true that the production of affect, the production of emotion limited to what suits a certain functionality of the system, is characteristic of capitalistic subjectivity (one has only to ask the indigenous peoples of the Americas, or the Africans, for example, what they think of white people, and one finds that they often describe whites as walking corpses). On the other hand, though, it strikes me as being utterly absurd to think that it might be possible to reconquer emotions in their original status. This has to do with the great postwar mythology that developed around a certain conception of ethnology, jazz, and so on—a sort of Third Worldism.

I think that it's preferable to elaborate what you call emotion, and what I would call affect, in relation to the assemblages of production of subjectivity nowadays. For example, an item that comes from modern technology, such as a Walkman, can be interpreted in different ways. We could say that it's an instrument for the subjection of young people to the dominant forms of music and technology, or that it's some kind of techno-aesthetic drug. But we could also consider it as an invention of a different musical world and a different perception.

Maria Tereza Aaron: It's like the muzak in elevators, mechanical music, which is the death of music. There are even radio stations that play nothing but elevator music.

Guattari: I don't agree that it's the death of music; you're judging it from the viewpoint of musical content, while I'm trying to talk about the mutation of affects. In different technological phases there are different kinds of musical affects, or image affects, whatever their content or message may be.

Interview by Pepe Escobar for the "Folhetim" section of the Folha de São Paulo, *September 5, 1982:*

Pepe Escobar: Instinctively—gauging the distance that, within so many people, separates all possible splendor from the misery that's reserved for us—adolescents seem to be the first to recognize the situation and try to confront it with their weapons. In some cultural circles there's a lot of talk about the affective knowledge, not involving language or reason, through which adolescents mainly express themselves.

Guattari: I think there are many elements of expression that don't involve language as it's manufactured by school, university, the media, and all the formations of power. The expression of the body, the expression of grace, dance, laughter, and the will to change the world, to circulate, or to codify things in a different way are languages that can't be reduced to quantitative global impulses. They constitute the difference. In their ways of seeing, feeling, and expressing, the young generations have increasingly elaborate semiotic chains or systems. When my grandfather talked on the telephone, he didn't feel comfortable. Nor do I, when I have one of these technological gadgets in my hands. But for children who are five or six years old it isn't a problem. In other words, *these forms of affective language are not something similar to Rousseau's noble savage or his return to nature.* Look at how nowadays, in old Europe, there's a radical cut-off between the postwar generation that literally plunged passionately into films, technology, and knowledge of jazz and African art, and the university generation that followed. There's a different language, different ways of making films, video, and politics, that correspond to the real possibility of doing something *different*, something that gets away from the standard labels, something that isn't at all about doing something more primitive. The possibilities that open up are endless, even on a political level. My son does politics by setting up free radio stations—a highly specialized technology—and playing guitar. In New York, for example, things already happen from the viewpoint to which you referred, the viewpoint of affective knowledge, on the level of the sensibility inherent in the relation beneath immediate perception. But in so-called cultural milieus, in France, for example, it's all tedious, there isn't any kind of richness. I think that in Brazil, and in other countries, on the contrary, there's the emergence of a new kind of possible, which of course is coopted and framed by the great formations of power, the media, and so on, but it continues to proliferate in all its margins.

I have always been irritated by the litany about the theme of science with no conscience—"wouldn't it be good if we could place a bit of soul in science and technology," and that sort of thing. It's nonsense, because it is from this same subjectivity, which is moving toward an irreversible, accelerated degeneration, that machinic systems were able to develop. And also, isn't it a bit silly to want to improve the human species, which is one of the most vulgar, evil, and aggressive that exist? As for me, machines don't frighten me, because they broaden the perception and simplify human behavior. What frightens me is when they are reduced to the level of human foolishness.

I am not postmodern. I don't think that scientific progress and technology are necessarily accompanied by a reinforcement of the schiz in relation to the values of desire, of creation. On the contrary, I believe that it's necessary to use machines, all machines, concrete and abstract, technical, scientific and artistic, to do much more than revolutionize the world: to recreate it from point to point.

I am, of course, totally in favor of defending the environment. That's not the issue. But we have to admit that technoscientific expansion has an irreversible character. The question is that of carrying out the molecular and molar revolutions that can totally change its objectives, because—it has to be repeated—this mutation does not necessarily have to go in the catastrophic direction in which it is now heading. The increasingly artificial character of the processes of subjective production could very well be associated with the new forms of sociability and creation. That's where you could find the "cursor" of the molecular revolutions that I talk about nonstop, at the risk of breaking my friends' eardrums.

It's all very well to say that ideas come from the body, but then one would have to explain what is "the body." In a way, we could say that language comes from the body, insofar as we talk with the mouth. But language is not a biological function as such, and if we take other examples—such as sensibility, the relation with the world, etc.—we see that they do not sprout from the body, like a plant. Precisely because, if it were so, history would not be in the situation in which it is: if this kind of problem could be resolved by simply "cultivating one's garden," as Voltaire said, there would be a logic of historical transformation of a kind entirely different than what we are witnessing.

Perhaps there is a need for greater reflection on this notion of the body. In "developed" industrial societies, things are represented as if we had a body, but it's not as obvious as that. I think that they attribute a body to us, they produce a body for us, a body capable of developing in a social space, a productive space, for which we are responsible. There are other anthropological systems where this notion of an individuated body does not function in the same way; in fact, in those places the very notion of the body, the natural body, does not exist as such. The archaic body, for example, is never a naked body, it is always a subset of a social body, traversed by the marks of the *socius*, by tattoos, by initiations, and so on. This body does not comprise individuated organs: it is itself pervaded by souls, by spirits that belong to the whole set of collective assemblages.

In our societies, the great phases of the initiation of childhood to capitalistic flows consist precisely in interiorizing the following notion of the body: "You have a naked body, a shameful body, you have a body that must be inscribed within a certain kind of functioning of the domestic economy, the social economy." *The body, the face, the way of behaving in each detail of the movements of social insertion is always something that has to do with the mode of insertion in the dominant subjectivity.* And when the body emerges as such—for example, as a problematic of neurosis, as a problematic of anguish, or as a problematic of love, which, by the way, is often the same thing—it's because we find ourselves at a certain crossroads of articulation between, on the one hand, assemblages that are potentially productive of a singular possible and, on the other hand, social assemblages, collective facilities that expect a certain normalizing adaptation.

Meeting at the Freudian Psychoanalysis Institute, Rio de Janeiro, September 10, 1982:

Rose M. Muraro: We carried out a study on the body and social class in Brazil, more specifically on women's sexuality in different social classes. We interviewed people ranging from the upper bourgeoisie (rich people, the owners of the financial market, industry, and commerce) to peasants, people who don't live in the capitalist mode of production, people who circulate simple consumer goods, in the Zona da Mata, in Pernambuco. We also interviewed male and female assembly line workers in São Paulo. I want to report that the notion of the body that we found in these three social classes is radically different. There's almost a pathology of class, a paranoid pole, in the dominant class, and a divided, schizophrenic pole in the working class, for example.

Guattari: I want to thank you for enriching the debate with this data. However, I'm not so sure that the sociological categorization that you took as a reference is entirely relevant. The projection of notions such as schizophrenia on these categories doesn't seem to me to be very clear. I ask myself whether the tri-partition that you propose shouldn't be compared, for example, with a cross-section by age, and with a cross-section that operates in terms of ethnic ties. A different questioning of the sociological categorization would consist in distinguishing not only urban areas from rural areas, but also all the areas that can't be classified in terms of either of these two elements. Urban systems that are not cities, and rural systems that are not rural—such as the case of the vast areas of *favelas* that are so common in Latin America. There is also the fact that a certain number of capitalistic facilities have actually been inserted into this whole system of sociological categories—with the establishment, for example, of health systems, educational systems, the media, and so on. *I think that, if we don't reject cross-sections that are too simplistic from a sociological viewpoint, we risk finding only the level of assemblage that functions according to that system of categorization.* Such systems of categorization should only serve as a means for us to discern what the real assemblages are. My methodological perspective is therefore the opposite of one that relates descriptive elements to sociological categories.

In restricting the issues concerning desire in the social field to an issue such as that of sexuality, and to a particular technique, such as sexology (and perhaps also family psychotherapy, group psychotherapy, the hundreds of such technologies that are proliferating at present), it seems to me that we let the essential escape. If Gilles Deleuze and I have adopted the position of practically not speaking of sexuality, and instead speaking of desire, it's because we consider that the problems of life and creation are never reducible to physiological functions, reproductive functions, to some particular dimension of the body. They always involve elements that are either beyond the individual in the social or political field, or else before the individual level. These elements are not as easy to capture as the psychoanalysts thought, with their notion of stereotyped complexes and general, universal structures. In this aspect, before the individual and the body, there are complex singularities that can't be labeled.

Interview by Pepe Escobar, unpublished, São Paulo, August 26, 1982:

Pepe Escobar: What do you think of sexual liberalization as a normalization of sexuality?

Guattari: Sexuality is normalized in all societies. That's nothing new. What is interesting is the way that it is used and incorporated in the constitution of collective labor power, in the production of consumers, in the totality of production systems inherent in capitalism. Sexuality was previously kept to the private domain, to individual initiatives, to clans and families. *Now the machine of desiring is a machine of working.* It's on this level of investments of desire that there are reserves of capacity to express the revolt. And the system acts on this in a preventive manner, like an insurance company.

6

LOVE, TERRITORIES OF DESIRE,

AND A NEW SMOOTHNESS

LOVING DESIRE HAS NOTHING TO DO with animality or with any kind of ethological issue. When it assumes that form we are dealing with something that is precisely of the nature of the treatment of desire in capitalistic subjectivity. *There is a certain serial and universalizing treatment of desire that consists precisely in reducing the feeling of love to this kind of appropriation of the other, an appropriation of the image of the other, an appropriation of the body of the other, the becoming of the other, the feeling of the other.* And through this mechanism of appropriation there is the constitution of closed, opaque territories that are inaccessible precisely to the processes of singularization, whether they are of the order of personal sensibility or of creation, whether they are of the order of the social field or the invention of a different mode of social relation, a different conception of social work, culture, and so on.

The sometimes terrible struggles of neurosis, of conjugality, which cause the most promising feelings of love to fall occasionally into territories of hell—these struggles participate in the field of molecular revolutions. This may seem somewhat fantastic if we set out with the idea of psychoanalysis in which the phenomena that it calls the superego are of the nature of an intrapsychic agency. But if we consider such phenomena as really constituting a certain micropolitics of subjectivity, we understand why these Oedipal-type relations that I mentioned are specific micropolitics and not the embodiment of supposedly universal models.

Interview by Pepe Escobar, unpublished, São Paulo, August 26, 1982:

Pepe Escobar: Is it still possible for two people to live together? To reconstruct the structure or the sequence of structures of a relation? To maintain a kind of interpersonal anarchism that renews itself creatively against all pressures?

Guattari: I don't believe that freedom is anarchy. It's true that living as a couple has an element of being totally controlled. For a salaried worker, for example, it's practically impossible to live alone; there has to be at least one more salary—and so it's necessary to live as a couple. But life as a couple does not come down to this. It can also constitute a completely original way of understanding the world.

Pepe Escobar: Does familialism continue to be a cheap drug?

Guattari: In many cases the woman becomes a slave, a kind of assistant to the promotional sector of the husband. This is typical in the case of bureaucratic employees. But there's no point in making a moral evaluation of this kind of phenomenon. There's no point in looking down on people who take up drugs in order to protect themselves—whether conjugal drugs or not. What is important is that in *every* situation there is still—methodologically, in principle—the possibility of trying.

Informal conversation, São Paulo, September 8, 1982:

Question: The way that you and Deleuze found for working together reminds me a little of Montaigne and La Boétie, and what Montaigne said about his relation with La Boétie: "If a man urge me to tell wherefore I loved him, I feel it cannot be expressed but by answering: because it was he, because it was me." Taking this as a starting point, the question that I want to ask you is whether, in order not to fall into a black hole, it isn't essential that there should be someone with whom one can go on through the process. Someone who, in a way, helps us a little to keep our feet on the ground from time to time, and whom we also support, from time to time, so that he or she doesn't fall into a black hole. I ask myself whether people like Lenz, Artaud, and Nietzsche didn't fall precisely because they were totally alone.

Guattari: You have already answered your own question. I think that, really, one can never dissociate machinic processes from the structures of reterritorialization—to adopt a language that may be more complicated, sophisticated, or pedantic. The question of the assemblage of expression, of machinic assemblage—which changes the data, which reworks it, which drives forward new references, new universes—is inseparable from the question of the territories or the "bodies without organs" on which the machinic becomings, the incorporeal processes, are inscribed, marked, and embodied. But it's precisely here that we find all this ambiguity of territory, of deterritorialization and reterritorializations. A couple can have (I am convinced) an extraordinary productivity in a certain kind of assemblage, and it can also lead to a hell "between four walls" (going back to Sartre's expression), to a systematic impotentialization.

Informal conversation in Salvador, September 13, 1982:

Mauricio Lissovski: And this mysterious "new smoothness"[1] that you speak of in one of the texts in *Molecular Revolution*?

Guattari: The "new smoothness" is part of this theme that we are constantly discussing, which is that of the invention of a different relation—with the body, for example—a relation that is present in becoming-animal. To get away from all these modes of subjectivation of the naked body, the conjugal territory, the will for power over the body of the other, the possession of one age group by another, and so on. So, for me, the new smoothness is the fact that, really, a becoming-woman, a becoming-plant, a becoming-animal, a becoming-cosmos can be inserted in the rhizomes of modes of semiotization, without thereby threatening the development of a society, the development of productive forces and things like that. I mean that, earlier, war machines, military machines, and the great machines of industry were the only condition for the development of societies. It was physical force, military force, the affirmation of manly values that functioned as a guarantee of the consistency of a society. Without them, there was total devastation. This still exists in Russia, in all fascist countries, in the United States, etc. But nowadays the margins (the *marginati*), the new forms of subjectivity, can also affirm themselves in their vocation to manage society, to invent a new social order, without thereby having to take their directions from these phallocratic, competitive, brutal values. They can express themselves through their becomings of desire.

Letter from Guattari to Suely Rolnik, September 1983:

The sexual semiotics of the domain of "nature," of animal ethology, are hard and cruel. The territories that are constituted there, the *graspings*, are circumscribed. The new smoothness corresponds, on the contrary, to new coefficients of transversality, to the invention of new constellations of universe (becoming-woman, becoming-music, etc.). I had the impression that there is something like that in Brazil. I could be wrong, and the Brazilians are terrible machos! But there's a certain smoothness in the intonations... the music... In any case, it's a micropolitical objective and not an objective fact.

A New Smoothness?
Suely Rolnik

The fact that a certain figure of the family has imploded is something we already know. It is not new: it becomes deterritorialized in the same speed of Integrated World Capitalism, spurred in fact by its very logic. What is left of it is an empty repetition of the post-Fordist conjugal cell and its Hollywoodian characters—a certain figure of man, a certain figure of woman; a certain heterossexuality—entirely devoid of sense. Left without compass, diverse are the paths that we experiment. From obsessive attachment to the forms that the new capitalistic regime has hollowed out (artificially restored territories) to the creation of other territories of desire, the dangers that we confront are many, and sometimes fatal.

At one of the extremes it is fear of deterritorialization to which we succumb: we lock ourselves into symbiosis, we intoxicate ourselves with familialism, we anesthetize ourselves to every sensation of the world; in short, we become hard. At the other extreme, resistance to deterritorialization becomes impossible and, plunging into its movement, we become pure intensity, pure emotion of the world—yet there, another danger stalks us. The fascination that deterritorialization exercises on us may now be fatal; instead of experiencing it as an element in the creation of territories, without which we weaken to the point of, sometimes definitive, dissolution; we take it as an end in itself.

Between these two extremes, or these different ways of dying, other ways of living are clumsily rehearsed. And all these cases coexist, often in the life of the same person.

In the first case, Penelope and Ulysses—survivors of the shipwreck of the family—are embodied within us, dragging us into the accursed symbiosis that pursues us all, men and women. The accursed wish to mirror. The insatiable thirst for the absolute, the eternal. A thirst that gives us no respite and that separates us from all the strands of the world—whether human or not—with which we could be weaving other territories, with which we could be weaving ourselves in becoming-other. In the sullen immobility of Penelope (who weaves, but eternally the same threads), or in the compulsive movement of Ulysses (who weaves nothing, always returning to the cell), there is always the same tedium, the same impotence, the same suffocation.

Penelopes weave, but always the same thing: love for Ulysses. Threads, whether human or not, are nothing for Penelope: she rejects them all, or does not even see them. Her argument is the eternal presentness of the fabric that she weaves for (and with) Ulysses, a work that takes all her time and space. A fabric unraveled every night, reinvented every day. It is not for the taste of weaving that she weaves, but for the taste of reproducing this fabric—the image of this kind of love. Thus the world becomes absolute: she and the other (Ulysses) within her. Penelopes are eternally condemned to the wish to remain.

Ulysses travel, they go everywhere, without being anywhere. The threads of world they stumble across, whether human or not, are for them no more than bits of mirror that they try to possess at each adventure, in the expectation that a whole will be composed:

image of an absolute world; portrait of oneself as master of this world, a complete and stable self. But this imaginary whole is never composed. Ulysses are eternally condemned to the wish to depart.

Penelopes reject adventure, because it is in adventure that deterritorialization, the focus of their panic, becomes evident to them. Fervent followers and, in their own way, propagators of faith in the absolute, Penelopes do not recognize themselves in the discontinuity of outlines, and do not recognize this discontinuity as inevitable. Every time they feel it, they consider it a mere accident and, as such, transitory and definitely surpassable—an "accident" attributed to the lack of the other. Deterritorialization is translated as a sensation of falling apart because of longing for Ulysses. Melancholically, Penelope accuses him: "You destroy me with your desire for absence."

But this sensation of destruction (in absence) is inseparable from hope of reconstruction (in presence)—a condition of existence for Penelopes. The so bitterly bewailed threat of losing Ulysses is a threat of losing herself; a threat appeased at each of Ulysses's returns, for they bring her back this *self*. It is as if, to exist, she were infinitely condemned to repeat this ritual sequence culminating in the act that founds her as *a Woman*, a ritual always recommenced. And she hums: "Each of your returns has to wipe out what your absence caused me..."[2] With each of your returns, I will know again... and again... and again... that *I exist*. It is through the sobs that punctuate the anguished waiting for Ulysses—a cultivation of symbiosis—that Penelope safeguards her mirror.

For Ulysses the evidence of deterritorialization—the focus of his panic—is in the weaving. So it is weaving that Ulysses rejects. Fervent followers and, in a different way, propagators of faith in the absolute, Ulysses do not recognize themselves in the discontinuity of outlines, and do not recognize this discontinuity as inevitable. Every time they feel it, they consider it a mere accident and, as such, transitory and definitely surpassable. The "accident," here, is attributed to the excess of presence of the other, which prevent access to all the others in their illusory quest for the absolute. Deterritorialization is translated as a sensation of being devoured by Penelope. And Ulysses phobically accuses her: "You destroy me with this demand of yours, your insatiable desire for presence."

Here, the sensation of destruction (in presence) is inseparable from hope of reconstruction (in absence)—a condition of existence for Ulysses, Penelope's inverse complement. He needs to depart in order to keep Penelope subject to the threat of losing him, and with that threat keep her desire for him alive, a desire in which he is mirrored. And he feeds off the tearful song Penelope sings from the depths of her despair: "I don't exist without you...," "without you, my love, I am no one...," "I fall asleep thinking of you... I wake up thinking of you..."[3] When he hears this, Ulysses is relieved: he is consoled by the certitude of her eternal disconsolateness. Reassured, he now knows: "At each of my absences, *I exist* in her tearful waiting, which I see and see again at each return." It is in this repeated ritual, forged of an eternal flight and an eternal return—the other vector of symbiosis—that Ulysses safeguards his mirror.

His aggressive escapades (the journeys of Ulysses) are a condition for her existence. In her waiting, Penelope needs to complain of "the other woman"—all women (real or imaginary) he seduces in his drifts. In this complaint, she asks herself: "Mirror, mirror of mine, is there anyone more woman than me?" And the eternal return of Ulysses, the mirror's response, gives her the certainty of being *The Woman*, only object of the desire of "her" man, the condition of her existence.

The melancholy waiting (Penelope's weaving and reweaving) is a condition of his existence. In the irritation with Penelope's demand, Ulysses founds himself as a *Man*. He needs to complain of her inconsolable despair, because in this complaint he makes sure of the permanence of his ground, the ground of his perpetual reterritorialization. In fact, in his travels, Ulysses is never really deterritorialized: it is always—and only—on the secret *terra firma* of Penelope's incessant lament that he strides.

Ulysses's panic at Penelope's demand generates Penelope's panic at Ulysses's flight, which in turn generates the panic of Ulysses. But Ulysses is born of Penelope's panic, which itself is born of Ulysses's…

He seems to be the villain of the story, and she the nuisance: to all intents, he is the one who flees, and she the one who clings. But in reality, both of them need the abandonment and the clinging— in- and outside of a symbiotic pact. They both need this intermittence: in the dead of night, silently, the fabric unravels, establishing the threat of the unraveling of the *union*—and consequently of each of them, who are inexistent outside this cell. In the morning light, visibly, the threads are woven. In this alternation, what is sought is the certainty that the mesh of this drama will endure. It is necessary to ceaselessly repeat the danger of unraveling, in order to be sure of the absolute, eternal nature of this mesh.

Penelope controls time: she weaves the mesh of eternity. Ulysses controls space: he assembles the image of totality. Two complementary styles of the wish for the absolute: lukewarm, sticky immobility; cold, dry mobility. It is the same sterility. One and the same neurosis: a homeostatic equilibrium. The fear of living. The will to hibernate outside time and space, in the eternal ennui of death.

It is not always the same Ulysses whose return Penelope awaits; it is not always the same Penelope that Ulysses abandons when he leaves—they are increasingly interchangeable. However, the scene is always the same: there is always a woman who plays the part of Penelope for him, always a man who plays the part of Ulysses for her (or vice-versa). Radioactive waste of a vanished family figure, whom we reproduce artificially in the most pathetic forms. Reterritorialization, being eternally condemned to "make couple scenes," stubborn in the belief that one day "this" will become a stable whole.

But there is more than just Ulysses and Penelopes imprisoned in their conjugal cells. Suddenly, unable to bear the terror of confinement, some quit. Never again will those Ulysses return; never again will these Penelopes always be there in waiting. They have overcome fear and given themselves to deterritorialization. It is the second case: a different scene takes over, that of the *bachelor machines*.[4]

With no fixed territory, the bachelor machines roam through the world. With each thread that is presented—whether human or not—they weave, and are woven. And with each new thread, they forget, they forget themselves, carried away in their becoming-other. Without identity, they are born from each fleeting state of intensity that they consume. Their flight, far from the suffocating world of Ulysses and Penelope, reaches unsuspected universes. Life expands. There is a giddiness in this expansion. *Bachelor magnificence*.

However, there is also a new misery in this: in this fury of weaving with so many threads, so quickly replaced, the bachelor machines tend to lose the capacity to stop. No sooner are threads enlaced than they start fraying, never to become embodied in territories. Life, disarticulated, declines. And so the potential for expansion contained in the recently conquered freedom of movement is dispersed. Without time or space to weave anything at all, these erring body-souls gradually lose the capacity to weave. Immunological defenses invalidated, they become so vulnerable that at the slightest touch they fall apart. A new figure of death appears: AIDS. *Bachelor misery*.

It is true that sometimes the special passion that a thread arouses in them still leads to investment in a new weaving. But then what often happens is that, helplessly, they watch their fall into symbiosis—the very same. Once again they land on this soil; the bachelor machines become reterritorialized in the grisly symbiotic conjugal cell.

Two scenes, two dangers, the same damage: between symbiosis of Ulysess and Penelope on the one hand and deterritorialization experienced by bachelor machines as an end in itself on the other, it is the possibility of loving itself that declines. So have love relationships become impossible? Not exactly.

Exhausted by so much repetition, we find that both scenes are equally negative. Being like Penelope, exalting the return to the comfort of the home (conjugal confinement), or being like Ulysses, exalting the freedom of adventure (which only exists in relation to his eternal return to the nest), just masks the fear of deterritorialization, through a wish for the absolute. But also, in the other extreme, the act of exalting like bachelor machines this freedom to circulate disembodied eventually disembodies us from life itself. In consternation we discover that the result of having sought to free ourselves from symbiosis is that in the end we lose the very possibility of assembling territories—as if the only possible assemblage were symbiotic-specular.

Saturated by having our sensibility limited to these frequencies—the fear and/or fascination of deterritorialization—we tune in (as a question of survival… and of humor) to other frequencies, which until recently were ignored. One day one goes to the cinema and in a film chosen entirely by chance—Ridley Scott's *Blade Runner*[5]—this becomes more finely tuned.

In a city of the future—already vitually here, in fact—one discovers a new element in this plot that makes it even more intolerable, and us even more impotent. At the same time, however, we see the rise of a violent reaction to this situation and a whole experimentation in the construction of territories of desire beyond the trodden paths. In it we are introduced to the "replicants," clones of humans programmed by a leading high-tech corporation to colonize space. One finds here that at the very heart of the turbulence of bachelor machines and the crisis of the Fordist world of Hollywood they had caused, capital had found its new figure, from which it can extract new, more powerful than ever, forces. It is the IWC that had grounded itself on the appropriation of this drift, turning it into the source of its wealth and power. A new character walks onto the scene: the capitalistic bachelor machines, for whom the other is only a spare part for an insatiable narcissic machine. In truth, all vital energy of this flexible, deterritorialized self acquired by the Ulysseses and Penelopes who had bravely deserted their scene has been drained by the market.

The operation has achieved its degree of maximum perfection with the production of replicants. Perfect replicas of capitalistic bachelor machines in which, so as to make them more profitable, one had eliminated the sensible apparatus of vulnerability to the other on which the production of affects, compass for the production of territories, depends. To maintain such an apparatus would have compromised their free circulation between planets, indispensable for the accomplishment of their task: to elevate the operation of instrumentalisation of life from which they resulted to its intergalactic power.

However, they do not accept their mission with the neutrality one would expect from technical machines: when their time of existence is about to expire, they rebel. They replicate. At the start of the film they have just come back to Earth, precisely in order to avert their destiny. They want to overcome their artificial intelligence of slavery and, above all, their affect-less condition. They already sense the existence of those frequencies for which man, their creator, deliberately refused to equip them. They attack their creator's company: they want to *live*. But life, not allowed by their composition, is not for them—their doom is sealed. The revolt will only be successful if the replicants can contaminate the humans with its virus, so that the latter can themselves fight against the anaesthesia that has been sneakingly imposed on them and put an end to the expansion of this perverse enterprise.

Deckard, a man hired by the enterprise to eliminate the replicants and their rebellion, is the one they choose to contaminate with the awakening of the vulnerability that humans are capable of. Roy, chief of the band of replicants, about to win a life-and-death struggle with Deckard, saves him, contaminates him, and dies. Their revolt has been victorious: Deckard awakens. He decides to betray his all too human mission. To be a human, they say in the film, is to be either persecuted (man) or persecutor (policeman). From now on, Deckard will be neither. First quasi-replicant human, he bonds with Rachael, the last quasi-human replicant. They save themselves. Accomplices and lovers, they leave together and the film ends.

Will they invent another kind of love relationship? Other scenes? Other myths? We know nothing. But this does not prevent us from dreaming of something beyond the Ulysses/Penelope couple and their *all too human* love. Invention of territories freed from the vice of reducing the other to that through which our outline is sketched. But also something beyond the bachelor machines dedicated to deterritorializing in pure loss, these abstract invidualities and their *all too inhumane* love. Invention of terriories cured of the vice of reducing the other to a fleeting landscape with which, become sterile, we can create nothing. But we dream, above all, of a something beyond capitalistic bachelor machines and their voluptuous abandon to the exploitation of their own vital energy of creation by the IWC. Invention of territories freed from the vice, even more *inhumane*, of reducing the other to a rival in the market whose failure is the condition of our success.

We imagine *something beyond man (human and/or unhuman)*, in which fields of intimacy of another kind are established and our journey is no longer either the (attached) one of Ulysses/Penelope or the (dettached) one of bachelor machines, and even less the instrumentalised one of their capitalistic version. But thus far we know little about what this journey is like, which may be little but a vague memory of the initial inspiration that pushed us to leave the conjugal cell behind and to create bachelor machines before their miserable capitalisation. The desire for this autonomy of flight, where one would open up to the otherness of the world, allowing the affects mobilised by this openness to deterritorialize us. Above all, however, this desire to invent new territories by following the trace of affects produced in the course of encounters. A solitary journey, but a solitude populated by the encounters with the irreducibly other. Suddenly, we realise that the difference between the journey of bachelor machines before and after their capitalisation is precisely there. A first hint to follow.

It is not a matter of going back, in any case: we are in a different time, different affects convoke us, different strategies are necessary to carry out the rebellion of the replicants. And one is nevertheless ill-prepared. We have just been contaminated by Roy, chief replicant, and what we are living is the very first encounter of a quasi-replicant human and a quasi-human replicant. We are starting to invest desire into the creation of this new scene (scenes?), but we are still a bit tentative; the frequency ranges of this unusual journey are not yet tuned properly. There are noises, inarticulate sounds, and often we cannot bear to wait for a composition to be created: in our hurry to hear it, we risk composing those sounds with old clichés. It is difficult not to lapse into the sentimentality of a happy ending, these images that haunt us from everywhere with the trappings of the desire for eternity they bring and that makes us easy prey for the IWC.

We are always partly Penelope and partly Ulysses, partly capitalistic bachelor machine; but also partly replicant and, irrevocably, "none of the above." Caught unawares, what we really cannot bear is the stridency of those inarticulate sounds. And yet, in those rare moments when we just manage to bear it, we glimpse with a certain relief that, in the paradoxical encounter of these figures that come together in us in different degrees, almost ineffable, a *new smoothness* is already emanating.

7

LOOKING BACK ON

THE BRAZILIAN JOURNEY

CONVERSATION AT THE AIRPORT
São Paulo, September 19, 1982:

Suely Rolnik: How about talking a bit about the trip before you board the plane?

Guattari: You must be dead tired.

Suely Rolnik: Aren't you the one who's dead tired? The marathon certainly wasn't easy. But I didn't feel overburdened at any point. On the contrary, the trip just left me invigorated. Firstly because it enabled me to reflect on various sets of problems, whose urgency demanded a work of cartography and at the same time made it more difficult. And then because there were so many surprising encounters, so much adventure, so much that was worked out in these busy thirty days.

Guattari: It's true that we invented a kind of assemblage of enunciation, and not just the two of us. We invented a kind of exploratory machine that tries to penetrate different areas, different fields; to penetrate and at the same time invent, because, along the way, we had the impression of unleashing certain encounters, and perhaps even (why not) catalyzing certain microevents. That was an important dimension. Another thing that you said, and that I would emphasize, is that this stroll through different social areas in Brazil—often a frenetic stroll—gave me an opportunity to reflect on certain themes, to work on them and go deeper into them. I must say, incidentally, that this took place essentially in the debates that we had with groups of people, much more than in the lectures—which for me were a bit awkward, almost disturbing… as well as being tedious. For example, during the meeting yesterday in Florianópolis, I was very interested to have to go back to two questions that paradoxically had been left out from the very beginning: the question of a "lack," and the question of class struggle. People who approach us, myself and Gilles, know that we've made a break with Lacanism, a break with Marxism, and strictly speaking they no longer raise that kind of question with us any more. But here the question of a lack arose again, and that made me go back to the subject, trying above all to *redefine it in terms of a politics introduced by the division between guaranteed and nonguaranteed, the politics of culpabilization and castration that is peculiar to capitalistic subjectivity*. To redefine the lack not as something that constitutes us a priori (the essential lack of the relation of the subject with the signifier), but as an effect of the market, an effect of the production of consumption: a lack produced, invented and injected.

The second question was that of class struggle. Unlike many contemporary intellectuals, we were led to reaffirm and relegitimate the validity of social struggles, class struggles. I insisted a great deal on this point throughout the trip because I think that we have to stop thinking about the relation between autonomy and large-scale social struggles in terms of a dualist logic, because we know very well where that leads us. We have enough information to recognize that the two phenomena in question, of equal importance, operate according to forms of logic that cannot be reduced to one another: they cannot coexist except in a contradictory mode, in the knowledge that the antagonistic terms will never be "resolved dialectically" in this kind of thing. What perhaps allows us to advance in relation to this antinomy is the idea that *in any case, the political dimension drifts toward a micropolitical and analytic dimension, which is basically inapprehensible in terms of militancy*. This doesn't mean that the micropolitical dimension implies an oppositional implosion that prohibits each and every possibility of organization of speech, action, etc. It simply means that this dimension continuously reinjects all the asignifying elements, all the elements of singularity; it makes the questions complex at the very moment when they finally seemed to be quite simple: the moment when people thought they had reached an agreement. It's precisely at that moment that one sees that it's not like that, because *existence itself reemerges in its singularity*. This is the dimension—I would say the line of flight—of micropolitics outside the field of militancy. As for the apparatuses, if we confront them with these analytic lines of flight they appear precisely as they are. "Long live the Workers Party" until November, somewhat as if we were to say "Long live March 22nd" until the time comes when we're finished with it, until the time comes when we dissolve it.

What's dramatic in militancy is the fact that it has a religious function, a function of eternity. People engage in the structure of an organization thinking that they are investing in a kind of manna, religious power, or numen. They reify themselves in precisely the same way as in any church that promises salvation through the mere fact of adhering to its ritual. This is the idea that permeates all the organizations in the world. But things change once it becomes clear that they are precarious, provisional contracts, subject to revision, and that in any case history will make them disappear, will reconsider the problems in other terms and sweep away all the conceptions, all the ideological, theoretical, organizational references that history itself created. This idea was already present some time ago in the text about "transversality,"[1] when I said that the subject-group is defined by assuming its finite nature. It's an enormous problem for an individual to accept his finiteness, that is, the fact that he's delimited between his life and his death. However, this problem is part of any human undertaking, whatever its nature (political or aesthetic): to find that it is a sequence, a process, and that this limitation does not decrease the importance of the undertaking but, on the contrary, increases its value. This reminds me of Kierkegaard, in *Fear and Trembling* if I'm not mistaken, when he talks about leaving the sphere of the general and confronting what he calls the religious, which he defines as contingency, as a seal of singularity. It's what I would call the process of singularization: what makes it impossible to understand the meaning of the act. It's precisely because of the existence of the limit contained in the fact that we are necessarily going to die, and that the groups that we create in order to struggle, to change life, are necessarily going to fail—that's precisely what permits the processual character of the undertaking, its creative character, its engendering of new universes, its engendering of rhizomes of all kinds. This is an example of themes that were gradually becoming more precise during our meetings.

Suely Rolnik: It doesn't surprise me that those are the themes that appeared most during the trip, because basically that was why I thought of calling you at that moment. This intense agitation that we're experiencing seems to be asking us to work with these kinds of themes. Firstly, because in addition to this process of formalization of democracy on the macropolitical plane, a kind of boldness of social expression that didn't exist before is emerging: new forms of sensibility seem to be insinuating themselves. This probably has to do with the "crisis" into which capitalist development and its deterritorializing force has plunged us, causing certain patterns of sociability to lose their meaning. An example of this is the fact that the population (at least some sectors of it) is beginning to demystify rigidly hierarchized relations—a kind of servile respect, an active memory of "the masters and the slaves"[2]—which has always characterized, and still characterizes, sociability in Brazil. (Actually, living here has this unbearable element: as far as I can remember, I haven't come across any country in the world where the domination is so blatant and the servitude so "voluntary"). This divestment from the position of subservience appears both in small, everyday gestures (especially, of course, in the big metropolitan regions), and in this proliferation of social movements of the most diverse kinds and in the most diverse contexts. To reorganize oneself in this unprecedented situation, to recognize its disruptive potential, to think of it in its relation with macropolitics, certainly requires a renewal of parameters. This is the kind of situation that you like, and in which your presence fits like a glove: one of your greatest talents is the flair that you have for detecting movements of social vitalization—whether they're tiny or extensive, whether they're in Paris or Tokyo—to get involved with them, to seek their mode of rupture, to help to mobilize certain articulations at once in the situation and, indissociably, in your own thought. I would even say that this is your art: the art of the cartography of desire, the art of the analyst, of the schizoanalyst. In fact, understanding the exercise of analysis as this flair for the politico-libidinal economy of social life in its various nuances—in other words, as the exercise of micropolitics—is another set of themes whose urgency made me call you then. Psychoanalysis has been going through a process of rapid expansion in Brazil. This is probably due to the fact that Brazilian society is reaching a certain degree of capitalist "development" to which I referred, which involves approaching a dangerous threshold of dissolution of existing forms. The need to deal with this situation is an unavoidable task, a matter of survival. However, the way in which psychoanalysis is being practiced in Brazil, in general, doesn't seem to me to be able to respond to this kind of questioning.

In São Paulo, for example, until a short time ago there was only the Society of Psychoanalysis, linked to the International Society, with all the orthodoxy of its reading of Freud, all its disinformation about what's happening in psychoanalysis throughout the world, all the sclerosis of its structures of transmission. With the exception of a few isolated individuals, to my knowledge one of the only groups for preparing psychoanalysts that escaped this situation consisted of people—varying considerably over time—who revolved informally around the figure of Regina Schnaiderman. It was also largely due to her effort and the collaboration of Argentinean psychoanalysts who were exiled in Brazil at this point that, later on, the Sedes Sapientiae Institute's Psychoanalysis School was created, a school that still exist. That's on the educational side, because, if we were to consider the theoretical production of psychoanalysis and, more specifically, the reflection about the political and social implication of the concept of the unconscious, we would have to recognize that the situation is even more discouraging. If even the strictly Freudian or Freudian-Marxist treatment of these issues seems, with rare exceptions, to have passed by our coast and landed directly in Argentina, then just imagine the attempts at theoretical construction of such issues on a level beyond Freudian Marxism, where the work of Deleuze and yourself is situated?

Then recently, the movement broadened considerably: various independent groups arose, especially Lacanian ones; the Society of Psychoanalysis itself began to be shaken up by its new generations; and in addition, psychoanalysis has been gaining ground in the public health care institutions, the university, and in elite and mass culture. Given this situation, your arrival at this time also seems interesting to me as a way of mobilizing a certain reading of analytic thought and practice that preserves its disruptive character, within and outside the walls of consultation rooms, or even the borders of what's conventionally called the field of "mental health." When I speak of the disruptive character of analysis, I'm referring to this detailed work which consists in removing from territories—individual, group, institutional, etc.—the accumulated refuse of frozen images, which, by impeding access to the consistency of the processes that are being experimented with, obstruct passages, jamming each and every possibility of movement. The dissolution of these images—to escape from a merely defensive position—is necessary to recover the sensibility of the processes, without which there can be no creation of new territories of life. *In short, I'm defining analytic thought and practice as a certain way of exercising sensibility which allows the expansion of processes of singularization—and not as a prerogative of some kind of specialized work (although I have nothing against this kind of specialty), and even less as the monopoly of certain associations.* I was saying to myself that your presence could have an effect in these types of practice manifesting themselves, becoming articulated and advancing, because I feel that this demand already existed; it didn't wait for your arrival, reality itself imposed it. To understand and deal with the accelerated capitalist development that we are experiencing, and the "crisis" that is peculiar to it—this deregulation of the modes of social semiotization—demands, among other things, new instruments for the analysis of desire.

I feel that your trip was a success, because these matters were discussed from many different angles and in relation to many different situations: it encouraged things like agglutinations, confrontations, collective projects, the elaboration of processes, etc. But at the same time, who knows whether this means that it was a "success." It's impossible to foresee the effect of an encounter, however revitalizing it may be, at the time when it's being experienced.

Guattari: I agree. In my view, there's an inevitable discrepancy between the immediate apprehension that can be had of a direct intervention in the field and what it may come to be later, what I would call its "semiotic efficiency." They're assemblages that don't coincide. If they succeed in intersecting, so much the better. But it's possible that the semiotic efficiency comes, not from what you're thinking, but from a phrase, from a statement that will have repercussions precisely in the field of singularities. Something that moved me considerably was when Yone, in the context of a warm group welcome, took me over to a corner and said "Félix, you said something that unsettled me, that really gave me something. In your interview for *Folhetim* you said you believe that there's always a totally incommunicable basis to what happens between people." That's what caught her attention. That was what she connected with. It's a bit paradoxical, because we come to communicate, to stir up ideas, to liven up the molecular revolution, and then someone comes and says: "Oh, so there's something... a threshold beyond meanings." That's why *we can't claim to be transmitting messages or ideas: there's always also a kind of asignifying threshold, a kind of relation of apprehension which is of the order of affect, of the order of silent interrogation.* This can also have a semiotic efficiency, perhaps even greater than the fact that we catalyze ideas, the taking of decisions like "let's make free radio stations," "let's hold a big alternative Latin American meeting," and so on. Well, it might even be so, but it seems to me to be necessary to underline the existence of these two dimensions. To suppose that the only dimension of efficiency is of the nature of group relations, inductions of ideas, etc. is a bit suspect, it means being ignorant of the existence of another dimension: something that I would prefer not even to call knowledge, something that is more of the nature of an apprehension, an assemblage, the invention of a singular reality. In any case, in this passage there is the invention of a reality that for me will remain singular, thanks to you and all our friends, and that possibly, for some people, will also mark points of singularization. I mean that for me it isn't a trip connected with militancy or propaganda. It's precisely for this reason that my attitude in relation to the media is always very ambiguous.

Suely Rolnik: In the same way that your relation with the university audiences is ambiguous, or with any other mundane or mystifying situation. I think that what bothers you on these occasions is a demand that you should occupy the position of the "foreign intellectual" who comes to bring the latest word from Paris, the latest slogan. Or else there is a kind of projection of this image on you, which comes accompanied with accusations, as though you were occupying that place, or wished to occupy it (there were situations when you were fiercely attacked for that reason). Deep down, it comes to the same thing: in both cases it has to do with a demand for cultural paternity, a kind of academic/colonial Oedipus that needs to establish you in that role, either to exalt it or to attack it. Whenever it happened, you answered from another place, insisting that people should express their different positions and tell their experiences, formulate their questions. What you wanted was a dialogue.

Guattari: It's the least one can ask.

Suely Rolnik: Sometimes it just wasn't possible, and then you clammed up, which might be understood as arrogance, when really you were simply deserting the position that some people insisted on attributing to you in this colonized politics of subjectivity. It may be that on some occasions, your attitude had analytic effects. But that's the kind of thing there's no way of guaranteeing. Well, it's almost time for you to go. Before we say goodbye, would you like to say something about the book that I'm planning to make with the material from this trip?

Guattari: No. I think that this book is entirely yours. I'm interested in it, but it's yours, just as the first book is unquestionably yours.[3] To see my ideas worked on and presented in that way, for a start in the titles you invented, seems to me to be a small miracle. The impression that I have is that I didn't write any of it. Translation is production, it's creation, especially in the way that you collected and commented on texts from different sources, translating them by carefully choosing each semantic option, and so on. It's like what happens with a musician who takes a theme from another musician to make a different interpretation. It belongs to the domain of borrowings. In that book, you borrow my texts to make a text that's yours. As for this new book of yours, far removed from a collection or a mere work of editing text, for me it will be a complete surprise.

GUATTARI'S JOURNEY TO BRAZIL ACCORDING TO HIMSELF

Informal conversation in São Paulo, September 19, 1982:

Question: What is your desire in relation to Brazil?

Guattari: I think it's to be listened to a bit, to be heard as I think I could never be in France and in Europe in general. But that's not the complete answer. I'm also here because I'd like to create for myself a territory in Brazil where it would be possible to unite dimensions of myself that have always been separated in my mode of functioning in Europe.

Question: What dimensions?

Guattari: In particular, dimensions of writing, but not only writing, dimensions of all kinds.

Question: We perceive a certain movement of interest about Brazil, on the part of some French people who belong to the intelligentsia—Roustang, De Certeau, Jacques-Alain Miller, Castoriadis, Piera Aulagnier. Can you say something about the meaning of this?

Guattari: I don't know.

Question: It's happening in relation to the whole of Latin America. Could it be the language?

Guattari: That's the broad view of Lang, with his Latin cultures project. Perhaps what is behind this is really the invention, the mutations, of universes of Latin America. Latin America is undoubtedly also the continent that has taken off, from the viewpoint of capital flows—Brazil, for example, is already a great world industrial power.

Question: On the fringe.

Guattari: Oh, no, I don't think so. In any case, increasingly less so. And along with this, it's a country where there are, I don't know exactly, some 80 or 100 million subjects in atrocious poverty, in total underdevelopment. So Latin America seems to me to be the only place where certain problematics are being conjugated. Latin America is Africa, Asia, and Europe at the same time.

I've really had the good fortune to travel a lot in recent years. I've made many visits to Japan, Mexico, the United States, and recently to Poland. These trips have a very important function for me, which is to try to apprehend how the social problematics concerning what I call "formations of the unconscious" are captured and articulated, or simply ignored. What I call Integrated World

Capitalism projects its impasses in different situations in very diverse ways. I think that the very nature of the world crisis that is pervading all societies is raising the same kind of problematics everywhere, but not necessarily the same kind of questions. What interests me in these trips is not to have an academic or dogmatic position, but precisely to try to get to know the way in which what seems to me to be a general problem of the world crisis is apprehended, semiotized, and mapped in the various contexts.

What I am interested in understanding here is the distinctive traces of the various alternative experiences that are being developed and also the possible lines of flight, the lines of possible, that are being triggered off by these processes over the middle term.

I always consider it to be a privilege to be able to talk to real interlocutors, into whose problematics we wish to plunge. It's somewhat of the nature of processes, in which what is produced is not a repetition of ideas but a will to create, to change the order of thought, to change affects and—why not?—to change the social reality around us. I don't think that I'm being very demanding. I'm simply proposing that we try to play this game and see if we are able to put into operation a little communication machine capable of allowing us to advance in our respective problematics.

I would not give a lecture or an academic talk, firstly because I don't like doing so, and secondly because, for me, the only way to enter into a dialectical process of understanding is always to proceed through what I call a "collective assemblage of enunciation." The systems of traditional conferences and colloquiums have the failing of making people speak from written texts. This causes oral interventions to be based totally on writing, thus losing all the resources of information and communication that operate through different, nonwritten elements. This is precisely the kind of element that can be irreplaceable in debate, as has happened in the discussions that Suely and I have had with various groups since I arrived in Brazil. It's something that does not belong only to the domain of transmission of information. It's a feeling of capturing the intrinsic rhythms, the particular sensibilities, capturing the impact produced by a certain kind of problem in certain groups of people, in certain situations, capturing the way in which we're attracted to one direction, repelled by another, etc. Really, for me, what's taking place through this journey in Brazil is a debate in twenty or thirty parts.

There are two possible scripts: I could give a lecture in the appropriate terms, and afterwards there could be questions, some polished, others aggressive. In any case, there would only be an investment of sadomasochistic affects, the most classic result in this kind of situation. I'm a professor, I come from Europe, I have the means to travel, and I've come to bore you. Some of you would look at me as a kind of media image; others, a very small minority, might use me as a figure that serves as a kind of imaginary punching-bag. But it seems that the script that was drawn up here is different. Irrespective of the fact that the debate didn't take place in a kind of miraculous progression, there was the creation of a climate of expression. There were also, probably, lessons that I'll work on tonight, for example, in a dream, or two months from now in something else.

Round-table discussion at the ICBA, Salvador, September 13, 1982:

Question: Since the theme here is desire, when you make your presentation I would like you to explain a bit about the question of your desire to be on this panel.

Guattari: What you are asking requires a highly acrobatic exercise. Even so, I'm ready to go along with all the risks involved. When I arrived in Salvador yesterday, I didn't want to give a lecture at all, but I decided to do so because otherwise I would have placed my friends who organized yesterday's and today's meetings in an embarrassing situation. It's true that there's a custom of putting foreign speakers in the middle of an arena and making them talk as if they were in a bullfight. And that aspect wasn't entirely absent from yesterday's meeting. At some points in the discussion I felt that there was a wish, not so much to cut the speaker into little pieces, as to pick him up with pincers, as if he were a strange insect just arrived from Europe. There may even be a collective pleasure in this, but I wouldn't like to lend myself to that kind of pleasure.

This is a first part of the reply. The second is the fact that Suely told me, in letters and phone calls, that it would be good for me to come to Brazil now, not only because the collection of my texts that she edited was published a few months ago and was raising questions that were worth discussing, but above all because this is a time of intense political, cultural, and social agitation. As I have known Suely for a long time, I realized that, if she was insisting, it was because I really did have to come. Then she set up a plan for a university invitation to finance the trip, but I was tormented by the program of speeches and so on that the invitation implied. So I asked Suely if we could just do the meetings she was organizing with the groups, movements, minorities, community projects, etc., and leave aside the academic commitments: I'd pay for the trip to Brazil myself. That's what we did, and to my surprise, when I arrived, the thing took on proportions far beyond what I expected. I was literally captured by groups of all kinds. Suely had organized meetings with alternative schools, gay and feminist movements of various tendencies, people interested in setting up free radio stations, various groups of alternative experiments in psychiatry (including meetings with the Network[4] in some states), PT groups concerned with the issue of autonomy, and so on. There was even a lecture in a very austere academic environment—an enormous hall at a university in Rio de Janeiro, with photographs of all the chancellors on the wall—which became a passionate meeting with people from many different milieus. That was the mood in which we arrived in Bahia, where we felt that there was a different situation in relation to the agitation that I perceived in Rio and São Paulo. So my desire is, together with you, to try to get a better understanding of the meaning of this difference.

After a meeting with some alternative preschools, Suely commented that she was impressed by the fact that the meeting had triggered off a movement of articulation between those schools. What's going on? It's obvious that things don't happen like this. The meeting may have been a catalyst, but that's quite accidental. Perhaps the catalyzing element was not the meeting, the dialogue, but something else. In any case, other elements were needed to trigger off the movement: a certain economy acting at the level of a general questioning of the stratified economies, the abstract machinisms, that, in the current social order, govern the relations between work and leisure, between pedagogy, children, and adults; the whole electoral movement that's operating independently from my discourse; and there's also the indispensable fact that groups have come to me with their rituals and their problems. Well, it's true that there is an effect, but, if we don't want to be paranoid, we can't ignore certain conditions that create possibilities of change, and that may disappear. I might very well return to Brazil six months from now saying precisely the same things, in the same situations, and that discourse would be totally rejected because the fields of effectuation may no longer be the same, and other types of semiotic registers may be at work.

Interview by Sonia Goldfeder, São Paulo, August 31, 1982:

Sonia Goldfeder: Who is Félix Guattari?

Guattari: I'm French, I've worked in the field of psychiatry for a long time, I'm a psychoanalyst, and I run a psychiatric clinic 120 km from Paris. I don't work at the University, and I don't really like that kind of thing or have a talent for it. Ever since I was a teenager I've been interested in social movements, militant movements. I've always remained interested in them, which may be a remnant of childishness, or immaturity, because generally these things stop at a certain age.

Sonia Goldfeder: Let's talk a bit about what you call "your childishness," of this need that you have to act in various sectors, in various places at the same time.

Guattari: First of all, I do it because I can. Not everyone has this good fortune. There are a lot of people planted like mushrooms, like trees stuck in the ground, without being able to move. I have the good fortune to be able to take advantage of this kind of situation, to travel. And I'm not going to give it up. It's one thing to go to a country and give a series of talks (it's like going to Club Med: taking a trip without going outside). Another thing is doing what I do: going to all sorts of meetings. I would never go and talk at a university in France (and they don't invite me). But Deleuze, for example, is planted, tied like a goat to the university. You're tied to a newspaper.

Sonia Goldfeder: And La Borde? How do you organize your work, to be able to travel so much?

Guattari: I'm tied to La Borde, but with an extremely light, elastic rope that allows me to go away, to travel. I can't give a rational response to your question: for me, it's a question of affect, of desire, of doing things that interest me, and of not doing things that don't interest me. When the groups of alternative psychiatry communities in the southeast ask me to go to Nîmes—actually, they don't ask me, they summon me—or a free radio group asks me to do something, or friends in Lausanne (who are now being tried) call me, it seems to me absolutely natural that I should appear. For me this is clear, they're my family.

Sonia Goldfeder: How are you seen by French intellectuals?

Guattari: When I have the opportunity to come to Brazil or other countries, a dialogue is established. We're in a reality in which the little things that Deleuze and I have done have a large effect. People don't necessarily agree with what we say, but it always triggers off a discussion. The French aren't at all interested. There's no life on that level. We're not even criticized. The French intellectual milieu is monstrously pretentious. They think that they're the center of the world. France is a kind of narcissistic country where fewer and fewer things are happening. It's a kind of poor Switzerland. It's inconceivable that I could conduct a debate there like the one that I did here with the PT last week, for example.

Sonia Goldfeder: How does your activity tie in with the Mitterrand government?

Guattari: I'm a member of a research group that's trying to define a new form of funding for research in the social sciences. We're trying to create new paths for the development of what we call the "third sector," the associative sector (everything that isn't the state, or private capital, or even cooperatives). In fact, I have friends who are now in power, which doesn't mean that I'm a socialist. If I were to join a party now, it would be the PT and not the French Socialist Party.

Informal conversation, Rio de Janeiro, September 10, 1982:

Question: Taking your conception of analytic thought and practice as a starting point, would you consider your trip, or some parts of it, analytic?

Guattari: There's a perfectly definable trip that one can do with Air France and Varig; in principle, I should be in Paris on the planned date if all goes well. But this trajectory in the coordinates of space and time bypassed certain assemblages: it linked up with some of them, although without really making a connection, because it didn't find the means of discernibility,[5] or else it made a connection, but it will have a delayed effect, and so on; it found other assemblages, for which it triggerred off a processual system; others it literally invented, with all the retroactions that exist, because *there are no assemblages lodged as objects in space-time closets.* Therefore, one cannot say that a trip is analytic. We can, however, consider that we were taken up, Suely and I, by what took place on the borders of this process, we lost or avoided some analytic processes, some processes of assemblage. At the same time, we have the impression that perhaps there has been a process that may have changed something in some place, in the modes of individual and collective semiotization. But it's the process itself that will determine this. For example, it may be that the process will say: "it's nothing like that, you two are utterly delirious, you've experienced this trip in a state of exaltation, you believe that you stirred up heaven and earth, that you changed something, that you discovered America and the PT, and you really didn't discover anything." It's very possible that that's the way it is, but who can say for sure? I would question anyone who says so, starting with myself. What can one know about it?

We can generalize this in terms of analysis: when you intervene, when you say something, or when you say nothing, you place yourself in a position of interpretation, but it's obvious that you have no guarantee that your intervention has any validity. You'll find out, perhaps, through the process itself, through what happens later. There isn't any validation at the level of a corpus of signifying statements on the basis of which I can be sure that I've said the right word, at the right time. In fact, I'm sure that my attitude to people here, in conversations and in relations that I established, was sometimes paralyzing, inhibiting from a molecular viewpoint, and it's important to try to detect this. I think (and hope) that this is not all that happened, but, once again, only time will tell. As I said before, I don't believe that there's a system of guarantees in this field; instead, there's a constant, radical precariousness.

As far as Indians are concerned, whether Metropolitan or Tupiniquim, European countries are very underdeveloped. It's obvious that one can always reassure oneself by saying that history isn't linear, and that sudden ruptures can be expected. I'm convinced of that, and especially of the fact that *if you continue at the present pace of transformation in Brazil, you'll probably be the ones to set us back on the path of molecular revolutions.*

GUATTARI'S JOURNEY ACCORDING TO THE BRAZILIANS

Meeting at the premises of the Grupo de Ação Lésbico-Feminista, São Paulo, September 2, 1982:

Maria Tereza Aaron: Guattari gives me the impression of being a kind of comet. At one point he spends some time in Poland; at another, he's in Japan; at yet another, he is French, a therapist at a clinic in the country, an author we read a lot here and who is even translated into Japanese.

Suely Rolnik: At yet another moment he's hosting the Italian autonomists in his Paris apartment, while Radio Tomate is being broadcast from the kitchen, and in the living room he's playing Chopin duets with some American friend, for example.

Round-table discussion at the Folha de São Paulo, *September 3, 1982:*

José Miguel Wisnik: When I read what Guattari writes—for example, in *Molecular Revolution*—or when I hear what he's saying here, I feel as if I'm in the presence of a discourse that has a prophetic element, although totally desacralized, and not compromised by a prophet figure.

When he talks about the molecular revolution, he's referring to a process of gigantic growth of capital, which expanded from Europe and was practically enveloping the planet, dominating and insinuating itself into the lives of all human beings. This process now seems to have turned round and bitten its own tail: it's as if Europe was now in some way receiving the leftovers, the ricochet, the backfire of what it launched upon the world. In Europe now, the question of ethnocentrism arises: as the center of a world that is being decentered, it basically discusses the issues raised by decentering at a world level. What I am calling decentering is the fact that power takes on gigantic proportions, spreading everywhere, and at the same time it is miniaturized in each focus. So it's curious that the reflection on this process comes from France, the center of European thinking. Guattari's visit to Brazil now, and his interest in seeing what's happening here, forms part of this reflection. This will certainly have an impact on his theory and his practice in France.

What gives Guattari's diagnosis a prophetic dimension is the fact that he believes that, insofar as capital has expanded to this point (dominating all social relations and material and subjective processes, mobilizing cybernetic resources and the most sophisticated technology, becoming capillary and appearing everywhere), this expansion has made capital ambivalent: it's extremely powerful and at the same time extremely fragile. This process, which involves the mass media at a world level, makes each individual, from birth, a producer/consumer whose desire is completely captured by the production process. And at the same time, contradictorily, this process unleashes molecular mutations and proliferations.

I think that it's curious, creative, and stimulating that the things that we're experiencing in Brazil now are being taken into this kind of process: a process of global domination that at the same time can trigger off a reversal of this whole machinery. Whether this does or doesn't happen, whether these flows of desire end up precipitating themselves and uniting toward a true break with the despotic system installed in the country, remains an open question. It seems to me that the thing to which Guattari calls attention is the fact that it is not a question of asking whether this can happen or not but of committing oneself to it, staking on the possibility that desire will emerge and reverse these power relations.

Meeting with groups working with communities on the outskirts of the city, Olinda, September 16, 1982:

Comment: I think that Guattari's presence here is very interesting. He's working as a facilitator for the discussion of certain questions that are fundamental, but that have been experienced in an isolated manner. Here in Olinda, it's the first time that all the groups—of women, homosexuals, blacks, community activists, independent literature, etc.—are getting together. What stuck with me from yesterday's meeting is the realization that the question of micropolitics is latent, it's exploding and being discussed, even if not with the same conceptualization. What fascinates me most is the fact that it's being discussed not only among minority groups, but in a much broader territory, the territory of what's generally called the "popular movement."

Round-table discussion at the Folha de São Paulo, *September 3, 1982:*

Arlindo Machado: I think that Guattari's role among us is basically one of intervention. Most of the debates that he's provoked permit or stimulate greater knowledge, a deeper exploration of the issue of the mutations that Brazilian society is producing now.

Talk given at the Pontifical Catholic University, São Paulo, August 30, 1982:

Comment: I think that what nearly everyone here is interested in is for Guattari to talk a bit about the transition that he makes from an academic theoretician to a practitioner of politics. What I've noticed is that his own attitude in the meetings, debates, and conferences is this transition in action, even if the issue is not raised.

Informal conversation, São Paulo, September 8, 1982:

Question: In the work that you and Gilles Deleuze are doing there's something that irritates me a bit: you always present yourselves as people who are developing a kind of philosophy that's antisystemic or asystemic, I'm not sure which. At some moments I have the impression that it really is asystemic—that is, there's no project of totalization, precisely because totalization would be impossible. At other moments I have more of an impression that it's an antisystemism, or an antisystemization, but that even so it's philosophy. I don't know if you understand: what I mean is that, really, there's a kind of liquidation of dialectics. The two of you say: "the dialectic doesn't allow us to think any longer, or it only allows us to think through images—it's precisely this thinking through images that has to be overcome." But I have the impression that, despite this, the dialectic is reintroduced from time to time and eventually produces a kind of antisystemism (which would be the reverse side of a system), and we continue within the system.

Guattari: On this point in particular, I can't answer for two people. There are two types of functioning of desire, which are very different from each other, in this process of writing with Deleuze. Deleuze is a philosopher, I'm not a philosopher. I assemble reference signs, I try out ploys, like people who try to rob banks—I venture into maneuvers of expression in a certain context, in a certain situation. Later, I abandon it all and go and do something else. There's certainly a philosophical desire in Gilles, which definitely doesn't belong to the tradition of the history of philosophy, but which participates in a philosophical territory—at any rate, the philosophers are in Deleuze's family, not mine. So I think that this aspect of systematic antisystemism—if I've understood correctly— is first of all an event of writing, an event of creation: a dimension almost like a work of art, which work with Deleuze always acquires. So, in the final analysis, I want to say to you that this question doesn't concern me. I don't know whether your irritation is still there.

Question: I think it is, in a way. Because this issue that I'm raising touches on something that disorients me considerably, and sometimes I have the impression that really it's a crazy business: I'm referring to a certain kind of appropriation—which in my view is implicit in your work—which consists in receiving this philosophy (or whatever it is that you do) as a kind of model, a model to be followed, with its instructions for use, and so on. So what I ask myself is precisely this: doesn't the mere fact of adopting your work as a model mean falling into a Hegelian position, with no way out?

Guattari: You already know that I'm going to say that it doesn't, but I suppose that's not enough: if you're asking the question, it's because you can't be satisfied with that response. So, once again, I'm going to answer for myself. I have to tell you something that may be more than a formal denial: the fact is that I can't stand rereading a text that I've written, whether on my own or with Deleuze. Only yesterday I had a very unpleasant experience: someone read me a research project full of words, ideas, expressions, things that I'd written some ten or twenty years ago, and it made me terribly uncomfortable. This kind of thing annoys me, it shocks me in a way. That's all I can say. So I can see very clearly that there really is not only the risk, but to some extent even the reality of a modelizing action like the one that you're criticizing, and that's how I react.

Question: Precisely. The impression that I have is that one can't redo *Capitalism and Schizophrenia*, because it's a process that involves both of you, an approach that belongs to both of you, and it can't be taken up just like that and applied somewhere else. It's a kind of singular itinerary, if one can say that.

Guattari: Without wishing to make comparisons, one can't relive the Brothers Karamazov. I think that a work—which can't be called philosophical, though it doesn't bother me at all if it's called philosophical—can't be repeated. It can't be repeated, not only in its general movement—which situates it at a certain cross-roads, in a certain historical phylum—but even in its detail. I mean that no one repeats the mastery of the hand of a Picasso, or a Chagall, or a Pollock—otherwise, it would be easy to copy the brushstrokes of Pollock, for example, because he was filmed, and the film shows certain stages in his method of working. But why isn't it possible? Because this general movement, these brush-strokes, belong to assemblages that go right beyond the confinement of an act of creation. The assemblage of creation of a philosophical work, or an artistic work, depends on a climate, a potential audience, an attendant language—in short, it depends on thousands of things that are not reproducible, any more than the Paris Commune or May 1968.

Interview by Laymert Garcia dos Santos, São Paulo, September 8, 1982:

Laymert Garcia dos Santos: There's an issue that I would like to raise. What you see in Brazil as a kind of hope, I see, on the con-trary, as a kind of horror. I'm referring to the fact that different components of the people have not yet been totally integrated into capitalism, which makes the differences very powerful, and they're still not totally homogenized; something which is no longer the case in France, for example (which one can see very clearly in art and creative movements). Living in Brazil is a kind of horror. For example, when I prepared the text to speak in the debate at the *Folha*, I tried to put on paper something that I've felt since I came back to Brazil: a kind of very powerful malaise, which constantly irritates me, preventing me from living in this country. It's the thing that I referred to on that occasion as "persons."[6] In Brazil, one is obliged to be a person, whereas in France people are totally anonymous in relation to this abstract individuality. This means that in France your discourse can be worked with (I'm not saying that we can recognize ourselves in it, that's not the issue). Whereas here one can't work with your discourse in the same way, while at the same time our destiny is to become industrialized. The day that we are completely industrialized, we'll be semiotized by capitalism—as you say—but everything will remain the way it is. I believe that's how it is, and increasingly so. And there's no going back. So I don't understand what charm you find in these movements, the future of which is necessarily capitalistic abstract individuality. I don't know whether you understand what I'm trying to say... it's all a bit confusing for me... but at the same time, the difference is so clear.

Guattari: Brazil isn't Cambodia. It isn't a small territorial and human entity that is fenced in, isolated, totally the prisoner of the great international power relations. Brazil is for me what the economists call a "large market." It's on the basis of large markets like this that a new kind of entity has developed, called the United States, the Soviet Union, etc. Something that's constituted in a terrain of options for capitalistic flows, much more than the old Spain, for example. So that's already happened. This preponderance of capitalistic flows and capitalistic unconscious has already happened. This mutation has already happened. I understand very well that you may talk about residual areas, areas of resistance, and so on—great, enthralling. But for me, the people who practice *candomblé* participate integrally in capitalistic flows, even if there are all kinds of resurgences and reinventions of religions of African origin.

On this basis, if you consider what's happening in the systems devastated by the mode of production of capitalist subjectivity—the United States, for a start—it's clear that this vitality of the economy of desire exists especially among blacks, Puerto Ricans, Chicanos, etc. There's no destiny of being crushed because, on the contrary, at the same rate as the diffusion of machinic systems of any nature, they invent and conjugate instruments, bodies, and elements of expression, a certain kind of affectivity and of human relations, with the most modern machinery. So that they are the true inventors of the subjectivity of the mutants in the United States. Even the Burroughs, the Ginsbergs, etc. participate in a "becoming-black," in a "becoming-Puerto-Rican," in a "becoming-homosexual," and so on.

In my opinion, the real United States now is actually Brazil, or perhaps Mexico or Venezuela, who knows? They're the people who made this capitalist mutation and who, nevertheless, are totally engulfed in a black hole process on a large scale, like the Soviet Union. Although, really, if we change our perspective we see that this issue must exist with the very same intensity—but in territorial entities that are much more reduced—in the United States, Poland, Czechoslovakia, East Germany, etc.

I think, a bit like Braudel, that there are, not exactly "world cities," but productive centers—at any rate, in the production of subjectivity; centers that are the emergence of a process that is created and later dies, like the stars. It may be Brazil—perhaps I'm wrong, perhaps I'm delirious or stupid—and later, in ten or fifteen years, it might be China or India, who knows?

In any case, it seems to me that the conditions have been met for the development of a kind of huge machine, a kind of huge cyclotron of production of mutant subjectivities. I also think that Japan satisfies these conditions, and I wouldn't be at all surprised if, in the coming years, centers of extraordinary cultural revolution appeared in Japan. That's what interests me. Any objections?

Laymert G. dos Santos: I have no objection, I totally agree. But I'm not certain that what you say is being heard by people in this way. Listening to what you were saying, there were moments when I thought I was going completely mad. It was absolutely impossible to hear what you were saying inasmuch as people were taking precisely the opposite path: setting out in search of black identity, women's identity, homosexual identity, etc. And at the same time, people didn't understand that the search for a black identity and so on was already (or still) the introduction of capitalism.

Guattari: That's precisely what I tried to say about the film that we saw the other day—*Ylê Xoroquê*, by Raquel Gerber. There was that extraordinarily pretty, fluid girl, with a richness that embodied ancient worship and which, at the same time, gave the whole erotic dynamic to the film. She's really a mutant character; she's definitely not a character that exists in ancient societies, or in traditional systems of religious functioning.

Laymert G. dos Santos: Then I don't know if you understood what I wanted to say. I have no objection at all to your discourse, or to the process (which is fascinating): seeing how things are placed to work together, and how they evolve. But people understand this as a defense. What you call singularity is, for them, a sort of "step back," in search of identity, or even in search of the hope of being able to crystallize this, by finding an instrument—such as cynicism, for example—which is neutral and can serve archaism.

Guattari: For the last twelve or fifteen years, Gilles Deleuze and I haven't stopped talking about desiring machinisms—and not in order to speak of archaism. We often repeat that it isn't a metaphor, that it really is a machine, a machinic phylum, and so on. A machine that is as abstract as it is concrete, and affective, and social. So, underlying what you're saying, there's the idea of a certain dissatisfaction because our discourse isn't being heard. The question is not whether the discourse is being heard or not, the question is whether the process is being deciphered, insofar as that's possible—amidst the stammering, and arguing, and traveling around. The question is whether the process corresponds to something or not. As for the way in which people map their social production, as far as I'm concerned...

Perhaps that might be a first level. Another level is the fact that there is also this opaque core, this quasi-tragic core, this horror story that you were talking about. At any rate, one thing is certain: when I go to Mexico or Brazil, there's an enormous richness, whereas in France, as you know very well, they're not very much switched on to this kind of thing. Could this be a narcissistic trap? It might be.

Laymert G. dos Santos: That's right, I think that it's no accident that people like Luís Melodia or Julinho Bressane—people who capture all of this—are totally isolated in Brazil. I think that you made a kind of "faulty" contact, which led you to believe that positions like yours could be accepted in Brazil. On a certain level they can be, on the level of "what you're saying is so interesting," but if we look a little closer, we're left with just another talk. But getting back to this horror story, one can see very clearly that the situation is increasingly desperate (and you and Deleuze sense this—I say sense, because it happens on the level of intensity), but at the same time it's true that there's something that makes one envision possibles. However, that doesn't mean that we have a people behind us. As you yourselves say, it's like Klee or Artaud: "Really what we lack is a people, so that we may not fall into this huge black hole; in fact, that's what we lack most." So, basically, I can see what leads to an affirmation of optimism—there are possibles. But it's crazy because, at the same time, we can't go toward those possibles—I have the impression that the other machine is stronger.

Guattari: As I see it, this doesn't arise in terms of conflict, because if we take it to a schizophrenic level, a Lewis Carroll-type level of apprehensions, we'd say "it's very difficult, there's nothing to be done, but at the same time all that's needed is just the littlest thing for the possible to be truly within reach." It has nothing to do with "we have to wait, we have to mature," or "it's a catastrophe," "it's not a catastrophe." So there's the idea, not of gratuity, but of a possible mutation; and believing in it doesn't mean we're delirious, because in the scientific order and the aesthetic or the social order we do sometimes find unexpected changes in the situation.

Laymert G. dos Santos: This business of the people that is lacking reminds me of La Boétie. I believe he said "a few people"—he no longer had any hope of finding "a" people; but, at the same time, he depended on a people to liberate from servitude.

Guattari: That's right. Perhaps that's what I've been looking for with all my recent traveling. That's what took me to Palestine, and then Poland, Mexico, Brazil, and Japan. Is it possible that there's a deterritorialized people that traverses all these systems of capitalistic reterritorialization? It certainly isn't the proletariat or the myth of autonomy that will provide an answer. Yes, I believe that there is a multiple people, a people of mutants, a people of potentialities that appears and disappears, that is embodied in social events, literary events, and musical events. I'm often accused of being exaggeratedly, stupidly, stubbornly optimistic, and of not seeing people's wretchedness. I can see it, but... I don't know, perhaps I'm raving, but I think that we're in a period of productivity, proliferation, creation, utterly fabulous revolutions from the viewpoint of this emergence of a people. That's molecular revolution: it isn't a slogan or a program, it's something that I feel, that I live, in meetings, in institutions, in affects, and also through some reflections.

Laymert G. dos Santos: Taking you up on what you've just said, I would like to know if you aren't looking for a reaction against industrialization in this people? The word I used was reaction.

Guattari: Explain what you mean. What you're saying is very serious.

Laymert G. dos Santos: I mean that you may be looking for a kind of reaction, that is, looking for people who haven't yet been completely taken over by this process of realization of abstraction as such, and who refuse to go into this abstraction—because, once they go into it, there's no going back. Perhaps you're looking for a people with this kind of reaction, in order to activate it in some way, and also in order to show that what must not be done is to succumb to this realization of abstraction.

Guattari: If that's what you mean, I disagree completely. On the contrary, I think that I shall never tire of presenting a defense of abstract machines. I have absolutely no fear of the procedure of abstraction in question; in fact, it's what most fascinates me. I shall illustrate what I'm saying with the example of the Japanese, who conjugate structures that, from a social viewpoint, are archaic with an absolutely fascinating machinic madness in a totally ambiguous situation. It's the same as what we were discussing the other day about Brazil, with its dual register: widespread archaisms (which actually aren't archaisms, because they enjoy a very great creative vitality) and, at the same time, this relatively weak impregnation of machinic processes. I always trust in the people, in *childhood*, in the madness of what is most differentiated, that is, most machinic. So I didn't come, like Illich, to plead for the structures of togetherness, for returns to a bit more unity. No, I'm truly fascinated by machinic processes, and I'm thinking precisely about what they bring to these pseudosystems of territorialization and, at the same time, of undifferentiation. So, as I say, the primitives, the people, children, the insane, and so on are the bearers of the most elaborate and the most creative abstract machines. That's why I can't accept what you're saying. I have no people. *I think that the human masses will and must be radically deterritorialized precisely so that they can cease being masses and engender unaccustomed rhizomes of processes of singularization.*

Informal conversation, São Paulo, September 18, 1982:

Suely Rolnik: When Laymert suggests that even though you say the people doesn't exist, you're still looking for a people to save, I partly agree with him. It's true that there is in you a kind of air of communist youth, summer camp, "onward comrades!" and all that. It's leftist kitsch. But this is only one of your aspects, because, on the other hand, what moves you in all of this is a kind of passion for the currents of active energy that blow gusts of air into the social body, which then starts to pulsate, in an alternation between the destabilization of the reigning cartographies and the mobilization of a blast of collective intelligence which invents new forms of life. Every time it happens, you become chidlike. Godard said that men don't have much childhood and are very childish.[7] Well, if what mobilizes your childhood can be called a "people," making you radiant, running in all directions, in this case the "people" isn't a thing—it isn't a class, or group, or nation. "People" is the name of these currents, which are not to be confused with the places that they agitate, with the historical contexts that they help to create.

For example, on this trip, for you the "people" was located in the PT: a vibrating surface of the paradox between the readiness to organize in terms of parties, to struggle under macropolitical banners like "overthrowing the dictatorship," and, on the other hand, the willingness to allow oneself to be captured by a sensibility for the molecular, by a sensibility for destabilization and the creation of forms of sociability, subjectivity, etc., just as, yet differently essential. The PT as a medium for this sensibility and this paradox led you to participate in an electoral campaign and even to publish a book during the trip, containing a conversation that you just had with Lula.[8] But that didn't make you a supporter of the PT. It wasn't the PT that motivated you to conduct a campaign, but what the PT is being now. Afterwards is afterwards. The fleeting currents may continue to pass through these places, but they may also start passing through others, creating other situations not necessarily connected with political parties.

It's toward these currents that you have spent your life traveling. It has more to do with comets, as Teca said, with a "becoming-comet," than with a "becoming-scout" or a "becoming-priest." Perhaps the boy scout and the priest appear because they are the only way, or the age-old way, that we have for dealing with this kind of thing, which lacks a language of its own. That's why they're so kitsch. But, behind or through this priest and/or scout, what most draws the attention in the quality of your presence is precisely the opposite of these figures: your insistence on the importance of being attentive to the creation of a different logic, new languages—"minor languages" as you and Gilles call them—your desire to participate actively in this creation.

Your journeys are occasions for the exercise of this creation. For you and Gilles, this is not just the focus of a reflection, but a politics of thinking exercised in highly varied fields of experimentation. It's fascinating how you and Gilles succeed in doing this at the level of writing itself. It's fascinating how you individually succeed in doing this at the level of political and clinical practices. In this respect, both the "people" that you may be searching for, and the search itself, never cease to be deterritorialized in a "becoming-comet." It's all of that at the same time: one thing unfolding in another, in an infinite succession of masks that appear, and disappear, and reappear. It's what probably gives this ambiguous character to your optimism: the solemnity of this militant search for a "people," in a "leftist kitsch" style (which is your *childish, infantile* side, and at the same time the lightness and joy of the discovery of currents of active force, currents that deterritorialize even the people and the search, draining all of this into the tracing of new, untimely worlds (which is your *childhood*). In the final analysis, your quest consists, at the very least, of an austere becoming-priest or becoming-scout, a blazing becoming-comet, and the coexistence of all these characters and many more still.

Interview by Néstor Perlongher:

In a meeting with feminists and gays at the premises of the Grupo de Ação Lésbico-Feminista, Guattari dodged a question about why he had come to Brazil, saying that he hadn't come for any special reason. That didn't prevent him from saying that one doesn't catch a plane for no purpose. For me, personally, the novelty and the disturbing quality of Guattari's discourse resides in the possibility of making a reading of the social based on desire, making the passage from desire to politics within the framework of the modes of subjectivation. If Mr. Guattari came from Paris just to sow the seed of this restlessness, it's more than enough to make us happy.

Appendix

Notes about certain concepts[1]

Asignifying: We distinguish "signifying semiotics"—those that articulate signifying chains and signified contents—from "asignifying
semiotics," which work from syntagmatic chains without producing
effects of meaning in the linguistic sense, and which are capable of
entering into direct contact with their referents in the framework of
a diagrammatic interaction. Examples of asignifying semiotics
would be: musical notation, the mathematical corpus, the syntax of
computers or robots, etc.

Assemblage (Agencement): A broader notion than those of structure,
system, form, process, montage, etc. An assemblage comprises heterogeneous elements, which may be of a biological, social,
machinic, gnoseological or imaginary order. In the schizoanalytic
theory of the unconscious, assemblage is conceived as replacing the
Freudian "complex."

Becoming: A term related to the economy of desire. The flows of
desire proceed by affects and becomings, irrespective of whether
they can or cannot be applied to people, images, or identifications.
Thus an individual anthropologically labeled as masculine may be
pervaded with many apparently contradictory becomings: a becoming-feminine that coexists with a becoming-child, becoming-animal,
becoming-invisible, etc. A dominant language (a language that

operates in a national space) may be taken locally into a minority becoming. It would be characterized as a "minor language." For example: the German dialect of Prague used by Kafka. See Wagenbach, Klaus, *Franz Kafka. Pictures of a Life*, tr. Arthur S. Wensinger (New York: Pantheon Books, 1984).

Block (Bloc): A term close to that of "assemblage" (*agencement*), introduced with the notion of "block of childhood" in the book *Kafka. Toward a Minor Literature* by Deleuze and Guattari. It is not a question of childhood complexes, but of crystallizations of systems of intensities that go through the psychogenetic stages and are capable of operating through a great variety of perceptual, cognitive or affective systems. An example of a block of intensity would be the musical ritornellos in Proust, "Vinteuil's little phrase."

Body without organs: A notion that Gilles Deleuze takes from Antonin Artaud to mark the zero point of intensities. The idea of a "body without organs," unlike that of a "death drive," does not imply any kind of thermodynamic reference.

Code/overcoding: The idea of "code" is used here in a very broad sense; it could apply to semiotic systems or to social flows and material flows. The term "overcoding" corresponds to a second degree of coding. For example: primitive agrarian societies functioning according to their own territorialized system of coding are overcoded by a relatively deterritorialized imperial structure that imposes on them a hegemony that is military, religious, fiscal, etc.

Collective enunciation: Although language is essentially social and, moreover, diagrammatically connected to contextual realities, linguistic theories of enunciation center linguistic production on individuated subjects. Beyond individuated instances of enunciation, it must be made clear what "collective assemblages of enunciation" are. It must be emphasized that here "collective" should not be understood solely in the sense of a social group; it also implies the involvement of a variety of collections of technical objects, flows of matter and energy, incorporeal entities, mathematical or aesthetic idealities, etc.

Constellation of universes: References of representation are not quantifiable only in accordance with energy-space-time (EST) coordinates. They are also related to qualitative coordinates of existence. Universes of reference are not comparable to Platonic ideas: they vary according to their point of origin. They organize themselves into constellations that can appear or disappear with the constitution of assemblages of subjectivation.

Cut: "Desiring machines" are characterized as systems for cutting flows. In *Anti-Oedipus*, the term "cut" is inseparable from the term "flow": "Connecticut, Connect-I-cut!" cries Bettelheim's little Joey.[3]

Desiring production (desiring economy): Unlike the Freudian conception, here desire is not associated with representation. Independently of subjective and intersubjective relations, it is in a direct position to produce its objects and the modes of subjectivation that correspond to them.

Encoding: assemblage of code. A particular case of assemblage, which may be of molding, catalysis, identification, discursive enunciation, etc. In these conditions it is necessary to separate from encodings:

   a. "concrete machinic processes" (technical machines, economic machines, etc.);

b. "abstract machinic processes" (or machinic phyla). The "incorporeal universes" are nondiscursive universes of reference. They consist of traces of intensity that form relations between themselves according to the systems of coordinates, which do not depend on the logic of discursive ensembles, but on a logic of bodies without organs, or rather a "machinics of bodies without organs." Examples of abstract machines:

    —Chomsky's "deep structures" of transformational-generative syntax;

    —Mendeleyev's periodic table of chemical elements;

    —the various baroque machines that pervade art history.

Flow: Material and semiotic flows "precede" subjects and objects. As an economy of flows, desire is therefore not primarily subjective or representative.

Imaginary/fantasy: Insofar as the imaginary and the fantasy are no longer in the central position in the economics of desire in schizoanalysis, these agencies must be reformulated within notions such as "assemblage," "block," etc.

Machine (machinic): Here we distinguish between the machine and mechanics. Mechanics is relatively self-enclosed; it only maintains perfectly coded relations with exterior flows. Machines, on the other hand, considered in terms of their historical evolution, constitute a phylum comparable to those of living species. They generate each other, select each other, or eliminate each other, bringing out new lines of potentialities.

Machines in the broad sense (i.e., not only technical machines, but also theoretical machines, social machines, aesthetic machines, etc.) never operate in isolation, but by aggregation or assemblage. A technical machine in a factory, for example, interacts with a social machine, a training machine, a research machine, a marketing machine, etc.

Modelization/capitalistic subjectivation: It is only in current usage that these two terms can coalesce. But that is very imprecise: capitalistic subjectivation is always borderline, tangential, in relation to a "passion of abolition" of assemblages, in the sense that:

> a. Affects and Effects tend to be radically dissociated there, "dualized" (pure subjective affect, cut off from a pure diagrammatic effectuation), and
> b. relations of deterritorialization (discursive and nondiscursive paradigms) tend to be reduced to the strictly necessary. In fact, all subjectivation is modelization: the capitalistic model is a model of a model, a modelizing reduction.

Molecular/molar: The same elements that exist in flows, strata, and assemblages can be organized in accordance with a molar mode or a molecular mode. The molar order corresponds to the stratifications that delimit objects, subjects, representations, and their systems of reference. The molecular order, on the other hand, is that of flows, becomings, phase shifts, intensities. This molecular crossing of strata and levels by the various kinds of assemblage will be called "transversality."

Object "a": A term proposed by Lacan in the framework of a generalized theory of partial objects in psychoanalysis, designating a function that implies the oral object, the anal object, the penis, the gaze, the voice, etc. I (Guattari) had suggested to Lacan that to object "a" he should add objects "b," corresponding to Winnicott's "transitional objects," and objects "c," corresponding to institutional objects.

Persistence/transistence: I have changed the use of the word "persistence" several times. I see it now as the deterritorialized mode of existence that is established between flows and territories. "Transistence," on the other hand, is what is established, in parallel, between phyla and universes.

Personological: An adjective used to qualify molar relations in the subjective order. The emphasis placed on the role of people, identities, and identifications characterizes the theoretical conceptions of psychoanalysis. The psychoanalytic Oedipus brings into play people and typified characters; it reduces intensities and projects the molecular level of investments onto a "personological theater," that is, onto a system of representations cut off from the real desiring production (equivalent expression: Oedipal triangulation).

Phylum: The various kinds of machine—technical, living, abstract, aesthetic—are positioned in relation to space and time. In which case they constitute phyla, like living species in evolution. But these phyla do not start from a single point of origin: they are arranged in a rhizome.

Plane of consistency: Whatever differences there may be between the nature of flows, territories, machines, and universes of desire, they have to do with the same plane of consistency (or plane of immanence), which must not be confused with a plane of reference. Indeed, these various modalities of existence of the systems of intensities do not come within the scope of transcendental idealities, but within that of real processes of generation and transformation.

Process: A continuous sequence of events and operations that can lead to other sequences of events and operations. The process implies the idea of permanent breakdown of established equilibriums. The term is not used here in the sense in which classical psychiatry speaks of a schizophrenic process, for example, which always implies having reached a terminal state. On the contrary, here the term comes close to what Ilya Prigogine and Isabelle Stengers call "dissipative processes."

Production of subjectivity: Subjectivity is not envisaged here as a thing in itself, an unchanging essence. The existence of one subjectivity or another depends on whether an assemblage of enunciation produces it or not. (Example: modern capitalism produces a new kind of subjectivity on a large scale by means of the media and collective facilities.) Behind the appearance of individuated subjectivity one must try to locate the real processes of subjectivation.

Redundancy: A term created by theorists of communication and linguists. What we call redundancy is the unused capacity of a code. In *Différence et Répétition*,[4] Gilles Deleuze distinguishes between "empty repetition" and "complex repetition," inasmuch as the latter cannot be reduced to a mechanical or material repetition. To this distinction I add another: that which exists between a "signifying redundancy," deprived of any access to reality, and a "machinic redundancy," producing effect in reality.

Rhizome, rhizomatic: Arborescent diagrams proceed by successive hierarchies, starting from a central point to which each local element refers. On the other hand, systems in rhizomes or in "lattices"[5] can drift endlessly, establishing transversal connections that one cannot center or close. The term "rhizome" was taken from botany, where it defines the systems of underground stems of perennial plants that produce adventitious shoots and roots on their underside (example: an iris rhizome).[6]

Schiz: A system of cuts that are not merely the interruption of a process, but an intersection of processes. A schiz brings with it a new capital of potentiality.

Schizoanalysis: Whereas psychoanalysis set out from a model of the psyche based on a study of neuroses, focusing on the person and identifications and working on the basis of transference and interpretation, schizoanalysis takes its inspiration instead from research into psychosis; it refuses to reduce desire to personological systems; it denies that there is any efficacy whatever in transference and interpretation.

Schizoanalytic unconscious: Now I would say that the schizo unconscious is not just machinic. It also participates in four formations of meaning:

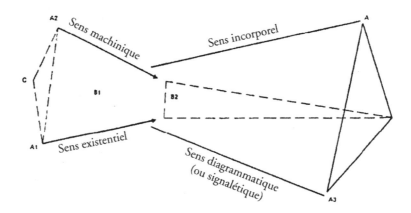

The formations of the unconscious are "staggered" on three random levels:

    a. the level of vectors of meaning (A);
    b. the level of the constitution of paradigmatic relations (B);

c. the level of the synapses of Affect and Effect (C), which "capture" intrinsic references (Systems and Structures).

Semiotic and diagrammatic interaction: "Diagram" is a term taken from Charles Sanders Peirce,[7] who classifies diagrams as icons, referring to them as "icons of relationship." Diagrammatic interactions (or semiotic interactions), in the present terminology, are the opposite of semiological redundancies. Diagrammatic interactions make sign systems work directly with the realities to which they refer, bringing about an existential production of referent, whereas semiological redundancies only represent, providing "equivalents" of realities, without any operational impact. Examples: mathematical algorithms, technological plans, and computer programs participate directly in the process of creating their object, whereas an advertising image can only give an extrinsic representation of its object (but then it is a producer of subjectivity).

Subject-group/subjected group: Subject-groups are the opposite of subjected groups. This opposition implies a micropolitical reference: the subject-group's vocation is to manage its relation to external determinations and its own internal law, as far as it is at all possible. The subjected group, on the other hand, tends to be manipulated by all the external determinations and to be dominated by its own internal law (superego).[8]

Territoriality/deterritorialization/reterritorialization: The notion of territory is understood here in a very broad sense, which goes beyond the use that ethology and ethnology make of it. Living beings organize themselves in terms of territories that bound them and articulate them to other living beings and cosmic flows. Territory can be related to an inhabited space or a perceived system within which an individual feels "at home." Territory is a synonym of appropriation, of self-enclosed subjectivation. It is the totality of the projects and representations to which a whole series of behaviors and investments leads, pragmatically, in social, cultural, aesthetic, and cognitive times and spaces.

Territory can be deterritorialized, that is, it can open up, engage in lines of flight, and even move off course and be destroyed. The human species is plunged into a vast movement of deterritorialization, in the sense that its "original" territories constantly dissolve through the action of the universal gods who surpass the frameworks of tribe and ethnicity, through machinic systems that lead it to traverse the stratifications of matter and mind at ever increasing speed.

Reterritorialization consists in attempting to recompose a territory engaged in a deterritorializing process.

Capitalism is a good example of a permanent system of reterritorialization: the capitalist classes are constantly seeking to "recapture" the processes of deterritorialization in the order of production and social relations. Thereby it seeks to control all the processual drives (or machinic phyla) that work on society.

Sources [9]

A. Program of events organized by Suely Rolnik for Guattari's visit to Brazil in 1982:

São Paulo   Date

1. 3rd Congress of Black Culture of the Americas, PUC: "Micropolitical   08/25
Analysis of Social Movements."

2. Meeting at the Freudian School of São Paulo: "Psychoanalysis and   08/26
Institution."

3. Meeting with "alternative" preschools.   08/08

4. Meeting with the International Network of Alternatives to Psychiatry   08/28
at the Sedes Sapientiae Institute.

5. Debate held by a branch of the PT: "Autonomy and Party."   08/29

6. Talk given at the Pontifical Catholic University: "Desire and Politics." 08/30

7. Talk given at the Psychoanalysis School of the Sedes Sapientiae Insti- 08/31
tute: "Psychoanalysis and Familialism."

8. Meeting at the premises of the Grupo de Ação Lésbico-Feminista.   09/02

9. Round-table discussion with PT candidates for the São Paulo City   09/02
Council and State Assembly: "Revolution and Desire."

10. Round-table discussion at the *Folha de São Paulo*: "Mass Culture and 09/03
Singularity."

Rio de Janeiro

11. Debate at the Pinel Hospital after a showing of Hugo Denizart's films *Região dos Desejos* (Region of Desires) and *Bispo*: "Mass Culture and Singularity."   09/09

12. Meeting at the Freudian Institute of Psychoanalysis: "Psychoanalysis and Familialism."   09/10

13. Debate held by the Institute of Philosophy and Social Sciences at the Federal University of Rio de Janeiro: "The Unconscious and History."   09/10

14. Debate held by a branch of the PT: "Autonomy and Party."   09/11

Bahia

15. Debate held by the PT: "Desire and Politics."   09/12

16. Round-table discussion at the ICBA (Brazil-Germany Cultural Institute): "Mass Culture and Singularity."   09/13

17. Meeting with a group of psychoanalysts belonging to the CEP.   09/14

18. Round-table discussion at the ICBA: "Desire and the Social."

Pernambuco

19. Debate at the Centro Social de Soledad: "The Unconscious and History."   09/14

20. Meeting with minority groups at the Luis Freire Center.   09/15

21. Meeting with groups working with communities on the outskirts of the city.   09/16

22. Meeting with the Network of Alternatives to Psychiatry at the Tamarineira Hospital.   09/16

Florianópolis

23. Debate at the Federal University of Santa Catarina: "Desire and History."   09/17

24. Debate on the bandstand in the Praça de São José with students, minorities, and passers-by. — 09/18

Interviews and conversations[10]

25. Meeting with philosophers, São Paulo.

08/23

26. Interview about "free radio," Journalism Department, Pontifical Catholic University, São Paulo.

08/26

27. Interview with Pepe Escobar, unpublished, São Paulo.

08/26

28. Interview with Sonia Goldfeder for *Veja*.

08/31

29. Interview by Néstor Perlongher for *O inimigo do Rei* and *Persona*.

09/01

30. Meeting of Lula and Guattari.

09/02

31. Interview by Pepe Escobar for "Folhetim."

09/05

32. Interview with Laymert Garcia dos Santos in São Paulo.

09/08

33. Interview with João Luiz S. Ferreira for the Fundação Cultural Bahia.

09/13

34. Conversation with Tata Raminho, *candomblé* priest, in Recife.

09/16

35. Conversation with Suely Rolnik at the airport.

09/19

36. Informal conversations.

B. Other sources

37. Fragments of correspondence between Guattari and Suely Rolnik: letters from Guattari dated 02/08/83, 05/27/83, 09/10/83, 09/18/84, 06/26/85, and 05/10/86.

38. Guattari, Félix, "Les énergétiques sémiotiques" (Semiotic Energetics), talk given in the Cerisy Colloquium on the theme "Time and Becoming on the Basis of the Work of Ilya Prigogine," June 1983.

39. Guattari, Félix, "La guerre, la crise ou la vie," initially published in Portuguese in the *Folha de São Paulo*, 08/07/83, and included in Guattari, Félix, *Les années d'hiver: 1980-1985* (Paris: Bernard Barrault, 1986), pp. 34-38.

40. "Drogue, psychose et institution," interview with Félix Guattari by Antoinette Chauvenet and Janine Pierrot in *Sciences Sociales et Santé*, vol. II, nos. 3-4, Paris, October 1984.

41. Original texts of the glossary written by Guattari in 1984 for the English edition of *Molecular Revolution: Psychiatry and Politics* (New York: Penguin Books, 1984); correspondence concerning these originals; the version published in *Molecular Revolution: Psychiatry and Politics*; and the revised version of the same, published in Guattari, Félix, *Les années d'hiver: 1980-1985* (Paris: Bernard Barrault, 1986), pp. 287-295.

42. Interview with Félix Guattari by Michel Butel and Antoine Dulaure for *L'Autre Journal*, no. 6, Paris, 06/12/85; included in Guattari, Félix, *Les années d'hiver: 1980-1985* (Paris: Bernard Barrault, 1986), pp. 80-121.

43. Unpublished texts by Suely Rolnik.

44. Questions and comments arising in connection with the preparation of the book.

Notes

Preface to the 7th Brazilian edition

1. The dictatorship in question came to power in Brazil in 1964 by means of a military coup. A succession of generals remained in power until 1985, and the first direct presidential elections were reestablished in 1989.

2. "Integrated World Capitalism" (IWC) is a term coined by Félix Guattari as early as the late 1960s as an alternative to the term "globalization," which he considered to be excessively generic and which serves to hide the fundamentally economic, specifically capitalist and neoliberal senses of the phenomenon of transnationalization which began to be installed at that period. According to Guattari, "capitalism is worldwide and integrated because it potentially colonized the whole planet, because it currently lives in symbiosis with countries that historically appear to have escaped from it (the Soviet bloc countries and China) and because it tends to leave no human activity, no productive sector, outside its control." Cf. Guattari, Félix, "Le Capitalisme Mondial Intégré et la Révolution Moléculaire," unpublished report of a conference given at a 1980 CINEL group seminar. Published in Portuguese in: Rolnik, Suely, ed., "O Capitalismo Mundial Integrado e a Revolução Molecular," *Revolução Molecular: Pulsações políticas do desejo* (Brasiliense: São Paulo, 1981, 3rd ed. 1987, out of print), p. 211.

3. See Foreword.

4. The so-called "Paulo Delgado law" was approved by the Senate in 1996, but has been awaiting ratification by the Congress ever since.

5. Lula is the nickname of Luiz Inácio da Silva, elected as President of the Republic of Brazil in November 2002.

6. One could date this reactivation of critical forces from 1994, when the North American Free Trade Area was officially constituted and the Zapatista uprising began. Massive strikes in France in the winter of 1995–1996 (the largest since May 1968) helped prepare the ground for the initial phase of movements against the neoliberal

globalization of capital, culminating in the blockage of the WTO summit in Seattle in 1999, the demonstrations against the G8 meeting in Genoa in 2001, and the near-complete breakdown of the WTO program under the pressure of widespread social critique at the Cancún meeting in 2003. The powerful movement of deterritorialization launched by capitalist restructuring in the 1980s was finally appropriated by oppositional forces in the 1990s, giving rise to decentered, networked protests ("Global Days of Action") and to the emergence of a new organizational figure: the swarm of autonomous groups and individuals, operating without hierarchical structures, through horizontal coordination in real time. None of these developments has yet exhausted its potentials, despite the powerful repression articulated by the counter-terrorist policies forged after the events of September 11, 2001. (Note Brian Holmes)

7. PT is the acronym for Partido dos Trabalhadores (Workers' Party), of which Lula is one of the founding members and most important leaders.

8. The text has been fully revised, parts of it have been rewritten and many of the original 71 footnotes have been expanded. In addition to this, 79 new notes have been added to the foreign editions, 61 of which also appear in the seventh Brazilian edition (leaving aside 18 notes, specifically intended to explain certain references to the foreign reader).

9. Lula and Guattari met again, some years later, on August 20, 1990.

10. *Félix Guattari entrevista Lula* (São Paulo: Brasiliense, 1982, out of print).

11. A product of the labor union movement, Lula lost his first governmental election to Franco Montoro, the PSDB party candidate (Partido da Social Democracia Brasileira, or Brazilian Social Democratic Party). In his second try in 1986, Lula ran for Congress and was elected by the largest margin of votes in the country; he subsequently ran for presidential office on four occasions. Having suffered defeat in his first three tries (1989, 1994 and 1998), he was finally elected in 2002, again by a significant margin, as in his first election to Congress.

12. "Gilles Deleuze and Félix Guattari on *Anti-Oedipus*," in *Negotiations 1972–1990*, tr. Martin Joughin (New York: Columbia University Press, 1995), pp. 13–24.

Foreword

1. "Gilles Deleuze and Félix Guattari on *Anti-Oedipus*," in *Negotiations 1972–1990*, *op. cit.*

2. A complete timeline of the full schedule of activities may be found at the end of the book under the title "Sources."

3. "So What", an interview by Michel Butel, in *Chaosophy*, trans. Chet Wiener, ed. Sylvère Lotringer, New York, Semiotext(e), 1995,

4. 1. "Gilles Deleuze and Félix Guattari on *Anti-Oedipus*," in *Negotiations 1972–1990, op. cit.*

1. Culture: a reactionary concept?

1. Guattari adds the suffix "-ic" to "capitalist" because he finds it necessary to create a term to designate not only those societies considered to be capitalist, but also sectors of the so-called "Third World" or "peripheral" capitalism, as well as the ostensibly socialist economies of the Eastern countries that are either dependent or counterdependent on capitalism. According to Guattari, all such societies operate according to the same politics of desire in the social field; in other words, according to the same mode of producing subjectivity and relationship to the other. Variations on this theme are developed throughout the book in different ways.

2. Title of a panel discussion held on September 3, 1982, sponsored by the *Folha de São Paulo*, a newspaper published in São Paulo and accredited with one of the highest circulations in Brazil. Participants included Félix Guattari, Laymert G. dos Santos, José Miguel Wisnik, Modesto Carone and Arlindo Machado. The following text is a montage which includes a transcription of Guattari's words at this event and at other talks he gave during the trip that dealt with the same problematics. Contributions by other participants of the panel in question, as well as excerpts from the debate, appear in different parts of the book, according to the issues under discussion.

3. Mieczyslaw Rakowski was deputy prime minister of Poland in 1981.

4. Along with Santo André and São Caetano, São Bernardo is part of the so-called "ABC," an industrial belt in which the automobile industry is prominent. The three municipalities concentrate a strong labor union movement (of metalworkers especially) in the heart of which Lula began his political trajectory. It is the birthplace of the Partido dos Trabalhadores (PT), or "Workers' Party."

2. Subjectivity and history

1. *Orixá* (or *orisha*) is the generic designation of deities worshipped by the Yoruba (of Southeastern Nigeria, Benin and Northern Togo) and brought to Brazil by the African slaves who came from those areas. The *orixás* were incorporated into *candomblé*, an Afro-Brazilian religion.

2. Autonomia designates both a movement and a political theory developed in Italy during the 1960s and 1970s. See *Autonomia: Post-Political Politics*, ed. Sylvère Lotringer and Christian Marazzi, New York, Semiotext(e)/The MIT Press, (1980) 2007.

3. The term "psychiatrized" has been in use since the 1970s to designate individuals who have undergone successive psychiatric hospitalizations which define their fate under the sign of segregation. The term possesses a critical connotation which denounces the fact that, in transforming madness into a nosographically categorizable disease, confined to medical spaces, psychiatric knowledge produces both the identity of said individuals and the perspective through which society sees them and relates to them. In the game of marked cards instituted by the psychiatric apparatus, the "madman" is a card forever excluded from the deck of public life.

4. "Folhetim" was the name of a weekly cultural supplement, now defunct, of the *Folha de São Paulo*.

5. Anthropologist Roberto da Matta is widely acknowledged as one of the most prominent figures in Brazilian cultural and social studies. He has taught at the Universidade Federal do Rio de Janeiro/Museu Nacional (where he directed the graduate program in Social Anthropology, associated with Harvard University) and at Notre Dame University in the United States.

6. *Povo na TV* (The People on TV) is the name of an immensely popular television program hosted by Hilton Franco which has migrated from one Brazilian television network to another (it was first transmitted by Excelsior TV; later by Tupi TV, TVS, and then by the Bandeirantes network…). It is the forerunner of a certain genre of television journalism that has proliferated enormously in Brazil over the past few years and may be regarded as a significant trend in the country's mass culture. In *The People on TV*, the anonymous poor are granted space and a few minutes' notoriety in which to tell their stories, usually as victims of a dramatic situation. The perverse ambiguity inherent in such scenes is one of the features of the aforementioned trend in Brazilian mass culture. If, on one hand, a few minutes of media presence upgrade the value of individuals who are usually ignored by the official map of social rank distribution (one that is strongly influenced, to this day, by the country's colonial heritage and its slave-holding tradition), on the other hand, within the moralizing racial, class and gender prejudices which set the program's tone, such accounts become the object of irony and humiliation, to the delight of a collective voyeurism mobilized by the avid mass of viewers. The public existence gained by program participants is, therefore, nothing more than the confirmation of their anonymous place—the place of humiliation and contempt. Programs such as these may be regarded as a sort of public ritual afforded by the mass communication media in which the perverse social map that permeates Brazilian society is collectively claimed and reiterated, castigating those who dare to disobey it by attempting to leave their rank.

7. Gil Gomes is the host of *Aqui agora* (Here and Now), an immensely popular program broadcast over SBT (a Brazilian television network). Though different from *The People on TV*, it is one of the forerunners of a sensationalistic, cops-and-robbers style of TV journalism which may be classified within the same trend in Brazilian

mass culture within which that program is situated (cf. note 28). Cameras on their shoulders, breathing heavily, its reporters follow police as they hunt down lawbreakers in live broadcasts filled with classist, racist, macho anger. This genre of program has proliferated to such a degree on Brazilian national and local channels that, in February, 2004, the Lula government's Ministry of Justice vetoed the broadcasting of some programs of this nature before 9 p.m. and others before 11 p.m. Pressure from the television network lobbies was such that the veto was suspended on the very next day and the individual responsible for it fired from his job.

8. Luís Melodia is a well-known Brazilian singer/songwriter.

9. Júlio Bressane has directed one of the most original and refined bodies of work in Brazilian film. The 1970s film movement of which he was part became known as "Udigrudi" (the ironic Brazilian sound equivalent of "Underground") cinema, marked by an experimental aesthetic, alternative production methods and a universe of irreverent, amoral characters through which he distilled an intelligent, biting and witty micropolitical reading of Brazilian society light years away from ideological clichés. Bressane's films have been included in countless European and North American film festivals, those of Porto, Rotterdam, Syracuse, Paris, Venice and Toulouse, among others. Particularly appreciated by film buffs, Bressane's work has been accorded retrospectives by museums such as the Jeu de Paume in Paris (in 1974) and film festivals such as the Turin Festival, where a tribute to his work was held in November, 2002.

10. Franco Montoro was Minister of Labor during President João Goulart's government, deposed by the military dictatorship in 1964. A member of the PDC (Partido Democrático Cristão, or Christian Democratic Party), Montoro was an active participant in the struggle for Brazil's redemocratization, having been among the founding members of the PSDB. At the time Laymert G. dos Santos gave this presentation in 1982, Montoro had just been elected governor of the state of São Paulo in the country's first direct elections after nearly two decades of military dictatorship. Lula was his principal opponent.

11. Estácio is the name of a district in Rio de Janeiro's Northern Zone, near the city center. Luis Melodia hails from there and it is home to one of the city's most highly respected samba schools.

12. ICBA the acronym for the Instituto Cultural Brasil-Alemanha, known as the Goethe-Institut.

13. "Quebra-quebra" (the doubled imperative of the Portuguese verb "to break") is the popular designation for the sort of mass vandalism that took place over a period of some months in 1983 in the principal large cities of Brazil. A more detailed description of this popular manifestation may be found in the text itself.

14. See Guattari, Félix, and Toni Negri. *Les Nouveaux Espaces de Liberté* (Paris: Dominique Bedou, 1985). A free translation by Michael Ryan of the body of the text was published in English as "Postscript 1990," in Guattari, Félix, and Toni Negri, *Communists Like Us* (New York: Semiotext(e), 1990).

15. The acronym ABC designates the industrial belt of Greater São Paulo. It is made up by the municipalities of Santo André, São Bernardo and São Caetano.

16. The Anchieta and Imigrantes highways connect São Paulo to the ABC region.

17. "Iridescent surface of the hollow ball" and "like the heads of babies without bonnets" are verses from the previously mentioned Caetano Veloso song *Ele me deu um beijo na boca* (He kissed me on the mouth).

18. The reference is to the "Schreber case," one of Freud's most important studies of psychosis. In a letter Guattari sent me while we were writing the book, he made the following observation regarding Schreber's "miraculous gods": "…one could take advantage of President Schreber's use of the verb 'to miraculate' in order to replace 'to sublimate,' a term that implies a change of register. We make miracles, we make 'surreality' with everything that surrounds us…" (letter of September 18, 1984).

19. The Movimento Negro Unificado (MNU: Unified Black Movement) was organized around the Brazilian resurgence of political activity among sectors of the Afro-descendant population and fueled by the growth of racial awareness and collective actions among black and mulatto Brazilians. A similar phenomenon may be identified internationally in Afro-descendant populations of the so-called Third World of the period (the 1960s and 1970s). However, it can also be situated at a local level within the context of the social movements that emerged in Brazil between 1964 and 1985 in response to the military dictatorship, movements which are discussed at length in this book. Many of those who founded the Movimento Negro Unificado Contra Discriminação Racial in the early 1970s had been militant members of clandestine organizations committed to toppling the dictatorship. By the 1980s, the MNU had probably become Brazil's most important black political organization.

20. Guattari, Félix, "I have even met happy travelos," tr. R. McComas, *Semiotext(e)* IV/1, 80–81.

21. *Indiani Metropolitani* was the self-styled name used to describe certain groups of young students and casual workers in Italy's Movement of 1977 during the heyday of the Autonomia movement. The name refers to the fact that these groups defined themselves as inhabitants of a sort of cultural reservation with regard to the established order (of labor). See *Autonomia: Post-Political Politics*, ed. Sylvère Lotringer and Christian Marazzi, , *op. cit.*

22. The Lesbian-Feminist Action Group (GALF) was founded in 1981 by two ex-militants of the Lesbian-Feminist Group (LF), organized in São Paulo in 1979 as a

feminine subgroup of the gay SOMOS group. The LF split in 1980 and many of its members joined the SOS-Mulher feminist movement, while others formed the lesbian group Terra Maria and yet others the GALF, a study group which organized the first library on lesbianism in Brazil by acquiring the archives of the SOMOS group (SOMOS was dissolved in 1983), at a moment which coincided with the group's greater integration to the international networks of lesbian movements.

23. The text to which the question refers is "Trois milliards de pervers," originally published as "Trois milliards de pervers—Grande Encyclopédie des Homosexualités," in *Recherches* 12, Fontenay-sous-Bois, March, 1973, and republished under the title "Trois milliards de pervers à la barre," in Guattari, Félix, *La Révolution Moléculaire* (Fontenay-sous-Bois: Recherches, 1977), pp. 110–119. See Félix Guattari, "Letter to the tribunal," in *Soft Subversions*, trans. David L. Sweet and Chet Weiner, ed. Sylvère Lotringer, New York, Semiotext(e), 1996.

24. In Pierre Clastres, *La Société contre l'État* (Paris: Minuit, 1974). English edition: *Society against the State*, tr. Robert Hurley (New York: Urizen, 1977).

25. The word "grasping" here means "existential tension." (Note F. Guattari).

26. Founded in 1969, Lotta Continua was among the extraparliamentary groups of the extreme left formed in Italy between 1969 and 1973. See *Autonomia: Post-Political Politics, op. cit.*

27. Democratic Psychiatry was an association organized around Franco Basaglia in Italy in 1973. It played a fundamental part in the struggle to reform the country's structures within the field of mental health.

28. Italian psychiatrist Franco Basaglia (1924–1980) was one of the principal leaders of the movement which protested Italian psychiatric structures during the 1970s. Among the most well-known projects developed around Basaglia was the successful Trieste project in which psychiatric hospital and asylum treatment was replaced by a territorial care network which included community health services, psychiatric emergency wards in general hospitals, protected work cooperatives, community centers and out-patient residential centers. In 1973, the World Health Organization appointed the Trieste Psychiatric Service as the world standard for the reformulation of mental health care. But Basaglia's contribution went beyond these transformations within the field of mental health. He was also a key figure in the movement which led to the 1978 ratification of the so-called "Law 180" or "Italian Psychiatric Reform Law" (popularly known as the "Basaglia Law"), which brought about the transformation of mental health care structures in Italy. This legal-political accomplishment played a fundamental role in the struggles of psychiatry then taking place in many other countries.

In Brazil, Basaglia and the Italian mental health movement were one of the main influences on the strugle for Psychiatric Reform throughout the 1980s. Between the year immediately following the law's ratification (1979) and his death

(1980), Basaglia visited Brazil several times, giving seminars and conferences and participating directly in the country's movement. It was precisely during that same year (1979) that Guattari made the first of seven trips to Brazil, likewise participating in the struggles of the mental health field in which his ideas also functioned as theoretical references and fundamental pragmatics, strongly influencing the local psychoanalytic movement. Guattari's presence in the country continued over the course of thirteen years (until his death in 1992) and was not restricted to mental health, but extended to movements in various other fields, given the borderline location of his theory and practice. This book bears witness to Guattari's active participation in different actions and debates in Brazil.

29. Basaglia, Franco (ed.), *L'instituzione negata: Rapporto da un ospedale psichiatrico* (Torino: Einaudi, 1968). The book, a kind of bible for the transformations of Western asylums in the 1970s and 1980s, brings together a series of testimonials by the medical team, patients and collaborators of the psychiatric hospital of Gorizia, directed by Franco Basaglia from 1961 to 1972, before the experience in Trieste.

30. Guattari is referring to Italian filmmaker Marco Bellocchio's *Sbatti il mostro in prima pagina* (*Slap the Monster on Page One*, 1972). The film was based on a survey conducted by Belocchio in collaboration with specialists in the mental health care system, concerning violence in psychiatric institutions and the reintegration of the so-called mentally ill in society, a movement which was rapidly expanding at the time.

31. "Sectoral policy was established in France from 1960 onward. Public authorities, supported by progressive movements in institutional psychotherapy, wanted psychiatry to leave the large, repressive hospitals. The aim was to bring psychiatry closer to the city. This led to the creation of 'out-patient facilities': health centers, day hospitals, shelters, protected workshops, home visits, etc. This reformist experience transformed the external social appearance of psychiatry without leading to a genuine attempt at disalienation: psychiatric facilities were miniaturized, but fundamentally the relations of segregation and oppression did not change at all." Guattari, Félix, *Les années d'hiver* (Paris: Ed. Bernard Barrault, 1985).

32. The Clinic at Cour-Cheverny, better known as La Borde, was the major French reference-point for the revolution that took place in psychiatry everywhere during the 1970s. Installed in a countryside chateau 200 km from Paris in the *département* of Loir-et-Cher, the clinic was founded by Jean Oury in 1953. Oury's background came from the experience at Saint-Alban, the hospital where Institutional Psychiatry had been founded and the forerunner in France of the psychiatric revolution of the 1970s. Guattari worked at La Borde from its founding days and had a residence there from 1955 until the end of his life. He was its clinical director for many years. La Borde is a private institution, but it has an agreement with the French health insurance system and provides care to a hybrid population ranging from the region's peasants to members of the Parisian cultural scene. After the publication of *Anti-*

Oedipus (which inaugurated the partnership between Guattari and Deleuze), La Borde became associated with the work of these authors, while also serving as a theoretical reference for the clinical practice of institutional schizoanalysis. See: "La Borde: A Clinic Unlike Any Other," in Félix Guattari, *Chaosophy, op. cit.*

33. "Alternative" was the adjective used to describe certain pedagogical experiments carried out in São Paulo, especially between 1980 and 1983, at the core of a movement which moved beyond schools into various segments of the intellectualized, progressive middle-class of the day—a micropolitical movement that actively participated in the country's redemocratization, pragmatically questioning the dominant policies of subjectivity and sociability, and inventing or experimenting with other policies. In schools, it is possible to observe the continuity between these initiatives and centers of resistance in the field of education rising out of a reaction to AI-5 (the Fifth Institutional Act, promulgated by the military dictatorship on 12/13/1968, punished actions considered subversive with prison, without any right to *habeas corpus*). These centers of resistance continued to exist throughout the 1970s, and lasted to the beginning of the country's redemocratization.

34. Centre d'Initiative pour de Nouveaux Espaces de Liberté (Initiative Center for New Spaces of Freedom).

35. UNESCO conference held in Mexico in 1982, at which Jack Lang, then French Minister of Culture, gave a talk contesting the media hegemony of the United States, especially in the film industry.

36. *Rasga Coração* is the name of a play by Brazilian playwright Oduvaldo Viana Filho (a.k.a. Vianinha).

37. The Tupiniquim were one of the indigenous groups that inhabited Brazil at the time of its discovery by the Portuguese. Belonging to the Tupi-Guarani linguistic family, the name is also used, in a figurative sense, to designate a Brazilian style marked by an ambiguity somewhere between ironic self-deprecation and pride in a certain freedom or irreverence with regard to codes of knowledge and behavior of so-called developed countries.

38. Mário Juruna, a Xavante Indian chief who passed away in 2002, was elected to Congress by the Rio de Janeiro chapter of the PDT during the 1980s and was well known for the tape recorder he always carried with him to record the promises of politicians, and then call them to account in case of nonfulfilment.

39. Fundação Nacional do Índio (National Foundation of the Indigenous Peoples).

40. The notion of a "primary group" comes from US sociology and refers to noninstitutional groups that "shape" opinions. The use that Guattari makes of this notion broadens its meaning, incorporating, as he himself says, emotional components and elements of the "confection" of aesthetic existence.

41. The notion of "transversality" was present in Guattari's work from the outset. It is among those created within the context of what became known as "Institutional Analysis," when his thinking was still marked by Lacanian theory. His "classic" texts dealing with this particular concept include "Transversalité" and "Le transfert," both written in 1964 and included in a collection of his essays, *Psychanalyse et Transversalité* (Paris: Maspero, 1972), pp. 52–58 and 72–85. Published in English in *Molecular Revolution: Psychiatry and Politics* (New York: Penguin Books, 1984), pp.11–23.

3. Politics

1. Nelson Rodrigues was born in Recife in 1912 and died in Rio de Janeiro in 1980. Known primarily for his plays, Rodrigues authored a vast output of *crônicas* (a Brazilian journalistic genre related to the essay that uses art, politics, sports or everyday life as a basis for personal reflection), which were originally published in newspapers. A number of Brazilian directors have made films of his plays.

2. Rodrigues, Nelson, in *Dionysos*, vol. 1, a magazine published by the Serviço Nacional de Teatro, October 1949, quoted by Sábato Magaldi in Rodrigues, Nelson, *Teatro completo*, vol. 2 (Rio de Janeiro: Nova Fronteira, 1981), "Introdução," p. 13.

3. Rodrigues, Nelson, *Teatro completo*, vol. 2 (Rio de Janeiro: Nova Fronteira, 1981), "Álbum de Família," p. 87. English edition: *The Theater of Nelson Rodrigues*, 2 vols. (Ministry of Culture, 2001).

4. The expression was coined by Nelson Rodrigues and subsequently became a colloquialism.

5. Rodrigues, Nelson, *op. cit.*, p. 58.

6. Rodrigues, Nelson, *ibid.*

7. Rodrigues, Nelson, *op. cit.*, p. 59.

8. Rodrigues, Nelson, *op. cit.*, p. 95.

9. A Recife-based gay liberation group which existed from the late 1970s through to the early 1980s.

10. Guattari's encounter with Recife and Olinda feminists was organized by the SOS-Corpo. Founded in Recife in 1981, this group focused initially on such issues as women's body awareness and information-sharing regarding women's health and sexuality. It continued to exist and is currently among the country's largest and most consistent Brazilian feminist NGOs under the name of SOS Corpo Gênero e Cidadania (SOS Body Gender and Citizenship; the name is about to be changed to Instituto Feminista pela Democracia: SOS Corpo Gênero e Cidadania: Feminist Institute for Democracy: SOS Body Gender and Citizenship), which renders countless consulting services to the government and has international support. It is worth

noting that the feminist activity in Recife and Olinda is among the most intereesting in Brazil: not only the current mayor of Olinda is a feminist (a member of the Brazilian Communist Party), but also, the municipality of Recife, run by the PT, has just been awarded a UN prize for its women's programs, with the SOS Mulher Recife group being among those responsible.

Participants of the encounter with Guattari included women from the SOS-Corpo group and from SOS-Mulher, a feminist group formed in São Paulo in the early 1980s which quickly expanded to twelve other Brazilian cities (Recife among them). Dedicated to the legal, social and mental health care of female victims of violence, it was one of the first such services to have organized anonymous, confidential assistance to women. It grew out of the women's movement that flourished in Brazil during the mid-1970s (especially in 1978–79), when many Brazilians who had been exiled by the dictatorship returned to Brazil. At the time, the organization had already begun to denounce the judiciary system's acquittal of men who had killed women. Chapters of SOS-Mulher were autonomous, often existing under other names, and only infrequently shared their experiences at national conferences of the feminist mouvements. Among the consequences of the successful politicization of the theme of violence against women by SOS-Mulher and the feminist movement in general was the 1985 creation, in São Paulo, by the Franco Montoro government, of the first Women's Protection Precincts (Delegacias de Polícia da Defesa da Mulher), a result of the priority given to the theme of violence by the State Advisory Council on the Condition of Women created during the same government in 1983, a priority set in motion by the strong presence of the feminist movement and of SOS-Mulher in particular. Staffed by policewomen and specializing in crimes against women, there are over 300 Women's Protection Precincts throughout the country (cf. note 43).

11. Radio Alice was founded in February, 1976, by the editors of the Desiring Autonomy (or Creative Autonomy) newspaper *A/traverso*, which regarded Deleuze and Guattari's *Anti-Oedipus* as a major reference. The station was closed down by police in March, 1977; on the following day, the group went back on the air, only to have police close it down a second time, this time arresting several of its speakers. On this occasion, Bifo (Franco Berardi) sought refuge in Paris, where he met Guattari, who helped him launch a campaign against repression, censorship, etc., which led to the recommencement of Radio Alice in July of that year. The station continued to broadcast through 1981, but its first period (1976–1977) was the most creative one. Published in English as "Popular Free Radio," tr. David Sweet, *Semiotext(e)* ("Radiotext(e)"), vol. VI, no. 1, pp. 85–89 (cf. notes 23, 42, 47, 74, 75, 124).

12. The Red Brigades appeared in Italy in 1973, initially as the armed faction of certain labor confrontations. The Red Brigades became internationally known in 1979 for the kidnapping of Aldo Moro, the leader of the Christian Democrats and former Prime Minister of Italy. See *Autonomia: Post-Political Politics, op. cit.*

13. Prima Linea was the name of a guerilla group founded in 1976, the leaders of which came mostly from Lotta Continua after its dissolution. Its militants went underground in 1979. See *Autonomia: Post-Political Politics, op. cit.*

14. Guattari is referring to the counterculture.

15. *O Inimigo do Rei* (The King's Enemy) was a newspaper put out in the mid-1970s by anarchist youths from Salvador, the capital of Bahia. It lasted through the early 1980s. Its editorial base was itinerant, so to speak, Porto Alegre having been the last city out of which it was published. The articles and testimonials that appeared in this newspaper were not easily found in other Brazilian underground publications of the day.

16. "Gilles Deleuze and Félix Guattari on *Anti-Oedipus*," in *Negotiations 1972–1990, op. cit.*

17. Deleuze, Gilles, and Félix Guattari, *A Thousand Plateaus: Capitalism and Schizophrenia*, tr. Brian Massumi (Minneapolis: University of Minnesota Press, 1987).

18. "Gilles Deleuze and Félix Guattari on *Anti-Oedipus*," in *Negotiations 1972–1990, op. cit.*

19. PMDB is the acronym for Partido do Movimento Democrático Brasileiro, the Party of the Brazilian Democratic Movement.

20. Cf. information on pages 262 and sq. for the position that Autonomia-related groups in Italy during the 1970s took on the question of labor.

21. Néstor Perlongher interviewed Guattari in 1982 for *Persona*, a feminist journal edited by writer Maria Oddone and published in Buenos Aires from 1981 to 1983. However, the interview was only published eighteen years later, under the title "¿A qué vino de París Mr. Félix Guattari?" in *Tsé Tsé* 7/8, May 2000, a special issue posthumously dedicated to Néstor Perlongher.

22. The reference to Jorge Amado's *Capitães de Areia* (Captains of the Sands; New York, NY: Avon, 1988) concerns children's gangs as an example of a war machine. See: Deleuze, Gilles, and Félix Guattari, *Nomadology: The War Machine*, tr. Brian Massumi, New York, Semiotext(e), 1987.

23. Deleuze and Guattari borrow the notion of "segmentarity" from anthropology (where the term indicates the mode of operation of primitive societies, as opposed to modern ones) and broaden it. For them, segmentarity exists in any society, always being simultaneously of three types:

    1. "rigid" (this is how it is produced on the molar plane, which functions according to the "abstract machine of overcoding");
    2. "relatively supple" (this is how it is produced on the molecular plane, which functions according to the "abstract machine of mutation");

3. nonexistent (in pure flow, where the particles are free in pure movement of speed and slowness, constituting a "war machine").

What characterizes a moment in the life of an individual, a group, or a society, what distinguishes one society from another, or even one period of history from another, is the general economy of the reigning machine, that is, the relationship between the three machines that predominate in the libidinal and political economy of the individual, group, society, or period in question. *A Thousand Plateaus: Capitalism and Schizophrenia*, tr. Brian Massumi (Minneapolis: University of Minnesota Press, 1987). Cf. also Deleuze, Gilles, and Claire Parnet, *Dialogues*, tr. Hugh Tomlinson and Barbara Habberjam (New York: Columbia University Press).

24. Guattari, Félix, "La guerre, la crise ou la vie," in *Change International Un* (Paris: september 1983); reprinted in Guattari, Félix, *Les années d'hiver: 1980–1985* (Paris: Ed. Bernard Barrault, 1986), pp. 34–38.

25. Guattari borrows the concept of structures "far from equilibrium" from Ilya Prigogine (awarded the 1979 Nobel Prize for Chemistry) and Isabelle Stengers. The authors propose the idea of an "order by fluctuations." Instead of "calming down," so that the system might reestablish stability, such fluctuations lead it away from equilibrium until it undergoes an irreversible transformation. See esp. Prigogine, I. and I. Stengers, *Order Out of Chaos: Man's New Dialogue with Nature* (New York: Bantam Books, 1984).

26. Guattari borrows the notion of "strange attractors" from Stengers and Prigogine.

27. First meeting between Guattari and Lula, organized by myself and Marco Aurélio Garcia (who later became Municipal Secretary of Culture in the PT government of the Prefecture of São Paulo, under Marta Suplicy's administration, and later, Special Foreign Policy Counselor to the President of the Republic, under Lula's administration). Guattari and Lula met again, a few years later, on August 20, 1990.

28. In 1979, the period to which Guattari refers, Jacó Bittar was a union official for the workers of the petroleum industry. In 1982, when this conversation took place, Bittar was a candidate of the PT for the office of senator in the state of São Paulo.

29. Lula alludes to the meeting at Puebla, Mexico, in January of 1979, on the occasion of the Third Episcopal Conference of Latin American (CELAM), in the presence of Pope John Paul II.

30. Lula seems to distinguish here between a stage of "nationalization," corresponding to a politics of safeguarding the economy against the international domination, and a form of "statization" [*estatização*] strictly speaking. (Note F. Guattari)

31. *Lula, Entrevistas e Discursos* (São Paulo: Editora O Repórter de Guarulhos LTDA, 1981).

4. Desire and history

1. The term "reductionism" is used to describe the systematic reduction of any given field of knowledge to another, more formalized one (for instance, the reduction of mathematics to formal logic, with a consequent loss of depth and complexity). In this case, Guattari is referring to the psychoanalytic reduction of the rich and varied production of the unconscious to a few models which, according to him, were inaugurated by Freud himself. For Guattari, any model in this field is always the cartography of a given formation of the unconscious. To this extent, he is signaling the importance of preserving the possibility of inventing new models which, according to him, are a condition for listening to the productions of the unconscious. In the text that follows (a montage of various conferences and scattered commentaries on the subject), Guattari attempts to point out different reductionisms produced by psychoanalysis (in Freud's work especially).

2. Bertalanfy is the founder of systems theory.

3. Sylberer theorized the functional processes in dreams and developed an interpretation of an anagogical character. Freud refers to this, many times, in *The Interpretation of Dreams* (1900), in *The Standard Edition of the Complete Psychological Works of Sigmund Freud* (London: The Hogarth Press and The Institute of Psycho-analysis, 1991), vol. V.

4. The theme of the Cerisy Colloquium on this occasion was "Time and Becoming on the Basis of the Work of Ilya Prigogine."

5. From the Greek, meaning "matter."

6. "Irreversibility of time" and "order by fluctuation" are among the principal concepts of Prigogine and Stengers. The idea of irreversibility is of interest to Guattari in that it allows for the definition of a thermodynamics "far from equilibrium," thus countering the physics of classical clinical theory, which involves the idea of an always possible reversibility of processes (cf. notes 87, 88, 97, 100, 107, 120, 121, 122).

7. "Bifurcation" is also a term that Guattari has borrowed from Prigogine and Stengers: a bifurcation is established from the point of a singularity that causes a process to be derived outside the pathways of its equilibrium.

8. "Analysis Terminable and Interminable," in *The Standard Edition of the Complete Psychological Works of Sigmund Freud,* ed. James Strachey (London: Hogarth Press, 1953–1974), vol. 23.

9. Guattari is referring to the angry speeches against the university made by students at the Federal University at Santa Catarina on the occasion of his visit to Florianópolis. They complained that they had to organize Guattari's arrival without any support from the university administration, which, they felt, was merely taking advantage of his prestigious media presence.

10. Guattari is referring to "L'interprétation des énoncés," a text included in the pirate publication *Politique et psychanalyse* (Alençon: Bibliothèque des mots perdus, 1977); English edition: "The Interpretation of Utterances," in *Language, Sexuality and Subversion*, tr. Paul Foss and Meaghan Morris (Sydney: Feral Publications, 1978). It provides a detailed reading by Félix Guattari, Gilles Deleuze, Claire Parnet, and André Scala of three cases of child analysis—one from a sectoral institution and two classic cases: Freud's Little Hans, in "Analysis of a phobia in a five-year-old boy," *The Standard Edition of the Complete Psychological Works of Sigmund Freud*, vol. X (London: The Hogarth Press and The Institute of Psycho-Analysis, 1991, pp. 3–149) and Melanie Klein's Richard, in *Narrative of a Child Analysis* (London: The Hogarth Press, 1961) and *Writings of Melanie Klein* (New York: The Free Press, 1984, vol. IV). This is one of the only texts—if not the only one—in which Guattari and Deleuze do a reading of a clinical case together. Some of the ideas set out in this text recur throughout their work, especially in *Anti-Oedipus: Capitalism and Schizophrenia, op. cit.* Also see Deleuze, Gilles, and Claire Parnet, *Dialogues, op. cit.*

11. Vlado was the nickname of Vladimir Herzog, an important Brazilian journalist during the dictatorship, who proclaimed and practiced the concept of "the social responsibility of journalism," a professional journalism that would not be "servile" to the state. In 1975 he was summoned by the federal police to explain his involvement with the Brazilian Communist Party. He was brutally tortured and assassinated when he refused to sign the deposition; his body was then dragged to a cell and hung from the bars, simulating suicide. Herzog's assassination raised a national scandal and was one of the triggers of the movement that led to the democratic opening of Brazil. In 1978, the Justice Department declared the state to be responsible for his death.

12. The French use the verb "to follow" [*suivre*] to designate the process of medical or psychotherapeutic treatment.

13. A Paris hospital specialized in treating drug addicts.

14. Letter to Fliess of May 25, 1895, in *Naissance de la psychanalyse* (Paris: PUF, 1979), letter n. 24, p. 106 (this letter was not included in the English edition of their correspondence).

15. Draft E. "How Anxiety Originates" (June 1894) in *The Standard Edition of the Complete Psychological Works of Sigmund Freud* (London: The Hogarth Press and The Institute of Psycho-analysis, 1991), vol. I, p. 192.

16. *The Interpretation of Dreams* (1900), Chapter VII "The Psychology of the Dream-Processes, (A) The Forgetting of Dreams," in *The Standard Edition of the Complete Psychological Works of Sigmund Freud* (London: The Hogarth Press and The Institute of Psycho-analysis, 1991), vol. V, p. 516.

17. In a note, Guattari comments that Lacan—with a frankness rare in a psychoanalyst who claimed the Freudian heritage as his own—insisted on the fact that Freud never broke with his first scientist ties; cf. "La science et la vérité," in Lacan, Jacques, *Écrits, A Selection*, tr. Alan Sheridan (New York: Norton, 1977).

18. "...the intrasubjective field tends to be conceived of after the fashion of intersubjective relations, and the systems are pictured as relatively autonomous persons-within-the-person.... To this extent then, the scientific theory of the psychical apparatus tends to resemble the way the subject comprehends and perhaps even constructs himself in his phantasy-life." Laplanche J. and Pontalis, J.-B. *The language of psycho-analysis*, tr. Donald Nicholson-Smith (New York & London: W.W. Norton & Co., 1973), p. 452.

19. "As an *energetic concept*, on the contrary, libido is merely the symbolic notation of the equivalence between the dynamisms that images invest in behavior." Lacan, Jacques, "Au-delà du 'principe de réalité'," paper delivered at the Congress of Marienbad in 1936, published in *Écrits, A Selection, op. cit.*

20. "Energetics is nothing more than the cladding of the world of the network of signifiers, despite what engineers may believe in their naïve hearts." (Notes made by Guattari at Lacan's Seminar of Jan. 14, 1970).

21. "... the libido should be conceived as an organ in both senses of the term, organ as part of an organism and organ as tool," *The Seminar of Jacques Lacan*, ed. Jacques-Alain Miller, Book 11, *The Four Fundamental Concepts of Psychoanalysis*, tr. Alan Sheridan (New York & London: W.W. Norton, 1998). See also: "*Subversion du sujet et dialectique du désir,*" in *Écrits* (Seuil: Paris, 1960), p. 817; "*Position de l'inconscient,*" in *Écrits* (Seuil: Paris, 1960), p. 848.

22. *Écrits* (Paris: Seuil, 1960), p. 817.

23. *Ibid.*

24. *Le séminaire—Livre XI—Les quatre concepts fondamentaux de la psychanalyse*, Paris: Seuil, 1973, ch. XV, p. 179; English edition: *The Seminar of Jacques Lacan*, ed. Jacques-Alain Miller, Book 11, *The Four Fundamental Concepts of Psychoanalysis*, tr. Alan Sheridan (New York & London: W.W. Norton, 1998).

25. "Du 'Trieb' de Freud et du désir du psychanalyste," in Lacan, Jacques, *Écrits* (Paris: Seuil, 1960), p. 851; English edition.

26. Guattari borrows the notion of "dissipative processes" from Stengers and Prigogine.

27. Guattari borrows the notion of "reordering through fluctuation" from Stengers and Prigogine.

28. Guattari borrows the notion of "implosions without appeal" from Stengers and Prigogine.

29. Hjelmslev, Louis, *Prolegomena to a Theory of Language*, tr. Francis J. Whitfield (Madison: University of Wisconsin Press, 1961). According to Guattari, "despite the fact that Hjelmslev and the Linguistic Circle of Copenhagen rejected any possible translatability of the meaning of different systems of expression outside 'everyday language,' they intended to prepare a 'glossematic algebra' which, in their view, should be distinct both from the linguistics of spoken languages and from 'symbolic' logic."

30. The Italian physicist Franco Piperno was an active participant in the Autonomia movement of the 1970s. He had been one of the leaders of Potere Operaio (which preceded the movement) and, when that group dissolved, Piperno participated in Autonomia Possibile which published the newspaper *Metropoli*. He went into exile in Paris in 1979, and, soon afterward, was extradited to Italy, despite public protest by then president François Mitterrand. Acquitted, Piperno returned to Paris in 1980 on a Poincaré Institute fellowship and remained there until he received another fellowship from MIT. Denied entry to the United States, he moved to Canada, where he was hired by the University of Quebec and, later, by the University of Alberta in Edmonton, before finally returning to teach and serve as an elected official in the city of Cosenza in southern Italy.

6. Love, territories of desire and a new smoothness

1. In French, *nouvelle douceur*; in Guattari, Félix, "Les huits 'principes'," in *L'inconscient Machinique: Essais de Schizo-analyse* (Fontenay-sous-bois: Recherches, 1979), p. 201.

2. A verse from "Eu sei que vou te amar" ("I know I'm going to love you"), a well-known Brazilian song by Tom Jobim and Vinícius de Moraes.

3. Verses from several well-known Brazilian love songs.

4. "Bachelor machines" is a concept proposed by Michel Carrouges in his book *Les Machines célibataires* (Paris: Arcanes, 1954) to describe the fantastic machines that appear in the works of Kafka, Jarry, Edgar Allan Poe, Roussel, Duchamp, and others. The concept was reintroduced by Deleuze and Guattari in 1972 in *Anti-Oedipus: Capitalism and Schizophrenia*, *op. cit.* The authors use it to designate what they call the "third synthesis of the unconscious," which follows the "paranoiac machine" and the "miraculating machine."

5. The film *Blade Runner* was directed by Ridley Scott in 1982, based on the novel *Do Androids Dream of Electric Sheep?* by Philip K. Dick (1968).

7. Looking back on the Brazilian Journey

1. Guattari is referring to the text "Transversalité," written in 1964 and included in a collection of his essays, *Molecular Revolution: Psychiatry and Politics*, *op. cit.*

2. In the original, "casa grande e senzala" (the manor house and the slaves' village) is an expression borrowed from the title of a book by Gilberto Freyre, *Casa Grande e Senzala: Formação da família Brasileira sob o regime da Economia Patriarca* (Rio de Janeiro: Livraria José Olímpio Editora, 1984). An English translation was published in the United States as *The Masters and the Slaves: A Study in the development of Brazilian Civilization* (New York: Alfred Knopf, 1946). It was also published in England as *The Masters and the Slaves* (London: Wendenfeld & Nicholson, 1947). In 1956, the book was awarded the Anisfield-Wolf prize for best worldwide publication on "race relations." With the passage of time, the book's title became widely used in colloquial language as an expression designating the mark of slavery, strongly present in the country's social life.

3. Guattari is referring to the anthology edited by Suely Rolnik, *Revolução Molecular: Pulsações Políticas do Desejo* (São Paulo: Brasiliense, 1981, 3rd ed. 1987, out of print).

4. The International Network of Alternatives to Psychiatry. Cf. in this book Chapter II, Subjectivity and History, section 10b, Minority Experiments in Psychiatry, p. 125.

5. A term that Guattari borrows from the field of computer science—artificial intelligence—aimed at the reproduction of human strategies. In computer science, discernability designates the recognition of patterns. Guattari uses the term to designate the semiotic work of the apprehension of discursive traces specific to a material of expression.

6. Round-table discussion at the Folha de São Paulo: "Mass culture and singularity," São Paulo, September 3, 1982.

7. In *Sauve qui peut (la vie)*, a film made by Godard in 1980, released in the US as *Every Man for Himself.*

8. Cf. conversation between Lula and Guattari on p. 275 and sq.

Appendix: Notes about certain concepts

1. The following notes on some of Guattari's concepts have been put together from our three-year correspondence in preparation for the writing of this book as well as from the two versions of a glossary he wrote himself—the original text, not published in full, of the glossary he prepared for the American edition of his book *Molecular Revolution: Psychiatry and Politics* (New York: Penguin Books, 1984), which he sent me in 1983, plus a complete revised version of the same glossary prepared for a collection of his essays titled *Les années d'hiver* (Paris: Bernard Barrault, 1986).

2. In the original, *Kafka: Toward a Minor Literature* (Minneapolis: University of Minnesota Press, 1986).

3. Guattari is referring to a comment about little Joey—one of Bruno Bettelheim's clinical cases in *The Empty Fortress: Infantile Autism and the Birth of the Self* (New York: Free Press, 1967)—which he and Deleuze made in their book *Anti-Oedipus: Capitalism and Schizophrenia, op. cit.*, p. 37.

4. Deleuze, Gilles, *Difference and Repetition*, translated by Paul Patton (New York: Columbia University Press, 1994).

5. Guattari is probably referring to the wire or wooden trellises supporting climbing plants that are constructed progressively as the plants grow.

6. Cf. esp. Deleuze, Gilles, and Guattari, Félix, "Rhizome," in *On the Line*, tr. John Johnston, edited by Sylvère Lotringer, New York, Semiotext(e), 1983.

7. Peirce, Charles Sanders, "Principles of Philosophy. Elements of Logic," in *Collected Papers of Charles Sanders Peirce*, ed. Charles Hartshorne, Paul Weiss, and Arthur Burks, vol. 1 (Cambridge, Mass.: The Belknap Press of Harvard University Press, 1931).

8. The major texts by Guattari that deal with the notions of "subject-group" and "subjected group" can be found in a collection of his essays, *Molecular Revolution: Psychiatry and Politics, op. cit.*

9. Debates, meetings, conversations, conferences, panels, interviews, texts and correspondence used in the elaboration of the blocks of ideas, essays, and dialogues.

10. In the case of published interviews, the dates correspond to when the interviews took place and not when they were finally published.

ABOUT THE AUTHORS

Félix Guattari (1930–1992), post-'68 French psychoanalyst and philosopher, is the author of *Anti-Oedipus* (with Gilles Deleuze), *The Anti-Oedipus Papers* (Semiotext(e)), and other books. Semiotext(e) has published the first two volumes of his complete essays, *Chaosophy* (1995) and *Soft Subversions* (1996), and will publish the final volume, *Chaos and Complexity*, in 2008.

Suely Rolnik is a psychoanalyst, cultural critic, and full professor at the Catholic University of São Paulo, where she coordinates the Nucleous of Cross-Disciplinary Studies on Subjectivity, in the Clinical Psychology Doctoral Program. She sought exile in Paris in the "post-'68" period (1970–1979) where she studied philosophy, social sciences and psychology. In recent years, Rolnik's research has concentrated on contemporary art and its political and clinical links. She co-curated a Lygia Clark exhibition in France and Brazil (2005–2006). Among her publications is, *Cartografía Sentimental: Transformações contemporâneas do desejo* (1989, 3th ed. 2007). Among her translations into Portuguese is: Deleuze and Guattari's *Thousand Plateaus* (vol. III/IV). She also is a guest researcher at the INHA (Institut Nationale d'Histoire de l'Art) in Paris. She lives in São Paulo.